"There is a cliché in sport that you should look to where the ball is going to be, not where it is now. This book very much upholds that tradition by not just identifying the scope of the duty of care in the context of sports coaching, but by importantly identifying where it should be in the future. The book is insightful and thought-provoking, and I would recommend this to anyone involved in sports coaching or management, at every level, as well as students, teachers and practitioners involved in sports law."

Kris Lines, *Senior Lecturer in Law at Aston University, UK and performance coach in gymnastics and trampolining*

"This is the book that those interested in a coach's legal duty of care have been waiting for. It is lucid and thought-provoking and not everyone will agree with its arguments, but it is no less important for that. It is a timely contribution to a debate we need to have."

David McArdle, *Head of Law, Stirling University, UK*

"The publication of this text by Neil Partington is well timed. It follows on from the review of Duty of Care in sport undertaken by Baroness Tanni Grey-Thompson and the many investigations into the culture of performance sports in the UK. The relationship between coach and athlete was central to both. The legal and moral definition of duty of care and how it is interpreted and delivered is dynamic and ever changing. The insight and learning this book provides will help all involved in sport make better decisions about the role of coaching in the future and inform the practical delivery of duty of care. The detailed discussion provided by this text will act as a significant catalyst to bring people together to debate and discuss duty of care and will provide added strength to the crucial role of sport and physical activity to the wellbeing of our society."

Ian Braid, *founder and MD DOCIAsport, UK and former CEO of the British Athletes Commission*

"Coaches are powerful individuals in the lives of athletes in all contexts. They have the power to inspire, support, educate, and accordingly are tasked with a legal duty of care to sport participants. Existing texts have, however, rarely considered how coaches may enact their legal duties. This does not serve sports, coaches or athletes well. In response, Partington's text introduces and rigorously explains the key legal concepts relevant to all coaches. The cases he explores will help readers to apply these concepts to their own sport coaching contexts. The book therefore provides policy makers, coach educators and sport coaches with essential, robust and relevant knowledge. More importantly, the knowledge within the text will empower coaches to enact their duty of care."

Colum Cronin, *Senior Lecturer in Physical Education and Sport Coaching, School of Sport and Exercise Sciences, Liverpool John Moores University, UK*

COACHING, SPORT AND THE LAW

The interdependent coach–athlete relationship represents the most fundamental instance of a duty of care in sport. This book defines, analyses and clarifies the duty of care incumbent upon sports coaches and identifies important recommendations of real-world significance for coaching practice.

Given the dynamic relationship between coaching, sport and the law, it is imperative that coaches have an informed awareness of the evolving legal context in which they discharge their duty of care. Detailed analysis of a coach's duty of care has so far been lacking. The book addresses this gap by being the first to critically scrutinise the concept of duty of care in the specific context of sports coaching. Sustained analysis of the developing case law allows the scope and boundaries of the particular duties demanded of coaches to be rigorously examined. The legal principles and court decisions discussed relate to coaching delivered in a wide range of individual and team sports, at both amateur and professional levels of performance, and include common scenarios and challenges frequently encountered by sports coaches globally.

By adopting an interdisciplinary approach within a broader sociolegal methodological framework, this book's detailed analysis and original insights will prove highly instructive for practising coaches, coach educators and national governing bodies of sport. It also offers extremely valuable insights for students, teachers and practitioners involved in sports law, sports coaching, sports ethics, tort law, sports policy and development, sports studies and physical education.

Neil Partington is Lecturer in Law at the University of Sussex, UK. He teaches, conducts research and has published widely in the areas of sports law and tort law. Neil holds a PhD in Law and a Masters in Legal Science (with Distinction) from Queen's University Belfast, an MSc in Sports Coaching from Miami University (Ohio) and a BA(Ed) in Physical Education from the University of Exeter.

Ethics and Sport

Series editors
Mike McNamee
University of Wales Swansea
Jim Parry
Charles University, Prague, Czech Republic

The *Ethics and Sport* series aims to encourage critical reflection on the practice of sport, and to stimulate professional evaluation and development. Each volume explores new work relating to philosophical ethics and the social and cultural study of ethical issues. Each is different in scope, appeal, focus and treatment, but a balance is sought between local and international focus, perennial and contemporary issues, level of audience, teaching and research application, and variety of practical concerns.

Titles in the series:

The Philosophy of Football
Steffen Borge

Kinetic Beauty
The Philosophical Aesthetics of Sport
Jason Holt

Gym Culture, Identity and Performance-Enhancing Drugs
Tracing a typology of steroid use
Ask Vest Christiansen

Coaching, Sport and the Law
A Duty of Care
Neil Partington

For more information about this series, please visit: www.routledge.com/Ethics-and-Sport/book-series/EANDS

COACHING, SPORT AND THE LAW

A Duty of Care

Neil Partington

LONDON AND NEW YORK

First published 2021
by Routledge
2 Park Square, Milton Park, Abingdon, Oxon OX14 4RN

and by Routledge
52 Vanderbilt Avenue, New York, NY 10017

Routledge is an imprint of the Taylor & Francis Group, an informa business

© 2021 Neil Partington

The right of Neil Partington to be identified as author of this work has been asserted by him in accordance with sections 77 and 78 of the Copyright, Designs and Patents Act 1988.

All rights reserved. No part of this book may be reprinted or reproduced or utilised in any form or by any electronic, mechanical, or other means, now known or hereafter invented, including photocopying and recording, or in any information storage or retrieval system, without permission in writing from the publishers.

Trademark notice: Product or corporate names may be trademarks or registered trademarks, and are used only for identification and explanation without intent to infringe.

British Library Cataloguing-in-Publication Data
A catalogue record for this book is available from the British Library

Library of Congress Cataloging-in-Publication Data
A catalog record for this book has been requested

ISBN: 978-0-367-35993-5 (hbk)
ISBN: 978-1-032-00451-8 (pbk)
ISBN: 978-0-429-34314-8 (ebk)

Typeset in Bembo
by Apex CoVantage, LLC

This book is dedicated to Katie, Conor, Annie, Fionn and my parents.

CONTENTS

List of cases and legislation   xi
Foreword   xvi
Preface   xviii
Acknowledgements   xxi

    Introduction   1

PART I
Key concepts   15

1   Distinguishing duties of care of sports coaches   17

2   Legal duty of care: the law of negligence   40

3   Professional liability of amateurs   68

PART II
Duty of care in context   85

4   Duty of care in the context of sport   87

5   Duty of care of sports coaches   121

6   Case study: *Anderson v Lyotier*   168

PART III
Implications and future developments   183

7 Implications for coaching practice   185

    Conclusion   204

References   *219*
Index   *232*

CASES AND LEGISLATION

Cases

United Kingdom

Adams v Rhymney Valley DC [2001] PNLR 4 (CA), 76, 78, 80, 82
Affuto-Nartoy v Clarke (1984) Times, 9 February, 165
Ahmed v MacLean [2016] EWHC 2798, 131, 160–4, 178, 180, 192, 211
Allport v Wilbraham [2004] EWCA Civ 1668, 38, 107
Anderson v Lyotier [2008] EWHC 2790, 12, 13, 40, 62, 80, 82–3, 93, 135, 167, 168–82, 189, 192, 194, 210, 212
Barclays Bank v Various Claimants [2020] UKSC 13, 63
Barnett v Chelsea and Kensington Hospital Management Committee [1969] 1 QB 428, 59
Bartlett v English Cricket Board Association of Cricket Officials County Court (Birmingham), 27 August 2015, 23, 38, 63, 113, 119, 195, 215
Blair-Ford v CRS Adventures Ltd [2012] EWHC 2360, 66, 198, 199
Blake v Galloway [2004] EWCA Civ 814, 62, 88
Blyth v Birmingham Waterworks (1856) 11Ex 781, 46
Bolam v Friern Hospital Management Committee [1957] 1 WLR 582, 12, 28, 51, 64, 68, 78
Bolitho v City of Hackney Health Authority [1998] AC 232, 28, 65, 78, 194
Bolton v Stone [1951] AC 850, 52
Brady v Sunderland Association Football Club Limited, 2 April 1998 (QBD), 149–51, 192
Brady v Sunderland Association Football Club Ltd, 17 November 1998 (CA), 42, 149
Browning v Odyssey Trust Co Ltd [2014] NIQB 39, 9, 49, 61, 89
Caldwell v Maguire [2001] EWCA Civ 1054, 5, 12, 30, 44, 45, 55, 75, 88, 102–5, 106, 125, 126, 132, 139, 186, 189, 209, 210, 211
Caparo Industries Plc v Dickman [1990] 2 AC 605, 3, 216

Cassidy v Manchester CC, 12 July 1995 (CA), 155
Catholic Child Welfare Society v Institute of the Brothers of the Christian Schools [2012] UKSC 56, 62, 63, 212
Cavalier (Pauper) v Pope [1906] AC 428, 22
Condon v Basi (1985) 1 WLR 866 (CA), 4, 5, 12, 45, 56, 96, 98–101, 126, 211
Cox v Dundee CC [2014] CSOH 3, 60, 143–6, 199, 212, 215
Craig v Tullymurry Equestrian Centre [2019] NIQB 94, 167
D v East Berkshire Community Health Authority [2005] 2 AC 373, 70
Davenport v Farrow [2010] EWHC 550, 33, 42, 44, 45, 60, 76, 77, 83, 149, 151–5, 177, 192, 193, 194, 196
Davis Contractors Ltd v Fareham UDC [1956] AC 696, 7
Donoghue v Stevenson [1932] AC 562, 19, 24, 46, 101
Dorset Yacht Company v Home Office [1970] AC 1004, 28
Eckersley v Binnie [1988] 18 ConLR 1 (CA), 77, 190
Elliott v Saunders and Liverpool Football Club, Unreported, Queen's Bench Division 10 June 1994, 4, 9
Fairchild v Glenhaven Funeral Services [2003] 1 AC 32, 6
Fowles v Bedfordshire County Council [1995] PIQR P380 (CA), 4, 9, 12, 32, 40, 62, 76, 127–30, 137, 177, 194, 212, 215, 216
Froom v Butcher [1976] QB 286 (CA), 62
Gannon v Rotherham Metropolitan Borough Council Unreported, Crown Court (Nottingham), 6 February 1991, 130, 214
Glasgow Corporation v Muir [1943] AC 448, 56
Gold v Haringey Health Authority [1988] QB 481, 76
Goldstein v Levy Gee (A Firm) [2003] EWHC 1574, 80
Gravil v Carroll, Redruth Rugby Football Club [2008] EWCA Civ 689, 63
Hall v Brooklands Auto-Racing Club [1933] 1 KB 205 (CA), 89
Hammersley-Gonsalves v Redcar & Cleveland BC [2012] EWCA Civ 1135, 60, 130, 133
Harrison v Vincent [1982] RTR 8 (CA), 96–7, 119, 125, 189, 211
Hedley Byrne & Co Ltd v Heller & Partner Ltd [1964] AC 465, 32, 130
Hide v The Steeplechase Company (Cheltenham) Ltd [2013] EWCA Civ 545, 66
Honnor v Lewis [2005] EWHC 747, 62
Humphrey v Aegis Defence Services Ltd [2016] EWCA Civ 11, 53
James-Bowen v Commissioner of the Police of the Metropolis [2018] UKSC 40, 3
Kennedy v Cordia (Services) LLP [2016] UKSC 6, 179
Kent v Griffiths [2001] QB 36 (CA), 28
Letang v Cooper [1965] 1 QB 232 (CA), 42
Lewis v Buckpool Golf Club 1993 SCT 43, 58
MacFarlane v Tayside Health Board [2000] 2 AC 59, 7
MacIntyre v Ministry of Defence [2011] EWHC 1690, 53, 65, 142, 146–8, 179, 181, 193, 196, 198, 199, 212, 213
Maylin v Dacorum Sports Trust trading as XC Sportspace [2017] EWHC 378, 131
McErlean v MacAuley [2014] NIQB 1, 132
McMahon v Dear [2014] CSOH 100, 53

Michael v Chief Constable of South Wales Police [2015] UKSC 2, 32
Morrell v Owen (1993) Times, 14 December 1993, 56, 212, 215
Morrow v Dungannon and South Tyrone Borough Council [2012] NIQB 50, 29, 137–9, 193, 194, 210
Mountford v Newlands School [2007] EWCA Civ 21, 165
Mullin v Richards [1998] 1 WLR 1304 (CA), 62
Murray v Harringay Arena LD [1951] 2 KB 529 (CA), 89
Murray v McCullough [2016] NIQB 52, 131, 132
Nettleship v Weston [1971] 2 QB 691 (CA), 48, 52, 55
Orchard v Lee [2009] EWCA Civ 295, 62
Overseas Tankship (UK) Ltd v The Miller Steamship Co (Wagon Mound No 2) [1967] 1 AC 617, 52
Overseas Tankship (UK) Ltd v Morts Docks & Engineering Co Ltd (Wagon Mound No 1) [1961] AC 388, 59
Paris v Stepney BC [1951] AC 367, 52
Perry v Harris [2008] EWCA Civ 907, 53, 57, 213
Petrou v Bertoncello [2012] EWHC 2286, 32, 63, 64, 136–7, 212, 215
Phee v Gordon [2013] CSIH 18, 53
Phelps v Hillingdon London BC [2000] LGR 651, 76, 79
Pinchbeck v Craggy Island Ltd [2012] EWHC 2745, 10, 132, 133–5, 181
Pitcher v Huddersfield Town Football Club, 17 July 2001 (QBD), 77
Pook v Rossall School [2018] EWHC 522, 54, 66, 169, 176
Poppleton v Trustees of the Portsmouth Youth Activities Committee [2008] EWCA Civ 646, 32, 131
Porter v Barking and Dagenham LBC (1990) Times, 9 April, 131
R v Barnes [2004] EWCA Crim 3246, 5
Read v Lyons [1947] AC 156, 56
Regina (Daly) v Secretary of State for the Home Department [2001] 2 AC 532, 30, 55, 186
Risk v Rose Bruford College [2013] EWHC 3869, 179, 198
Robinson v Chief Constable of West Yorkshire Police [2018] UKSC 4, 3
Scout Association v Barnes [2010] EWCA Civ 1476, 54, 55, 63, 164, 196, 198, 209, 215
Shone v British Bobsleigh Limited [2018] 5 WLUK 226, 29, 131, 155–8, 211, 212, 215
Smith New Court Securities Ltd v Scimgeour Vickers (Asset Management) Ltd [1997] AC 254, 18
Smoldon v Whitworth [1997] ELR 115, 46
Smoldon v Whitworth [1997] PIQR P133 (CA), 4, 12, 38, 45, 46, 62, 105, 107–10, 125, 195, 210
Spartan Steel & Alloys Ltd v Martin & Co (Contractors) Ltd [1973] QB 27 (CA), 22
Stovin v Wise [1996] AC 923, 27
Sutton v Syston RFC Limited [2011] EWCA Civ 1182, 54, 140–2, 209, 213
Tomlinson v Congleton BC [2004] 1 AC 46, 54, 140
Uren v Corporate Leisure (UK) Limited [2010] EWHC 46, 53, 198, 199
Uren v Corporate Leisure (UK) Limited [2011] EWCA Civ 66, 55, 142, 179, 198, 212

Uren v Corporate Leisure (UK) Limited [2013] EWHC 353, 178, 179, 198, 199
Van Oppen v Clerk to the Bedford Charity Trustees [1989] 1 All ER 273, 50
Van Oppen v Clerk to the Bedford Charity Trustees [1989] 3 All ER 389 (CA), 50, 51, 130, 216
Vaughan v Menlove (1837) 3 Bing NC 468, 52
Villella v North Bedfordshire BC, 25 October 1983 (QBD), 49, 190
Vowles v Evans [2002] EWHC 2612, 112
Vowles v Evans [2003] EWCA Civ 318, 4, 12, 23, 38, 45, 46, 63, 68, 107, 113–17, 118, 119, 125, 189, 211, 215
Watson v British Boxing Board of Control [2001] QB 1134 (CA), 3, 213, 214
Watt v Hertfordshire CC [1954] 1 WLR 835 (CA), 52
Wattleworth v Goodwood Road Racing Co Ltd [2004] EWHC 140, 61
Wells v Full Moon Events Ltd [2020] EWHC 1265, 61
Whippey v Jones [2009] EWCA Civ 452, 53, 213
Whittet v Virgin Active Ltd [2019] 2 WLUK 779, 131
Wilkin-Shaw v Fuller [2012] EWHC 1777, 43, 50, 51, 196, 197, 198
Wilks v Cheltenham Homeguard Motor Cycle and Light Car Club [1971] 1 WLR 668 (CA), 8, 12, 93–5
Williams v Eady (1893) 10 TLR 41, 74
Wilsher v Essex AHA [1987] QB 730 (CA), 28, 51, 58, 77, 132, 195
Woodbridge School v Chittock [2002] EWCA Civ 915, 60, 65, 80, 124, 177, 194, 210
Woodland v Swimming Teachers Association [2013] UKSC 66, 52
Woodland v Maxwell [2015] EWHC 820, 214
Woodroffe-Hedley v Cuthbertson, 20 June 1997 (QBD), 60, 79, 124–6, 132, 176, 177, 181, 208, 211
Wooldridge v Sumner [1963] 2 QB 43 (CA), 2, 12, 44, 59, 61, 88–91, 95, 125, 210
Wright v Cheshire CC [1952] 2 ALL ER 789 (CA), 65, 130, 194
Young v Kent CC [2005] EWHC 1342, 180
Yuen Kun Yeu v Attorney-General of Hong Kong [1988] AC 175, 27

Australia

Agar v Hyde [2001] HCA 41, 4, 10
Canterbury Bankstown Rugby League Football Club Ltd. v Rogers [1993] Aust. Torts Reports 81–246, 64
Dickson v Northern Lakes Rugby League Sport & Recreation Club Inc & Anor (No 2) [2019] NSWDC 433, 9
Frazer v Johnston (1989) Aust Torts Reports 80–248, 8, 9
Goode v Angland [2016] NSWSC 1014, 8, 9
Hyde v Agar (1998) 45 NSWLR 487, 9
Papatonakis v Australian Telecommunications Commission (1985) 156 CLR 7, 7
Rootes v Shelton [1968] ALR 33, 4, 5, 99, 101, 102, 211
Sutherland Shire Council v Heyman (1985) 60 ALR 1, 3, 4
Woods v Multi-Sport holdings PTY Ltd [2002] HCA 9, 8, 9

Canada

Cooper v Hobart [2001] 3 SCR 537, 4
Dolby v McWhirter [1979] OJ No. 4154, 9
Dyck v Manitoba Snowmobile Assn [1982] MJ No. 13, 9
Fink et al. v Greeniaus [1973] OJ No. 2283, 9
Goshen v Larin [1974] NSJ No. 248, 9
Hamstra et al. v British Columbia Rugby Union [1989] 1 CCLT (2d) 78, 49
Mattheson v The Governors of Dalhusey University and College (1983) 57 NSR (2nd) 56; 25 CCLT 9l (SC), 4
Mocharski v Young Men's Christian Assn. of Greater Vancouver [2004] BCJ No. 1898, 8
Plumb (Guardian ad litem of) v Cowichan School District No. 65 [1991] BCJ No. 3709, 8
Potozny v Burnaby (City) [2001] BCJ No. 1224, 8
R v Cey (1989) 48 CCC (3d) 480, 5
Thornton v School Dist. No. 57 (Prince George) Bd. Of School Trustees [1976] 5 WWR 240, 73 DLR (3d) 35 (BCCA), 51
Unruh (Guardian ad litem of) v Webber (BCCA), [1994] BCJ No. 467, 8, 9

Hong Kong

Wai Yip Hin v Wong Po Kit (No 1) [2009] 3 HKC 362, 9, 131

New Zealand

Evans And Others v Waitemata District Pony Club, East Coast Bays Branch And Others [1972] NZLR 773, 8
R M Turton & Co (in liq) v Kerslake & Partners [2000] 3 NZLR 406, 4

United States

Austin v Miami University (2013) – Ohio – 5925, 9
McCarty v Pheasant Run Inc 826 F2d 1554 (1987), 53
US v Carroll Towing Co 159 F2d 169 (1947), 52

Table of legislation

Compensation Act 2006, s 1…21–2, 52, 54, 112, 135, 142, 209
Consumer Rights Act 2015, s 65…10
Law Reform (Contributory Negligence) Act 1945, s 1…62
Occupiers' Liability Act 1957…89, 140, 141
Senior Courts Act 1981, s 69…7
Social Action, Responsibility and Heroism Act 2015…22, 54, 111–12, 135, 209
Unfair Contract Terms Act 1977…10, 134

FOREWORD

The act of being a PhD supervisor is a bit like being a driving instructor. Many of those whom you supervise have some existing knowledge or even training in what they are about to engage in, though they will now engage more deeply; some are more confident and ready than others; a few seem to think they know it all already and one or two clamber out awkwardly before the lesson has even begun.

Equally though, there are those candidates who listen thoughtfully, engage with you critically and realise that what is about to occur is a process wherein the relationship must evolve from one of supervisor–student to one of peer-to-peer.

The author of this excellent text was originally one of the "self-drive" PhD students just described, that is, one who recognised the process at work. As one of his supervisory team (with Dr David Capper at Queen's University Belfast), we only had to point him vaguely in the right direction and he took off, cautiously at first but later confidently and all the way to his viva, which was that rare thing – a joy, for all involved. Thanks, enduringly, to the examiners, Dr Ciara Hackett (QUB) and Dr David McArdle (Stirling), for their assistance.

The driving instructor analogy is apt in that one of the standard cases wheeled out – sorry – by tort law lecturers yearly to discuss the constituent parts of negligence is, of course, *Nettleship v Weston*. That driving instruction did not end well when on that cold Sunday morning of 12 November 1967, Lavinia Weston (married woman) on her third lesson with Eric Nettleship, took a "vice-like" grip on the steering wheel, hit a lamp post and broke Eric's left kneecap. Professional, and presumably neighbourly, relations between the pair were sundered forever.

On that fateful day, Eric's duty of care towards Lavinia was to coach her in the art of driving. This book is, of course, about coaching in the sporting sense. A common experience for all of us who love and have played sport is often the influence of a teacher and/or coach who, at an early stage, fosters a love of our chosen sport – its skills, its difficulties, its glories – that endures a lifetime.

Parents like mine and yours – and now I, as a parent myself – trust coaches weekly with the care and sporting education of their children. It is an onerous and important task, the "professionalisation" of which is somewhat underestimated and misunderstood, though not by this seminal book.

The core legal aspect of this book – duty of care – is really predicated on the assumption of responsibility that a coach has over an individual or team. The scope of that assumption and the boundary of the responsibility within which a coach must operate is teased out in impressive detail in this book.

The level of trust that players (professional, amateur, youths, etc.) place in and assign to coaches – and not just their athletic capacity but also their health and well-being – is not only elemental to coaching and the profession's greatest strength; it is also where it is often at is most vulnerable.

At best, the coaching relationship prepares and inspires athletes to fully realise their potential; at worst, it can be abusive and both physically and psychologically damaging.

The key appeal of this book is that it analyses critically and with clarity how best to prevent, identify and redress in law and in practice the sometimes nefarious elements of coaching so that we can better support the "better angels" of our coaching nature and the good practices which the overwhelming majority of coaches adhere to daily.

Finally, the author and I met as PhD student and supervisor in Belfast. During the height of the troubles there, many sports, and particularly boxing gyms, remained resolutely, defiantly neutral. Coaches therein saw the athlete – the boy, the girl – and nothing more and took them under their care.

There are countless coaches globally, under varying circumstances, who do the same every day to the benefit of their charges. Such coaches, to paraphrase Teddy Roosevelt, do what they can with what they have, where they are. In other words, they discharge their duty, a duty of care.

Professor Jack Anderson
Director of Studies, Sports Law
University of Melbourne
August 2020

PREFACE

The following motivational passage by Sir Andrew Barton may be regarded as symbolic of the character, commitment and desire sports coaches frequently demand of athletes:

> Little I'm hurt, but yet not slaine,
> I'll lye downe and bleede awhile,
> And then I'll rise and fight againe.[1]

It has undoubtedly influenced and shaped my own approach to coaching, having experienced its sentiments modelled and reinforced by highly successful coaches. However, the ballad offers little by way of guidance when determining when it may be (un)reasonable to 'rise and fight againe'. Adopting a legal perspective, this distinction may prove decisive when establishing if coaches have effectively discharged their duty of care. In the context of sport, decisions regarding 'how hard to "push"' athletes and teams are often left to individual coaches. This reveals one of the core curiosities underpinning this book: the boundary between forging champions and committing a tort (i.e., by breaching the duty of care owed). More categorically, the subsequent pages critically consider the practical content of the specific duties required of modern sports coaches. By adopting an engaging interdisciplinary analysis, *Coaching, Sport and the Law: A Duty of Care* clarifies what precisely is meant by a legal duty of care in the context of sports coaching, thereby offering original and sustained treatment of this evolving complexity of coaching. As such, the book should be of considerable interest and value to all bodies, and individual practitioners, involved in sports coaching, coach education,

---

1 Adapted from the ballad by Sir Andrew Barton, LXIV <www.bartleby.com/243/130.html> accessed 16 December 2019.

sports policy, planning and development, and students and teachers in the following fields: sports ethics, sports studies, PE teaching, law and, most specifically, the developing academic disciplines of both sports law and sports coaching. Moreover, given the book's scrutiny of ordinary tort law principles in the distinctive context of sport, with its emphasis on the application of legal principles in practice, *Coaching, Sport and the Law: A Duty of Care* is intended to prove instructive for legal practitioners specialising in personal injury law, professional negligence and sports law.

Reinforcing the fact that duty of care considerations are integral to coaching behaviour and practice, comments made by Coach Bill Sweetenham, when interviewed for BBC R5L's sports week on 1 May 2016, are worth recalling in full:

> With any coaches, or a lot of coaches, they're gonna push boundaries and push them very hard and do things to motivate athletes that probably, on occasions, are gonna push the limits. . . . When you're pushing boundaries and you're trying to get athletes to express their potential at the highest level it can happen [doing or saying something inappropriate]. It's very easy to go. Coaches don't know what the athlete's capabilities are. You're trying to push the boundaries and hope that you get the result that's best for the athlete. Remember, coaches are pushing boundaries all the time to try and achieve the athlete's potential, or actually get the athlete to rise above their talent. So, if you can coach an athlete above their level of talent, and you've always got to have a skill level in there that's beyond the athlete's talent. To do that, it's not easy and there will be times that you push the boundaries a bit too hard and you think – nah, I've gone too hard on that situation. . . . I know that I've pushed the boundaries from time to time.
>
> I always insist that I have a person with me knowing what I'm gonna push and how I'm gonna push and the boundaries and the limits, how I'm gonna try and get every athlete to see their horizons and go beyond it and the coaching staff as well. I always have someone to work with me to pick up the pieces so to speak . . . their job will be [to] say: 'Bill, back off. It's time to stand away.' And sometimes you need that because in the heat of the moment, in the heat of the battle . . . the world is changing, the world, the wide generation is a different group of people to coach and the next generation will be more different than it was and it is now. Each generation is gonna bring to the senior and older coach great challenges and more challenges and they will have to, they can't change the culture, the coach will have to change.[2]

This book critically analyses a number of the issues alluded to by Coach Sweetenham in relation to the duty of care of modern sports coaches and the developing intersection between sports coaching and the law of negligence. These issues

---

2 Interview with Bill Sweetenham, *Sportsweek*, BBC R5L (1 May 2016) <www.bbc.co.uk/programmes/b078x676> accessed 1 May 2016.

include the health, safety and welfare of athletes; the boundary between reasonable and negligent coaching practice; the specificity of sports coaching; the mutually dependent coach–athlete relationship; the particular circumstances in which sports coaches perform their functions; defining regular and approved coaching practice that might be logically justifiable and the emerging challenges posed by respective and ever-evolving legal and coaching contexts.

Importantly, this book illustrates how the legal standard of care required of modern sports coaches, when exercising their duty of care, represents a fluid and malleable benchmark by conducting a rigorous and searching examination of the developing body of related case law and providing rich, insightful and engaging detailed extracts from relevant court judgments. This benchmark is prone to constant review due to advances brought about in the field of sports science, technical developments in certain sports, medico-legal issues in sport, societal expectations, general improvements likely to be facilitated by the further 'professionalisation' of sports coaching and evolutions in the law relating to duties of care. These factors will increase the scope and degree of the duty of care owed by coaches by progressively placing more responsibilities on coaches. Accordingly, conducting a detailed scrutiny of this hitherto often cited but seldom analysed fundamental aspect of coaching practice is both timely and necessary, not least because the concept of duty of care is increasingly latched onto by the media and members of the general public as an expression of legitimate and reasonable expectations in the particular circumstances of sport.

ACKNOWLEDGEMENTS

Grateful acknowledgement is made to all the authors and publishers of copyright material which appears in this book, and in particular to the following for permission to reprint material from the sources indicated.

SPRINGER NATURE: N Partington, 'Legal liability of coaches: a UK perspective' (2014) 14(3–4) *International Sports Law Journal* 232–241.

THOMPSON REUTERS (PROFESSIONAL) UK LIMITED: N Partington, 'Professional liability of amateurs: The context of sports coaching' (2015) 4 *Journal of Personal Injury Law* 232–242.

BLOOMSBURY PROFESSIONAL (an imprint of Bloomsbury Publishing Plc): N Partington, '"It's just not cricket". Or is it? (2016) 32(1) *Professional Negligence* 75–79.

TAYLOR & FRANCIS LTD (www.tandfonline.com): N Partington, 'Sports Coaching and the Law of Negligence: Implications for Coaching Practice' (2017) 6(1) *Sports Coaching Review* 36–56.

THOMPSON REUTERS (PROFESSIONAL) AUSTRALIA LIMITED: N Partington, 'Distinguishing Duties of Care of Sports Coaches in a UK Context' (2019) 27(1) *Tort Law Review* 62–77. This article was first published by Thomson Reuters in the *Tort Law Review* and should be cited as N Partington, 'Distinguishing Duties of Care of Sports Coaches in a UK Context', (2019). For all subscription inquiries please phone, from Australia: 1300 304 195, from Overseas: +61 2 8587 7980 or online at legal.thomsonreuters.com.au/search. The official PDF version of this article can also be purchased separately from Thomson Reuters.

I am tremendously grateful for the support, advice and encouragement given to me by colleagues at Sussex Law School, University of Sussex, during the writing of this book. In particular, Professor Jo Bridgeman, Dr Mark Davies, Dr Stavros Demetriou, Dr Kenny Veitch, Dr Verona Ni Drisceoil and both the present and previous Heads of Department, Professor Donald McGillivray and Professor Sue

Millns. Further, given this book's interdisciplinary focus, I am extremely appreciative of the constructive comments provided by Dr Colum Cronin, School of Sport and Exercise Sciences, Liverpool John Moores University, on a previous draft of the manuscript.

This book draws considerably from my PhD thesis completed at Queen's University Belfast (QUB) in 2016. As such, the outstanding supervision of my PhD by Professor Jack Anderson (now Director of Studies, Sports Law, University of Melbourne) and Dr David Capper (QUB) was instrumental in helping to develop this monograph, and I am most fortunate and privileged that they continue to encourage and support me and my research. I would also like to express my gratitude for the positive and constructive comments made by my PhD examiners, Dr Ciara Hackett (QUB) and Dr David McArdle (Stirling University), as well as instructive suggestions made by Professor Gordon Anthony (QUB).

Many thanks also go to all at Routledge for their patience, professionalism and courtesy, and especially to Simon Whitmore and the *Ethics and Sport* series editors, Professor Mike McNamee and Professor Jim Parry, for providing this opportunity. The extensive support offered throughout the writing process by Rebecca Connor was likewise very helpful.

Finally, I wish to thank my parents, along with Katie, Conor, Annie and Fionn, for their unreserved encouragement, backing and considerable understanding during completion of this book. This book is dedicated to them.

INTRODUCTION

The concept of duty of care is under unparalleled scrutiny in the context of sport and, more specifically, with regard to sports coaching. The need to critically analyse the emerging relationship between the law and sports coaching could not be more pressing, not least because of recent controversies suggesting that coaches may frequently breach the duty of care owed to athletes in order to achieve sporting success. This has led to independent investigations, reviews and concerns regarding the ethos and culture of numerous sports, including British Cycling, GB Bobsleigh, British Gymnastics, British Canoeing and, as articulately presented in evidence to the Department for Digital, Culture, Media and Sport (DCMS) by Eniola Aluko in October 2017, at the highest level of women's football. Moreover, in what appears likely to prove a landmark publication, 'Duty of Care in Sport: Independent Report to Government' (DoC in Sport Report), Baroness Tanni Grey-Thompson insightfully recognised that:

> Winning medals is, of course, really important, but should not be at the expense of the Duty of Care towards athletes, coaches and others involved in the system. . . . [I]t feels timely for the sport sector to consider Duty of Care in its fullest sense. . . . Questions are being asked about the price being paid for success.[1]

At its core, the DoC in Sport Report concentrated on the safety, well-being and welfare of all participants involved in sport, with a particular aim being to 'raise the profile of Duty of Care' and facilitate further discussion regarding its achievement and implementation. Crucially, the concept of duty of care appears ever more

---

1 Baroness Tanni Grey-Thompson, 'Duty of Care in Sport: Independent Report to Government', Department for Digital, Culture, Media & Sport, 21 April 2017, 4.

deeply engrained in everyday language and, as suggested by Norris, is increasingly latched onto by members of the general public in order to create a 'veneer of pseudo-legal authority'.[2] Thus, rather than being legal, its use often becomes metaphoric. Put bluntly, when the concept of the duty of care assumes both a legal and extralegal meaning in the context of sport, there is a danger, to borrow from the words of Diplock LJ in the leading UK authority for sports negligence, *Wooldridge v Sumner*, of mistaking 'aphorism for exegesis'.[3] As this book argues, this is problematic and may result in serious unintended consequences. This distinction emphasises the need for the concept of the duty of care in sport to be clearly defined and rigorously tested. Since it is at common law that the notion of a duty of care originates and continues to evolve,[4] the focus of this book is the intersection between the ordinary law of negligence and sports coaching.[5]

Coaches are the principal supervisors of organised sporting activities. The interdependent coach–athlete relationship represents perhaps the most obvious and commonly occurring instance of a duty of care in sport. Significantly, existing academic scholarship offers only limited detailed analysis of the duty of care incumbent upon coaches or what may amount to a breach of this duty. This book addresses this gap by offering sustained treatment of the concept of duty of care in the specific context of sports coaching. To this end, this book adopts an interdisciplinary approach within a broader sociolegal methodological framework which uncovers authentic insights of contemporary practical importance for the many stakeholders with a passion, enthusiasm and interest in sports coaching. Interdisciplinarity may be regarded as involving 'an integration or synthesis – an interconnection between different academic disciplines'.[6] Critical synthesis of literature from areas including law, sports coaching and sports ethics facilitates appropriate and effective interdisciplinary research. Moreover, a sociolegal perspective, or 'law in context' approach,[7]

---

2 W Norris, 'A Duty of Care in Sport: What It Actually Means' (2017) 3 *JPI Law* 154.
3 *Wooldridge v Sumner* [1963] 2 QB 43 (CA) 66. This case is discussed in detail in Chapter 4.
4 Norris (n 2).
5 Importantly, the legal framework dealing with child protection and safeguarding is predominantly directed at statutory bodies and involves both general criminal (e.g., Sexual Offences Act 2003) and civil law. Moreover, litigation in child abuse cases is most commonly brought against those deemed to be responsible for the actions of the perpetrator of the abuse and not against the individual perpetrator(s) of the abuse. As such, a specific consideration of the very serious issue of child safeguarding in sport is outside the scope of this text. See further, A Gray et al., 'Child Safeguarding' in A Lewis and J Taylor (eds), *Sport: Law and Practice* (3rd edn, London, Bloomsbury Professional 2014) Chapter C4.
6 D Vick, 'Interdisciplinarity and the Discipline of Law' in D Cowan et al. (eds), *Law And Society* (London, Routledge 2014) Vol I 314. For further discussions on what might be regarded as a 'discipline' and distinctions between interdisciplinary, multidisciplinary, cross-disciplinary and transdisciplinary, see: MH Stober, *Interdisciplinary Conversations: Challenging Habits of Thought* (Stanford, Stanford University Press 2011) 12–18.
7 F Cownie and A Bradney, 'Socio-Legal Studies: A Challenge to the Doctrinal Approach' in D Watkins and M Burton (eds), *Research Methods in Law* (London, Routledge 2013) 35.

speaks to 'an interface with a context within which law exists'.[8] Whilst this text's jurisdictional focus is predominantly the UK, as explained later, the relevance of this book's critical analysis will transcend geographical boundaries given the interchange of ideas in the field of sports negligence by courts in different countries and the compelling commonalities of reasonable coaching practice globally.

Common law family

There is well-established and extensive cross-pollination of tortious principles between countries of the wider common law family.[9] In determining whether a duty of care is owed by a particular defendant in certain circumstances, or duty test, UK courts apply the approach adopted by the High Court of Australia[10] in *Sutherland Shire Council v Heyman*.[11] In *Sutherland Shire Council*, Brennan J stated that:

> [i]t is preferable, in my view, that the law should develop novel categories of negligence incrementally and by analogy with established categories, rather than by a massive extension of a prima facie duty of care restrained only by indefinable considerations which ought to negative, or to reduce or limit the scope of the duty or the class of person to whom it is owed.[12]

As acknowledged by Lord Phillips MR in *Watson v British Boxing Board of Control*, both the House of Lords and Court of Appeal have approved these observations of Brennan J on many occasions.[13] This approach by the High Court of Australia was most recently endorsed by the UK Supreme Court in *Robinson v Chief Constable of West Yorkshire Police*[14] and *James-Bowen v Commissioner of the Police of the Metropolis*.[15] *Robinson* and *James-Bowen* reaffirmed that the leading authority regarding the establishment of a duty of care in the UK for novel situations remains *Caparo Industries Plc v Dickman*.[16] According to Witting, the *Caparo* test is also applied in Canada

---

8   S Wheeler and P Thomas, 'Socio-Legal Studies' in D Hayton (ed), *Law's Future(s)* (New York, Hart 2002) 271. See further, R Banakar and M Travers, *Theory and Method in Socio-Legal Research* (New York, Hart 2005) xii.
9   See generally, R Caddell, 'The Referee's Liability for Catastrophic Sports Injuries – A UK Perspective' (2005) 15 *Marq. Sports L. Rev.* 415, 424. Also see H Spamann, 'Contemporary Legal Transplants: Legal Families and the Diffusion of (Corporate) Law' (2009) *BYU L Rev* 1813, 1831–33.
10 Australia's highest court and the final court of appeal.
11 *Sutherland Shire Council v Heyman* (1985) 60 ALR 1. As discussed in Chapter 2, given it is now well established that a coach would ordinarily owe a duty of care to participants, the duty test in the context of sports coaching is typically straightforwardly satisfied.
12 Ibid, 43–44.
13 *Watson v British Boxing Board of Control* [2001] QB 1134 (CA) [7].
14 *Robinson v Chief Constable of West Yorkshire Police* [2018] UKSC 4 [25] (Lord Reed).
15 *James-Bowen v Commissioner of the Police of the Metropolis* [2018] UKSC 40 [23].
16 *Caparo Industries Plc v Dickman* [1990] 2 AC 605, 618 (Lord Bridge).

4 Introduction

and New Zealand.[17] Indeed, despite being reformulated in *Cooper v Hobart*, the Canadian Supreme Court has fashioned 'a test of duty very similar to that which emerges from Caparo',[18] such that it appears 'remarkably familiar to the "classic" incremental approach re-adopted by the House of Lords'.[19] This lends support to Witting's argument that *'Caparo Industries* is likely to remain an irresistible force in the law of negligence' in common law countries.[20]

Two further decisions of the High Court of Australia, *Rootes v Shelton*[21] and *Agar v Hyde*,[22] have also been cited by the English Court of Appeal in the respective leading judgments concerning the duty of care owed by sports officials,[23] *Smoldon v Whitworth*[24] and *Vowles v Evans*.[25] Most significantly, with regard to a coach's duty of care, and in further consolidating the submission that this book's analysis will be of considerable relevance beyond its primary jurisdictional focus, is the fact that the UK's leading authority for coach negligence, *Fowles v Bedfordshire County Council*, also refers to *Sutherland Shire Council*.[26] So whilst the law of negligence can sometimes be given a 'plural twist' to ensure that its development remains attuned to the circumstances of practical life in different common law jurisdictions,[27] the

---

17 C Witting, 'Tort Law, Policy and the High Court of Australia' (2007) 31 *Melb U L Rev* 569, 580. See *Cooper v Hobart* [2001] 3 SCR 537 and *R M Turton & Co (in liq) v Kerslake & Partners* [2000] 3 NZLR 406.
18 J Hartshorne, *'Confusion, Contradiction* and *Chaos within* the *House* of *Lords Post Caparo v. Dickman'* (2008) 16 *Tort Law Review* 8, 22.
19 J Neyers, 'Distilling Duty: The Supreme Court of Canada Amends Anns' (2002) 118 *LQR* 221.
20 C Witting, 'The Three-Stage Test Abandoned in Australia – Or Not?' (2002) 118 *LQR* 214, 221.
21 *Rootes v Shelton* [1968] ALR 33.
22 *Agar v Hyde* [2001] HCA 41.
23 In this book the term 'sports official' will be used to refer to individuals refereeing and/or umpiring competitive sporting activities.
24 *Smoldon v Whitworth* [1997] PIQR P133, P138. Lord Bingham CJ, when giving the judgment of the court, began by highlighting that *Rootes v Shelton* was one of the earliest cases to have explored the duty owed by one sporting participant to another. As discussed later, in *Condon v Basi* (1985) 1 WLR 866, the English Court of Appeal adopted the exact legal principles established in *Rootes*.
25 *Vowles v Evans* [2003] EWCA Civ 318 [15]-[20]. Although *Agar v Hyde* was ultimately distinguished from *Vowles* given the very different facts, in acknowledging the potential for decisions from another common law jurisdiction to prove persuasive before courts in England and Wales, Lord Phillips MR recognised that there were passages in *Agar* which lent support to the arguments submitted by counsel for the defendant rugby referee in *Vowles* (at [18]). In a similar fashion, this book's detailed examination and analysis of coach negligence case law involves judgments that will, no doubt, provide persuasive authority in certain circumstances for legal practitioners and scholars based in jurisdictions other than the UK. A further illustration of this particular submission is provided in *Elliott v Saunders and Liverpool Football Club,* Unreported, Queen's Bench Division 10 June 1994 when Drake J accepted that submissions made about the nature and extent of the duty of care owed by one professional football player towards another was supported by the Australian High Court case of *Rootes* (n 21) and, to a lesser degree, the Canadian case of *Mattheson v The Governors of Dalhusey University and College* (1983) 57 NSR (2nd) 56; 25 CCLT 9l (SC).
26 *Fowles v Bedfordshire CC* [1995] PIQR P380 (CA) P388–89 (Millett LJ). *Fowles* is discussed in detail in Chapter 5.
27 R Mullender, 'The Reasonable Person, The Pursuit of Justice, and Negligence Law' (2005) 68(4) *MLR* 681, 690–91.

contribution of persuasive authority from the wider common law family has been repeatedly drawn upon to assist the development of the law in the UK by the highest courts.[28] This interchange of ideas is argued to be especially prevalent in the evolution and establishment of the legal principles applied in cases of negligence during sporting activities.[29]

The influence afforded to legal principles established in the law of negligence in other Commonwealth countries is not limited to the question of whether a requisite duty of care exists. In *Condon v Basi*, the Court of Appeal adopted wholesale the decision and statements of law made in *Rootes v Shelton* when formulating the legal test for breach of duty by co-participants.[30] As revealed in Chapter 4, this test remains integral to the vast majority of sports negligence cases in the UK,[31] including claims of a breach of duty by coaches.[32] In following the reasoning of the court in *Rootes*, Sir John Donaldson MR in *Condon* essentially applied 'a general standard of care, namely the Lord Atkin approach in Donaghue v Stevenson [1932] AC 562 that you are under a duty to take all reasonable care, taking account of the circumstances in which you are placed'.[33] Fundamentally, this standard exacted by the law is premised on a benchmark of reasonableness and it is this generalised expression of the content of the duty of care that underscores the widespread relevance of this book's sociolegal analysis.

Reasonableness

As explained by Zipursky, law's use of the term 'reasonable' is legion.[34] Reasonableness represents 'a paradigmatic example of a standard in the law'.[35] It is the standard of conduct ordinarily required when individuals discharge their legal duties of care. As a ubiquitous fixture of the common law, enormous weight is afforded to the acts and/or omissions that the fictional 'reasonable person' would have displayed in claims of negligence due to a breach of duty.[36] Simply applied, common law negligence doctrine in the United Kingdom, the United States, and Commonwealth

---

28 Drawing upon persuasive authority from other common law jurisdictions is not restricted to the law of tort. For instance, when considering the issue of criminal liability for on-field violence, the Court of Appeal in *R v Barnes* [2004] EWCA Crim 3246 [12] approved the approach of the Saskatchewan Court of Appeal in *R v Cey* (1989) 48 CCC (3d) 480.
29 See further, Chapter 4 where the development of sports negligence jurisprudence in the UK is critically analysed.
30 *Condon* (n 24) 867–68. *Condon* is discussed in detail in Chapter 4.
31 As refined and further developed in *Caldwell v Maguire* [2001] EWCA Civ 1054.
32 See further, Chapter 5, where sustained treatment of the duty of care required of modern sports coaches is provided.
33 *Caldwell* (n 31) [16] (Tuckey LJ).
34 B Zipursky, 'Reasonableness In and Out of Negligence Law' (2015) 163 *U. of Pa. L. Rev.* 2131, 2132.
35 Ibid, 2133.
36 G Yaffe, 'Reasonableness in the Law and Second-Personal Address' (2007) 40 *Loy L A L Rev* 939. Also see Mullender (n 27).

countries is largely concerned with 'whether a defendant acted as a "reasonably prudent person" would act under the circumstances'.[37] Reliance on a reasonableness standard is not restricted to common law jurisdictions.[38] As argued by Fletcher, French, German and Soviet [now Russian] legal systems adopt terms parallel to the term 'reasonable'.[39] When considered alongside the earlier discussion concerning the persuasive force of authority from the High Court of Australia when fashioning the duty test to be applied by UK courts, for instance, this offers considerable weight to Magnus's observation that the law of negligence may be regarded as generally similar everywhere.[40]

The suggestion that the legal principles underpinning the law of negligence remain largely consistent throughout the world, and most notably with regard to the applicable standard of care or conduct element, is further concretised by Ahmed's comparative legal analysis of 'reasonableness' in South Africa, France, the USA and the UK.[41] For present purposes, South African law is a particularly interesting comparator since it is referred to as a hybrid system, or mixed jurisdiction, with the South African law of delict representing a mix of English common law and Roman-Dutch law.[42] As concluded by Ahmed, reasonableness is implicit in the element of conduct in both the South African and French laws of delict and in

---

37 Zipursky (n 34) 2134 & 2169.
38 The law in common law countries, including the UK, Australia, Canada and the US, is premised on the doctrine of precedent, whereby the previous decisions of courts, or case law, provides the basis for the development of the law. See, for instance, E Finch and S Fafinski, *Legal Skills* (7th edn, Oxford, OUP 2019) 139, and the further discussion in Chapter 4. Conversely, German and French law forms part of the civil law family where the applicable law is codified. See further, R Ahmed, 'The Influence of Reasonableness on the Element of Conduct in Delictual or Tort Liability – Comparative Conclusions' (2019) *Potchefstroom Elec. L.J.* 2–3: DOI: 10.17159/1727–3781/2019/v22i0a6122.
39 G Fletcher, 'The Right and the Reasonable' (1985) 98 *Harv L Rev* 949, though these parallel terms are not as prominent in legal discourse in these different jurisdictions. Also see B Markesinis, 'The not so Dissimilar Tort and Delict' (1977) 93 *LQR* 78, 115–16.
40 U Magnus, 'Tort law in general' in J Smits (ed), *Elgar Encyclopaedia of Comparative Law* (Cheltenham, Edward Elgar 2006) 725. Also see P Vines, 'Doping as Tort: Liability of Sport Supervisors and the Problem of Consent' in U Haas and D Healey (eds), *Doping in Sport and the Law* (Oxford, Hart 2016) 193. Interestingly, in *Fairchild v Glenhaven Funeral Services* [2003] 1 AC 32, when considering the law of negligence's control mechanism of causation (see further, Chapter 2), cases referred to in the opinions of their Lordships included decisions from both common and civil law jurisdictions. Indeed, the Commonwealth cases cited were supplemented by material describing the position in European legal systems, and when considering the wider jurisprudence, cases and textbooks on the German law were regarded by Lord Rodger as being particularly instructive (at [167]-[169]). Nonetheless, with specific regard to legal transplants, or diffusion of law, it may well be the case that legal principles and knowledge are more easily shared within legal families (e.g., common law and civil law), rather than as between them. See, for instance, Spamann (n 9).
41 Ahmed (n 38).
42 Ibid, 3–5; S Greenfield et al., 'Reconceptualising The Standard Of Care In Sport: The Case Of Youth Rugby In England And South Africa' (2015) 18(6) *Potchefstroom Elec. L.J.* 2183, 2188. As noted by Ahmed, 'tort' is synonymous with 'delict' and, moreover, French law represents a leading influential system in the civil law tradition.

US tort law.[43] Furthermore, Greenfield et al. have argued that despite a claim being framed differently, 'the original English common law approach to negligence, as inherited and developed in the South African context, is still valid and has persuasive power for delict claims in South Africa'.[44] Consequently, this book's detailed analysis of the nature and extent of the duty of care of coaches in English common law is intended to provide some pertinent insights for readers in common, civil and hybrid legal jurisdictions.

In emphasising the reasonable person's ordinariness, judges in the common law have referred to: the reasonable person on the Clapham omnibus;[45] the man [now person] on the street;[46] the reasonable commuter on the London underground;[47] the reasonable person on the Bondi tram;[48] 'the man [or person] who takes the magazines at home, and in the evening pushes the lawn mower in his [or her] shirt sleeves';[49] and the more modern standard juries are instructed to apply in routine negligence cases in the US, the actions expected of 'a reasonably careful person' or 'a reasonably prudent person'.[50] Lord Radcliffe eloquently and succinctly recognised that in law the reasonable person is the 'anthropomorphic conception of justice'.[51] In many respects, this book is concerned with a ubiquitous fixture of sport, that is, the ordinary reasonable coach and, more specifically, the conduct and practice that would ordinarily be displayed by this fictional coaching figure when discharging their duty of care. Given the established cross-pollination of tortious principles previously discussed, and in elaborating on comments made by Lord Radcliffe, it is argued that in defining the standards represented by the ordinary reasonable person/coach, the UK courts can to a large extent be regarded as the hypothetical reasonable person's/coach's spokesperson.[52] Accordingly, the observations of this judicial spokesperson would be directly applicable not only to the ordinary rugby coach on the playing fields at Rugby School but, given the strong persuasive influence of established authority from different jurisdictions, the requisite standards of this reasonably average rugby coach will have much in common with the ordinary basketball coach in Springfield, Massachusetts, USA, and the ordinary coach of Australian Football in Melbourne, Australia.[53] In short, all of

---

43 Ahmed (n 38) 5.
44 Greenfield et al. (n 42) 2187.
45 Mullender (n 27).
46 *Hall v Brooklands Auto-Racing Club* [1933] 1 KB 205, 224 (Greer LJ).
47 *MacFarlane v Tayside Health Board* [2000] 2 AC 59, 82 (Lord Steyn).
48 *Papatonakis v Australian Telecommunications Commission* (1985) 156 CLR 7, 36 (Deane J).
49 *Hall* (n 46), Greer LJ in 1933 citing an American author. For critical analysis of the reasonable man/person standard, see M Moran, *Rethinking the Reasonable Person: An Egalitarian Reconstruction of the Objective Standard* (Oxford, OUP 2003).
50 Zipursky (n 34) 2154. In the UK, a negligence claim brought to court no longer involves a jury. See section 69 of the Senior Courts Act 1981.
51 *Davis Contractors Ltd v Fareham UDC* [1956] AC 696, 728.
52 Ibid.
53 The same would be true of the ordinary reasonable coaches of lacrosse and ice hockey in Canada and so on.

8 Introduction

these coaches will have a legal duty of care to adopt reasonable coaching behaviour in the particular circumstances.

Whilst this book provides legal scholars with extensive and in-depth coverage of case law that will be of strong persuasive authority, the detailed analysis of this context-specific area of the law ensures that readers with a more precise interest in coaching practice are presented with engaging and instructive factual scenarios from which a judicial pronouncement of reasonableness was drawn. Increasingly, courts in the UK have been tasked with objectively considering many of the types of challenges and tensions frequently encountered by coaches and instructors throughout the world.[54] In ruling whether or not there has been a breach of duty, courts have to address questions of law (i.e., setting the legal standard of care) and questions of fact (i.e., application of this legal standard in a particular case).[55] Looking to another jurisdiction for guidance on a problem that has yet to be conclusively addressed domestically is a common approach adopted by the judiciary.

This technique, combined with the dual ubiquity of both sport and a legal standard of reasonableness, makes sports negligence cases generally and, coach negligence cases in particular, peculiarly suited to the interchange of legal principles and observations from different jurisdictions. For immediate purposes, the persuasive force of Anglo-Welsh case law within other common law jurisdictions when claims of sports negligence have been heard can be readily illustrated.

Persuasive authority

Chapter 4's detailed consideration of the evolution of sports negligence jurisprudence in the UK reveals the leading authorities in this field. These English authorities, most of which have already been mentioned, include *Wooldridge v Sumner*, *Wilks v Cheltenham Homeguard Motor Cycle and Light Car Club*,[56] *Condon v Basi*, *Smoldon v Whitworth* and *Caldwell v Maguire*. *Wooldridge* has been referred to and/or applied by the High Court of Australia,[57] the Supreme Court of New South Wales,[58] the Supreme Court Auckland,[59] the British Columbia Supreme Court,[60] the British Columbia Court of Appeal,[61] the Nova Scotia Supreme Court

---

54 See further, Chapter 2 and, more specifically, Chapters 5–7 where there is detailed engagement with the relevant case law.
55 S Deakin and Z Adams, *Markesinis and Deakin's Tort Law* (8th edn, Oxford, OUP 2019) 184.
56 *Wilks v Cheltenham Homeguard Motor Cycle and Light Car Club* [1971] 1 WLR 668 (CA).
57 *Woods v Multi-Sport holdings PTY Ltd* [2002] HCA 9.
58 *Goode v Angland* [2016] NSWSC 1014; *Frazer v Johnston* (1989) Aust Torts Reports 80–248.
59 *Evans and Others v Waitemata District Pony Club, East Coast Bays Branch and Others* [1972] NZLR 773. The Supreme Court Auckland is now referred to as the High Court.
60 *Mocharski v Young Men's Christian Assn. of Greater Vancouver*, [2004] BCJ No. 1898; *Potozny v Burnaby (City)*, [2001] BCJ No. 1224; *Plumb (Guardian ad litem of) v Cowichan School District No. 65*, [1991] BCJ No. 3709.
61 *Unruh (Guardian ad litem of) v Webber* (BCCA), [1994] BCJ No. 467.

Appeal Division,[62] the Manitoba Court of Appeal,[63] and the Ontario High Court of Justice.[64] *Wilks*,[65] *Condon*,[66] *Smoldon*[67] and *Caldwell*[68] have correspondingly been cited repeatedly in various jurisdictions. In a reciprocal manner, it is not only the higher courts in the UK that also engage with persuasive authority from other jurisdictions when determining liability in negligence during sporting activities.[69] Interestingly, academic commentary analysing UK sports negligence jurisprudence has also proved instructive and helpful to judges abroad.[70] On the more specific issue of coach negligence, a particularly strong illustration of a court in another jurisdiction applying the legal principles established in England and Wales is *Wai Yip Hin v Wong Po Kit*.[71] In *Wai Yip Hin*, Sakhrani J in the Hong Kong Court of First Instance applied *Fowles v Bedfordshire County Council* when defining the nature and extent of the duty of care incumbent upon the defendant Kendo (a Japanese martial art) instructor.[72]

Clearly, in scrutinising the scope of a sports coach's duty of care, this book's analysis of the emerging UK case law will be of relevance and interest to readers from a range of academic and/or professional backgrounds and will extend far beyond its main jurisdictional focus. Nonetheless, given the law of negligence is highly situation-dependent, determining whether or not there has been a breach of duty by a defendant will, as the following pages reveal, often be far from certain.[73]

---

62 *Goshen v Larin*, [1974] NSJ No. 248.
63 *Dyck v Manitoba Snowmobile Assn.*, [1982] MJ No. 13.
64 *Dolby v McWhirter*, [1979] OJ No. 4154; *Fink et al. v Greeniaus*, [1973] OJ No. 2283.
65 E.g., *Woods* (n 57); *Unruh* (n 61); *Frazer* (n 58); *Dyck* (n 63); *Evans* (n 59).
66 E.g., *Dickson v Northern Lakes Rugby League Sport & Recreation Club Inc & Anor* (No 2) [2019] NSWDC 433; *Woods* (n 57); *Unruh* (n 61); *Frazer* (n 58).
67 E.g., *Woods* (n 57); *Hyde v Agar* (1998) 45 NSWLR 487.
68 E.g., *Goode* (n 58); *Wai Yip Hin v Wong Po Kit* (No 1) [2009] 3 HKC 362.
69 See, for instance, *Browning v Odyssey Trust Company Limited* [2014] NIQB 39 [20] & [26], where Gillen J found the American authority of *Austin v Miami University*, (2013) – Ohio – 5925, and the New Zealand case of *Evans* (n 59) at 775, instructive when determining the duty of care owed to the injured spectator by the defendant. Also see *Elliott* (n 25).
70 For instance, in *Frazer* (n 58), Finlay J agreed with the observations made in AL Goodhart, 'The Sportsman's Charter' (1962) 78 LQR 490, 494. See further, Chapter 4. Interestingly, since 2002 there has been a biennial conference on the law of obligations which brings together scholars and practitioners from across the common law world to discuss current issues in areas including the law of torts. See: <www.obsconf.com/> accessed 14 August 2020.
71 *Wai Yip Hin* (n 68).
72 Ibid. [34]-[36]. This case is discussed further in Chapter 5.
73 The focus of this book is on the extent of the duty owed, or standard of care, hence the strong similarities between different legal jurisdictions and the wide application and relevance of the following pages when defining a coach's duty of care. This will enable coaches to reflect and make informed decisions about what constitutes reasonable coaching practice, regardless of the legal jurisdiction in which they coach. However, the further question of whether liability in negligence might be established will be more jurisdiction-specific, not least in view of different statutory provisions (e.g., Part 3 of the Civil Law (Miscellaneous Provisions) Act of 2011 in the Republic of Ireland, whereby legal liability is premised on a gross negligence standard for individual volunteers). See further,

10 Introduction

This underlines the importance of all coaches, when discharging their duties, taking full account of the prevailing circumstances in which they operate.[74] Moreover, an important issue for all readers to reflect on further, when contextualising the arguments presented in this text, is the relevance of broader cultural factors that might influence the standards expected of the ordinary coach in a particular 'sporting country'.[75] There will always be a requirement when analysing tortious issues, regardless of the methodological design utilised, to be cautious when aiming to draw qualified conclusions of general application in relation to standards of care. As all tort law scholars are fully aware, some uncertainty in deeming whether a requisite duty has been breached is an inherent characteristic of the law of negligence. Nonetheless, it is abundantly evident that in defining the practical content of the duty of care required of modern sports coaches it is essential to engage with the emerging case law and, whilst the hypothetical reasonable coach's spokesperson in this book might be predominantly based in the UK, her/his words warrant close and careful attention internationally.

Defining a coach's duty of care

In aiming to provide an authoritative and instructive reference point in the field of sports law generally, and coach negligence in particular, engaging in robust doctrinal research methods is a prerequisite. At first glance, this may appear an obstacle to readers from non-law backgrounds. However, defining the content of a sports coach's duty of care is highly context- and fact-specific and represents an evolving complexity of coaching practice. The practical application of the legal principles

---

N Partington, 'Beyond the "*Tomlinson* trap"': analysing the effectiveness of section 1 of the Compensation Act 2006' (2016) 37(1) *Liverpool L Rev* 33. There is also the potential application in a number of jurisdictions of waivers (e.g., in Australia, the US and Canada). See further, D Thorpe et al., *Sports Law* (Oxford, OUP 2009) 129–59; G Wong, *Essentials of Sports Law* (4th edn, Oxford, Praeger 2010); R Corbett et al., *Legal Issues in Sport: Tools and Techniques for the Sport Manager* (Toronto, Emond Montgomery Publications 2010) 31. In contrast, following section 2 of the Unfair Contract Terms Act 1977, and more recently section 65 of the Consumer Rights Act 2015, all exclusions of negligence liability causing death or physical injury are unenforceable in the course of a business in the UK. This was reiterated in *Pinchbeck v Craggy Island Ltd* [2012] EWHC 2745 [41]. See further, Chapters 2 and 5.

74 The centrality of context, when defining a coach's duty of care, is a theme consistently returned to throughout this book.

75 For instance, the individual would appear to be prioritised above community interests more so in the US than other legal systems (R Michaels 'American law (United States)' in Smits (n 40) 68). Also, commenting on *Agar* (n 22), Griffith-Jones has argued that: '[t]he judgments of the court are replete with the kind of statements of policy which may owe much to an Australian view that sport is good for you and rugby union is a sport played by men who delight in stretching themselves to meet the physical challenges which it poses and are prepared to run the risk of injury in order to do so' (D Griffith-Jones, 'Civil Liability Arising Out of Participation in Sport' in A Lewis and J Taylor *Sport: Law and Practice* (2nd edn, Haywards Heath, Tottel 2008) 745). That said, and as the previous discussion reveals, the strong persuasive force of Australian tort law principles in English law remains convincing.

derived from the existing jurisprudence are therefore brought into more meaningful and sharper focus when considered in conjunction with some of the related research findings from the relevant disciplines of sports coaching and sports ethics. In addition, to ensure that the following analysis of a coach's duty of care remains accessible and informative, detailed extracts from the developing case law are consistently highlighted. This provides authentic and necessary detail when determining the precise extent of a coach's duty of care since the law in this area is essentially judge-made.[76] Also, in addition to providing the most accurate account of the reasoning of courts tasked with determining the nature and scope of a coach's duty of care in particular circumstances, and so of the utmost legal importance, the cited passages discuss many actual and common scenarios frequently encountered by coaches. For instance, the court decisions considered involve coaching delivered in a wide range of individual and team sports at both amateur and professional levels of performance.[77] This bespoke and sustained engagement with the judgments of the UK courts offers a rigorous analysis of the pertinent legal issues whilst ensuring that the discussion and commentary remain broadly accessible, interesting and robust. Furthermore, given the analogous duties (e.g., providing adequate instruction and supervision) and corresponding mutually dependent and symbiotic relationship with participants which are integral to these similar roles, claims brought against sports instructors and sports leaders for a breach of duty also prove instructive and engaging.

Structure of the book

At present, discussions regarding the duty of care in sport often appear to conflate (aspirational) moral, ethical and social duties with (established) legal duties of care. Such terminological confusion is problematic. Accordingly, Chapter 1 distinguishes between legal, moral and ethical duties of care in this context. In arguing for a more definitive, nuanced and informed understanding of the legal duty of care in sport, Chapter 1 cautions against extending the scope of the duty of care of sports coaches by tacit assumption of responsibilities that, until now, have not explicitly been the responsibility of coaches. Chapter 1, therefore, concludes by warning against expanding a fundamental legal principle beyond its intended sphere of application. Having distinguished between legal, moral and ethical duties of care, Chapter 2

---

76 See generally, J Powell and R Stewart, *Jackson and Powell on Professional Liability* (7th edn, London, Sweet and Maxwell 2012) [2–089].
77 This book adopts the European Union's definition of sport, established by the Council of Europe, which encompasses 'all forms of physical activity which, through casual or organised participation, aim at expressing or improving physical fitness and mental well-being, forming social relationships or obtaining results in competition at all levels': see European Commission, *White Paper on Sport* [2007] COM(2007) 391 final, 2. Similarly, the terms 'athlete', 'player' and 'performer' will be used interchangeably to appropriately cover all participants involved in sport and at all levels of sporting performance.

situates the concept of the duty of care firmly within its originally intended and well-established confines – the tort of negligence. This allows for a more precise framing of the nature of a coach's duty of care. More specifically, since it is now well-settled law that coaches owe a duty of care to athletes,[78] this chapter turns to critically scrutinise the pivotal issue in coach negligence cases, the standard of care in all the circumstances, or the law of negligence's control mechanism of breach. This analysis is of considerable practical importance, as it allows the content of the duty of care to be defined. Since the extent of a coach's duty will be informed by the full factual matrix in which coaches operate, Chapter 2 also critiques the necessary balancing exercise demanded of courts when determining sports negligence cases. Moreover, since sports coaching requires special skill, the analysis undertaken in Chapter 2 demonstrates that establishing breach in this area is premised on the principles of professional negligence. Significantly, although the vast majority of coaches are amateur volunteers, the legal test for coach negligence is derived from the field of professional liability. This curiosity is examined in detail in Chapter 3 by critically analysing the issue of professional liability in the unique context of sports coaching. This acknowledges and reinforces the *Bolam* doctrine[79] as a control mechanism designed to protect both athlete claimants and defendant coaches when allegations of a breach of duty of care are made. Consequently, in ultimately framing the *Bolam* test as a quasi-defence, Chapter 3 concludes by emphasising that in discharging the heightened standard of care incumbent upon them, coaches must ensure that the coaching practices adopted are regular, approved and capable of withstanding logical and searching scrutiny.

Following the establishment in Chapters 1–3 of the key legal concepts relevant in this field, Chapter 4 focuses more specifically on the practical application of duty of care considerations in the particular context of sport. Chapter 4 analyses the reciprocal duty owed by co-participants,[80] the duty of participants towards spectators,[81] and given the strong analogy with the duty of care required of sports coaches, the duty of care of sports officials/referees.[82] The general legal principles applicable in sports negligence cases are subsequently explored, unpacked and scrutinised in Chapter 5 which concentrates specifically on the duty of care of sports coaches. Indeed, Chapter 5 engages in a detailed interdisciplinary analysis in order to provide an authentic and informative contextualisation of the particular duties of care of modern sports coaches. Importantly, this chapter highlights the tendency

---

78 E.g., *Fowles* (n 26); *Anderson v Lyotier* [2008] EWHC 2790.
79 *Bolam v Friern Hospital Management Committee* [1957] 1 WLR 582.
80 E.g., *Condon* (n 24); *Caldwell* (n 31).
81 E.g., *Wooldridge* (n 3); *Wilks* (n 56).
82 E.g., *Smoldon* (n 24); *Vowles* (n 25). Importantly, at trial in *Smoldon*, the injured player who brought the action was referred to as the 'plaintiff'. The term 'plaintiff' remains the preferred terminology in Northern Irish cases. However, in England and Wales, following the introduction of the Civil Procedure Rules in 1999, the term used for the injured party suing in negligence at first instance is 'claimant'.

for the standard of care barometer to be heightened over time, reinforcing the requirement for all coaches to acquire an informed awareness and understanding of the evolving legal context in which they discharge the duty of care incumbent upon them. In further developing and deepening the discussion provided, Chapter 6 aims to illustrate and test the practical application of the duty of care principles previously outlined by conducting a detailed case study of *Anderson v Lyotier*,[83] where a claim was brought in negligence against a ski instructor. The sustained treatment of the most relevant case law by means of a sociolegal analysis provides instructive and engaging insights into the specific and precise scope of the duty of care owed by modern sports coaches.

In drawing together the main findings from earlier chapters, Chapter 7 identifies implications for practising coaches when fulfilling their duty of care. Simply applied, the chapter recognises the hallmarks of reasonable coaching practice as encompassing: (i) regular and approved coaching practices; that are (ii) logically justifiable; and (iii) suitable for the post or position of the coach. Successfully satisfying these three legal propositions should better protect the safety and welfare of athletes by ensuring that coaches effectively discharge their duty of care. Nonetheless, since there may on occasion be a fine line between reasonable and negligent coaching, some of the pertinent dilemmas faced by modern coaches (e.g., determination of training intensity levels) are considered. Ultimately, Chapter 7 reinforces the legal duty and obligation of all coaches to adopt objectively reasonable and justifiable coaching practices when interacting with athletes, and for the duty of care incumbent upon modern sports coaches to become a more pronounced and detailed topic within the education, training and continuing development of all coaches. Consequently, the book's conclusion highlights the importance of coaches discharging their duty of care in sport with the necessary care and skill to safeguard the legitimate right of athletes not to be exposed to unreasonable or unacceptable risk. This duty to protect the safety of athletes is integral to all coach–athlete interactions. So raising the profile of the duty of care in sport generally, and a coach's duty of care in particular, is both necessary and long overdue. Moreover, coaches must be attuned to duty of care being a dynamic concept. As such, it is continually becoming more challenging to effectively discharge. This reveals further notable ramifications for the continuing 'professional' development of coaches. In making an important contribution to further advances in this field, this book cautions against a pervading duty of care in sport narrative, framed in terms of loose quasi-legal authority and, crucially, calls for a more precise and informed future discussion regarding the duty of care incumbent upon modern sports coaches.

---

83 *Anderson* (n 78).

PART I
Key concepts

1
DISTINGUISHING DUTIES OF CARE OF SPORTS COACHES

Introduction

Duty of care considerations are under unprecedented scrutiny in the context of sport.[1] Coaches owe a duty of care to athletes. This duty of care may involve legal, moral and ethical considerations. It was argued by Baroness Tanni Grey-Thompson in the Duty of Care in Sport: Independent Report to Government' (DoC in Sport Report) in 2017 that sporting success:

> should not be at the expense of the Duty of Care [owed] towards athletes, coaches and others involved in the system. . . . [I]t feels timely for the sport sector to consider Duty of Care in its fullest sense.[2]

The DoC in Sport Report adopted 'a deliberately broad definition of "Duty of Care"– covering everything from personal safety and injury, to mental health issues, to the support given to people at the elite level'.[3] High-profile controversies about a breach of duty of care in various sports, and accusations of a culture of bullying, continue to come to light.[4] The growing number of athlete complaints of

---

1 See, for instance, Baroness Tanni Grey-Thompson, 'Duty of Care in Sport: Independent Report to Government', Department for Digital, Culture, Media & Sport, 21 April 2017 (DoC in Sport Report) 4; D Roan, 'Was 2017 the Year British Sport Lost Its Way?' (BBC News, 29 December 2017) <www.bbc.com/news/uk-42353175> accessed 9 November 2019.
2 DoC in Sport Report (n 1) 4. In December 2015, as part of the Sporting Future strategy, the Minister for Sport asked Baroness Grey-Thompson to conduct an independent review into the Duty of Care sport has towards its participants.
3 Ibid.
4 J Anderson and N Partington, 'Duty of Care in Sport: Time for a Sports Ombudsman?' (2018) 1 *International Sports Law Review* 3, 7–8.

this nature has also resulted in coaches being made to feel 'vulnerable', prompting leading coaches in Britain to form an association to protect their interests.[5] In these circumstances, practical reasoning determining coaching conduct, performance goals and what sort of person or coach to be may be shaped by both law and morality. This is the case because, as argued by Cane, 'both law and morality are about right and wrong, good and bad, virtue and vice. These contrasts are "normative": they express value judgments'.[6]

Problematically, whilst it has been suggested by Lord Steyn that '[t]he law and morality are inextricably interwoven',[7] Hart's seminal jurisprudential discussion of the nature of morality[8] contends that 'there is no necessary connection between law and morals'.[9] At first glance, this seems somewhat contradictory and confusing, not least for non-lawyers making repeated value judgements about what might constitute reasonable coaching practice. For instance, is a coach's duty of care, derived from the tort of negligence, plainly informed by law, essentially informed by morality or informed by a combination of both law and morality? At present, legal scholarship tends to approach the issue of a coach's duty in broad terms,[10] often with an emphasis on school sport,[11] thereby offering only limited detailed analysis of the extent of a coach's duty of care. The intersection between the law of negligence and sports coaching is also seldom discussed in the extant academic literature on sports coaching.[12] This misses important emerging complexities that can only be understood by an analysis that highlights the necessity of separating legal and moral duties of care. In order to achieve this sort of analysis, the one undertaken in this chapter is set within the context of the classic jurisprudential debate surrounding the relationship between law and morality. By drawing on some of that scholarship, existing gaps in the duty of care in sport literature are addressed, with the nuanced arguments developed also being of more general application and relevance, particularly in the mainstream field of professional negligence.

---

5 M Dickinson, 'Coaches Unite Over Bullying', *The Times,* 21 November 2018 <www.thetimes.co.uk/article/coaches-unite-over-bullying-by-forming-new-group-c7wp7jnxx> accessed 9 January 2019.
6 P Cane, 'Morality, Law and Conflicting Reasons for Action' (2012) 71(1) *CLJ* 59, 60.
7 *Smith New Court Securities Ltd v Scrimgeour Vickers (Asset Management) Ltd* [1997] AC 254 (HL), 280. Also see, T Honoré, 'The Dependence of Morality on Law' (1993) 13 *Oxford J Legal Stud* 1, 3.
8 P Cane, *Responsibility in Law and Morality* (Oxford, Hart 2002) 6.
9 HLA Hart, 'Positivism and the Separation of Law and Morals' (1959) 71 *Harvard Law Review* 593, 601 (footnote).
10 E.g., J Anderson, *Modern Sports Law: A Textbook* (Oxford, Hart 2010) 248; M James, *Sports Law* (2nd edn, Basingstoke, Palgrave Macmillan 2013) 92–97; S Greenfield et al., 'Reconceptualising The Standard Of Care In Sport: The Case Of Youth Rugby In England And South Africa' (2015) 18(6) *Potchefstroom Elec. L.J.* 2183.
11 E.g., M Beloff et al., *Sports Law* (2nd edn, Oxford, Hart 2012) 146–48; D Griffith-Jones, 'Civil Liability Arising Out of Participation in A Lewis and J Taylor, *Sport: Law and Practice* (2nd edn, Haywards Heath, Tottel 2008) 737–42; E Grayson, *Sport and the Law* (3rd edn, Haywards Heath, Tottel 1999) 190–99; N Cox and A Schuster, *Sport and the Law* (Dublin, Firstlaw 2004) 230–47; H Hartley, *Sport, Physical Recreation and the Law* (Abingdon, Routledge 2009) 55–63.
12 N Partington, 'Sports Coaching and the Law of Negligence: Implications for Coaching Practice' (2017) 6(1) *Sports Coaching Review* 36, 37.

The chapter begins by discussing the context in which the concepts of law and morality, broadly applied, are critically explored. In cautioning against conflation of the legal and moral duties of coaches, since these vary in scope and content, the chapter next conducts a more detailed consideration of the concepts of duty of care and standard of care. A more precise understanding of this area of the law, since the seminal case of *Donoghue v Stevenson*,[13] allows distinctions between legal and moral duties of care to be better understood and critiqued. Following this, in considering the subsequent development of the law of negligence, analysis of its modern application reveals a significant shift away from its origins as a general moral principle. Accordingly, the no-duty-to-assist a stranger in distress at common law is posited as a forceful illustration of the crucial distinction between moral and legal duties of care. The intricacies and interrelationship between these respective duties is then subjected to sustained treatment in the specific circumstances of sports coaching. This reinforces how the doctrine of assumption of responsibility has the potential to bring what might otherwise ought to be distinct moral duties, within the confines of the standard of care required of coaches, thereby creating legal obligations. Ultimately, this unique vantage point proves instrumental in uncovering original insights that are of importance not merely in the context of sport but, given the apparent tendency for duty of care terminology to be increasingly employed in contemporary society, will be of much more widespread significance and application. By revealing somewhat concealed and unintended potential repercussions likely to result from an uncritical conflation of legal and moral duties of care, the implications uncovered in this chapter are of considerable relevance to sports coaches and in additional areas including: (i) other sectors largely reliant upon volunteers, since the 'neighbour principle' appears peculiarly susceptible to influence by moral and social considerations in such contexts (i.e., education sector; recreation and leisure sector); (ii) the broader sphere of professional negligence, not least given instances of professional liability 'must be viewed against a background of constant change';[14] and (iii) by government departments, most notably, the UK's Department for Digital, Culture, Media & Sport (DCMS), with the Minister of Sport having tasked Baroness Tanni Grey-Thompson with looking 'into issues surrounding the so-called "Duty of Care" that sports have towards their participants'.[15]

Context

Modern sports coaches are faced with a multitude of moral, legal and ethical duties, with the degeneration of the moral standards of some coaches fuelling contemporary interest in the ethics of sport.[16] For present purposes, and as identified by

---

13 *Donoghue v Stevenson* [1932] AC 562.
14 R Jackson, 'The Professions: Power, Privilege and Legal Liability' (2015) 31(3) *Professional Negligence* 122, 122–23.
15 DoC in Sport Report (n 1) 4.
16 M McNamee and S Parry, *Ethics & Sport* (London, E & FN Spon 1998) xvii; H Appenzeller, *Ethical Behavior in Sport* (Durham, Carolina Academic Press 2011) xi.

McNamee, morality might broadly be regarded as the 'rules, guidelines, mores or principles of living . . . that exist in time and space', with 'the systematic reflection upon them' referring to ethics.[17] This is entirely consistent with Honoré's submission that morality concerns 'conduct that has a significant impact on other people . . . and with the restraints on behaviour that we should accept because of this. Moral criticism assesses behaviour in the light of its impact on others'.[18] Given the interdependent relationship between a coach and athlete, and for instance, in view of recent investigations and controversies, there has rightly been moral criticism of some non-recent and contemporary coaching conduct. Viewed through the prism of descriptive or empirical sports ethics,[19] the terms ethics and morality seem sometimes to be used interchangeably and might be regarded 'to mean that aspect of human concern related to the incidence of good and evil in people's lives, and thus too the moral duties . . . that affect such outcomes'.[20] Indeed, research in the field of sports ethics, including moral issues encountered when coaching sports, makes frequent reference to notions of morality, justice, righteousness and virtue.[21] More specifically, in contemporary sports coaching scholarship Roberts et al. have suggested 'that care should not be limited to the minimum legal requirement, but . . . coaches should embrace a more aspirational and holistic caring ethic'.[22]

In contrast, and more discretely, when conceptualising law, Lucy succinctly recognised that:

> law is a more formal and detailed body of standards for conduct than morality, dealing with bad outcomes rather than good and which, broadly speaking, maintains minimal rather than aspirational standards for conduct. Given such differences between law and morality, it would be folly to assume that legal and moral liability-responsibility are synonymous, yet equally wrong to think that they never overlap.[23]

Whilst highlighting important distinctions between law and morality that will be subsequently further explored, this passage reaffirms the elusive nature of attempts

---

17 M McNamee (ed.), *The Ethics of Sport: A Reader* (Abingdon, Routledge 2010) 3.
18 Honoré (n 7) 2
19 McNamee (n 17) 3.
20 R Scott Kretchmar, 'Soft Metaphysics: A Precursor to Good Sports Ethics' in McNamee and Parry (n 16) 20.
21 Appenzeller, (n 16) xi.
22 S Roberts et al., 'Lifting the Veil of Depression and Alcoholism in Sport Coaching: How Do We Care for Carers? (2018) *Qualitative Research in Sport, Exercise and Health*, 2: DOI: 10.1080/2159676X.2018.1556182. See further, R Jones, 'Coaching as Caring (The Smiling Gallery): Accessing Hidden Knowledge' (2009) 14(4) *Physical Education and Sport Pedagogy* 377; C Cronin and K Armour, '"Being" in the Coaching World: New Insights on Youth Performance Coaching from an Interpretative Phenomenological Approach' (2017) 22(8) *Sport, Education and Society* 919.
23 W Lucy, *Philosophy of Private Law* (Oxford, OUP 2007) 47.

to clearly demarcate the potential overlap between law and morality. Indeed, if we employ the concepts of a morality of duty (i.e., legal liability-responsibility), and a morality of aspiration (i.e., moral liability-responsibility), it has been suggested by Fuller that 'there is neither occasion nor warrant for drawing a clear line between the[se] two moralities'.[24] This chapter argues otherwise, submitting that a coach's legal liability and moral responsibility vary significantly in scope and content. Simply applied, a deeper understanding of the intersection between the tort of negligence and modern sports coaching cautions against conflation of the concepts of legal and moral duties of care. Making a distinction between legal and moral duties is of immediate importance and significance when the concept of the duty of care is employed in a general manner which fails to appreciate and ascertain the limits set by legal standards of care. Nonetheless, and as will be argued, this blurring of boundaries has the potential to give rise to legal obligations in circumstances where coaches assume responsibility for what might otherwise be more accurately regarded as moral duties. It is contended that this may include duties that should be categorised, from a purely legal standpoint, and prior to the assumption of responsibility for such duties by the coach, as falling beyond the direct responsibility of coaches lacking the necessary specialist skill, competence, training, qualifications and experience (e.g., administering basic first aid; decisions regarding return-to-play following participant injury). So whilst courts are no doubt alive to distinctions between legal and moral duties of care – with determination of the standard of care in all the circumstances allowing further mitigation of such differences by the judiciary, even in situations where the duty test is met – many sports coaches, officials and administrators are unlikely to be aware of these control measures or nuances. However, and somewhat curiously, a coach sued in negligence for breach of what without some additional reason might more aptly be viewed as a moral duty of care, and so typically extending beyond the reasonable standards ordinarily expected of coaches, may well be vulnerable to liability in negligence should the actions of the coach create a legal obligation. Adopting a broad definition of duty of care, as an expression of best practice in an extralegal context, may unwittingly promote the widening of such legal obligations and limits. This scenario is problematic, not least since the courts would then be tasked with defining the standard of care in the particular circumstances where a conflation of moral and legal duties has already essentially been established in law. Put simply, there appears limited recourse in this context for judges to distinguish between moral and legal duties of care, for instance, by defining the content of the duty imposed (i.e., standard of care) narrowly in order to avoid setting unrealistic standards. Furthermore, despite being intended to provide reassurance to volunteers functioning to promote desirable activities, including sport, engagement of s.1 Compensation 2006 '[i]s not concerned with and does not alter the standard of care, nor the circumstances in

---

24 L Fuller, *The Morality of Law* (Revised edition, New Haven, Yale University Press 1969) 10.

which a duty to take care will be owed'.[25] In this context, the impact of s.1 Compensation Act 2006 is therefore limited.[26] Accordingly, since conflation of legal and moral duties may potentially transform moral duties of care into legal obligations, there is limited room for judicial manoeuvre or discretion in order to guard against associated unintended and undesirable outcomes. To more fully develop this point, it proves necessary and instructive to examine the doctrinal foundations at the root of this submission.

Duty of care or standard of care?

Despite both law and morality serving to channel our behaviour,[27] moral guilt may play little or no role in many cases of liability in negligence.[28] A legal rule might be thought to be morally desirable, but it in no way follows from this mere fact that something morally desirable should be regarded as a rule of law.[29] Lord James made this abundantly clear in *Cavalier (Pauper) v Pope*,[30] when he observed '[b]ut moral responsibility, however clearly established, is not identical with legal liability'. Conversely, when determining a case concerning the legal liability of a learner driver in *Nettleship v Weston*,[31] Lord Denning in the Court of Appeal expressed the view that '[m]orally the learner driver is not at fault; but legally she is liable because she is insured and the risk should fall on her'.[32] Since taking all reasonable care in the circumstances seems to exonerate defendants from moral blame,[33] as noted by Stevens, the (legal) standard of care expected of the learner driver is somewhat puzzling when contrasted with the submission that the law and morality are inextricably interwoven.[34] By analogy, the issue of coach negligence is argued to be of

---

25 Explanatory Notes to the Compensation Act 2006, [11] <www.legislation.gov.uk/ukpga/2006/29/notes> accessed 16 April 2019. Interestingly, this note speaks to both the imposition of a duty of care and a further control mechanism within the law of negligence, the standard of care. Arguably, this is perhaps somewhat indicative of the limitations of pigeonholing and conclusively separating issues of whether to impose a duty, and the standard of reasonable care and skill expected in all the circumstances: see generally, *Spartan Steel & Alloys Ltd v Martin & Co (Contractors) Ltd* [1973] QB 27, 37 (Lord Denning MR). No doubt this has the potential to create considerable conceptual confusion in this context, most particularly when duty of care terminology attracts a non-legal meaning with clear potential legal implications.
26 See further, N Partington, 'Beyond the "*Tomlinson* Trap": Analysing the Effectiveness of Section 1 of the Compensation Act 2006' (2016) 37(1) *Liverpool L Rev* 33. Recent enactment of the Social Action, Responsibility and Heroism Act 2015 would appear not to alter this view. For sustained treatment of the SARAH Act 2015, see J Goudkamp, 'Restating the Common Law? The Social Action, Responsibility and Heroism Act 2015' (2017) 37 *Legal Studies* 577.
27 S Shavell, 'Law Versus Morality as Regulators of Conduct' (2002) 4(2) *American Law and Economics Review* 227, 257.
28 S Deakin et al., *Markesinis and Deakin's Tort Law* (7th edn, Oxford, OUP 2013) 43.
29 Hart (n 9) 626.
30 [1906] AC 428 (HL).
31 [1971] 2 QB 691 (CA). Also see, the foreword to this book.
32 Ibid. 700.
33 HLA Hart, *The Concept of Law* (3rd edn, Oxford, OUP 2013) 173.
34 R Stevens, *Torts and Rights* (Oxford, OUP 2007) 97.

Distinguishing duties of care of coaches 23

direct relevance to this tension. Should an amateur volunteer sports coach be sued in negligence, since the legal test applied would be informed by the principles of professional negligence,[35] there is the possibility of a potentially serious disconnect between legal and moral blameworthiness.[36] This is an argument Lord Phillips appeared mindful of in *Vowles v Evans* (though the defendant was a rugby union referee) when he stated:

> There is scope for argument as to the extent to which the degree of skill to be expected of a referee depends upon the grade of the referee or of the match that he has agreed to referee. In the course of argument it was pointed out that sometimes in the case of amateur sport, the referee fails to turn up, or is injured in the course of the game, and a volunteer referee is called for from the spectators. In such circumstances the volunteer cannot reasonably be expected to show the skill of one who holds himself out as referee, or perhaps even to be fully conversant with the laws of the game.[37]

In this scenario described by Lord Phillips, whilst the question of possible legal liability remains arguable,[38] it would be an altogether more difficult task to regard the actions of the volunteer referee (or coach[39]) as being morally at fault. Nonetheless, by identifying the standard of care, or control device of breach or fault, as the mechanism by which the volunteer will be adequately safeguarded from negligence liability, the existence of a duty of care must be incontrovertible. In which case, and as a point previously mentioned and subsequently further developed in this chapter, should assumption of responsibility for moral duties by volunteer coaches (and referees) limit the application of judicial discretion when defining the standard of care at a reasonable level, the possible scope of legal liability becomes materially wider.

The significant distinction between a duty owed in law, and actions deemed morally desirable/justifiable in a more general sense, might be blurred by the widespread modern-day usage of the phrase duty of care. Importantly, Norris notes that the words 'duty of care' are frequently 'used to characterise whatever the speaker thinks should or should not have been done by authorities or individuals in a particular set of circumstances'.[40] Peculiarly, should expressions of duties of care in sport encapsulate both legal and moral duties in this fashion, this may pose serious

---

35 N Partington, 'Professional Liability of Amateurs: The Context of Sports Coaching' (2015) 4 *JPI Law* 232. See further, Chapter 3.
36 Partington (n 26) 48–54.
37 *Vowles v Evans* [2003] EWCA Civ 318 [28]. Problematically, this seems to conceal the fact that an individual assuming a duty requiring the exercise of a special skill would, in fact, be subject to the ordinary principles of the law of negligence if sued.
38 N Partington, '"It's Just Not Cricket"'. Or Is It?' (2016) 32(1) *Professional Negligence* 75, 79–80. See further, the approach adopted by HHJ Lopez in *Bartlett v English Cricket Board Association of Cricket Officials* (unreported), County Court (Birmingham), 27 August 2015.
39 N Partington, 'Legal Liability of Coaches: A UK Perspective' (2014) 14(3–4) *International Sports Law Journal* 232, 238.
40 W Norris, 'A Duty of Care in Sport: What It Actually Means' (2017) 3 *JPI Law* 154.

ramifications. Put simply, the implications of failing to more precisely frame these two respective duties, thereby potentially extending the scope of legal responsibility beyond its current constraints,[41] may not be obvious to the ordinary reasonable person. Accordingly, since it is in law that the concept of a duty of care originates and continues to evolve,[42] a more precise understanding of its legal roots, and subsequent development since the seminal case of *Donoghue v Stevenson*,[43] proves both necessary and fruitful in order to better understand distinctions between a coach's legal and moral duty of care towards athletes.

Donoghue v Stevenson is best known for 'introducing into the law a general moral principle of "good neighbourliness"'.[44] In this House of Lords judgment, Lord Atkin stated:

> The liability for negligence, whether you style it such or treat it as in other systems as a species of 'culpa', is no doubt based upon a general public sentiment of moral wrongdoing for which the offender must pay. But acts or omissions which any moral code would censure cannot in a practical world be treated so as to give a right to every person injured by them to demand relief. In this way rules of law arise which limit the range of complainants and the extent of their remedy. The rule that you are to love your neighbour becomes in law, you must not injure your neighbour; and the lawyer's question, Who is my neighbour? receives a restricted reply. You must take reasonable care to avoid acts or omissions which you can reasonably foresee would be likely to injure your neighbour. Who, then, in law is my neighbour? The answer seems to be – persons who are so closely and directly affected by my act that I ought reasonably to have them in contemplation as being so affected when I am directing my mind to the acts or omissions which are called in question.[45]

In alluding to Lord Atkin's carefully chosen and extremely precise language, when formulating this said duty, Heuston recognised that '[i]t would be a very strange reasonable man who could comprehend all its implications and subtleties without instruction from a lawyer'.[46] Given the interdependent relationship between a sports coach and athlete, Lord Atkin's 'neighbour principle' is clearly relevant in the context of sports coaching.[47] Simply applied, the law of negligence's control mechanism of duty would be straightforwardly satisfied in the circumstances of organised sporting activities led by coaches. But also of central relevance to the application of

---

41 Ibid. 154–55.
42 Ibid. 154.
43 *Donoghue* (n 13).
44 M Lunney et al., *Tort Law: Text and Materials* (6th edn, Oxford, OUP 2017) 117.
45 *Donoghue* (n 13) 580.
46 R Heuston, 'Donoghue v Stevenson in Retrospect' (1957) 20(1) *Mod L Rev*, 1, 16.
47 D Griffith-Jones and N Randall, 'Civil Liability Arising Out of Participation in Sport' in A Lewis and J Taylor, *Sport: Law and Practice* (3rd edn, Haywards Heath, Tottel 2014) 1638–39; Beloff et al. (n 11), 146.

this principle in a claim in negligence are the associated restrictions that define the content or extent of the duty owed (i.e., standard of care). This further crystallises the need to unpack and scrutinise the subtleties of a concept, where at first glance, legal and moral duties of care may intuitively appear to overlap and be inextricably interwoven. Moreover, given the apparent increasing tendency to refer to the concept of duty of care in order to create a 'veneer of pseudo-legal authority',[48] greater consideration should be given to the seemingly concealed consequences of an uncritical and unwitting conflation of legal and moral duties of care (e.g., by policy-makers). As just indicated, this poses significant implications when the term duty of care assumes both an extralegal and legal meaning, thereby perhaps setting in motion a peculiar interplay between moral duties of care and legal standards of care.

A shift from moral standards

Since the law of negligence is fluid and dynamic, reflecting variations in the prevailing 'social conditions and habits of life',[49] a more current consideration of its development and application reveals a significant shift from its origins as a general moral principle. Interestingly, Lord Atkin himself was acutely aware of distinctions between law and morality, recognising prior to his speech in *Donoghue v Stevenson* the following:

> It is quite true that the law and morality do not cover identical fields. No doubt morality extends beyond the more limited range in which you can lay down the definite prohibitions of law; but, apart from that, the British law has always necessarily ingrained in it moral teaching in this sense: that it lays down standards of honesty and plain dealing between man and man.[50]

More recently, it has been suggested by Deakin et al. that basing negligence liability upon a general public sentiment of moral wrongdoing 'takes a wholly exaggerated view of the degree to which the legal concept of carelessness is based on moral fault and pays no regard at all to the aims of loss shifting and accident prevention'.[51] Put simply, since Lord Atkin's celebrated dictum, it is argued by Deakin et al. that there has been a:

> transformation of the notion of negligence from a concept with strong moral overtones into a legal notion in which wider policy considerations determine the existence of a duty to take care, its breach, and even the extent of the consequences.[52]

---

48 Norris (n 40).
49 R Percy and C Walton (eds), *Charlesworth & Percy on Negligence* (9th edn, London, Sweet & Maxwell 1997) [6–04].
50 Lord Atkin, 'Law as an Educational Subject' (1932) *J Soc'y Pub Tchrs L* 27, 30.
51 Deakin et al. (n 28) 248.
52 Ibid. 50.

This apparent general erosion of the weight afforded by courts to moral codes, when determining cases brought in negligence, has created a certain amount of conceptual confusion for lawyers.[53] Such a lack of clarity may also have contributed to a framing of the concept of the duty of care in a more general and overarching sense outside of the law by non-lawyers. According to Montrose, since the legal test of negligence concerns what *ought* to be done in the particular circumstances, presuming a duty of care is found to be owed, it may still be regarded as an ethical concept.[54] As such, it is little wonder that, for instance, Baroness Tanni Grey-Thompson, having been asked by the Minister of Sport to examine issues surrounding the 'so-called "Duty of Care" that sports have towards their participants', adopted a deliberately broad definition.

It appears uncontroversial to accept that, and as argued by Cane, engaging moral considerations may very well prove instructive in establishing what the law ought to be.[55] Conversely, and in providing valuable reinforcement to morality,[56] law might be regarded as acting as a 'moral educator'.[57] However, and in cautioning against conflating moral standards with legal requirements, Weir observes that whilst there may be an 'understandable urge to bring legal standards up to those of delicate morality . . . [this] should be resisted, or there would be no room for generosity or for people to go beyond the call of legal duty'.[58] More bluntly, there remains no legal compulsion for individuals to display the excellences of which they might be capable when interacting with others, requiring the law to turn to 'its blood cousin, the morality of duty' (as distinct from the previously mentioned morality of aspiration) for workable standards of judgement (i.e., defining the standard of care).[59] Crucially, this speaks to the fact that law may in actual fact often represent the lowest denominator of behavioural standards, whereas morality establishes higher behavioural standards.[60] Furthermore, it is not always necessary, in order to satisfy widely accepted moral requirements, to do what is legally required.[61] Such a 'separation thesis'[62] has important ramifications for the duty of care incumbent upon modern sports coaches. For instance, should the deliberately broad definition of the concept of duty of care in the DoC in Sport Report gain unquestioning traction, the contended (moral) aspirations with regard to issues including the transition of athletes through the system (i.e., entering and leaving top-level sport),

---

53 Ibid.
54 J Montrose, 'Is Negligence an Ethical or a Sociological Concept?' (1958) 21 *Mod L Rev* 259.
55 Cane (n 8) 14; Law Reform Commission of Ireland, Civil Liability of Good Samaritans and Volunteers (LRC 93 2009) [2.07].
56 Ibid. 15.
57 J Braithwaite, 'Negotiation Versus Litigation: Industry Regulation in Great Britain and the United States' (1987) *American Bar Foundation Research* J 559, cited in Cane (n 8) 15.
58 J Weir, *An Introduction to Tort Law* (2nd edn, Oxford, OUP 2006) 1.
59 Fuller (n 24) 9.
60 J Herring, *Medical law and ethics* (5th edn, Oxford, OUP 2014) 3.
61 Honoré (n 7) 17.
62 Cane (n 6) 60.

education (e.g., in football academies), mental welfare concerns and, of most present concern, safety, injury and medical issues, may well extend the scope of the duty of care incumbent upon modern sports coaches.[63]

No-duty-to-assist

Perhaps the strongest illustration of the distinction between moral and legal duties concerns the void of a legal duty to rescue a stranger in distress at common law.[64] According to Williams, this is despite whatever moral decency may require, the seriousness of the emergency or the ease in which effective assistance may be rendered.[65] In *Stovin v Wise*,[66] Lord Nicholls provided a number of classic examples to illustrate this point that are worth recalling in full:

> The classic example of the absence of a legal duty to take positive action is where a grown person stands by while a young child drowns in a shallow pool. Another instance is where a person watches a nearby pedestrian stroll into the path of an oncoming vehicle. In both instances the callous bystander can foresee serious injury if he does nothing. He does not control the source of the danger, but he has control of the means to avert a dreadful accident. The child or pedestrian is dependent on the bystander: the child is unable to save himself, and the pedestrian is unaware of his danger. The prospective injury is out of all proportion to the burden imposed by having to take preventive steps. All that would be called for is the simplest exertion or a warning shout.
>
> Despite this, the recognised legal position is that the bystander does not owe the drowning child or the heedless pedestrian a duty to take steps to save him. Something more is required than being a bystander. There must be some additional reason why it is fair and reasonable that one person should be regarded as his brother's keeper and have legal obligations in that regard. When this additional reason exists, there is said to be sufficient proximity.[67]

A further widely cited example of this nature is provided in *Yuen Kun Yeu v Attorney-General of Hong Kong*,[68] where Lord Keith makes plain that there would not be liability in negligence should an individual refrain from shouting a warning

---

63 See generally, Norris (n 40) 155, noting that in this context there is a need to be careful what we wish for.
64 J Barr Ames, 'Law and Morals' (1908) 22 *Harvard Law Review* 97, 109; Q Bu, 'The Good Samaritan in the Chinese Society: Morality vis-à-vis Law' (2017) 38 *Liverpool L Rev* 135, 144.
65 K Williams, 'Doctors as Good Samaritans: Some Empirical Evidence Concerning Emergency Medical Treatment in Britain' (2003) 30 *Journal of Law & Society* 258, 258–59.
66 [1996] AC 923.
67 Ibid. 931.
68 [1988] AC 175.

to a stranger about to walk over a cliff with his head in the air.[69] As suggested by Heuston, no matter how grievous the consequences may be to others, individuals are fully entitled to do nothing in the absence of a legally recognised duty.[70] Simply applied:

> When a person has done nothing to put himself in any relationship with another person in distress or with his property mere accidental propinquity does not require him to go to that person's assistance. There may be a moral duty to do so, but it is not practicable to make it a legal duty.[71]

Clearly, UK courts take the view that the general no-duty-to-assist rule in English common law makes 'good sense',[72] it being 'one thing to disapprove of and criticise failure to rescue but another to impose legal liability and to award monetary compensation for failing to rescue'.[73] In echoing the sentiments of Lord Reid in *Dorset Yacht Company v Home Office*, it is contended that it is both impracticable and undesirable to equate the moral duties of sports coaches with their legal duties of care. Defining and subjecting a coach's duty of care to detailed scrutiny illustrates the importance of this fundamental distinction.

Duty of care of modern sports coaches

Modern sports coaches are under a legal duty of care to adopt objectively reasonable coaching practice, in the prevailing circumstances, so that athletes are reasonably safe and not exposed to unreasonable risk of personal injury.[74] In view of the specialist skill required of coaches, and consistent with the legal principles established in instances of professional negligence,[75] this duty demands a standard of care and skill consistent with the ordinarily competent coach occupying the same role and/or coaching at the same level.[76] When defining this said duty, or more precisely, the required standard of objective reasonable coaching practice, considerable weight would be attached to regular and approved coaching practices advocated by a responsible coaching organisation or national governing body of sport (NGB).[77] There is also a corresponding requirement for such endorsed practice to be logically justifiable.[78] The most recent reported judgment regarding coach negligence

---

69 Ibid. 192. Also see, Norris (n 40) 155.
70 Heuston (n 47) 18.
71 *Dorset Yacht Company v Home Office* [1970] AC 1004, 1027 (Lord Reid).
72 *Kent v Griffiths* [2001] QB 36 (CA) [18]-[19]; R Mulheron, *Principles of Tort Law* (Cambridge, CUP 2016) 99.
73 Cane (n 6) 74.
74 Partington (n 12). See further, Chapter 2.
75 Partington (n 35).
76 *Wilsher v Essex Area Health Authority* [1987] QB 730. See further, Chapter 3.
77 *Bolam v Friern Hospital Management Committee* [1957] 1 WLR 582. For instance, coaching manuals and guidelines published by sports governing bodies.
78 *Bolitho v City of Hackney Health Authority* [1998] AC 232.

in the UK proves informative and helpful in illustrating the practical application of these principles in context.

In *Shone v British Bobsleigh Limited*,[79] the essence of the claim was that the British Bobsleigh and Skeleton Association (BBSA), essentially through the actions of its coaches:[80]

> owed the claimant a duty to take reasonable care for her safety, and that it negligently allowed the claimant to ride as brakeman in a two-man bobsleigh which had not been customised for her, or at least which did not enable her to brace herself adequately within the bobsleigh by holding on to handles and by pressing her feet against foot pegs or against the back of the driver's seat, as a result of which she suffered injury in the crash.[81]

With specific regard to the scope of the BBSA's duty of care, developed through discussions between experienced counsel during the trial, it was held:

> that it owed a duty of care to the claimant to take all reasonable actions to ensure she was reasonably safe in the course of her activities on the bobsleigh run, in accordance with the prevailing standard of reasonable practice in the sport of national bobsleigh.[82]

In defining the required standard of care of the coach in the prevailing circumstances, and ultimately finding a breach of duty by the BBSA, HHJ Parkes ruled:

> It seems to me quite clear, on my findings of fact, that the BBSA, through Mr Woolley [GB Performance Coach], breached its duty to the claimant by allowing a frightened novice to go down the run from the top start when (to his knowledge) she could not brace with either hands or feet and felt unsafe to slide.[83]

Put simply, and as illustrated in *Shone v British Bobsleigh Limited*, the duty of a coach is premised on the notion of reasonableness. As such, the duty of a coach is to adopt *reasonable* coaching practice so that *reasonable* care is taken to ensure the

---

79 *Shone v British Bobsleigh Limited* [2018] 5 WLUK 226. This case is considered more fully in Chapter 5.
80 Ibid. [67]: It being accepted 'on behalf of the BBSA that the level of control which it exercised over the bobsleigh teams was sufficient to impute liability to it for the actions of its coaches, especially Mr Woolley'. Mr Woolley, the GB Performance Coach, had 'been involved in training the claimant at Bath and in managing her training and performance' (at [50]).
81 Ibid. [2].
82 Ibid. [4]. The prevailing standard of reasonable practice in the sport of national bobsleigh being indicative of the *Bolam* test and reflective of an instance of professional negligence.
83 Ibid. [68]. For a further framing of the legal test for breach of duty in cases of coach negligence, see *Morrow v Dungannon and South Tyrone BC* [2012] NIQB 50 [20]. See further, Chapter 5.

reasonable safety of athletes. This reasonableness standard is strikingly fact-sensitive,[84] and as argued by Clancy, as a legal test reasonableness may be regarded as an elusive, vague and somewhat woolly notion which fails to provide much by way of guidance when attempts are made to define the standard of care.[85] Indeed, as succinctly noted by the Court of Appeal when determining the sports negligence case of *Caldwell v Maguire*, 'the issue of negligence cannot be resolved in a vacuum. It is fact specific'.[86] Moreover, since sports coaching involves a 'continua of highly complex, context-dependent and historically situated behaviours',[87] ascertaining precise moral and ethical duties of coaches is also somewhat problematic. Further, given the assumption that ethical considerations regarding coaching practice will be understood and grasped intuitively by coaches,[88] by analogy, the DoC in Sport Report's broad definition of duty of care may similarly promote intuitive expectations of coaches. As an aspirational expression reflective of best practice, it seems incontrovertible that the Report's terminology in relation to duty of care is geared towards an improvement in coaching standards and practice. However, as this chapter argues, should such implicit assumptions fail to reflect and account for the more subtle nuances between moral and legal obligations, this may unwittingly expose coaches to a greater risk of legal liability by potentially extending the scope of legal responsibility beyond its current limits. Most obviously, it may result in coaches assuming duties which may not presently be expected of them. Should this be the case, it is likely there would be a legal expectation for such duties to be discharged properly, regardless of coaches being categorised as amateur, professional, 'professional amateur', qualified, (in)experienced or accredited by an NGB.[89]

Standards of care in coaching

Although terminology associated with 'specific (legal) duties' may be regarded as technically misleading,[90] since the precise degree and scope of responsibilities owed by coaches more accurately define the standard of care, as noted by Clerk and Lindsell on Torts, this approach can be useful in a descriptive way.[91] So whilst the

---

84 W Norris, 'The Duty of Care to Prevent Personal Injury' (2009) 2 *JPI Law* 126.
85 R Clancy, 'Judo Mats, Climbing Walls, Trampolines and Pole Vaulters' (1995) 3(1) *Sport and the Law Journal* 28.
86 *Caldwell v Maguire* [2001] EWCA Civ 1054 [30] (Judge LJ). See further, Chapter 4. This echoes Lord Steyn's earlier submission that '[i]n law context is everything' (*Regina (Daly) v Secretary of State for the Home Department* [2001] 2 AC 532 [28]).
87 A Hardman and C Jones, 'Sports Coaching and Virtue Ethics' in A Hardman and C Jones, *The Ethics of Sports Coaching* (Abingdon, Routledge 2011) 78.
88 H Telfer, 'Coaching Practice and Practice Ethics' in J Lyle and C Cushion (eds), *Sports Coaching: Professionalisation and Practice* (Edinburgh, Elsevier 2010) 210–11.
89 Partington (n 35) 242
90 The duty remains that of reasonable care to ensure the reasonable safety of athletes.
91 MA Jones and AM Dugdale (eds), *Clerk and Lindsell on Torts* (20th edn, London, Sweet and Maxwell 2010) [8–137].

standard expected of sports coaches is fixed conceptually as the duty to take reasonable care, as argued by McCaskey and Biedzynski, specific duties required of coaches have evolved.[92] As a result of advances brought about by factors including those in the field of sports science, technical developments in certain sports and societal expectations, such legal duties are broadening.[93] Importantly, such advances may increase the scope and degree of the duty of care owed by progressively placing more responsibilities on coaches.[94] Correspondingly, as athletes progress to elite and excellence levels the required emphasis on more specialised training programmes creates new risks requiring coaches to ensure that they possess the necessary competence and expertise to operate safely in these amended circumstances.[95] Moreover, there may also be general improvements in the standards of skill and care provided by particular professions, regardless of associated advances in knowledge, similarly heightening the standard of the reasonably competent practitioner.[96] Accordingly, as the principles of coaching are constantly assessed and revised,[97] so too is the legal standard of care required of coaches.[98] This is due to reasons both devoid (e.g., scientific and technical developments in sport) and inclusive (e.g., societal expectations) of social and moral considerations. In general, the emerging case law in the UK reveals that the specific duties of coaches when managing the risk of injury to athletes predominantly relates to the reasonableness of supervision, training and instruction.[99] With this in mind, the example in the next paragraph offers a stark illustration of possible unintended consequences when conflation of legal and moral duties of care leads to a situation in which meeting the requisite standard of care may prove problematic.

Volunteering is commonplace and generally 'expected' in the provision of community and recreational sport.[100] The vast majority of sports coaches in the UK are volunteers,[101] this being reflective of the bulk of countries in the world.[102] Individual volunteers at community sports clubs may willingly embrace a social or

---

92 AS McCaskey and KW Biedzynski, 'A Guide to the Legal Liability of Coaches for a Sports Participant's Injuries' (1996) 6 *Seton Hall J. Sport L.* 7, 15.
93 R Ver Steeg, 'Negligence in the Air: Safety, Legal Liability, and the Pole Vault' (2003) 4 *Tex. Rev. Ent. & Sports L.* 109, 113.
94 J Labuschagne and J Skea, 'The Liability of a Coach for a Sport Participant's Injury' (1999) 10 *Stellenbosch Law Review* 158.
95 Ibid. 166.
96 J Powell and R Stewart, *Jackson and Powell on Professional Liability* (7th edn, London, Sweet and Maxwell 2012) [2–135].
97 T Cassidy et al., *Understanding Sports Coaching: The Social, Cultural and Pedagogical Foundations of Coaching Practice* (2nd edn, London, Routledge 2009) 130–31.
98 See generally, Powell and Stewart (n 96) [2–135].
99 See Chapter 5.
100 C Nash, 'Volunteering in Sports Coaching – A Tayside Study' in M Graham and M Foley (eds), *Volunteering in Leisure: Marginal or Inclusive?* (Eastbourne, LSA 2001) 44.
101 Sports coach UK, 'Coach Tracking Study: A four-year study of coaching in the UK' (2012) 17.
102 P Duffy et al., 'Sport Coaching as a "Profession": Challenges and Future Directions' (2011) 5(2) *International Journal of Coaching Science* 93, 94.

moral duty to support and assist other club members by organising, for instance, practice sessions for junior or less experienced players. In such a situation, it appears highly probable that these same volunteers will on occasion assume the responsibility for not only arranging the practice session but also supervising it and, if competent and experienced players (as opposed to coaches) themselves, providing some level of instruction. In such a scenario, and following *Fowles v Bedfordshire CC*,[103] the existence of an *assumption of responsibility* by the volunteer 'coach', and *reliance* on this supervision and/or instruction by the younger or more inexperienced players, would most typically give rise to a common law duty of care. Simply applied, the initial social or moral duty assumed by the volunteer 'coach', perhaps underpinned by altruistic motivations[104] and an associated aspirational and holistic caring ethic,[105] would probably be transformed into a more formal legal duty of care should 'specialist' advice be offered and acted upon. As noted by Gardiner, since the volunteer 'coach' would provide 'gratuitous advice on a matter within his particular skill or knowledge, and knows or ought to have known that the person asking for the advice will rely on it and act accordingly', a duty of care at common law would be established.[106] Consequently, the standard of care required of the volunteer 'coach' in these amended circumstances would be commensurate with that of the ordinarily competent coach. Put bluntly, the original social or moral duty is extended to become a more formalised duty to adopt *reasonable* coaching practice so that *reasonable* care is taken to ensure the *reasonable* safety of players (i.e., fellow club members). For the average reasonable club member, player and/or parent, without up-to-date training or a coaching qualification, this may well represent a surprising exposure to legal liability, and an unusual instance of professional negligence, should the duty of care be breached. More fundamentally, it signifies a realistic and important illustration

103 *Fowles v Bedfordshire CC* [1995] PIQR P380 (CA), and most notably, the judgment of Millett LJ at P390. This proposition was endorsed by the Court of Appeal in the later decision of *Poppleton v Trustees of the Portsmouth Youth Activities Committee* [2008] EWCA Civ 646 [17] (May LJ). Also see, Norris (n 40), 157. More recently, this line of reasoning was adopted by counsel for the claimant in *Petrou v Bertoncello* [2012] EWHC 2286 [22], [27]. See further, Chapter 5.
104 See, for instance, Law Reform Commission of Ireland (n 55) [2.79], noting that 'in the main, volunteers usually act for altruistic reasons and because they have a moral, rather than legal, duty'.
105 Roberts et al. (n 22).
106 J Gardiner, 'Should Coaches Take Care?' (1993) 143 *NLJ* 1598. Interestingly, this principle derived from *Hedley Byrne & Co Ltd v Heller & Partner Ltd* [1964] AC 465 rests on an assumption of responsibility by the defendant towards the claimant and is coupled by the claimant's reliance on the exercise by the defendant of due skill and care. The principle has been applied by the courts to a range of scenarios extending beyond mere negligent misstatements. In recently reiterating this 'underlying wider principle', Lord Toulson in the Supreme Court in *Michael v Chief Constable of South Wales Police* [2015] UKSC 2 at [67] repeated that '[t]he principle that a duty of care could arise in that way was not limited to a case concerned with the giving of information and advice (Hedley Byrne) but could include the performance of other services'. See further, S Peyer and R Heywood, 'Walking on Thin Ice: The Perception of Tortious Liability Rules and the Effect on Altruistic Behaviour' (2019) *Legal Studies* 1–18, 6. https://doi.org/10.1017/lst.2018.39.

of the necessity to explicitly distinguish between legal and moral/social duties of care in the context of sports coaching. On more searching examination of the context of sports coaching, appreciation of this crucial distinction becomes even more pronounced.

Sports coaching practice

Protecting the health and safety of athletes poses coaches with legal, moral and ethical obligations.[107] For instance, bullying coaches violate their moral duty, both to treat athletes with respect and dignity and to safeguard athletes' welfare, health and safety.[108] Correspondingly, the dividing line between training intended to maximise sporting potential, as contrasted with abuse or exploitation of athletes, can be a thin one.[109] A significant ethical dilemma facing modern sports coaches, not least when working with young athletes, concerns determination of training intensity levels.[110] This is generally a judgement call left to the discretion of individual coaches, based on the specific circumstances, and an area where coaches have to be trusted to make the right (or reasonable) decisions.[111] Further contentious issues concern the scope of the duty of coaches to protect athletes from themselves,[112] and determination of what constitutes reasonable encouragement when reintroducing previously injured athletes into activities and training,[113] with the scenario of an injured star athlete desperate to compete being a challenging dilemma frequently encountered by coaches.[114] Moreover, coaches are expected to deliver 'cutting edge' guidance and advice to athletes,[115] potentially challenging the threshold between harm and

---

107 R Simon, 'Coaching, Compliance, and the Law' in Simon (n 20) 188; M Mitten, 'The Coach and the Safety of Athletes: Ethical and Legal Issues' in Simon (n 20) 232.
108 M Hamilton, 'Coaching, Gamesmanship, and Intimidation' in Simon (n 20) 144.
109 P David, 'Sharp Practice: Intensive Training and Child Abuse' in McNamee (n 17) 426.
110 See, for instance, A Miles and R Tong, 'Sports Medicine For Coaches' in RL Jones and K Kingston (eds), *An Introduction to Sports Coaching: Connecting Theory to Practice* (2nd edn, Abingdon, Routledge 2013) 188–89; J Lyle, *Sports Coaching Concepts: A Framework for Coaches' Behaviour* (London, Routledge 2002) 240. Also see, *Davenport v Farrow* [2010] EWHC 550 [59], where based on the defendant's training log, the intensity of training expected of the claimant was found to be within the range of acceptable coaching (level 4) for an athlete of his ability and aspirations. See further, Chapters 2 and 5. Interestingly, Norris (n 40, 158) notes that:

> [w]hat may be perfectly acceptable treatment of a seasoned professional may be wholly inadequate when dealing with a vulnerable teenager . . . it is commonplace that coaches or clubs may expect their players to "go through the pain barrier" or "run off" an injury or to continue to play having taken pain-killing injections or drugs but without much regard for the harmful long-term consequences.

111 Cassidy et al. (n 97) 154–55.
112 Hartley (n 11) 89.
113 A Hecht, 'Legal and Ethical Aspects of Sports-Related Concussions: The Merril Hoge story' (2002) 12 *Seton Hall J. Sports L.* 17, 40–41.
114 D Healey, *Sport and the Law* (4th edn, Sydney, UNSW Press 2009) 156.
115 C Mallett, 'Becoming a High Performing Coach: Pathways and Communities' in Lyle and Cushion (n 87) 119.

reasonable endeavour when pushing the human body to its physical and emotional limits within training and performance.[116] Viewed from a legal perspective, these matters provide a clear illustration of the need for coaches to have regard to 'the likely boundary between coaches forging champions or committing a tort'[117] and, moreover, for the requirement for coaching practice and behaviours to be reasonable.[118] The DoC in Sport Report appeared to be acutely aware of such tensions in coaching:

> While a concentration on qualifications is important it should be noted that being qualified to teach a technical skill does not always mean having the appropriate skills to work with athletes (of any age) in sport. Having the responsibility for safeguarding participants' emotional, psychological and physical well-being means that those individuals require continuous professional development in these areas. There should be a greater focus on behaviours and keeping up to date with relevant information.[119]

Clearly, this benchmark of reasonable, ethical or morally justifiable coaching conduct and practice, and associated tensions and difficult borderline cases, remains a constant source of enquiry and curiosity which coaches have a responsibility to be mindful of.[120] Interestingly, in the same way in which it may be acceptable to use the terms ethics and morality interchangeably, a coach's moral and ethical obligation not to expose athletes to unacceptable levels of risk is '[c]onsistent with the legal duty of reasonable care established by the negligence standard'.[121] However, of absolutely crucial relevance is the fact that the moral and ethical obligations incumbent upon coaches are *broader* than the legal standard of care.[122] Consistent with what Raz labels the 'semantic thesis', in the context of the duty of care owed by a sports coach to those under the coach's charge, the term duty 'cannot be used in the same meaning in legal and moral contexts'.[123]

It has been suggested by Honoré that, technically speaking, this is not so much a difference of meaning but, 'a difference between formal, institutionally recognised duties and rights [i.e., legal context] and their informal, non-institutional equivalents [i.e., moral context]'.[124] Herein lies the fundamental and dangerous pitfall likely to pose significant unintended repercussions unless it is made more explicit and

---

116 Telfer (n 88) 214. As noted by Telfer, this is certainly an enduring debate, particularly in relation to the coaching of young performers. See further, Chapter 7.
117 TR Hurst and JN Knight, 'Coaches' Liability for Athletes' Injuries and Deaths' (2003) 13 *Seton Hall J. Sports L.* 27, 29.
118 See further, Chapters 5, 6 and 7.
119 Doc in Sport Report (n 1) 21.
120 Partington (n 12).
121 Mitten (n 107) 216.
122 Ibid. 232; Lucy (n 23) 47
123 J Raz, 'Legal Positivism and the Sources of Law' in J Raz, *The Authority of Law. Essays on Law and Morality* (Oxford, Clarendon Press 1979) 38.
124 T Honoré, 'The Necessary Connection between Law and Morality' (2002) 22(3) *Oxford J Legal Studies* 489.

transparent. Certainly, when adopting a deliberately broad expression in the DoC in Sport Report, and in much of the subsequent and continuing media coverage in this field,[125] the crucial distinction between formal and institutionally recognised legal duties, as contrasted with informal and non-institutional moral duties, is not made plain. But in elaborating on the earlier caveat alluded to by Heuston, when exposed to sustained scrutiny from a legal perspective, the critically informed reasonable coach may be somewhat surprised and alarmed when the potential ramifications of associated inferences are revealed. Indeed, in emphasising the significance of this distinction in the context of sport, Norris convincingly cautions against framing policies in terms of expressions of 'duty of care', given the possible associated enhanced exposure to negligence liability claims.[126] In this regard, ministers and sports bodies need to be alerted to the importance of employing more precise terminology, given the important dividing line between legal and moral duties of care.

Implications

As already mentioned, the vast majority of the volunteer coaches in the UK have limited training,[127] with approximately half of the coaches in this jurisdiction not holding a coaching qualification.[128] Previous experience as players and enthusiasm are often regarded as sufficient prerequisites for volunteer coaches.[129] Further, there is evidence to suggest that some parents volunteer as coaches to assist their children, thereby ensuring that opportunities to participate continue.[130] This commitment and desire to help by former athletes and parents at the entry level is representative of the motivations widely held in voluntary activity.[131] In short, the sports coaching 'workforce' may be regarded as largely unregulated and in the absence of a 'validated threshold level of expertise or a commonality of occupational practice and expectations'.[132] Despite this, it remains axiomatic that coaches are driven by social and moral considerations, this being at the very core of the notion of the volunteer ethic.[133]

---

125 E.g., D Roan, 'Player Welfare: How Big a Problem Is Football Facing? And What Is Being Done?' (BBC News, 10 August 2018) <www.bbc.co.uk/sport/football/45171563> accessed 17 July 2019.
126 Norris (n 40) 155.
127 G Nygaard and T Boone, *Coaches' Guide to Sport Law* (Champaign, Human Kinetics 1985) 13.
128 Sports Coach UK (n 101) 17. The national average of coaches holding a coaching qualification in 2012 being around 53%.
129 Healey (n 114) 159.
130 Nash (n 100) 51. Also see, R Groom et al., 'Volunteering Insight: Report for Sport England' (Manchester Metropolitan University 2014) 6. In addition to child involvement, other motivating factors for volunteers (not necessarily coaches), included: love of sport, giving something back to sport, social connection, career aspirations, and education/employment based volunteering.
131 A Lynn and J Lyle, 'Coaching Workforce Development' in Lyle and Cushion (n 88) 206.
132 Ibid. 205.
133 See, for instance, Study on Volunteering in the European Union (2010), Report for DG EAC Submitted by GHK, 149 <http://ec.europa.eu/citizenship/pdf/doc1018_en.pdf> accessed 3 January 2019. The report notes that the desire to help others is a key motivating factor amongst volunteers.

Importantly, as the principal supervisors of organised sporting activities, coaches must appreciate that participation in sport frequently leads to injury.[134] Theme 7 of the DoC in Sport Report concentrates on 'Safety, injury and medical issues'. Recommendations from Theme 7 include:

- Development of a standard first aid course specifically for sport;
- Sports to provide guidance to clubs with understanding their health and safety obligations;
- NGBs to provide and promote online access to basic first aid guidance (which should include CPR and concussion protocols);
- Consideration should be given to the development of a training module including content about Sudden Cardiac Arrest (SCA) symptoms;
- NGBs to work together on improving awareness of cardiac screening at community sport level. Consideration should be given to producing online materials and also inclusion in coaching courses or participant inductions;
- All sports (even those who may not be readily thought susceptible to concussion) need to be aware of concussion protocols and work together to ensure they have something in place and communicate with other organisations; and
- All contact sports to consider pre-season concussion awareness courses.[135]

Coaches generally operate in isolation,[136] without immediate access to the services of a doctor or physiotherapist, this being a common situation in amateur sport.[137] Moreover, there is no requirement in the UK at present for coaches to have first aid or life-support training,[138] despite the coach frequently being the first person to attend to an injured athlete.[139] Understanding the health and safety obligations of coaches demands a clear distinction between duties maintaining minimal rather than aspirational standards for conduct. Should all coaches be required to attend a standard first aid course specifically for sport (and appropriately supported in order to do so), the standard of care required when dealing with safety, injury and medical issues involving athletes may, quite deliberately and understandably, become explicitly heightened. For instance, using the analogy of sport managers, should the use of automated external defibrillators (AEDs) continue to become more commonplace, 'the bar will continue to be raised regarding the standard of care that

---

134 Miles and Tong (n 110) 178.
135 DoC in Sport Report (n 1) 25.
136 P Trudel et al., 'Coach Education and Effectiveness' in Lyle and Cushion (n 88) 141.
137 M McNamee et al., 'Concussion in Sport: Conceptual and Ethical issues' (2015) 4 *Kinesiology Review* 190, 199.
138 Miles and Tong (n 110) 189. In this scenario, it would be reasonable for the coach to have contingency plans in place for the management of foreseeable risk and make appropriate and timely referral to a qualified medical practitioner or nominated first aider.
139 See, for instance, S Broglio et al., 'Concussion Occurrence and Knowledge in Italian Football (Soccer)' (2010) 9 *Journal of Sports Science and Medicine* 418, 419–20.

organizations and facilities are expected to provide'.[140] Put simply, formalised standard first aid training should equip coaches with an ordinary level of competence that satisfies a 'basic level of awareness among those on the scene about what immediate action to take, whether that be calling for further assistance or administering basic first aid'.[141] Significantly, by providing appropriate and mandatory training, the extent of the coach's duty of care would be extended in confined situations in a deliberate, informed and incremental fashion. However, whilst it might be strongly desirable for coaches to be educated on CPR, concussion and SCA symptoms and protocols, at present, and very much depending upon the particular circumstances (e.g., professional versus amateur sport; type of sport), coaches are not always educated about these subjects. Thus, and reflective of the more general necessity for (volunteer) coaches to assume only legal obligations commensurate with their level of competence, a number of the DoC in Sport Report recommendations should be regarded as 'good practice – an expression of a moral, but certainly not a legal, duty'.[142]

Consequently, when defining the duty of care incumbent upon sports coaches, it is imperative that a distinction is drawn between a legal duty of care and broader moral, ethical and aspirational considerations. Failing to make this distinction, and consistent with the volunteer ethic, it is possible that intuitively moral and social duties may be transformed from aspirational standards of conduct, into legal ones in a somewhat haphazard and informal manner. Clearly, this would result in the unintended consequence of potentially exposing coaches to a greater risk of negligence liability. In principle, extending the scope of a coach's duty of care should be done in a more systematically planned and explicit manner. At the very least, an extension in the scope of a coach's duty of care should involve a process of informed dialogue,[143] coach education and qualification, continuing 'professional' development and corresponding support so that such provision and measures are accessible for all coaches. Moreover, the DoC in Sport Report recognised that '[a]n understanding of Duty of Care should be included in any leadership training in sport, in order to help and support a new diverse generation of leaders'.[144] Accordingly, the necessity for such training to address and unpack distinctions between legal or moral duties of care, by perhaps emphasising and discussing the significance of coaches assuming only duties for which they are ordinarily competent, seems compelling. More fundamentally, an aim of such training should be to proactively ensure that all of sport's stakeholders are aware of the danger of conflating moral and legal duties of care. Appropriate strategies could then be adopted to prevent coaches from being compromised in this regard.

---

140 J Spengler et al., *Risk Management in Sport and Recreation* (Champaign, Human Kinetics 2006) 64.
141 DoC in Sport Report (n 1) 26.
142 Norris (n 40) 154.
143 For instance, between NGBs, sports coach UK, coaching organisations, coach educators and coaches.
144 DoC in Sport Report (n 1) 16.

Conclusion

Critical analysis of a sports coach's duty of care reveals a context where the law and morality are not necessarily inextricably interwoven. Failure to appreciate this subtlety, blurred by connotations that likely flow from the pseudo-legal gloss of duty of care terminology, may unwittingly expose (mainly volunteer) coaches to an unreasonable future risk of legal liability. Whilst this submission is in no way intended to detract from the extremely worthwhile recommendations of the DoC in Sport Report, or a commitment to the highest standards in athlete safety and welfare, it is intended to make a valuable contribution to Baroness Tanni Grey-Thompson's hope of stimulating further discussion on the application of duty of care principles in the specific context of sport. Moreover, the original insights revealed by scrutinising distinctions between legal and moral duties of care in a somewhat novel context is submitted to be of significance beyond the confines of sport. So whilst the concerns highlighted in this chapter may also be of immediate and direct relevance to the duties of care incumbent upon sports referees and officials, this also representing an area with developing and recent case law in the UK,[145] the important implications discussed are likely to be of more widespread relevance. For instance, given the considerable reliance on volunteers in the EU – most notably in the sectors of sport; social, welfare and health activities; religious organisations; culture; recreation and leisure; and education, training and research[146] – and in view of the likely relevance and application of the 'neighbour principle' in these contexts, explicitly distinguishing between legal and moral duties is both prudent and necessary. More specifically, since the issue of breach of duty by coaches represents a distinctively nuanced issue of professional liability, this chapter's uncovering of distinctions between legal and moral duties of care is of relevance and merit in the area of professional negligence more generally. This appears a particularly convincing submission since moral and ethical considerations may become indicative of the prevailing 'social conditions and habits of life' that impact upon standard of care enquiries,[147] and which regardless of associated advances in knowledge, may similarly heighten the standard of the reasonably competent practitioner.[148] Further, given the increasing propensity for the concept of the duty of care to be employed in order to create a gloss of pseudo-legal authority, ordinary reasonable persons, recognised bodies, and indeed government departments (i.e., DCMS) should be advised to be acutely aware of the potential implications should legal and moral duties of care become regarded as being one and the same.

---

145 E.g., *Bartlett* (n 38); *Allport v Wilbraham* [2004] EWCA Civ 1668; *Vowles* (n 37); *Smoldon v Whitworth* [1997] PIQR P133 (CA); See further, Partington (n 38).
146 Study on Volunteering in the European Union (n 133) 9.
147 Percy and Walton (n 49) [6–04].
148 See further, Powell and Stewart (n 96) [2–135].

In calling for a more exact, nuanced and informed understanding of the legal duty of care in sport, this chapter cautions against potentially extending the scope and extent of the duty of care of sports coaches by expanding a fundamental legal principle beyond its intended sphere of application. Given this submission, the next chapter examines in detail this more precise intersection between the law of negligence and sports coaching.

2
LEGAL DUTY OF CARE
The law of negligence

Having distinguished between legal, moral and ethical duties of care in the previous chapter by expounding Lord Atkin's neighbour principle, this chapter situates the concept of the duty of care firmly within its originally intended, well-established and specific limits – the law of negligence. Doing this allows for a more precise framing of the practical content of the duty of care of modern sports coaches. More specifically, since it is now well-settled law that coaches owe a legal duty of care to athletes,[1] this chapter critically considers the decisive factor on which the vast majority of cases brought in negligence against coaches are decided, namely, the required standard of care in all the circumstances or control mechanism of breach. In short, analysing this core disputed issue at the intersection between the law of negligence and sports coaching enables the legal duty of care required of modern sports coaches to be defined, clarified and unpacked.

Introduction

Coaches push boundaries, are innovative and continuously search for an 'edge'. Working your team harder than opponents during preseason, strength and conditioning sessions, practices and games might provide a perceived controllable 'edge'. Indeed, some coaches may regard intense physical and mental conditioning as customary practice and the difference between success and failure. The approach of modern sports coaches in seeking a physiological and psychological 'edge' would likely encapsulate advances in sports science to optimise the sporting performance of athletes and teams: periodisation; sports nutrition; principles/types of training; biomechanics and sport psychology, to name but a few. Successful coaching is

---

1 E.g., *Fowles v Bedfordshire CC* [1995] PIQR P380 (CA); *Anderson v Lyotier* [2008] EWHC 2790.

a complex process. Crucially, one such important and hitherto under-analysed complexity of modern sports coaching, given the emerging relationship between coaching and the law of negligence, is the legal duty of care owed to athletes by coaches. For instance, should an athlete suffer serious personal injury when being pushed to their physiological and psychological limits to secure an 'edge', what might be regarded by the UK courts as objectively reasonable coaching in the circumstances? How is a legal test for breach of duty fashioned and formulated in order to appropriately reflect the specificity of coaching? Detailed analysis of case law and academic commentary reveals that both amateur and professional coaches in the UK may be unwittingly exposed to liability in negligence by potentially breaching their duty of care. This is problematic. Importantly, since the duties of coaches are broadly common and consistent,[2] and the law of negligence may be regarded to a large extent as generally similar everywhere,[3] although the primary jurisdictional focus of this book is the UK, as the introduction to this book makes plain, the ensuing discussion will be of much wider interest and relevance.

In analysing the legal duty of care as it relates to modern sports coaching, this chapter firstly considers relevant and important contextual issues. The chapter next engages critically with the law of negligence's control mechanisms of duty (of care), breach (of duty), causation and the most applicable defences to a claim of coach negligence. Significantly, in aiming to define and clarify the nature of a coach's legal duty of care, it is the practical content of this duty that requires the most detailed and searching scrutiny. Therefore, to facilitate a more rigorous and critical analysis, the content of a coach's duty of care is critiqued by means of an interdisciplinary analysis. Discrete scrutiny of the related doctrine of in loco parentis further extends the discussion. Following this, the standard of care required of modern sports coaches is exposed to sustained analysis by more precise and fuller engagement with the relevant case law and existing literature in order to analyse how courts determine whether there has been a breach of duty. Accordingly, it is argued that the dynamic relationship between a coach and those under the coach's instruction is reflective of the emerging interface between sport and the law of negligence and, crucially, that this relationship is progressively placing more responsibilities on coaches. This results in the duty of care demanded of modern sports coaches becoming more challenging to effectively discharge over time. Furthermore, by analysing the doctrine of customary practice (i.e., *Bolam* test), the chapter emphasises the importance of coaches ensuring that the coaching practices adopted are recognised, approved and capable of withstanding logical analysis, as a means of avoiding a breach of duty of care due to negligent entrenched practice.

---

2 The specific duties of coaches are discussed in detail in Chapter 5.
3 U Magnus, 'Tort Law in General' in JM Smits (ed), *Elgar Encyclopedia of Comparative Law* (Cheltenham, Edward Elgar 2006) 725. See further, the detailed discussion on this issue in the introduction to this book and, in particular, with regard to the well-established and extensive cross-pollination of tortious principles between countries of the wider common law family.

Context

Legal liability for athlete injury caused by a breach of duty of care is a significant issue facing all coaches,[4] not least given the increasingly visible interface between the law of negligence and sport in this area.[5] Clarifying the legal duty of care incumbent upon modern sports coaches represents a serious gap in both the (emerging) case law and the academic literature relating to the UK.[6] The narrow legal principles derived from judgments directly in point establish that, for instance, at the elite level, coaching that is 'robust' and 'fairly tough' would 'not begin to amount to negligence'.[7] Of more universal application, is the recognition by the courts that overtraining, or training requiring an unreasonable level of intensity, may provide the basis for a cause of action[8] for a claim in negligence.[9] Nevertheless, the pivotal question of what constitutes reasonableness in all the circumstances has yet to be fully scrutinised, allowing only speculative conclusions,[10] with academic commentary tending to address the issue more generally.[11] Often, the emphasis has been on school sport.[12] This compounds the age-old problem of predicting conduct deemed 'negligent'.[13] Moreover, this absence of legal authority and guidelines concerning the standard of care required of sports coaches, thereby failing to identify the practical content of the duty of care owed,[14] presents a lack of clarity in this area of sports law.

---

4 AS McCaskey and KW Biedzynski, 'A Guide to the Legal Liability of Coaches for a Sports Participant's Injuries' (1996) 6 *Seton Hall J. Sport L.* 7, 9.
5 S Greenfield et al., 'Reconceptualising The Standard of Care in Sport: The Case of Youth Rugby in England and South Africa' (2015) 18(6) *Potchefstroom Elec. L.J.* 2183, 2186.
6 See generally, M James, *Sports Law* (New York, Palgrave Macmillan 2010) 93.
7 *Brady v Sunderland Association Football Club Ltd*, 17 November 1998 (CA). Importantly, in the 18 years since this judgment was delivered, coaching practices and methods (including the tracking and monitoring of performance and injuries) have developed considerably.
8 A cause of action describes 'the various categories of factual situations which entitle[d] one person to obtain from the court a remedy against another': *Letang v Cooper* [1965] 1 QB 232 (CA) 242 (Diplock LJ). See further, CT Watson and R Hyde (eds), *Charlesworth & Percy on Negligence, First Supplement to the Thirteenth Edition* (London, Sweet and Maxwell 2015) [2–05].
9 *Davenport v Farrow* [2010] EWHC 550. This case is considered in detail in Chapter 5. The overtraining of elite young athletes may constitute a child protection issue, particularly in the context of elite international sport: see further, A Gray and A-M Blakeley, 'Child Protection' in A Lewis and J Taylor, *Sport: Law and Practice* (2nd edn, Haywards Heath, Tottel 2008) 813.
10 S Gardiner et al., *Sports Law* (3rd edn, London, Cavendish 2006) 649.
11 E.g., J Anderson, *Modern Sports Law: A Textbook* (Hart 2010) 248; M James, *Sports Law* (2nd edn, New York, Palgrave Macmillan 2013) 92–97; Greenfield et al. (n 5).
12 E.g., D Griffith-Jones, 'Civil Liability Arising Out of Participation in Sport' in Lewis and Taylor (n 9) 737–42; E Grayson, *Sport and the Law* (3rd edn, Haywards Heath, Tottel 1999) 190–99; N Cox and A Schuster, *Sport and the Law* (Dublin, Firstlaw 2004) 230–47; H Hartley, *Sport, Physical Recreation and the Law* (London, Routledge 2009) 55–63; M Beloff et al., *Sports Law* (2nd edn, Oxford, Hart 2012) 146–48.
13 A Morris, '"Common Sense Common Safety": The Compensation Culture Perspective' (2011) 27(2) *Professional Negligence* 82, 92–93.
14 See generally, J Steele, *Tort Law: Text, Cases and Materials* (2nd edn, Oxford, OUP 2010) 115.

Legal duty of care 43

The liability of coaches is arguably the least explored area of sports negligence.[15] Without clarification of the scope and reach of the tort of negligence into the domain of sports coaching there is a realistic prospect that some coaches might resort to defensive measures/practices that would have a chilling effect on a wide range of activities, or worse still, abandon their involvement in sports coaching altogether in order to negate potential exposure to perceived liability.[16] Indeed, Anderson has suggested that the current jurisprudence questions why volunteers would be willing to become involved in sports coaching,[17] likely compounded by a perceived (more) litigious society and 'compensation culture',[18] potentially removing from sport its 'most important and focal participant'.[19] As noted by Lord Falconer in 2005, 'the idea of a compensation culture can impact on volunteers – by discouraging people to give their time or by organisations restricting the activities people can do for fear – often a misplaced fear – of a claim'.[20]

Although it may be trite law to recognise that establishing what may be regarded as acceptable risk taking by coaches will be incapable of definition,[21] coaches are nevertheless required to have a familiarity with the emerging case law relating to sports coaching and instructing,[22] since this awareness and knowledge provides necessary guidelines for reasonable practice.[23] As argued by Champion, by identifying common situations that satisfy/fail to satisfy the criteria of negligence, consideration of individual cases offers 'a barometer of acceptable behaviour'.[24] Such illustrations of acceptable coaching behaviour can be used to promote and develop a proactive risk assessment lens that can subsequently be incorporated into the practices of coaches, sports leaders, sports instructors and physical education (PE) teachers.[25] Moreover, 'identification of the specific duties [incumbent upon coaches] is essential for understanding and evaluating what is required of coaches',[26] since it has been recognised that the sometimes impossible pressures and expectations placed upon some modern coaches forces the search for 'ever more extreme measures'.[27] It is comprehensible that coaches working in the context

---

15 Gardiner et al. (n 10) 649. An overview of the development of sports negligence case law is provided in Chapter 4.
16 J Fulbrook, *Outdoor Activities, Negligence and the Law* (London, Ashgate 2005) 105.
17 Anderson (n 11) 249; R Heywood and P Charlish, 'Schoolmaster Tackled Hard Over Rugby Incident' (2007) 15 *Tort Law Review* 162, 171.
18 Steele (n 14) 16; *Wilkin-Shaw v Fuller* [2012] EWHC 1777 [42] (Owen J).
19 McCaskey and Biedzynski (n 4) 9.
20 Lord Falconer, 'Compensation Culture', (Health and Safety Executive Event, 22 March 2005) 4.
21 Griffith-Jones (n 12) 717 & 725.
22 Chapter 7 contends that discussion of engaging scenarios derived from case law, as part of coach education and training, would be instructive in this regard.
23 G Nygaard and T Boone, *Coaches' Guide to Sport Law* (Champaign, Human Kinetics 1985) ix.
24 WT Champion, 'The Evolution of a Standard of Care for Injured College Athletes: A Review of Kleinknecht and Progeny' (1999) 1 *Va. J. Sports & L.* 290, 295.
25 Hartley (n 12) 56.
26 McCaskey and Biedzynski (n 4) 15.
27 P Craig and P Beedie (eds), *Sport Sociology* (2nd edn, Learning Matters 2010) 119.

of elite sport, seeking to optimise the performance levels of the athletes being coached, for instance, by repeatedly pushing players to the limit of their physical and mental performance thresholds,[28] may be reluctant to take extra precautions in practice.[29] Nevertheless, as convincingly recognised by Hurst and Knight, such coaches must have regard to 'the likely boundary between coaches forging champions or committing a tort'.[30]

Some coaching practitioners may be reticent and resistant to acknowledge that litigation risk, due to a breach of duty, should be of some considerable importance when planning, delivering and evaluating sessions, practices and competitive fixtures and events. For example, there is some evidence to indicate that soccer coaching behaviours can often be belligerent. Cushion and Jones contend that this hostility is reflective of the culture in professional soccer, with preparation for the rigours of the game regarded by certain coaches as requiring young players to be exposed to such harsh and authoritarian approaches to coaching.[31] It is further suggested that '[w]inning coaches often achieve results through techniques that could legally be considered "wanton" or "grossly negligent" in any other context'.[32] Clearly, should personal injury to an athlete be caused by coaching techniques evincing a reckless disregard for the well-being and safety of those under the coach's charge, there would be strong and justifiable grounds for establishing a breach of the legal duty of care owed by the coach.[33]

More generally, a lack of regard to potential civil liability may be reflected in much coach education,[34] given the tendency to focus on the bioscientific aspects of sports science,[35] with facilitation of such a mechanistic approach a potential barrier to the appreciation of the complexities of coaching.[36] This emphasis on practical

---

28 Interestingly, the coaching style adopted in the circumstances would be a factor likely scrutinised by the court in claims brought against coaches in negligence: see, for example, *Davenport* (n 9), where Owen J considered in some depth the claimant's submission that the coach was 'a forceful and controlling personality who demanded a high level of control over the young athletes whom he coached' (at [27]). See further, Chapter 5.
29 K Lines, 'Thinking Outside The Box(-Ing Ring): The Implications for Sports Governing Bodies Following Watson' (2007) 4 *International Sports Law Review* 67, 73.
30 TR Hurst and JN Knight, 'Coaches' Liability for Athletes' Injuries and Deaths' (2003) 13 *Seton Hall J. Sports L.* 27, 29.
31 C Cushion and R Jones, 'Power, Discourse, and Symbolic Violence in Professional Youth Soccer: The Case of Albion Football Club' (2006) 23 *Sociology of Sport Journal* 142, 148.
32 Hurst and Knight (n 30) 28.
33 See *Wooldridge v Sumner* [1963] 2 QB 43 (CA); *Caldwell v Maguire* [2001] EWCA Civ 1054. As noted by McArdle and James, as a standard of misbehavior, reckless disregard provides a sufficient, but not necessary, evidential guide in claims of sports negligence: D McArdle and M James, 'Are You Experienced? "Playing Cultures", Sporting Rules and Personal Injury Litigation After Caldwell v Maguire' (2005) 13(3) *Tort Law Review* 193, 207. See further, Chapter 4.
34 Greenfield et al. (n 5) 2201.
35 D Kirk, 'Towards a Socio-Pedagogy of Sports Coaching' in J Lyle and C Cushion (eds), *Sports Coaching: Professionalisation and Practice* (Edinburgh, Elsevier 2010) 165.
36 T Cassidy et al., *Understanding Sports Coaching: The Social, Cultural and Pedagogical Foundations of Coaching Practice* (2nd edn, London, Routledge 2009) 93–94.

skills and knowledge[37] may be regarded as perpetuating 'an academic orthodoxy in sports coaching, often branded as "coaching science", that endorses a practice-based profession assumed at improving athletic performance'.[38] Whilst practice-based skills and knowledge are integral to effective coaching behaviour, an overemphasis on bioscientific discourse focused on improving athletic performance may fail to fully account for the complex and dynamic context in which modern sports coaches discharge their duty of care. The evolving intersection between the law of negligence and sports coaching represents one such significant and emerging complexity of coaching that appears less frequently highlighted in both coach education and the extant academic literature of 'coaching science'. Importantly, unlike the reactive development of child protection safeguarding procedures and legal provision,[39] a fundamental aim of this book is to clarify and heighten awareness of the extent of a coach's legal duty of care, advocating for a proactive approach to risk management in order to better protect and safeguard coaches from legal liability and, as a result, improve the health, safety and welfare of all athletes in structured and supervised coaching environments.

Having identified some important contextual issues that are relevant to the legal duty of care of modern sports coaches, this chapter next engages critically with the law of negligence's control devices of duty, standard of care and breach, causation and the most applicable defences.

Law of negligence

In the context of sport, including the specific circumstances of sports coaching,[40] it is clear that the ordinary principles of the law of negligence are applicable.[41] One of the leading authorities in this area of sports law, *Caldwell v Maguire*,[42] relates to the liability for injury caused by co-participants. *Caldwell* establishes that the prevailing circumstances that the court would consider when applying ordinary principles of negligence may include: 'its object, the demands inevitably made upon its contestants, its inherent dangers (if any), its rules, conventions and customs, and the standards, skills and judgment reasonably to be expected of a contestant'.[43] Crucially, this proposition from *Caldwell*, by identifying the indicative criteria constituting the prevalent circumstances and enabling reasonableness to be defined, essentially formulates the legal test to be applied for injury caused by co-participants.

---

37 J Lyle, 'Coaching Philosophy and Coaching Behaviour' in N Cross and J Lyle (eds), *The Coaching Process: Principles and Practice for Sport* (Philadelphia, Butterworth-Heinemann 1999) 31.
38 A Hardman and C Jones (eds), *The Ethics of Sports Coaching* (Abingdon, Routledge 2011) 1.
39 Gray and Blakeley (n 9) 779.
40 E.g., *Davenport* (n 9).
41 E.g., *Smoldon v Whitworth* [1997] PIQR P133 (CA); *Vowles v Evans* [2003] EWCA Civ 318. See generally, Griffith-Jones (n 12) 715 & 740.
42 *Caldwell* (n 33). Also see, *Condon v Basi* (1985) 1 WLR 866 (CA).
43 *Caldwell* (n 33) [11].

Significantly, the prevailing circumstances will vary enormously the appropriate degree of care required of sports coaches.[44] For instance, when considering the analogous duty and standard of care expected of a rugby referee in *Smoldon v Whitworth*, Lord Bingham emphasised the significance of scrutiny of the full factual scenario in the court's deliberations. Thus, the Court of Appeal in *Smoldon* accepted that given the specific functions of a referee there would not be negligence liability 'for errors of judgment, oversights or lapses of which any referee might be guilty in the context of a fast-moving and vigorous contest. The threshold of liability is a high one. It will not easily be crossed'.[45] Whilst recognising from the outset that this book's focus concerns a highly fact-sensitive area of the law, a sports coach may be found liable in negligence in the UK where it can be established by the claimant that the coach:

(i) Owed the claimant a duty of care;
(ii) That this duty of care was breached;
(iii) The breach in question caused foreseeable personal injury to the claimant; and
(iv) The coach is unable to rely on an applicable defence(s)

In concentrating on defining a coach's duty of care, the following detailed analysis pays particular attention to the practical content of a coach's duty of care, or the standard of care, and the fashioning of the legal test for breach of duty by courts. Close attention is also paid to the seemingly interrelated legal doctrines of in loco parentis and customary practice.

Duty of care

Given the tort of negligence is underpinned by the neighbour principle,[46] requiring the exercise of reasonable care to avoid injuring anyone who ought reasonably to be considered as being affected by one's actions or omissions,[47] it is immediately apparent that coaches must display reasonable care when assuming such a role.[48] By analogy, given a similar interdependent relationship to that between coach–athlete, and a likewise heavy reliance on amateur volunteers, it has previously been argued that imposing a duty of care on rugby union referees is harsh, unjust and would lead to undesirable 'defensive' refereeing.[49] Nonetheless, despite further arguments indicating that holding that an amateur referee owes a duty of care to the players under their charge would have a 'chilling effect', by discouraging volunteers from being prepared to serve as referees, the Court of Appeal has ruled otherwise.[50]

---

44 Anderson (n 11) 248.
45 *Smoldon* (n 41) P139. The analogous duty of care of referees is discussed in detail in Chapter 4.
46 *Donoghue v Stevenson* [1932] AC 562. See further, Chapter 1.
47 *Blyth v Birmingham Waterworks* (1856) 11Ex 781, 784; *Donoghue* (n 46) 580.
48 Griffith-Jones (n 12) 737–38; Beloff et al. (n 12) [5.52]; James (n 11) 93.
49 *Smoldon v Whitworth* [1997] ELR 115, 122–23.
50 *Vowles* (n 41) [49].

Given the supervisory, instructional and safety functions of a coach, providing the foundation of the coach–athlete relationship, it is just, fair and reasonable that coaches may be held liable for a breach of their duty of care that causes personal injury to athletes.[51]

Content of a coach's duty of care

It is the coach's responsibility to be up-to-date with sport-specific knowledge and sports science, since techniques in sport can change remarkably over a couple of decades or so.[52] Should a claim be brought against a sports coach for negligence, the most critical determining factor in the vast majority of cases would be whether the coach fulfilled the duty to exercise reasonable care for the protection of the athlete.[53] Although the standard expected of sports coaches is fixed conceptually as the duty to take reasonable care,[54] specific duties required of coaches have evolved,[55] it being suggested by Barnes that coaches are required to discharge responsibilities that may be classified under three main headings which include: facilities and organisation; instruction and supervision; and medical care.[56] Unpacking these categories reveals the need for coaches to deliver safe practices with appropriate use of required protective equipment, the avoidance of coaching practices that might aggravate lingering injury and the need for supervision to reflect inherent risks that

---

51 Chapter 5 considers in detail the relevant body of coach negligence case law. The kind of injury suffered by claimants in all of these reported cases concerns physical harm. To date, there appears to be no reported case in the UK of a coach being sued by an athlete for a breach of duty of care resulting in negligently inflicted psychiatric illness. The closest connected case is *GB v Stoke City Football Club Limited* [2015] EWHC 2862. In *GB*, the claimant alleged that he suffered psychiatric/psychological injury due to an 'initiation ritual' or punishment known as 'gloving', whereby a goalkeeper's glove was smeared with heat cream and used in an 'intimate physical assault'. The court held that if there was a practice of 'gloving' at the club the coaches had no actual knowledge or suspicion of it. Ultimately, the claim failed due to a lack of credible evidence. Deakin and Adams argue convincingly that psychiatric harm is 'not yet placed on a par with bodily injury or the loss of a limb' and is 'only recoverable under exceptional circumstances' (S Deakin and Z Adams, *Markesinis and Deakin's Tort Law* (8th edn, Oxford, OUP 2019) 107–08). Indeed, as explained by Mulheron, it is much easier for a claimant to recover damages where psychiatric injury is negligently inflicted and consequential upon physical injury (R Mulheron, *Principles of Tort Law* (Cambridge, CUP 2016) 220). For detailed coverage of the issue of negligently inflicted pure psychiatric illness, see Mulheron, *Principles of Tort Law*, 218–89.
52 Nygaard and Boone (n 23) 24.
53 J Labuschagne and J Skea, 'The Liability of a Coach for a Sport Participant's Injury' (1999) 10 *Stellenbosch Law Review* 158, 159; W Norris, '*Perry v Harris* – Case Comment Following the Ruling in the Court of Appeal' (2008) 4 *JPI Law* 258, 259; N Partington, 'Legal Liability of Coaches: A UK Perspective' (2014) 14(3–4) *International Sports Law Journal* 232, 236.
54 See generally, D Howarth, 'Many Duties of Care – Or a Duty of Care? Notes from the Underground' (2006) 26(3) *Oxford J Legal Studies* 449.
55 McCaskey and Biedzynski (n 4) 15. Although the adoption of terminology making reference to 'specific duties' may be regarded as technically misleading, formulating the standard of care in terms of a particular duty can be useful in a descriptive way: see MA Jones and AM Dugdale (eds), *Clerk and Lindsell on Torts* (20th edn, London, Sweet and Maxwell 2010) [8–137].
56 J Barnes, *Sports and the Law in Canada* (3rd edn, Toronto, Butterworths 1996) 302.

are foreseeable.[57] As recognised by McCaskey and Biedzynski, it appears generally well established that the specific duties of care of coaches when managing the risk of injury to athletes relate to: (i) supervision; (ii) training and instruction (including organisation); (iii) ensuring the proper use of safe equipment; (iv) providing competent and responsible personnel; (v) warning of latent dangers; (vi) providing prompt and proper medical care; (vii) preventing injured athletes from competing; and (viii) matching athletes of similar competitive levels.[58] These criteria could be further elaborated upon. For instance, and as highlighted by Labuschagne and Skea, seven factors to be considered by coaches when matching performers include the athletes': (i) skill; (ii) experience; (iii) injuries; (iv) maturity: physical, emotional and mental; (v) height and weight;[59] (vi) age; and (vii) mental state.[60]

Traditionally, the assumption has been that the coach's 'primary duty' is the safety of the individual athlete,[61] which according to Healey would appear to remain the case when coaching children.[62] However, given the diverse contexts in which coaches now operate, including the highly commercialised circumstances of some professional elite sport, might there be occasion whereby the 'primary duty' of the coach is winning?[63] Whilst accepting that the terminology of 'primary duty' may be regarded as facilitating consideration of variable standards of care,[64] which have not been well received by the courts in the UK,[65] it concentrates attention on the highly fact-sensitive and sometimes conflicting responsibilities faced by coaches in diverse contexts such as school sport, amateur sport and professional sport. Further, since a volunteer coach working independently is unlikely to be a medical expert or have access to specialist medical advice, balancing the duty of reasonable care to individual players with responsibilities to the entire team generates a difficult judgement call, as coaches 'are forced to rely on imperfect information while upholding a series of competing obligations'.[66]

---

57 J Kessler, 'Dollar Signs on the Muscle . . . And the Ligament, Tendon, and Ulnar Nerve: Institutional Liability Arising from Injuries to Student-Athletes' (2001) 3 *Va. J Sports & L* 80, 99.
58 McCaskey and Biedzynski (n 4) 15–16. These specific duties are more fully examined, and further developed, in Chapters 5 & 6.
59 E.g., HAP Archbold et al., 'RISUS study: Rugby Injury Surveillance in Ulster Schools' (2015) *Br J Sports Med* 1, 6 Published Online First: 23 December 2015. DOI: 10.1136/bjsports-2015-095491, recognising that '[t]he trend for an increased risk of injury in higher level, older, heavier schoolboy players who regularly undertake weight training is worrying'.
60 Labuschagne and Skea (n 53) 175–77. Further considerations include the fitness levels of athletes, athletes with disabilities and participants returning after recovering from injury: see further, R Martens, *Successful Coaching* (3rd edn, Champaign, Human Kinetics 2004) 482.
61 McCaskey and Biedzynski (n 4) 15.
62 D Healey, *Sport and the Law* (4th edn, Sydney, UNSW Press 2009) 157.
63 Ibid. 156.
64 As noted earlier (n 55), terminology making reference to 'specific duties' may be regarded as technically misleading. The duty incumbent upon coaches is to discharge their functions with reasonable care and skill.
65 *Nettleship v Weston* [1971] 2 QB 691 (CA); Beloff et al. (n 12) 143.
66 Kessler (n 57) 100.

The practical content of a coach's duty of care is premised on a reasonableness standard.[67] Reasonableness is reflective of the circumstances at the material time,[68] with the standard of care being subject to variations in the prevailing 'social conditions and habits of life'.[69] The duties incumbent upon coaches have evolved, and as a result of advances brought about by factors including those in the field of sports science, technical developments in certain sports and societal expectations, such legal duties appear to be undergoing extension.[70] Put simply, and as identified by Cassidy et al., the principles of coaching are constantly assessed and revised.[71] These developments require courts to be mindful of coaching as a dynamic social practice that is responsive to new information and knowledge. Evidence of the tendency to extend the scope of a coach's duty of care, or to heighten the standard of care barometer, was articulated in *Hamstra et al. v British Columbia Rugby Union* when the court ruled that:

> the standard of care as it relates to the risk of serious debilitating cervical spine injury in British Columbia in May 1986 is . . . a lower one than the Court would apply in British Columbia were the same injury to occur today in similar circumstances.[72]

The management of sport-related concussion provides a further modern example of how the requirements of coaches are reflective of new information, knowledge and stipulated best practice protocols. As argued by Labuschagne and Skea, such related advances may increase the degree of the duty of care owed by progressively placing more responsibilities on coaches.[73] Problematically, and as critically analysed in Chapter 1, conflating the legal, ethical and moral duties of coaches may by implication, and unintentionally, also extend a coach's legal duty of care. In short, the specific duties of modern sports coaches, and the evidential threshold necessary to establish breach of these said duties, requires contemporary analysis, with critical scrutiny of the doctrine of in loco parentis providing an insightful illustration of developments in this area of the law.

---

67 The prevalence of a legal standard of reasonableness, or its equivalent, in countries throughout the world is discussed in this book's introduction.
68 Griffith-Jones (n 12) 716.
69 R Percy and C Walton (eds), *Charlesworth & Percy on Negligence* (9th edn, London, Sweet & Maxwell 1997) [6–04].
70 R VerSteeg, 'Negligence in the Air: Safety, Legal Liability, and the Pole Vault' (2003) 4 *Tex. Rev. Ent. & Sports L.* 109, 113. Labuschagne and Skea (n 53) 158.
71 Cassidy et al. (n 36) 130–31.
72 *Hamstra et al. v British Columbia Rugby Union* [1989] 1 CCLT (2d) 78. See 'The Standard of Care of Coaches Towards Athletes', 16 June 1995 <https://sportlaw.ca/what-is-the-standard-in-the-standard-of-care/> accessed 6 November 2019. Also see *Browning v Odyssey Trust Company Limited* [2014] NIQB 39 [23]; *Villella v North Bedfordshire BC*, 25 October 1983 (QBD).
73 Labuschagne and Skea (n 53) 158

In loco parentis

Since the test adopted in *Williams v Eady*,[74] that of a careful parent, the legal doctrine of in loco parentis, pronouncement of which varies with different age groups and generations,[75] has been recognised as providing a useful benchmark for the duty of care owed by both teachers[76] and sports coaches.[77] Certainly, from an ethical perspective, the doctrine of in loco parentis may appear useful.[78] For instance, although the concept of in loco parentis provides a rather unusual instance of 'tort law Latin' known and sometimes latched onto by parents and the general public,[79] when used in such a manner to describe the requirements of a duty of care, as argued by Hall and Mannis, rather than being legal, its use is metaphoric.[80] As discussed in Chapter 1, this misunderstanding reiterates the importance of distinguishing between the precise content of ethical, moral and legal duties of care. Correspondingly, the predominate tendency by the courts to raise the general standard of care expected of schoolteachers,[81] with the responsibilities of teachers no longer compared to those of parents, but rather the benchmark appropriate to a competent professional person,[82] renders the modern application of the term in loco parentis problematic. This was succinctly articulated by Lord Justice Croom-Johnson when *Van Oppen v Clerk to the Bedford Charity Trustees* was considered by the Court of Appeal:

> The background to the case is that the duty of care which the school owes to its pupils is not simply that of the prudent parent. In some respects it goes beyond mere parental duty, because it may have special knowledge about some matters which the parent does not or cannot have. The average parent cannot know of unusual dangers which may arise in the playing of certain sports, of which rugby football may be one. That is why the school undertakes to see that proper coaching and refereeing must be enforced. It might know that some types of equipment in, for example, gymnastics have their dangers. But this is all part of the duty placed on the school to take reasonable care of the safety of the person and property of each pupil.[83]

---

74 *Williams v Eady* (1893) 10 TLR 41.
75 Grayson (n 12) 191.
76 E.g., *Van Oppen v Clerk to the Bedford Charity Trustees* [1989] 1 All ER 273, 277; *Wilkin-Shaw* (n 18) [39]; A Chappell, 'Teaching Safely and Safety in PE' in S Capel and M Whitehead (eds), *Learning to Teach Physical Education in the Secondary School: A Companion to School Experience* (4th edn, London, Routledge 2015) 190.
77 Cassidy et al. (n 36) 150.
78 A Hall and M Mannis, 'In Loco Parentis and the Professional Responsibilities of Teachers' (2001) 7 *Waikato Journal of Education* 117.
79 Ibid. 125; T Petts, 'Visualising a Parent with a Very Large Family: The Liability' (2017) 1 *JPI Law* 13.
80 Hall and Mannis (n 78) 125.
81 G Barrell, *Teachers and the Law* (5th edn, London, Methuen 1978) 275.
82 P Whitlam, *Safe Practice in Physical Education and Sport* (8th edn, Leeds, Coachwise 2012) 57. E.g., *Wilkin-Shaw* (n 18) [40].
83 *Van Oppen v Clerk to the Bedford Charity Trustees* [1989] 3 All ER 389 (CA) 414–15. See further, N Partington, '*Murray v McCullough (as Nominee on Behalf of the Trustees and on Behalf of the Board of Governors of Rainey Endowed School)*' (2016) 67(2) *NILQ* 251.

Consequently, due to the 'special skill or competence' required by the teaching and coaching 'professions',[84] and the potential hazardous circumstances in which these roles are performed,[85] it is clear that a PE teacher, and sports coach, would be judged by an 'enhanced standard of foresight'.[86] In Canada the careful parent test also provides a benchmark for gymnastics teachers,[87] but significantly, this standard of care is judicially modified 'to allow for the larger-than-family size of the physical education class and the supraparental expertise commanded of a gymnastics instructor'.[88] Although this specialist knowledge or expertise does not enlarge the duty of care owed, it brings into consideration factors concerning the scope and degree of that duty which may be essential in deciding whether or not the duty of care has been discharged.[89] Importantly, an inexperienced PE teacher, coach or volunteer would be judged at the same standard as more experienced colleagues when discharging their duty of care in the same situation.[90] As argued by Cox and Schuster, this standard might prove peculiarly troublesome in circumstances where non-specialist teachers and coaches with an interest and enthusiasm for sport provide instruction that may be inadequate.[91] Overall, the initial (teacher) training requirements and continuing professional development (CPD) of PE teachers, and coaches, combined with curriculum developments and the 'professionalisation' of sports coaching, has extended 'supraparental expertise' to such an extent that judicial modification of the in loco parentis doctrine renders it somewhat artificial, restrictive and outdated. For instance, although Owen J in *Wilkin-Shaw v Fuller* accepted that the nature of the duty of the teacher responsible for the training of pupils for the Ten Tors Expedition was to show such care as would be exercised by a reasonably careful parent,[92] in recognising the duty of the school, he continued:

> [T]he school was under a duty to ensure that the first defendant was competent to organise and to supervise the training, and that the team of adults assisting him in the training exercise had the appropriate level of experience and appropriate level of competence to discharge any role required of them.[93]

---

84 *Bolam v Friern Hospital Management Committee* [1957] 1 WLR 582, 586. The test for negligence being 'the standard of the ordinary skilled man exercising and professing to have that special skill'. This test of professional negligence, as applied to sports coaching, is critically considered in the next chapter.
85 *Wilsher v Essex Area Health Authority* [1987] QB 730 (CA). See also, N Harris, *The Law Relating to Schools* (2nd edn, Croydon, Tolley 1995) 330.
86 Whitlam (n 82) 58.
87 Barnes (n 56) 299.
88 *Thornton v School Dist. No. 57 (Prince George) Bd. Of School Trustees* [1976] 5 WWR 240, 73 DLR (3d) 35 (BCCA) [74].
89 *Van Oppen* (n 76) 287.
90 *Wilsher* (n 85). See further, Whitlam (n 82) 57.
91 Cox and Schuster (n 12) 235. This issue is returned to in later chapters.
92 *Wilkin-Shaw* (n 18) [39].
93 Ibid. [40].

Such a level of competence and expertise would appear to extend beyond that of the reasonably careful parent. It is therefore contended that reference to the reasonably careful parent, in this particular instance, is somewhat superfluous to the court's reasoning.

Moreover, the Supreme Court in *Woodland v Swimming Teachers Association* reinforced the limitations of attempts to apply the notion of in loco parentis in the educational context,[94] the judgment imputing on schools 'a greater responsibility than any which the law presently recognises as being owed by parents'.[95] This is indicative of a shift away from courts viewing teachers as stand-in parents.[96] Put simply, both the teaching of PE, and coaching of sport, require a specialist skill not ordinarily possessed by the average reasonable parent. Teaching and coaching demand a higher standard of care, or in adopting the words of Lady Hale in *Woodland v Swimming Teachers Association*, 'more than' what might be expected of a reasonable parent. Accordingly, whilst arguably of some possible residual merit as a more narrow and distinct ethical metaphor,[97] in loco parentis essentially appears to be an anachronism of extremely limited contemporary legal relevance when defining/determining the duty of care of teachers, coaches and sports instructors.[98]

Standard of care and breach

For a finding of coach negligence it would need to be established that a sports coach's conduct had fallen below the required objective standard ascertained by the court,[99] when guarding against reasonably foreseeable risk,[100] in the specific circumstances.[101] Application of the law of negligence adopts similar principles to the 'Learned Hand' test in the US.[102] This recognises that a certain level of accidents will be tolerated by society,[103] approaching issues of a breach in the duty of care by determining if the burden of avoidance or precautions (B) was less than the injury (L) multiplied by

---

94 *Woodland v Swimming Teachers Association* [2013] UKSC 66 [41], Lady Hale stating 'it is not particularly helpful to plead that the school is *in loco parentis*. The school clearly does owe its pupils at least the duty of care which a reasonable parent owes to her children. But it may owe them more than that'.
95 Ibid. [25].
96 Petts (n 79).
97 Hall and Mannis (n 78) 125.
98 See generally, Hall and Mannis (n 78) 117.
99 *Vaughan v Menlove* (1837) 3 Bing NC 468; *Nettleship* (n 65). The test of reasonableness is objective since it 'is said to treat [virtually] all defendants equally' (Deakin and Adams (n 51) 182).
100 *Overseas Tankship (UK) Ltd v The Miller Steamship Co (Wagon Mound No 2)* [1967] 1 AC 617.
101 E.g., see *Bolton v Stone* [1951] AC 850; *Paris v Stepney BC* [1951] AC 367; *Watt v Hertfordshire CC* [1954] 1 WLR 835 (CA); Compensation Act 2006, s 1; Social Action, Responsibility and Heroism (SARAH) Act 2015, ss 2 & 3.
102 *US v Carroll Towing Co* 159 F2d 169 (1947). See, Steele (n 14) 138; S Deakin et al., *Markesinis and Deakin's Tort Law* (7th edn, OUP 2013) 200.
103 Deakin et al. (n 102) 199.

the probability (P).[104] Although courts in the UK do not engage with such a mathematical or purely economic analysis, it being difficult to equate an economic value with the risk of personal injury,[105] and with judges also mindful of sport's social utility and public interest benefits,[106] these elements remain important considerations in judicial reasoning.[107] Therefore, for there to be liability in negligence in the context of sports coaching, the risks of injury would be regarded as unreasonable, unnecessary and sufficiently substantial.[108] Further, for a breach of duty to be established, there should be sufficient probability of injury to lead a reasonable coach to anticipate it.[109] This reinforces the fact that when courts employ a calculus of risk in order to define reasonableness, the nature of the foreseeable harm must be a factor taken into account.[110] For instance, in *Perry v Harris*, a case where the 11-year-old claimant suffered a fractured skull by reason of a collision with an older boy who was performing a somersault while playing on a bouncy castle, Lord Phillips, when delivering the Court of Appeal's judgment, highlighted that:

> [a] reasonable parent could foresee that if children indulged in boisterous behaviour on a bouncy castle, there would be a risk that, sooner or later, one child might collide with another and cause that child some physical injury of a type that can be an incident of some contact sports. We do not consider that it was reasonably foreseeable that such injury would be likely to be serious, let alone as severe as the injury sustained by the claimant.[111]

Contextualisation of the duty of care of sports coaches in the UK recognises sport's social utility and public interest benefits. This includes physical and psychological well-being and civic participation,[112] with appreciation that PE and school sport promote health and fitness and the psychological and emotional development of participants.[113] Support for the social utility of desirable activities can be

---

104 Liability being established where B<PL.
105 Deakin et al. (n 102) 209. In *McCarty v Pheasant Run Inc* 826 F2d 1554 (1987), Posner J highlighted that the Hand formula has greater analytical than operational utility. See further, W Rogers, *Winfield and Jolowicz: Tort* (18th edn, London, Sweet & Maxwell 2010) 296.
106 E.g., *Uren v Corporate Leisure (UK) Ltd* [2010] EWHC 46 [59], Field J stating '[t]his means that a balance has to be struck between the level of risk involved and the benefits the activity confers on the participants and thereby on society generally'. See further later.
107 Steele (n 14) 138. In the UK, the 'calculus of risk' is a phrase sometimes adopted by courts to reflect the balancing of the magnitude of risk (i.e., likelihood and severity of injury) against the cost of preventative measures and the social utility of the activity giving rise to the risk. See, for instance, *McMahon v Dear* [2014] CSOH 100 [196]; *Phee v Gordon* [2013] CSIH 18.
108 See generally, Deakin et al. (n 102) 210.
109 *MacIntyre v MoD* [2011] EWHC 1690 [70], citing with approval *Whippey v Jones* [2009] EWCA Civ 452 at [16]. *MacIntyre* is discussed in detail in Chapter 5.
110 *Humphrey v Aegis Defence Services Ltd* [2016] EWCA Civ 11 [14].
111 *Perry v Harris* [2008] EWCA Civ 907 [38].
112 Anderson (n 11) 238.
113 Cox and Schuster (n 12) 235.

found in the drafting of section 1 of the Compensation Act of 2006, Lord Young's report 'Common Sense, Common Safety'[114] and more recently the Social Action, Responsibility and Heroism (SARAH) Act 2015. A number of Court of Appeal judgments have endorsed the social utility of sport.[115] Indeed, when *Scout Association v Barnes*[116] was heard in 2010, Jackson LJ forcefully stated that '[i]t is not the function of the law of tort to eliminate every iota of risk or to stamp out socially desirable activities'.[117] Similarly, Lord Hoffmann appeared mindful of balancing the foreseeable risks with the socially desirable aspects of certain physical activities in *Tomlinson v Congleton BC*:

> [T]he question of what amounts to 'such care as in all the circumstances of the case is reasonable' depends upon assessing, as in the case of common law negligence, not only the likelihood that someone may be injured and the seriousness of the injury which may occur, but also the social value of the activity which gives rise to the risk and the cost of preventative measures. These factors have to be balanced against each other.[118]

Following enactment of section 1 of the Compensation Act 2006, considerable weight should be afforded to the specific contribution of (volunteer) coaches when determining the standard of reasonable care in order to: (a) prevent a desirable activity from being undertaken at all, to a particular extent or in a particular way; or (b) discourage persons from undertaking functions in connection with a desirable activity.[119] Arguably, this underscores the necessity for courts to appreciate the sometimes slender distinction between negligent and non-negligent coaching,[120] affording coaches considerable latitude and leeway in their discretionary decision-making practices,[121] this appearing to be in accordance with the

---

114 Lord Young, *Common Sense Common Safety* (October 2010) <www.gov.uk/government/uploads/system/uploads/attachment_data/file/60905/402906_CommonSense_acc.pdf> accessed 6 November 2019.
115 E.g., *Sutton v Syston RFC Limited* [2011] EWCA Civ 1182; *Scout Association v Barnes* [2010] EWCA Civ 1476.
116 *Scout Association* (n 115).
117 Ibid. [34] (dissenting).
118 *Tomlinson v Congleton BC* [2004] 1 AC 46 [34].
119 See further, N Partington, 'Beyond the "*Tomlinson* Trap": Analysing the Effectiveness of Section 1 of the Compensation Act 2006' (2016) 37(1) *Liverpool L Rev* 33.
120 MJ Dobberstein, '"Give Me the Ball Coach": A Scouting Report on the Liability of High Schools and Coaches for Injuries to High School Pitchers' Arms' (2007) 14 *Sports Law Journal* 49, 69.
121 See, for instance, *Pook v Rossall School* [2018] EWHC 522 [33] (Spencer J):

> 'I reject the notion that the duty of a school is to reduce the risk to the lowest level reasonably practicable ... there will be situations in between which allow for a measure of discretion and judgment on the part of the [PE] teachers. In those circumstances, the court should be slow to condemn a [PE] teacher as negligent and to substitute its own judgment for that of the teacher where the teacher can be expected to have knowledge of the school, the environment, the particular children in her charge and her experience.

See further, Chapter 6.

will of Parliament in order to ensure that the standard of care is set at a realistic and appropriate level. Nevertheless, the weight afforded to 'desirable activities' is largely a value judgement based upon 'fact, degree and judgment, which must be decided on an individual basis and not by a broad brush approach'.[122] Such a subjective determination of what may satisfy the test of socially desirable activity has already revealed discrepancies in the case law.[123] Further, since most judges are unlikely to be trained coaches, a resulting limited understanding of the pressures and demands placed on coaches may perhaps prove a hindrance when determining the standard of reasonable care and skill owed in the particular circumstances.[124]

In *Nettleship v Weston*, Megaw LJ recognised that 'it is preferable that there should be a reasonably certain and reasonably ascertainable standard of care'.[125] However, according to Clancy, the nebulous and woolly nature of reasonableness as a legal test fails to provide much by way of guidance when attempts are made to define the standard of care.[126] As argued by Fulbrook, judicial clarification of the standard of care required of coaches would present a transparent illustration of the level of due care necessary to avoid breaching the duty of care owed to athletes.[127] At first glance, such an observation might appear to merit little serious consideration since it is trite law to recognise that the standard of care is incapable of lending itself to being defined, not least because '[i]n law context is everything'.[128] As noted by Judge LJ in *Caldwell*, '[T]he issue of negligence cannot be resolved in a vacuum. It is fact specific'.[129] Anticipating the likelihood of foreseeable risks will depend upon the unique circumstances of the sporting activity in question,[130] a heightened standard of care being demanded in circumstances where injury is more foreseeable.[131] These prevalent circumstances informing the standard expected of the reasonable, competent and prudent coach include factors such as the nature and inherent risks of the particular sport and the skill level, age, size and experience of the participants.[132]

---

122 *Scout Association* (n 115) [49] (Smith LJ).
123 *Uren v Corporate Leisure (UK) Ltd* [2011] EWCA Civ 66 [69], Smith LJ confessing that 'I personally would not have assessed the social value of this game in quite such glowing terms'. See further, Partington (n 119).
124 Nygaard and Boone (n 23) 3.
125 *Nettleship* (n 65) 709.
126 R Clancy, 'Judo Mats, Climbing Walls, Trampolines and Pole Vaulters' (1995) 3(1) *Sport and the Law Journal* 28.
127 Fulbrook (n 16) 142.
128 *Regina (Daly) v Secretary of State for the Home Department* [2001] 2 AC 532 (HL) [28] (Lord Steyn).
129 *Caldwell* (n 33) [30]. Also see W Norris, 'The Duty of Care to Prevent Personal Injury' (2009) 2 *JPI Law* 126. The extremely fact sensitive nature of this area of the law is examined in detail in subsequent chapters.
130 Kessler (n 57) 100.
131 Champion (n 24) 295.
132 Cox and Schuster (n 12) 233.

In *Morrell v Owen*,[133] the practical content of the duty owed by the coaches organising and delivering a sports training event for disabled athletes, given the obligation of the coaches to take account of the athlete's disabilities, was more stringent than it would have been when coaching non-disabled athletes.[134] As explained by Harwood, since the court regarded the accident as being entirely foreseeable in the particular circumstances, the standard of care required of the supervising coaches was higher.[135] This was the case because the prevailing circumstances posed greater risks for wheelchair athletes. As a general legal principle, this is plainly correct, since although '[t]here is no absolute standard . . . it may be said that the degree of care required varies directly with the risk involved'.[136] For instance, when coaching younger participants, a higher standard of care will ordinarily be required of coaches.[137] In *Morrell*, archery and discus training were being conducted at the same time in a sports hall separated by a curtain during a British Les Autres Sports Association (BLASA) training weekend.[138] No instructions or warnings had been provided to athletes on how to safely enter or leave the archery area of the hall by crossing the curtain, that is, whilst disci were being thrown in the other half of the hall. This was despite particular problems associated with crossing the curtain for wheelchair archers due to a restricted view of the discus side of the hall (i.e., they could neither see nor be seen through the lower canvas section of the curtain).[139] In emphasising aspects of the evidence presented by the expert witness for the plaintiff, the court approved the view that '[y]ou cannot simply apply normal safety standards to disabled sport activities. The disabled are not always ambulant. In any event, movement can take longer and there will always be a range of disabilities involved'. Mitchell J was particularly unimpressed by one of the defendant coaches indicating that his priority was to treat the athletes as athletes, with disability argued by the coach to be a secondary consideration. In terms of safety precautions, and the need for workable and explicable procedures, the judge regarded such an attitude by the coach as being 'absurd'. The High Court ruled that the duty of the coaches supervising the activities included a responsibility to ensure, so far as reasonably possible, that the wheelchair athletes could enter and leave the hall in safety and, more

---

133 *Morrell v Owen* (1993) Times, 14 December.
134 D Griffith-Jones and N Randall, 'Civil Liability Arising Out of Participation in Sport' in A Lewis and J Taylor, *Sport: Law and Practice* (3rd edn, Haywards Heath, Tottel 2014) 1632.
135 V Harpwood, *Modern Tort Law* (6th edn, London, Cavendish 2005) 135.
136 *Glasgow Corporation v Muir* [1943] AC 448, 456 (Lord Macmillan). In *Read v Lyons* [1947] AC 156, 173, Lord Macmillan later stated that the law 'exacts a degree of care commensurate with the risk created'. Sir John Donaldson MR expressed this principle in *Condon* (n 42), 868, in the following terms: 'The standard is objective, but objective in a different set of circumstances. Thus there will of course be a higher degree of care required of a player in a First Division football match than of a player in a local league football match'.
137 Greenfield et al. (n 5), 2189.
138 BLASA later became part of The British Amputee and Les Autres Sports Association (BALASA).
139 The duty of coaches to provide warnings is more fully considered in Chapter 5.

specifically, that they would not be exposed to an unnecessary risk of being hit by a discus when passing from the archery section into the discus section and vice versa. The judge determined that the risk of injury to anyone on the archers' side who was near to the curtain when disci were being thrown was obviously great and that accordingly an injury was 'an utterly foreseeable incident' and an accident 'waiting to happen'. By failing to take adequate precautions to prevent clearly foreseeable risks from materialising, the coaches were in breach of their duties of care.[140]

The vagueness of a reasonableness standard is compounded by the lack of strong authority with reference to the liability of sports coaches. This, no doubt, contributes to Cox and Schuster's assertion that coaches are required to act in accordance with 'informed common sense' when discharging their duties.[141] According to Spengler et al., common sense may be regarded as 'the natural ability of a person, absent study, investigation, or research'.[142] Paradoxically, an emphasis on the application of common sense principles[143] may reinforce and perpetuate the tendency for coaches to adopt negligent entrenched practice, since common sense may be regarded as 'to a large extent a shorthand for dominant cultural values, the ideology – or sets of ideologies – into which we are socialised from an early age'.[144] Since many coaches are inclined to reproduce and model coaching methods and discourse reflective of their experience of coaching as players,[145] it is hypothesised that a significant number of coaches may unwittingly breach their duty of care when entrenched practice (previously regarded as routine practice) creates an unreasonable risk resulting in athlete injury.

Enhancing or optimising the level of performance is a common goal for coaches working in a broad range of environments within the sports development pyramid, whether the focus is on enjoyment and basic fundamental skills, advancement of foundational movement proficiencies, long-term athlete development and participation or peak performance at particular events. As athletes progress to elite and excellence levels, the required emphasis on more specialised training programmes creates new risks requiring coaches to ensure that they possess the competence and expertise needed to operate safely in these amended circumstances.[146] Although the distinctions of school, amateur and professional (elite) sport are undoubtedly

---

140 As highlighted by Mitchell J, the problem would have been solved by the simple provision of an ambulant ad hoc escort of appropriate authority at the net. Since the coaches were appointed by the BLASA, the BLASA was found to be vicariously liable. Vicarious liability is discussed later.
141 Cox and Schuster (n 12) 235.
142 J Spengler et al., *Introduction to Sport Law* (Champaign, Human Kinetics 2009) 53.
143 E.g., *Perry* (n 111) [47], their Lordships adopting an instinctive approach to principles of common sense and fairness, recognising that 'to a large extent a case of this nature properly turns on first impressions'.
144 N Thompson, *Theory and Practice in Human Services* (Oxford, OUP 2003) 97. See further, Cassidy et al. (n 36) 164.
145 Cassidy et al. (n 36) 4.
146 Labuschagne and Skea (n 53) 166.

important considerations when contextualising coaching and teaching,[147] these categories may deceptively oversimplify the multidimensional roles performed by coaches, with Academies, Centres of Excellence and Specialist Sports Colleges in the UK providing some instances of educational sporting provision, both curricular and extracurricular, where sporting excellence may, on occasion, be the objective.[148]

Similarly, amateur sporting provision encapsulates an extremely wide spectrum of sporting ability and aspiration levels, groupings frequently labelled beginner, improver, intermediate and advanced.[149] The predominantly voluntary nature of sports coaching suggests that it does not necessarily follow that there would be a correlation between the classification of athlete performance level and the qualification award held by the coach.[150] Consequently, scrutiny of the actual post held by the coach,[151] and the corresponding level at which the coaching is conducted, provides a crucial material factor to support the court in accurately defining a coach's duty of care. Nevertheless, as argued by Beloff et al., whether varying standards of care are applicable depending on whether the context in which the sport is being conducted is professional or amateur would appear to remain an issue of controversy, certainly with reference to participant liability for sporting injury.[152]

Analysis of performance differentials also presents the important issue of whether there may be occasion where (elite) athletes assume responsibility for enhanced risks involved, it being likely that high-performing and experienced athletes have a greater appreciation of foreseeable dangers.[153] Support for such a submission recognises that the awareness and foreseeability of risks on a golf course, and specifically the duty to warn fellow players of such potential dangers, may be related to the level of skill possessed by an individual golfer.[154] Straightforwardly, highly proficient and trained athletes, more experienced in performing challenging skills and techniques safely, and taking evasive action to prevent injury to themselves and

---

147 S Drewe, 'An Examination of the Relationship Between Coaching and Teaching' (2000) 52 *Quest* 79, 81.
148 For instance, in Ireland, some schools employ professional coaches and/or strength and conditioning specialists. Interestingly, Archbold et al. (n 59) have highlighted that should this result in a significant development of athlete physique and power (i.e., by a combination of intense training and nutritional supplementation), this may perhaps be an important contributory factor towards the risk of injury.
149 Interestingly, this may reveal little in terms of the athlete's expectations and aspirations, an 'ambitious' intermediate athlete perhaps desiring to be challenged more than a 'comfortable/settled' advanced athlete.
150 For instance, the demand/availability of coaches may result in performance coaches (level 3 or above) also being involved in the delivery of sessions for beginners.
151 *Wilsher* (n 85).
152 Beloff et al. (n 12) 143. See (n 136). This issue is more fully explored in Chapter 4.
153 T Davis, 'Tort Liability of Coaches for Injuries to Professional Athletes: Overcoming Policy and Doctrinal Barriers' (2008) 76 *UMKC L. Rev.* 571, 580.
154 J Kircher, 'Golf and Torts: An Interesting Twosome' (2001) 12 *Marq. Sports L. Rev* 347, 352. Beloff et al. (n 12) 143; *Lewis v Buckpool Golf Club* 1993 SCT 43.

opponents, may be able to take greater risks.[155] Indeed, a relevant consideration in establishing the necessary standard of care required of coaches, or the nature of the duty of care owed, includes 'the reasonable expectations of the victim of injury'.[156] Clearly, when performing a balancing exercise to determine what risks are reasonable and necessary in the circumstances, coaches must be mindful of the competence, aspirations and expectations of athletes, this being foundational to the interdependent and collaborative coach–athlete relationship.

This section has critically discussed the legal duty of care incumbent upon modern sports coaches. In order to define a coach's duty of care, it proves necessary to clarify the practical content of the duty owed in the particular circumstances. Establishing the nature of a coach's duty of care allows courts to ascertain the standard of reasonable care required and whether or not this standard has been met (i.e., the duty has been effectively discharged) or not (i.e., there has been a breach of duty) by the coach. Expressed as a legal test, this appears uncomplicated. However, the emerging relationship between the law of negligence and sports coaching is fluid and highly fact specific. So whilst it may be 'preferable that there should be a reasonably certain and reasonably ascertainable standard of care' set for coaches, defining a coach's duty of care presents a considerably more nuanced, vague and elusive challenge. As such, defining a coach's duty of care requires a detailed understanding and appreciation of the emerging interface between sport and the law of negligence. Moreover, the combined tendency over time for both the standard of care demanded of coaches in law to be heightened, and correspondingly, for the coaching practices of the ordinary competent coach to be constantly assessed, revised and improved, gradually places more responsibilities on coaches. Given this dynamic interaction, the issue of negligent entrenched practice is argued to be especially problematic.

Causation

Establishing both causation in fact,[157] and legal causation,[158] is generally straightforward for participant liability.[159] An interesting and informative insight into judicial consideration of causation, following alleged breach of duty of care by a very experienced high-performance athletics coach, was provided by Owen J in *Davenport v Farrow* and is worth recalling in full:

> Secondly his [the athlete's] case was advanced upon the basis that the probable cause of an acute spondyloyses was a marked increase in the intensity of his training from September 2004. There was an increase in the number of

---

155 Nygaard and Boone (n 24) 27; James (n 6) 75.
156 *Wooldridge* (n 33) 67; Deakin et al. (n 102).
157 *Barnett v Chelsea and Kensington Hospital ManagementCommittee* [1969] 1 QB 428.
158 *Overseas Tankship v Morts Docks & Engineering Co Ltd (Wagon Mound No 1)* [1961] AC 388.
159 James (n 11) 80.

sessions as the Claimant had begun training on a full time basis; but I accept the evidence of the Defendant, given by reference to his training programmes for the Claimant, that it was a moderate increase from the same period in the previous year, and was not therefore significantly more than he had done in the past. It is also to be noted that in this context that in their joint statement, the coaching experts whose reports were before the court, agreed that the regime undertaken in 2004–2005, based on the Defendant's training log, was within the range of acceptable coaching (level 4) for an athlete of his ability and aspirations. I am not persuaded that there was a change in the level and intensity of training in September 2004 such as to provide an explanation for the development of spondyloyses.[160]

Significantly, Owen J found that the increased level of intensity of training was reasonable according to the joint statement of the expert witnesses and that the coaching was 'within a reasonable range of options'.[161] Furthermore, the court's judgment was mindful of the level of coaching qualification held by the defendant coach and the claimant athlete's ability and aspirations.

Whilst accepting in the main that causation inquiries for coach negligence should also be relatively uncomplicated,[162] the Court of Appeal in *Mountford v Newlands School* appeared to apply a lowered standard of causation, whereas at first instance the judge may have overlooked this fundamental requirement of the tort of negligence by equating a breach of duty of the PE teacher with a finding of negligence.[163] Also, the trial judge in *Hammersley-Gonsalves v Redcar and Cleveland BC* appears to have made the same omission, it being emphasised by Pill LJ on appeal that:

> [e]ven if Mr Fowle's failure to observe the swing [with a golf club] was negligent, it would have been necessary for the respondent also to establish that the failure was causative of the accident that actually happened. With respect, the judge has not adequately addressed that question in the paragraph cited. There is no finding that on a balance of probabilities, action by Mr Fowle would have prevented the accident.[164]

Despite the control device of causation generally appearing to pose few difficulties in this context, evidence that the breach of duty was causative of the injury suffered is an essential component of any negligence claim brought against coaches. Unless this evidential threshold is considered, and on the balance of probabilities

---

160 *Davenport* (n 9) [59]. This case is considered more fully in Chapter 5.
161 *Woodbridge School v Chittock* [2002] EWCA Civ 915. See further, Chapters 3 & 5–7.
162 E.g., *Woodroffe-Hedley v Cuthbertson*, 20 June 1997 (QBD); *Cox v Dundee CC* [2014] CSOH 3. These cases are discussed in detail in Chapter 5.
163 Heywood and Charlish (n 17) 166–67.
164 *Hammersley-Gonsalves v Redcar and Cleveland BC* [2012] EWCA Civ 1135 [13].

satisfied, there ought to be no finding of liability. This would certainly appear from the case law a tort of negligence control mechanism, when being applied in cases brought against coaches and PE teachers, which must be fully considered and established to afford coaches the fairness and protection they are legally entitled to.

Defences

Volenti non fit injuria

The defence of volenti non fit injuria, or voluntary assumption of risk, is premised upon the notion of consent, and since it is reflected in the scope of the practical content of the duty owed in all of the circumstances,[165] its application in this particular area of the law appears essentially redundant.[166] As argued by James and McArdle, volenti will not operate as a defence in the vast majority of sports negligence cases in the UK since the determinative issue will typically be breach of duty.[167] Accordingly, for a sports tort, the only legally sustainable denial of liability appears to be establishing that the duty of care has not been breached.[168] Doing this further reinforces the significance and centrality of the law of negligence's control device of breach to the issue of coach negligence and attempts to define a coach's duty of care.

In *Wooldridge v Sumner*, Diplock LJ stated that 'the consent that is relevant is not consent to the risk of injury but consent to the lack of reasonable care that may produce that risk'.[169] Clearly, the relevant consent in this context is to the negligence itself,[170] not to the general risk of injury,[171] the doctrine of volenti now seldom applied.[172] For instance, Lord Bingham in *Smoldon v Whitworth* noted that:

> [t]he plaintiff had of course consented to the ordinary incidents of a game of rugby football of the kind in which he was taking part. Given, however, that the rules were framed for the protection of him and other players in the same position, he cannot possibly be said to have consented to a breach of duty on the part of the official whose duty it was to apply the rules and ensure so far

---

165 Griffith-Jones (n 12) 748.
166 Gardiner et al. (n 10) 643.
167 M James and D McArdle, 'Player Violence, or Violent Players? Vicarious Liability for Sports Participants' (2004) 12(3) *Tort Law Review* 131, 133. Interestingly, in sometimes adopting the phrase 'inherent risk' in the context of sporting activities, it could be argued that courts may on occasion consider a quasi-volenti defence. See, for instance, *Browning* (n 72) [25] & [30] and, most recently, *Wells v Full Moon Events Ltd* [2020] EWHC 1265 [137] & [141]-[143].
168 McArdle and James (n 33) 200–01.
169 *Wooldridge* (n 33) 69.
170 *Wattleworth v Goodwood Road Racing Co Ltd* [2004] EWHC 140 [174].
171 Steele (n 14) 290.
172 R Kidner, 'The Variable Standard of Care, Contributory Negligence and Volenti' (1991) 11(1) *Legal Studies* 1, 17.

62 Key concepts

as possible that they were observed. If the plaintiff were identified as a prime culprit in causing the collapse of the scrums, then this defence (and contributory negligence) might call for consideration.[173]

Nevertheless, the defence may be applicable in circumstances where a coach is utilising novel and innovative training techniques and coaching methods not endorsed by a responsible body such as a national governing body of sport (NGB), the athlete having specifically accepted the risk of injury.[174]

Contributory negligence

The issue of contributory negligence poses the question of what the hypothetical 'reasonable person' would have done in the same circumstances for their own safety.[175] Although not technically varying the standard of care, the application of contributory negligence,[176] by reflecting the relationship between the parties, performs a similar function.[177] In the context of sports coaching and instructing,[178] where the coaching of children is commonplace, it is important to note that children as young as 11 years old[179] and 12 years old[180] have been found contributory negligent. However, since children will be judged by the actions considered to be reasonable for a child of the same age,[181] it is clear that very young children would be unlikely to be regarded as partly responsible for injury suffered.

Vicarious liability

Vicarious liability may be regarded as a type of secondary liability,[182] shifting liability to the employer in circumstances where the coach is acting in the capacity of employee.[183] As recognised by Lord Phillips, in the vast majority of cases the relationship that gives rise to vicarious liability is that of employer and employee under a contract of employment.[184] Since the majority of sports coaches are unpaid volunteers, this doctrine has been suggested to be of limited application when coaches are sued

---

173 *Smoldon* (n 41) P147.
174 James (n 11) 96.
175 *Anderson* (n 1) [141]. This decision provides the case study examined in Chapter 6. As expressed by Lord Denning in *Froom v Butcher* [1976] QB 286 (CA) 291: 'Contributory negligence is a man's carelessness in looking after his own safety' (original emphasis).
176 Law Reform (Contributory Negligence) Act 1945, s 1.
177 Kidner (n 172) 22.
178 See, for instance, *Fowles* (n 1). This case is discussed in detail in Chapter 5.
179 *Honnor v Lewis* [2005] EWHC 747.
180 *Young v Kent CC* [2005] EWHC 1342.
181 *Mullin v Richards* [1998] 1 WLR 1304 (CA); *Blake v Galloway* [2004] EWCA Civ 814; *Orchard v Lee* [2009] EWCA Civ 295.
182 Steele (n 14) 572.
183 James (n 11) 81. Also see generally, Anderson (n 11) 242–45.
184 *Catholic Child Welfare Society v Various Claimants* (the '*Christian Brothers*' case) [2012] UKSC 56 [35].

in negligence for a breach of duty of care.[185] Nonetheless, there may be situations in which coaches employed, or appointed centrally by NGBs, satisfy the necessary requirements for the doctrine of vicarious liability to be applicable.[186] Furthermore, following acceptance by the Welsh Rugby Union that they would be vicariously liable for the negligence of their appointed amateur referee in *Vowles v Evans*,[187] the English Cricket Board Association of Officials,[188] and the Scout Association,[189] have likewise agreed in principle to potentially being vicariously liable in respect of the tortious acts or omissions committed by their agents/members in certain circumstances. Moreover, in regard to volunteer coaches, in *Petrou v Bertoncello*[190] Griffith Williams J ruled that on paper there appeared strong grounds for possibly finding the membership and/or the committee of Dunstable Hang-gliding and Paragliding Club (an unincorporated members' club) vicariously liable for the negligence of its (amateur volunteer) coach(es) when performing an 'Airspace' test.[191]

These decisions are consistent with the relatively recent expanded doctrine of vicarious liability. Following the Supreme Court's ruling in the *Christian Brothers* case in 2012, it is clear that even in the absence of a contract of employment, should the relationship between the defendant (e.g., sports club; NGB) and individual committing the tortious act (e.g., coach) have the same incidents of the relationship between employer and employee, 'that relationship can properly give rise to vicarious liability on the ground that it is "akin to that between an employer and an employee"'.[192] Lord Phillips' analysis in *Christian Brothers* was recognised by Lord Reed in *Cox v Ministry of Justice* as developing a 'modern theory of vicarious liability'.[193] In applying this modern theory in *Cox*, the Supreme Court further

---

185 Gardiner et al. (n 10) 646.
186 An interesting illustration of the application of the doctrine of vicarious liability in the circumstances of sport was provided by *Gravil v Carroll, Redruth Rugby Football Club* [2008] EWCA CIV 689. *Gravil* concerned a semi-professional rugby player employed by Redruth RFC. During a stoppage in play, the player threw a punch during an altercation following a scrum. In finding Redruth RFC vicariously liable, the Court of Appeal ruled (at [40]) that 'the tort was so closely connected with the employment, namely the playing of rugby for the club, that it would be fair and just to hold the club vicariously responsible for the injury to the claimant in the affirmative. The punch is fairly and properly regarded as having been carried out while the first defendant was acting in the ordinary course of his employment, albeit part time employment, as a rugby player. Looking at the matter broadly, it is fair and just to hold the club liable for the punch in circumstances in which it can fairly be regarded as a reasonably incidental risk to the playing of rugby pursuant to the contract'.
187 *Vowles* (n 41) [1].
188 *Bartlett v English Cricket Board Association of Cricket Officials*, County Court (Birmingham), 27 August 2015 [31].
189 *Scout Association* (n 115) [13].
190 *Petrou v Bertoncello* [2012] EWHC 2286.
191 It being possible for an unincorporated association to be vicariously liable for the tortious acts of one or more of its members: see further, *Christian Brothers* (n 184). For detailed treatment of the issue of the vicarious liability of members of unincorporated societies in the context of sports see: P Morgan, 'Vicarious Liability and the Beautiful Game – Liability for Professional and Amateur Footballers?' (2018) 38(2) *Legal Studies* 242, 255–58.
192 *Christian Brothers* (n 184) [47]. Also see *Barclays Bank v Various Claimants* [2020] UKSC 13.
193 *Cox v Ministry of Justice* [2016] UKSC 10 [24].

crystallised the 'akin to employment' category. As argued by Morgan, the essence of this category of 'akin to employment' has been distilled by the Supreme Court in such a way that it will encompass some amateur sportspersons.[194]

For claimants injured by the carelessness of formal volunteers who may not be worth pursuing personally for financial reasons, suing the defendant club or recognised body may appear attractive since a successful vicarious liability claim may provide compensation underwritten by an insurance company.[195] However, although there may appear scope for the shifting of liability for some formal volunteers attached to a recognised organisation or club, the doctrine of vicarious liability is likely to be of more limited application when coaches are informal volunteers and/or attached to clubs not affiliated to relevant regional or national bodies.[196] At the professional level, a club may be vicariously liable for the tactics or training methods employed by its coach,[197] which may include the targeting of opposing athletes,[198] instructing a player to fight or injure opponents,[199] and the over-arousal/'psyching-up' of performers.[200] More fundamentally, despite the possible advantages for some coaches of this type of secondary liability in certain circumstances, it does not in any way interfere with a coach's legal obligation to discharge their functions with reasonable care and skill. Put bluntly, in the majority of cases concerning coach negligence, arguments will remain focused on the issue of whether or not the duty of care has been breached by the coach's conduct.

During such arguments about a breach of duty of care, customary practice acts as a forceful justification for the coaching practices adopted, and so in view of the specialist nature of sports coaching, the *Bolam* test[201] warrants particular consideration in this context.

Customary practice

When teachers face a claim of negligence, a common argument is that the act causing the harm was in accordance with general and approved practice in the circumstances, often referred to as the custom of the trade,[202] or *Bolam* test. This position is

---

194 Morgan (n 191) 253. As noted by Morgan, to determine if the 'akin to employment' test is met, each relationship will need to be examined in detail.
195 See further, James and McArdle (n 167).
196 Importantly, in *Petrou* (n 190), Dunstable Hang-gliding and Paragliding Club was a member of the British Hang-Gliding and Paragliding Association, the governing body of the sport, and therefore more likely to have appropriate insurance provision ('deep pockets') for members acting on its behalf.
197 Gardiner et al. (n 10) 629.
198 A Epstein, *Sports Law* (Mason, Cengage Learning 2013) 137. An illustration of potential vicarious liability for a coach concerned the Temple University basketball coach John Chaney, who ordered a player substituted into the game to 'send a message' to the opposition by committing hard fouls, one of which resulted in a broken arm for an opposing player.
199 G Wong, *Essentials of Sports Law* (4th edn, Oxford, Praeger 2010) 123.
200 *Canterbury Bankstown Rugby League Football Club Ltd. v Rogers* [1993] Aust. Torts Reports 81–246.
201 *Bolam* (n 84).
202 Barrell (n 81) 289.

premised on the use of regular and approved practices that are logically justifiable[203] and operates as a strong justification for teachers and coaches[204] provided strict supervision has been implemented.[205] The professional negligence tests, and legal principles, developed from *Bolam* and *Bolitho* (and *Wilsher*) are applicable in cases of coach negligence.[206] Accordingly, if the coach has used a reasonable technique, approved by a body of informed opinion, there should be no liability or breach of duty,[207] with discretionary decision-making accepted 'within a range of reasonable options'.[208] Regular and approved practice is regarded as that conducted nationally rather than locally and may be evident in the publications of NGBs and the schemes of work produced by local education authorities.[209] In short, customary practice may safeguard coaches by means of a quasi-defence.[210]

To be best placed to avail of the *Bolam* 'defence', coaches should always be advised to balance the benefits of the activity at hand with the reasonably foreseeable harm, this being acknowledged as routine good practice. Doing this would ensure that the practice adopted by the coach is not only recognised and approved but is capable of being justified and withstanding logical analysis. Effectively, this requires a two-stage test. The second limb of 'justifiable' requires coaches to operate as critical and reflective practitioners. This requirement may be potentially difficult to satisfy for coaches failing to keep up-to-date with their own CPD in order to keep abreast of the latest coach education. The second limb of the test ensures that negligent entrenched practice should be prevented,[211] with this modern statement of the *Bolam* principle demanding a more rigorous analysis than the coach merely following routine practice. As argued by Mitten, it is entirely appropriate and necessary that such a standard (or legal test) would scrutinise 'customary coaching practices unduly emphasiz[ing] winning or athletic performance and expos[ing] young athletes to the risk of serious injuries'.[212]

Conclusion

Should a coach's legal duty of care be judicially scrutinised, in accordance with the law of negligence, the pivotal issue determinative of legal liability in the vast majority of cases concerns the required standard of care. This objectively ascertained

---

203 *Bolitho v City of Hackney Health Authority* [1998] AC 232.
204 E.g., *Wright v Cheshire CC* [1952] 2 All ER 789 (CA); *MacIntyre* (n 113): *Woodbridge* (n 161).
205 D Glendenning, *Education and the Law* (Dublin, Butterworths 1999) 310.
206 N Partington, 'Professional Liability of Amateurs: The Context of Sports Coaching' (2015) 4 *JPI Law* 232. These tests are examined in detail in the next chapter.
207 Barnes (n 56) 303.
208 *Woodbridge* (n 161) [18] (Auld LJ). This will be referred to as the *Woodbridge* principle and its practical application is more fully considered in Chapter 6.
209 P Whitlam, *Case Law in Physical Education and School Sport* (Worcester, BAALPE 2005) 26.
210 The *Bolam* 'defence' is discussed in detail in Chapter 3.
211 James (n 6) 91.
212 M Mitten, 'The Coach and the Safety of Athletes: Ethical and Legal Issues' in RL Simon (ed), *The Ethics of Coaching Sports: Moral, Social, and Legal Issues* (Colorado, Westview Press 2013) 222.

standard of ordinary competence is that of the reasonable coach in the same circumstances as the defendant, with coaches expected to take all reasonable care to avoid foreseeable risks. Since it is not possible to do any kind of sport without some inherent risk, or 'consequential foreseeable hazard',[213] reasonable coaching practice will involve acceptable risks in circumstances where such foreseeable risk is regarded by coaches as being necessary, worthwhile and beneficial. This is indicative of the balancing exercise inherent in law of negligence in the UK. Accordingly, effective coaching and teaching will be conducted in an environment where the activity is delivered 'as safe as necessary', crucially, distinguished from 'as safe as possible',[214] to ensure that the benefits of the activity and the cost of preventative measures outweigh the magnitude of risk. In these circumstances, conscientious application of the calculus of risk by coaches should endorse the particular coaching practice or conduct adopted.

As previously highlighted, the characteristics (and reasonable expectations) of athletes also shape the standard of care expected in the specific circumstances,[215] with assumption of risk by participants likely only to be of relevance to reasonable risks that are inherent to the specific activity. Determination of whether foreseeable and sufficiently substantial risks taken by coaches might be deemed reasonable in all the circumstances is highly fact-sensitive. Reasonable coaching practice is contextualised by the specificity of sports coaching, the prevailing tendency for courts to raise the general standard of care demanded of coaches over time, the symbiotic and interrelated relationship between coach and athlete, and by the rapidly advancing environment in which coaches perform. These factors clearly establish that a coach's duty of care is reflective of the emerging interaction between sport and the law. In short, this represents a developing area of sports law that cannot be effectively considered in a social or historical vacuum, it being imperative that modern coaches maintain an up-to-date and informed awareness of their legal duty of care. A better understanding and appreciation of this evolving legal duty of care would enable the modelling of best practice to protect and safeguard coaches from potential exposure to civil liability without compromising the core legitimate objective of enhancing performance.

Problematically, the elusive nature of reasonableness as a legal test means that it provides only limited guidance when defining the content of the duty of care demanded of coaches in particular circumstances. Further, the weight to be afforded

---

213 *Hide v The Steeplechase Company (Cheltenham) Ltd.* [2013] EWCA Civ 545 [36] (Davis LJ).
214 Whitlam (n 82) 18 & 20. See, for instance, *Pook* (n 121) [33] (Spencer J): 'I reject the notion that the duty of a school is to reduce the risk to the lowest level reasonably practicable. I agree with Mr Lemmy that whilst there are some risks which no reasonable school or teacher would allow a pupil to run (running in corridors between classes for example), and other risks which it will almost always be reasonable to allow a pupil to run (for example, the risk arising from contact and other sports), there will be situations in between which allow for a measure of discretion and judgment on the part of the teachers'.
215 *Blair-Ford v CRS Adventures Ltd* [2012] EWHC 2360 [47].

to the social utility and socially desirable aspects of sporting activities is predominantly determined by the individual trial judge, common sense judicial reasoning not necessarily being the most consistent benchmark on which coaches might ascertain what constitutes reasonable coaching. Moreover, whilst acknowledging that successful coaches will be creative and innovative in the coaching practices they adopt, the law is clear: changing established and approved practice should only be implemented following careful evaluation, completion of a risk assessment,[216] and ideally, with approval by a more experienced colleague(s).

Crucially, the need for coaches to avoid negligent entrenched practice, by ensuring that their practices are recognised, approved and can withstand logical analysis, cannot be overstated.[217] The prevailing tendency for courts to raise the necessary standard of care barometer, intensified by advances in sports science and coaching techniques, indicates that what may have been accepted practice up until quite recently may no longer be logically justifiable today. Arguably, this may pose a pitfall for talented and experienced coaches, perhaps even former professional players themselves, working in isolation or unreceptive to the latest developments in coaching and the law. Despite a logical touchstone of acceptable practice often being informed by common sense, judicial scrutiny necessitates a more robust consideration of reasonableness, perhaps challenging preconceived and stereotypical notions internalised by coaches about standardised practices. The progressively heightened standard of care required of modern sports coaches would be best satisfied by maximising coach education opportunities, seeking to share good practice with peers and mentors whenever possible, and operating as critical and reflective practitioners. Such self-scrutiny involves coaches analysing their own performance through a lens that recognises the dangers associated with negligent entrenched practice. Furthermore, a commitment to CPD would ensure that coaches keep abreast of the latest information regarding their sport, including common injuries and appropriate developments in technique and equipment.[218]

From this chapter's detailed scrutiny of the relevant legal principles that inform the extent of a coach's duty of care, it is evident that adopting common practice, or satisfying the *Bolam* test, appears indicative of coaches effectively discharging their duty of care. Nonetheless, as the next chapter's analysis reveals, meeting this standard may not always be straightforward, not least since the issue of coach negligence is revealed to represent a somewhat novel and curious instance of professional negligence.

216 Risk assessments are discussed in more detail in Chapters 5–7.
217 As revealed in Chapter 3, satisfying these requirements would enable coaches to rely on a common practice or *Bolam* 'defence'.
218 D Healey, 'Risk Management for Coaches' in S Pyke, *Better Coaching: Advanced Coach's Manual* (2nd edn, Champaign, Human Kinetics 2001) 41.

3
PROFESSIONAL LIABILITY OF AMATEURS

Introduction

> [W]here you get the situation which involves the use of some special skill or competence, then the test as to whether there has been negligence or not is not the test of the man on the top of the Clapham omnibus, because he has not got this special skill. The test is the standard of the ordinary skilled man exercising and professing to have that special skill. A man need not possess the highest expert skill; it is well established law that it is sufficient if he exercises the ordinary skill of an ordinary competent man exercising that particular art.[1]

In situations where a person undertakes a task requiring some special skill, this legal statement is repeatedly applied.[2] As a foundational component of the *Bolam* test, it represents a basic threshold measurement of reasonableness in claims of professional liability.[3] Interestingly, sports coaching requires the exercise of some special skill or competence and aspires to be classified as a 'profession'.[4] This chapter's careful scrutiny of the developing jurisprudence in this field confirms the negligence liability of coaches as being governed by the legal principles of professional liability, regardless of whether or not sports coaching should be legitimately classified as a

---

1 *Bolam v Friern Hospital Management Committee* [1957] 1 WLR 582, 586 (McNair J).
2 *Vowles v Evans* [2003] EWCA Civ 318 [27].
3 M Jones, 'The Bolam Test and the Responsible Expert' (1999) 7 *Tort Law Review* 226.
4 See generally, P Duffy et al., 'Sport Coaching as a "Profession": Challenges and Future Directions' (2011) 5(2) *International Journal of Coaching Science* 93–123; B Taylor and D Garratt, 'The Professionalisation of Sports Coaching: Relations of Power, Resistance and Compliance' 15(1) *Sport, Education and Society* 121–139.

profession.[5] Paradoxically, despite the majority of sports coaches being volunteers,[6] both amateur and professional coaches assume the same duty to coach properly in the particular circumstances. Consequently, the evolving 'profession' of sports coaching provides an intriguing and novel context in which to critically analyse the characteristics of professional liability. Importantly, this detailed analysis reveals some serious concerns relating to the emerging issue of the negligence liability of coaches.[7]

In further developing key aspects of Chapter 2, this chapter begins by providing a general introduction to professional liability, revealing it to be a flourishing aspect of the law of negligence. The peculiarity of applying a test of professional negligence in a context where defendants are predominantly volunteers and where the professionalisation of sports coaching remains fragmented is an issue considered next. Following this, the *Bolam* test, the celebrated benchmark of the standard of skill and care incumbent upon ordinarily competent and average professionals, is examined in considerable detail. Crucially, this examination reinforces the necessary function of this well-established legal control mechanism to protect the legitimate and genuine interests of *both* claimants (injured athletes) and defendants (coaches) alike.[8] Importantly, searching scrutiny of the relevant case law reveals significant implications for the education, training and continuing professional development (CPD) of modern sports coaches with regard to legal and ethical issues.[9] More generally, since professional liability is confirmed as a developing and fluid aspect of the law of negligence, this chapter's focus on a 'profession' profoundly distinctive in relation to the more traditional learned professions provides a critical commentary of relevance to not only sports coaching but to a broader range of duty of care inquiries.

Professional liability

Professionals by most conventional interpretations are regarded as 'knowledgeable others'– they 'profess'.[10] Nevertheless, the definition of profession remains a

---

5 See further, D Mangan, 'The Curiosity of Professional Status' (2014) 30(2) *Professional Negligence* 74.
6 Sports Coach UK, *Coach Tracking Study: A Four-Year Study of Coaching in the UK* (Leeds, Coachwise 2012) 17, the employment status of coaches in the UK classifying 76% as volunteers (unpaid), with the national average for coaches holding a coaching qualification being 53%.
7 Also see N Partington, 'Legal Liability of Coaches: A UK Perspective' (2014) 14(3–4) *International Sports Law Journal* 232. See further, Chapter 2.
8 R Kidner, 'The Variable Standard of Care, Contributory Negligence and Volenti' (1991) 11(1) *Legal Studies* 1, 23.
9 These implications are discussed further in Chapter 7.
10 B Taylor and D Garratt, 'The Professionalization of Sports Coaching: Definitions, Challenges and Critique' in J Lyle and C Cushion (eds), *Sports Coaching: Professionalisation and Practice* (Edinburgh, Elsevier 2010) 104.

contested concept,[11] and is inconclusive.[12] As argued by Powell and Stewart, perceptions about what might constitute a 'professional', or profession, are 'indistinct, subjective, and continually changing'.[13] As a result, there is a contemporary widened catchment of 'profession',[14] with sports coaching appearing determined to satisfy this designation.[15] General endorsement of sports coaching being classified as a profession includes: the moral aspect of coaching, reflected in codes of conduct and ethics produced by national governing bodies of sport (NGBs), and additionally, by the 'community' context in which much coaching is delivered; opportunities (or requirements) for membership of professional associations (e.g., for coach accreditation/CPD/insurance); and the apparent enhanced status of sports coaches in modern society.[16] Analysis of these factors, or indicators, reveals important ramifications linked to professional liability. For instance, despite publication of ethical guiding principles being integral to all professions,[17] mere production of a code of ethics is certainly not sufficient for sports coaching to be regarded as a profession.[18]

Fundamentally, as highlighted by *Clerk and Lindsell on Torts*, 'the rules governing a professional person's liability for negligence are no different from those governing the liability of anyone else who undertakes a specific task and professes some special skill in carrying out that task'.[19] Since success and safety cannot be guaranteed, this seems entirely sensible, demanding a certain minimum degree of competence from professional persons discharging their duties.[20] As made plain in Chapter 2, the pivotal issue in cases brought against coaches for a breach of duty would be determination by the court of the objective standard of skill and care required in the prevailing circumstances. Crucially, this would reflect, and be shaped by, the special skill or competence expected of the ordinary coach, with the imposition of this responsibility or duty of care often regarded as 'a badge of professional status'.[21] Determination of the legal standard of care incumbent on different professionals in particular circumstances and, more specifically, the weight to be attributed to guidelines and standards published by NGBs in individual cases, is instrumental to the thriving area of professional liability.[22] This intersection between professional liability and sports

---

11 K Armour, 'The Learning Coach . . . the Learning Approach: Professional Development for Sports Coach Professionals' in Lyle & Cushion (n 10) 154.
12 M Jones and A Dugdale (eds), *Clerk and Lindsell on Torts* (20th edn, London, Sweet and Maxwell 2010) [10–01].
13 J Powell and R Stewart, *Jackson and Powell on Professional Liability* (7th edn, London, Sweet and Maxwell 2012) [2–002].
14 Mangan (n 5) 74–5.
15 Duffy et al. (n 4); Taylor and Garratt (n 4).
16 See generally, Powell and Stewart (n 13) [1–005] – [1–006].
17 H Telfer, 'Coaching Practice and Practice Ethics' in Lyle and Cushion (n 10) 210.
18 Duffy et al. (n 4) 104.
19 Jones and Dugdale (n 12) [10–03].
20 Powell and Stewart (n 13) [1–004].
21 *D v East Berkshire Community Health Authority* [2005] 2 AC 373 [40] (Lord Bingham).
22 See generally, M Lunney and K Oliphant, *Tort Law: Test and Materials* (5th edn, Oxford, OUP 2013) 199.

coaching is contextualised by the varied, and somewhat unique, categorisation of coaches as volunteers, professionals and 'professional volunteers'. These distinctions may be further complicated and intensified by the particular coaching domains in which coaches operate, for instance, 'participation', 'development' and 'performance' pathways.[23] In short, the negligence liability of coaches represents an important, evolving and fascinating instance of professional liability in a unique context.

Context of sports coaching

Volunteering is commonplace in the provision of community and recreational sport.[24] The vast majority of sports coaches in the UK are volunteers,[25] this being consistent with most other countries in the world.[26] Coaches often receive limited training,[27] with approximately half of the coaches in the UK being unqualified.[28] Further, in contrast to traditional professions, including law and medicine, instead of required extended academic study and professional assimilation being requirements and markers of professional status, prime candidates for coaching positions may have acquired valued experience in the unique environment of elite sport.[29] This signifies an important distinction between formal qualifications and practical experience as admission requirements for professional practice.[30]

Coaching practitioners often operate in isolation,[31] likely restricting opportunities for professional discussion, dialogue and the sharing of best practice. This limitation may be compounded by the diverse performance spectrum of sport, requiring coaches to operate across an increasingly challenging range of performance levels.[32] Consequently, and as argued by Telfer:

> Identifying appropriate ethical decisions and behaviours at each stage of the performance spectrum can be problematic, both for the individual practitioner and also the coaching profession. The implication is that coaching practice, in relation to ethical judgement, is complex, situationally dependent, and offers a dynamic set of practice catalysts.[33]

---

23 See further, Chapter 2.
24 C Nash, 'Volunteering in Sports Coaching – A Tayside Study' in M Graham and M Foley (eds), *Volunteering in Leisure: Marginal or Inclusive?* (Eastbourne, LSA 2001) 44; N Partington, 'Volunteering and EU Sports Law and Policy' in J Anderson, R Parrish and B Garcia (eds), *Handbook on EU Sports Law* (Cheltenham, Edward Elgar 2018) 98–119.
25 Sports Coach UK (n 6).
26 Duffy et al. (n 4) 94.
27 See, for instance, Nash (n 24) 50: 57.8% of the sample of coaches surveyed having never participated in a National Coaching Foundation/Sports Coach UK Coach Education Course. Also see G Nygaard and T Boone, *Coaches Guide to Sport Law* (Champaign, Human Kinetics 1985) 13.
28 Sports Coach UK (n 6).
29 Duffy et al. (n 4) 110.
30 Ibid.
31 P Trudel et al., 'Coach Education and Effectiveness' in Lyle and Cushion (n 10) 141.
32 Telfer (n 17) 210.
33 Ibid.

For instance, and as highlighted in Chapter 1, there is pressure on elite level coaches to provide 'cutting edge' guidance to athletes,[34] which may on occasion test the boundary between harm and reasonable endeavour (for athletes) within both practice sessions and competitive events.[35] This clearly illustrates the requirement for coaches to be mindful of the boundary between 'forging champions or committing a tort' when discharging the duty of care incumbent upon them.[36] As revealed in subsequent chapters, this crucial distinction has particular resonance whenever coaches push athletes outside of their comfort zones.

The sports coaching 'workforce' may be regarded as largely unregulated and absent of a 'validated threshold level of expertise or a commonality of occupational practice and expectations'.[37] The somewhat unique aspects of coaching when presented as a 'profession' include the predominant reliance on volunteers; a lack of necessary formal accreditation and qualification; varying and flexible indicators of competence; seemingly reduced opportunities for professional dialogue, collaboration and the sharing of best practice; and the differentiated sporting contexts of participation, development and performance in which coaches work. Collectively, these factors represent a stark contrast with other more traditional professions such as doctor, accountant or lawyer. This contrast creates peculiar challenges when attempts are made to define the standard of care and skill required of coaches when discharging their duty of care.

Whilst accepting the presumption that, in terms of responsibility, passion and commitment, the majority of volunteer coaches would quite justifiably defend their practice as being intrinsically 'professional',[38] the dynamic intersection between coaching, sport and the law creates some uncertainty for practitioners coaching in the field.[39] Despite the majority of personal injury claims being settled before reaching the courts,[40] there is an increasing body of recent related case law.[41] More than ever, it would appear that coaches are concerned and mindful about the prospect of legal liability,[42] with alleged breach of duty providing by far the most common cause of action. For instance, since coaches at grassroots levels

---

34 C Mallett, 'Becoming a High Performing Coach: Pathways and Communities' in Lyle and Cushion (n 10) 119.
35 Telfer (n 17) 214. As noted by Telfer, this is certainly an enduring debate, particularly in relation to the coaching of young performers.
36 TR Hurst and JN Knight, 'Coaches' Liability for Athletes' Injuries and Deaths' (2003) 13 *Seton Hall J. Sports L.* 27, 29.
37 A Lynn and J Lyle, 'Coaching workforce development' in Lyle and Cushion (n 10) 205. As further noted by Lynn and Lyle, '[t]his absence of cohesion and the lack of clear "markers" of what being a coach means are limitations that the professionalisation process has yet to overcome'.
38 Taylor and Garratt (n 10) 111.
39 S Greenfield, 'Law's Impact on Youth Sport: Should Coaches Be "Concerned About Litigation"?' (2013) 2(2) *Sports Coaching Review* 114, 117; Partington (n 7) 235–36.
40 Lord Dyson MR, 'Compensation Culture: Fact or Fantasy?' Holdsworth Lecture (15 March 2013) [34].
41 See further, Chapter 2 and Chapters 5–6.
42 Greenfield (n 39) 121.

may be regarded as less confident and more vulnerable,[43] fears of perceived professional malpractice may be having a particular impact in displacing considerations of coaching pedagogy.[44]

Professionalisation of coaching

The creation of the International Council for Coaching Excellence (ICCE) in 1997 has provided a catalyst for a stronger focus on the position of sports coaching as a 'profession', this being further consolidated by the adoption of the Magglingen Declaration.[45] Twenty-nine countries at a general assembly meeting approved this declaration, which emphasised the importance of central challenges, including those related to: (i) coach education; (ii) clarity in the identification of coaching competencies; and (iii) the need to promote standards of ethical behaviour and the need for mechanisms for monitoring compliance.[46] Curiously, this shift towards professionalisation may be construed as an attack on the very ethos of community based volunteerism by some coaches,[47] there appearing to be some justification to the suggestion that the true nature of professionalism remains somewhat confused.[48] Indeed, there is considerable force in Lyle's assertion that:

> [c]oaching is not yet a formal profession; access/gateway requirements, a professional body with specific requirements for membership, self-regulation, the need for a licence to operate, and career structures and training are not yet in place. There are codes of ethics and conduct but, in the absence of a professional body, these are not implemented in any universally systematic fashion.[49]

It is anticipated that this book's analysis of a coach's duty of care might prove instructive in contributing to discussions centred on coach education, coaching competencies and the promotion of ethical behaviour, since fulfilment of the legal duty of discharging reasonable care may be regarded as consistent with the ethical obligation not to expose athletes to unreasonable risks of injury.[50] Indeed, whilst

---

43 For instance, a professional coach would be expected to have appropriate insurance indemnity and also be able to shift liability to the employer (vicarious liability) in circumstances where the coach is acting in the capacity of employee: M James, *Sports Law* (2nd edn, New York, Palgrave Macmillan 2013) 81. See further, J Anderson, 'Personal Injury Liability in Sport: Emerging Trends' (2008) 16 *Tort Law Review* 95, 112–13. Also see, Chapter 2.
44 D Garratt et al., '"Safeguarding" Sports Coaching: Foucault, Geneology and Critique' (2012) 18(5) *Sport, Education and Society* 615, 626.
45 Duffy et al. (n 4).
46 Ibid.
47 Taylor and Garratt (n 4) 132.
48 Taylor and Garratt (n 10) 101.
49 J Lyle, 'Coaching Philosophy and Coaching Behaviour' in N Cross and J Lyle (eds), *The Coaching Process: Principles and Practice for Sport* (Philadelphia, Butterworth-Heinemann 1999) 44.
50 M Mitten, 'The Coach and the Safety of Athletes: Ethical and Legal Issues' in R Simon (ed), *The Ethics of Coaching Sports: Moral, Social, and Legal Issues* (Colorado, Westview Press 2013) 216.

the crucial distinction between legal and moral duties of care discussed in Chapter 1 remains significant, concepts such as duty and obligations are nonetheless relevant to an understanding of ethical (and best) practice.[51]

Consequently, the professional development and training of coaches must appropriately address the implications of relevant ethical considerations on coaching principles and practice,[52] and more specifically, given the substantial growth in claims of coach negligence, familiarise coaches with their legal duty of care owed to athletes. Duffy et al. have recognised the importance of the need for the legal and ethical aspects of sports coaching to become more enhanced topics within the continuing professional development (CPD) provision of coaches.[53] There is also corresponding evidence to indicate a demand from coaches for more training on health and safety issues, including risk management and (ir)responsible coaching.[54] In short, there appears to be strong endorsement for a greater awareness and knowledge of the related developing case law by coaching practitioners, since this familiarity would provide coaches with useful illustrations of what would likely constitute (un)reasonable coaching practice. Fundamentally, these judgments define the practical content of the duty of care demanded of modern sports coaches, thereby providing important insights regarding the standards expected of individuals professing to have a specialist skill. Indeed, since the legal principles derived from the area of professional liability are engaged when establishing reasonable coaching practice, and as the following analysis of the *Bolam* test reveals, it appears axiomatic that an informed understanding of this area of the law will prove instructive when reflecting on the further professionalisation of sports coaching.

Bolam test

General

The *Bolam* test may be regarded as a control device designed to set the limits of liability.[55] As a crucial preliminary issue, it should be noted that when courts inquire whether a defendant may have been careless and in breach of duty, ascertaining the standard of care required in law in the particular circumstances protects *both* claimants and defendants.[56] This benchmark of objective reasonableness is defined to safeguard the legitimate and genuine right of claimants (athletes) not to be exposed to unreasonable risks but, importantly, providing that defendants

---

51 Telfer (n 17) 211.
52 Ibid.
53 Duffy et al. (n 4) 118.
54 A Stirling et al., 'An Evaluation of Canada's National Coaching Certification Program's Make Ethical Decisions Coach Education Module' (2012) 6(2) *International Journal of Coaching Science* 45, 46.
55 P de Prez, 'Something "Old" Something "New", Something Borrowed. . . . The Continued Evolution of Bolam' (2001) 17 *Professional Negligence* 75.
56 Kidner (n 8) 23.

(coaches) discharge and meet this standard of skill and care, there can be no liability in negligence. Nonetheless, since the law of tort's primary goal may be regarded as compensation,[57] operating in a contemporary social context mindful of a perceived 'compensation culture',[58] it is arguable whether the full significance of the standard of care's dual function and capacity is always fully articulated or emphasised. To somewhat bluntly borrow a maxim from contract law, the standard of care may be regarded as a sword for claimants in seeking to establish breach but, correspondingly, a protective shield for defendants, providing conduct and practices are essentially reasonable. At first glance, this may appear trite law. However, given this book's aim to be of practical utility and beneficial impact, considerable reassurance may be acquired from this knowledge and awareness by sports coaches. In short, providing coaches satisfy this threshold of regular, approved, responsible and justifiable practice, and thereby effectively discharge their duty of care, they would be protected and shielded from liability in negligence.

In this context, although the *Bolam* test may not formally be regarded as a 'defence',[59] successful satisfaction of the *Bolam* test by professionals essentially shields and defends practitioners from professional liability. On a purely technical analysis of the law of negligence, the court's scrutiny of the *Bolam* test relates to the control mechanisms of standard and care and breach, not partial or absolute defences, including contributory negligence and volenti non fit injuria respectively.[60] However, adopting the viewpoint of coaches facing a professional liability action (for a breach of duty of care), reference to the *Bolam* test as a quasi-defence appears likely to be a source of readily understood encouragement, without fundamentally misrepresenting judicial reasoning or compromising the final judgments made by courts. Simply applied, framing the *Bolam* test as a 'defence' encompasses the intricacies of contextualised factors informing determination of the applicable standard of care (e.g., when coaching children; coaching more hazardous activities). It also accounts for additional discrepancies between the legal principle of objective reasonableness and the sports torts related evidential threshold of 'reckless disregard',[61] without over-complicating matters for defendants.[62] This is because reasonable and responsible coaching would be reflective of the full factual matrix of individual cases. In short, a detailed examination of the case law confirms adoption

---

57 De Prez (n 55) 84. In this regard, tort law may be regarded as distributing loss increasingly by means of insurance provision. Further, tort law can prove instrumental in setting acceptable minimum standards and practices by defining what might constitute reasonable skill and care in particular circumstances.
58 A Morris, 'Spiralling or Stabilising? The Compensation Culture and Our Propensity to Claim Damages for Personal Injury' (2007) 70 *Mod L Rev* 349, 350.
59 Mangan (n 5) 85.
60 See further, Chapter 2.
61 *Caldwell v Maguire* [2001] EWCA Civ 1054 [11]. The relevance and applicability of an evidential threshold of 'reckless disregard' in instances of sports negligence is discussed in detail in Chapter 4.
62 See generally, J Steele, *Tort Law: Text, Cases and Materials* (2nd edn, Oxford, OUP 2010) 114–5, recognising the merit of efforts to make the law in this area easier to grasp.

of practice found to be universal, approved and logically justifiable by professionals as affording conclusive and absolute protection from liability in negligence. As such, there appears some merit and usefulness in referring to the *Bolam* test as a 'defence' in appropriate circumstances, including the education, training and CPD of coaches.

Importantly, the *Bolam* test is not confined to cases of medical negligence,[63] it being of general application when defendants exercise or profess to have a particular skill.[64] Despite attempts to define profession appearing to prove inconclusive, should a coach be sued in negligence, the required standard of skill and care would be determined by reference to other members of the coaching 'profession', not the objective reasonable person on top of the 'Clapham omnibus'.[65] Simply applied, any profession requiring special skill, knowledge, or experience, including the coaching of sport,[66] requires a higher standard of care to be displayed than would be expected of the ordinary reasonable person.[67] This recognises the enhanced difficulty and skill in the working practices of professionals.[68] The *Bolam* test is also applicable to individuals not regarded as being members of a profession but whose functions demand the exercise of a special skill.[69] This will include volunteer coaches. Further, whether or not the coach may have some formal recognition of her/his specialisation would appear immaterial,[70] as would classification as amateur or professional,[71] the standard required remaining appropriate to specialists in that designated field. Accordingly, the core dispute in professional negligence cases tends to concentrate on determining what might constitute 'proper practice' or 'ordinary competence' with reference to the particular practices being contested.[72]

'Reasonable average'

Enunciation of the *Bolam* test over 25 years ago by Bingham LJ is highly informative and worth recalling in full:

> a professional man should command the corpus of knowledge which forms part of the professional equipment of the ordinary member of his profession.

---

63 Lunney and Oliphant (n 22) 198.
64 *Gold v Haringey Health Authority* [1988] QB 481, 489 (Lloyd LJ); *Adams v Rhymney Valley DC* [2001] PNLR 4 [57] (Morritt LJ); *Phelps v Hillingdon LBC* [2000] LGR 651.
65 Powell and Stewart (n 13) [2–128].
66 E.g., *Fowles v Bedfordshire CC* [1995] PIQR P380 (CA); *Davenport v Farrow* [2010] EWHC 550. See further, Chapter 5.
67 Lunney and Oliphant (n 22) 198; Jones and Dugdale (n 12) [10–03].
68 Mangan (n 5) 85.
69 Lunney and Oliphant (n 22) 198.
70 Powell and Stewart (n 13) [2–130].
71 J Gardiner, 'Should Coaches Take Care?' (1993) 143 *NLJ* 1598.
72 M Brazier and J Miola, 'Bye-Bye Bolam: A Medical Litigation Revolution?' (2000) 8(1) *Med Law Rev* 85, 87.

He should not lag behind other ordinarily assiduous and intelligent members of his profession in knowledge of new advances, discoveries and developments in his field. He should have such awareness as an ordinarily competent practitioner would have of the deficiencies in his knowledge and the limitations on his skill. He should be alert to the hazards and risks inherent in any professional task he undertakes to the extent that other ordinarily competent members of the profession would be alert. He must bring to any professional task he undertakes no less expertise, skill and care than other ordinarily competent members of his profession would bring, but need bring no more. The standard is that of the reasonable average.[73]

Whilst reinforcing the fundamental barometer of the 'reasonable average', it is revealing that Bingham LJ's paragon of professionalism is committed to their own continuous improvement and ongoing (professional) development necessitated by relevant developments in their area of expertise. Further, this reasonably average person is ordinarily aware of deficiencies in their knowledge and the limitations on their skill. In a coaching context, this translates to the reasonable expectation that coaches will be committed to coach education, CPD and, significantly, perform only at a level consistent with their competence, experience and qualifications.[74] Interestingly, and as already alluded to in Chapter 2, as performers progress to elite and excellence levels the required emphasis on more specialised training programmes creates new risks requiring coaches to ensure that they possess the necessary competence and expertise to operate safely in these amended circumstances.[75] For instance, determination of the range of acceptable increases in the intensity of training programmes for athletes of international potential may be best satisfied by a coach with the highest level of formal qualification.[76] Simply applied, the personified reasonably average professional would be mindful of, and effectively account for, any possible skills gap.[77]

Further, in modern parlance, this reasonably average practitioner creates the impression of being an ordinarily alert and reflective practitioner, endorsing the assertion that the *Bolam* doctrine 'is not a licence for professionals to take obvious

---

73 *Eckersley v Binnie* [1988] 18 ConLR 1, 80 (Bingham LJ).
74 *Wilsher v Essex AHA* [1987] QB 730 (CA). Scrutiny of the actual post held by the coach, and the corresponding level at which the coaching is conducted, provides a crucial material factor to support the court in accurately defining the required standard of care in the circumstances. See, for instance, *Pitcher v Huddersfield Town Football* Club, Queen's Bench Division 17 July 2001, Hallet J citing with approval *Wilsher* for authority that the level of performance (in this instance, a Nationwide Division 1 professional footballer) is a factor to be taken into account in assessing all the circumstances when determining the standard of care and skill expected.
75 J Labuschagne and J Skea, 'The Liability of a Coach for a Sport Participant's Injury' (1999) 10 *Stellenbosch Law Review* 158, 166.
76 See generally, *Davenport* (n 66) [59].
77 See further, Chapter 7.

risks which can be guarded against'.[78] Put simply, as emphasised by *Bolitho v City of Hackney Health Authority*, the practices of this hypothetical reasonably average professional would no doubt be logically justifiable.[79] Correspondingly, there now appears an increasingly general trend for courts to more closely question the practices of the professions.[80] Although evidence of general and approved practice remains of significant importance, it is not automatically conclusive evidence of the exercise of due skill and care.[81] Indeed, while the law accounts for the considerable mechanisms of professional self-regulation,[82] courts may not be as hesitant to declare a widespread practice to be negligent as they were in cases (previously) brought against medical practitioners.[83] Following *Bolitho*, peer professional opinion which purportedly represents evidence of responsible practice can be discounted by the court in instances where that opinion is determined by the judge to be incapable of withstanding logical analysis, or is otherwise unreasonable or irresponsible. This observation may be of particular relevance to 'new' or aspiring professions, including sports coaching, with validation of regular and ethical practices a key hallmark of professionalisation.[84] As a result, the outcome may be a more searching and rigorous judicial scrutiny of practice submitted to be proper or approved by coaches. More generally, an informed appreciation of this legal requirement for the practices of modern sports coaches to be reflective of ordinarily evolving and contemporary standards should inform the shift towards professionalisation in coaching.

Common practice

A coach would not be:

> guilty of negligence if he has acted in accordance with a practice accepted as proper by a responsible body [of medical men] skilled in that particular art. . . . Putting it the other way round, a man is not negligent, if he is acting in accordance with such a practice, merely because there is a body of opinion who would take a contrary view'[85]

Modern coaching methods and domains are often varied and complex, requiring 'structured improvisation' by coaches.[86] As in the related field of education,

---

78 *Adams* (n 64) [40] (Sir Christopher Staughton).
79 *Bolitho v City of Hackney Health Authority* [1998] AC 232.
80 Powell and Stewart (n 13) [2–128].
81 Ibid.
82 Jones and Dugdale (n 12) [10–03]. This lack of professional self-regulation appears to remain a major obstacle to the legitimate classification of sports coaching as a profession: see J Lyle, *Sports Coaching Concepts: A Framework for Coaches' Behaviour* (London, Routledge 2002) 203–05.
83 Jones and Dugdale (n 12) [10–03].
84 Telfer (n 17) 219.
85 *Bolam* (n 1) 587.
86 See generally, Lyle & Cushion (n 10).

there will be occasions where substantiating a case of fault against coaches for a breach of duty will be set against a backdrop of a variety of professional practices.[87] Framed differently, in light of the dynamic environment in which coaches operate, it must always be appreciated that there may be a number of perfectly proper standards.[88] Accordingly, the discretionary professional judgement of coaches must be acknowledged and respected when defining a standard of skill and care representative of the prevailing standards of this particular 'art'.[89]

Despite these flexible parameters, or latitude afforded towards professional judgement, in *Woodroffe-Hedley v Cuthbertson*[90] the court had little difficulty in finding a professional mountain guide negligent for failure to take adequate safety precautions, leading to the death of another climber. Dyson J came to the clear conclusion that the guide owed a duty of care to the fellow climber,[91] and further, that:

> in deciding to dispense with the second screw, Mr Cuthbertson fell below the standard to be expected of a reasonably competent and careful alpine guide. He was also negligent when he compounded that error by his decision not to use a running belay. . . . It is for the very reason that the consequences of a fall in such circumstances are so catastrophic that it is universally recognised good practice that two screws should be used in making a belay, and that running belays should be used.[92]

In crystallising a finding of negligence by benchmarking the acts or omissions of Mr Cuthbertson against that objectively expected of a reasonably competent mountain guide, the court acknowledged that a potentially catastrophic accident was plainly foreseeable. In other words, an ordinarily competent coach or instructor in the same circumstances, being aware of the importance of adopting recognised and approved practice, would have been expected to contemplate and anticipate that their acts or omissions were likely to result in very serious personal injury. Given the precise facts of *Woodroffe-Hedley v Cuthbertson* and, in particular, a failure to adopt regular and approved practice in the circumstances, establishing a breach of duty by the mountain guide appears somewhat straightforward. However, since the majority of cases that litigate may not be (arguably) so clear-cut,[93] a fuller analysis of the *Bolam* test is necessary in order to further clarify its application and the approach taken by courts when there may be a range of perfectly proper standards.

---

87 *Phelps* (n 64) 685.
88 J Montrose, 'Is Negligence an Ethical or a Sociological Concept?' (1958) 21 *Mod L Rev* 259, 262.
89 See generally, De Prez (n 55) 84.
90 *Woodroffe-Hedley v Cuthbertson*, 20 June 1997. This case is discussed in detail in Chapter 5.
91 Ibid.
92 Ibid.
93 R Heywood, 'The Logic of Bolitho' (2006) 22 *Professional Negligence* 225, 228.

Analysis of *Bolam* test

Two significant and interesting considerations revealed following a detailed examination of the *Bolam* test relate to, firstly, the approach of courts to the scope or leeway of discretionary professional judgement as approved in *Woodbridge School v Chittock*.[94] Secondly, and of considerable practical importance and merit in facilitating the use of the *Bolam* doctrine as a shield for defendants, are the issues of whether there is a necessary requirement for defendants (coaches) to: (i) possess a recognised formal qualification; and (ii) conduct a prospective conscientious analysis of the risks and benefits of a range of potential options or practices before making the decision or choice leading to the personal injury of the claimant. Critical scrutiny of case law determines whether failure to satisfy these preliminary requirements may in effect negate engagement of the *Bolam* 'defence'. These matters would likely be of crucial significance should coaches or instructors be sued in negligence. Accordingly, a thorough analysis of the relevant legal principles established by the higher courts is necessary.

The Court of Appeal's decision in *Woodbridge School v Chittock*, in recognising that the teacher's decisions when dealing with a sixth form student who had failed to follow instructions on a school ski trip were 'within a reasonable range of options',[95] appears to indicate that judges should afford appreciable latitude towards the professional judgement of teachers (and coaches). This proposition will be referred to as the *Woodbridge* principle.[96] This was certainly the view advanced by counsel for the defendant ski instructor in *Anderson v Lyotier*.[97] A corresponding argument submitted in *Anderson* was that the decision as to the suitability of the slope in relation to the ability and competence of the claimant was 'not negligent within the well-known *Bolam* principle'.[98] This argument forced the court to address the fundamental issue of whether reliance on the *Bolam* test can be made in circumstances where defendants may not have embarked upon a responsible decision-making process. This aspect of the *Bolam* test, or 'Rule',[99] led to a strong dissenting opinion in the Court of Appeal by Sedley LJ in *Adams v Rhymney Valley District Council*.[100] His Lordship was of the view that the *Bolam* test should have no relevance in a case where the defendant has failed altogether to exercise her/his professional skill, since a requirement of the *Bolam* test is that the defendant 'should have considered and reflected upon the alternative courses available and made a conscious choice between them'.[101] Nonetheless, in representing the majority

---

94 *Woodbridge School v Chittock* [2002] EWCA Civ 915.
95 Ibid. [18].
96 The practical application of this principle is considered further in Chapters 6 & 7.
97 *Anderson v Lyotier* [2008] EWHC 2790 [121]. Chapter 6 provides a detailed case study of this High Court decision.
98 Ibid.
99 H Evans, 'Negligence and Process' (2013) 29(4) *Professional Negligence* 212, 222.
100 *Adams* (n 64). Also see as authority for the 'Rule', *Goldstein v Levy Gee (A Firm)* [2003] EWHC 1574. See further, Evans (n 99) 213.
101 *Adams* (n 64) [19].

view, Sir Christopher Staughton's judgment addresses both the application of the 'Rule', and further, whether relevant professional qualifications are a precondition of the *Bolam* 'defence':

> The key question is whether the Bolam test still applies, although the particular defendant did not in fact have the qualifications of a professional in the relevant field of activity, and although he did not go through the process of reasoning which a qualified professional would consider before making a choice. I know of no authority that the benefit of the Bolam test should be refused in either of those cases. Nor do I think that it should be refused.[102]

In concurring with this view, Morritt LJ continued:

> If his action satisfies the Bolam test he is not liable: if it does not then he is liable however long and carefully he thought in advance about what to do. So in this case, the council is to be judged according to the standards of the reasonably skilful window designer and installer. Such a person would be entitled to the benefit of the Bolam test whether or not he had sat down and considered exactly which sort of lock to provide. The council is not to be made liable for selecting the same lock just because it did not make a reasoned choice.[103]

It has been suggested that utilisation of the 'Rule', allowing defendants that may not have completed a responsible decision-making process to rely on the *Bolam* test, promotes too lenient an operation of the *Bolam* test by failing to more firmly reflect the reasonable expectations of claimants (i.e., athletes). This view is to the detriment of the applicable tort standard of professional liability.[104] Further, it can be argued that concentrating on the outcome of the defendant's (i.e., coach's) decision-making process, as opposed to the reasonableness of this thinking, departs from 'common sense' notions of carelessness.[105] In this context, perhaps the principles of professional liability should be capable of regarding subjective carelessness, or flawed decision-making, as a 'wrong', thereby establishing negligence if damage can be proved.[106] Indeed, there appears some merit to the submission that:

> [w]hilst the defendant may have made no effort to comply with accepted standards of practice or to evaluate the proper course of action, the *Bolam* defence can be used as an escape route from liability if their conduct 'coincidentally' matches that of a responsible body of professional opinion. It is

---

102 Ibid. [42]. This assumption was endorsed by Morritt LJ at [59].
103 Ibid. [61].
104 Mangan (n 5) 86.
105 De Prez (n 55) 88.
106 Ibid, 89.

distasteful for negligence litigation, on facts where lives have been lost, to be successfully defended on the basis of 'coincidence' rather than 'competence'.[107]

Certainly, ordinarily competent coaches should not routinely seek to rely on the *Bolam* 'defence' on the basis of 'coincidence', it being contended that empowering coaches to become critical and reflective practitioners should become more of a priority for coach education and CPD. This approach would ensure that the practices adopted were responsible and capable of withstanding logical (and potentially legal) scrutiny. Nonetheless, as a matter of legal principle and coherence, the *Bolam* test is a control device designed to protect the legitimate interests of both claimants and defendants.

Accordingly, whilst insisting that the particular conduct resulting in personal injury is ultimately responsible and consistent with that of the reasonably competent professional, the reasoning of the majority *Adams v Rhymney Valley District Council* appears preferable. In practice, the 'Rule' is widely applicable and not confined to particular professions,[108] affording some certainty and consistency to this aspect of professional liability. Indeed, in the main, it does not appear obviously unjust to adopt it.[109] Further, permitting reliance on the *Bolam* 'defence', despite the possibility that the thought processes of defendants may be regarded as inadequate or mistaken, represents a realistic and efficient approach by courts to this issue, thereby negating associated evidential difficulties in order to ascertain what might amount to diligent consideration.[110] Simply applied, the alternative approach, requiring inquiry into varying degrees of conscientious reasoning,[111] may be regarded as somewhat flawed by preferring 'form to substance'.[112] Consequently, and of considerable significance to defendant coaches (and legal practitioners), application of the *Bolam* test should not be dependent on the actual possession of the relevant formal qualification, nor indeed is completion of reasoned and responsible decision-making a prerequisite of proper and approved practice.

In *Anderson v Lyotier*, Foskett J regarded a failure to evidence conscientious deliberation by the ski instructor as being problematic when stating:

> I do not see that enunciation of the [*Bolam*] test as having much application in a situation such as this where . . . the evidence does not permit me to find that M. Portejoie did weigh up the risks and benefits of what he asked the group to do.[113]

---

107 Ibid, 83.
108 Evans (n 99) 213.
109 Ibid, 217.
110 Ibid.
111 Ibid.
112 *Adams* (n 64) [50] (Sir Christopher Staughton).
113 *Anderson* (n 97) [123] (Foskett J).

Following *Adams v Rhymney Valley District Council*, this reasoning seems flawed. It is not a requirement of the *Bolam* test that the reasoning of a coach or instructor, in arriving at a decision as to what amounts to proper practice in the circumstances, must be adequate. The court's inquiry should centre on the eventual conclusion and not the decision-making process underpinning it.[114] On the facts of *Anderson*, this oversight would not appear to have been the pivotal issue since the slope in question was determined by the judge to be beyond the capability of the claimant. However, prematurely discounting the *Bolam* doctrine signifies a disservice to the application of the principles of professional liability. Whilst this chapter contends that the *Bolam* test remains an instructive and valuable tool in protecting defendant coaches from liability in negligence,[115] in instances where coaches may be regarded as having made an error of judgement, further detailed analysis of whether the injury suffered by the claimant was reasonably foreseeable may prove necessary.[116]

Ultimately, and in further developing Chapter 2's examination of the intersection between the law of negligence and sports coaching, this chapter's critical consideration of legal authority and academic commentary reveals the following important implications regarding application of the *Bolam* test in the context of sports coaching: (i) the principles of professional liability apply to all individuals exercising a special skill, including volunteers; (ii) the *Bolam* test remains the applicable legal control mechanism for determination of the appropriate standard of care demanded in the circumstances, irrespective of whether or not the defendant possesses formal qualifications; (iii) although a hallmark of best practice, failure by coaches to engage in mature, considered and reasoned decision-making should not prevent reliance on the *Bolam* principle; (iv) common and logically justifiable practice may, essentially, provide a conclusive and absolute 'defence' in cases of professional negligence; and finally (v) as in all instances of negligence liability, the specific context and particular facts of individual cases are of utmost importance.

Conclusion

The foregoing legal analysis of the somewhat novel issue of the professional liability of (predominantly) volunteer sports coaches uncovers significant implications for those exercising the 'art' of coaching. Most notably, established jurisprudence confirms that defendant coaches would be judged according to the benchmark of the

---

114 In *Anderson* (n 97), it was held that in order for the *Bolam* defence to have had any chance of succeeding, the skiing instructor was expected to have conducted a 'prospective conscientious analysis of [the performer's] capacity to undertake' the physical activity (at [112]), this evidential threshold not being met on the facts.
115 W Norris, 'The Duty of Care Owed by Instructors in a Sporting Context' (2010) 4 *JPI Law* 183, 186. See, for instance, *Davenport* (n 66) [59]. See further, Chapters 5 & 7.
116 Norris (n 115) 187–90. Importantly, the standards expected of ordinarily competent coaches, and informed by expert witness testimony, should have regard for the necessary precondition of foreseeability when defining the negligence standard in the particular circumstances.

ordinarily average competent coach if sued in negligence for a breach of duty of care, regardless of being categorised as amateur, professional, 'professional amateur', qualified, (in)experienced or accredited by an NGB. Further, as a 'new' and emerging profession, rigorous and searching judicial scrutiny of what might amount to proper or approved practice, or the *Bolam* 'defence', emphasises the requirement for coaches to adopt universal good practice whenever possible. Failing the adoption (or perhaps void) of universal practice, practices employed by coaches must be responsible and robustly justifiable. Whether application of the ordinary principles of professional liability in the context of voluntary sports coaching is just, fair and reasonable, or whether this establishes unrealistic expectations[117] will be subjected to further analysis in the following pages of this book.[118] Nonetheless, in view of the emerging relationship between sports coaching and the law of negligence,[119] as the law currently stands, coaches must be aware and informed of the heightened standard of care and skill required of the ordinarily competent coach. Importantly, this chapter's technical analysis of the legal obligations of professionals, derived from the law of tort,[120] reinforces the urgency of coach education and CPD affording considerably more importance to legal and ethical issues likely to be encountered by ordinary coaches. This is an issue returned to since it would maximise the application of the *Bolam* test as an informative and valuable mechanism in protecting defendant coaches from liability in negligence when discharging the duty of care incumbent upon them.

In view of the special skill required of the ordinary competent coach, this chapter has provided a detailed appreciation of how the legal duty of care required of modern sports coaches is defined. Put simply, should it be claimed that a coach has breached her/his duty of care, the context of sports coaching means that the principles of professional negligence would be engaged. However, this remains an extremely fact-sensitive area of the law. Indeed, such is the significance of the particular sporting circumstances in this field that it also proves necessary to have a knowledge and understanding of the more general and established body of sports negligence case law authority. Accordingly, given the importance and relevance of identifying the indicative criteria constituting the prevalent circumstances in the specific context of sport/sports coaching, which proves integral and highly instructive when defining the extent of a coach's duty of care, the next chapter considers the development of sports negligence jurisprudence in the UK.

---

117 See generally, G Nichols and P Taylor, 'The Balance of Benefit and Burden? The Impact of Child Protection Legislation on Volunteers in Scottish Sports Clubs' (2010) 10(1) *European Sport Management Quarterly* 31, 46.
118 Also see, N Partington, 'Beyond the "*Tomlinson* Trap": Analysing the Effectiveness of Section 1 of the Compensation Act 2006' (2016) 37(1) *Liverpool L Rev* 33.
119 Partington (n 7) 234–5.
120 See further, Mangan (n 5) 84.

PART II
Duty of care in context

4
DUTY OF CARE IN THE CONTEXT OF SPORT

This chapter analyses the development of sports negligence jurisprudence in the UK. By exploring duty of care considerations in the specific context of sport, it provides the foundations and framework used by courts to define the duty owed by defendants involved in the particular circumstances of sporting activity. Whilst seeking to uncover and identify established legal principles of more general application, the analysis remains mindful of the relevance of such principles when defining a sports coach's duty of care. The chapter considers seven of the most relevant Court of Appeal decisions in this area. This encompasses claims of a breach of duty by various defendants, from a range of sports and performance levels, including both amateur and professional sport. The chapter firstly discusses the duty of care owed by competitors to spectators. Next, and in referring to the most recent decision in this field from an appellate court,[1] the duty of care owed by sports participants to co-participants is critically examined. This analysis proves instructive in identifying the fashioning of the legal test used by the judiciary when tasked with ruling on the nature and extent of the duty owed in the prevailing circumstances of sport. Following this, the chapter is brought into even sharper focus, with regard to defining a coach's duty of care, by analysing the strong analogy of the duty of care owed by referees to players.

---

1 Cases are initially heard at first instance by Trial courts. Trial courts (e.g., High Court) make an appropriate ruling having considered the matters of fact and law in the relevant case. Once a case has been heard at first instance, appellate courts (e.g., Court of Appeal) can consider the application of legal principles to that case. On appeal, instead of referring to the parties as claimant/plaintiff and defendant, the names of the parties changes to 'appellant' (the person bringing an appeal) and 'respondent' (the person against whom the appeal is brought). See further, E Finch and S Fafinski, *Legal Skills* (7th edn, Oxford, OUP 2019) 93–95 & 130.

As established in previous chapters, the law of negligence is highly fact-dependant. With this fundamental point in mind, the subsequent discussion provides a detailed insight into the reasoning of courts by providing extensive extracts from the judgments of the Court of Appeal. As any law student or scholar will (sometimes 'painfully') be fully aware, grasping a full appreciation and understanding of the relevant legal principles derived from the case law demands that the relevant judgments are carefully and thoughtfully read in full.[2] In making this body of case law more accessible for readers with a background in law, as well as for those from different fields and those with practical coaching experience, the following in-depth analysis makes no compromise on the searching and rigorous scrutiny afforded. The interesting and varied facts generated by these leading cases offers engaging scenarios from which informative insights can be ascertained. Moreover, the judgments considered establish how this area of judge-made law has been developed and refined over the last half century. This process involves the Court of Appeal considering, citing with approval and clarifying earlier authority in accordance with the doctrine of precedent. As noted by Finch and Fafinski, in order to maintain legal certainty and consistency in the application of the law, judicial precedent is premised on the principle that like cases should be treated alike. As such, the essence of the doctrine of precedent is that 'once a decision has been reached in a particular case, it stands as good law and should be relied upon in other cases as an accurate statement of law'.[3] This doctrine has proved integral to the incremental development of sports negligence jurisprudence,[4] and so in maintaining an authentic insight into judicial reasoning in this area, it proves both necessary and highly instructive to recall at length some of the key paragraphs from the leading authorities.

Duty of care owed by competitors to spectators

Wooldridge v Sumner [1963] 2 QB 43 (CA)

In terms of defining the duty of care in sports negligence cases, and as revealed by the following doctrinal analysis of predominantly Court of Appeal judgments, the leading UK authority appears to be *Wooldridge v Sumner*.[5] The plaintiff in

---

2 Interestingly, Dyson LJ in *Blake v Galloway* [2004] EWCA Civ 814 provided an instructive review of the sports negligence case law.
3 Finch and Fafinski (n 1) 139. It may sometimes be necessary for courts to consider whether the precedents should be departed from.
4 For instance, see *Caldwell v Maguire* [2001] EWCA Civ 1054 [21] (Tuckey LJ): 'The relevant principles to be applied to a case of this kind emerge clearly from the decision of this court in Condon and Smoldon, which are binding on us.' This leading authority for sports negligence is discussed in detail later.
5 J Anderson, *Modern Sports Law: A Textbook* (New York, Hart 2010) 223. As discussed in the introduction to this book, the extensive reference to *Wooldridge* by courts of the wider common law family also supports this view. Courts have also heard cases brought by injured spectators against owners and occupiers of sports venues in situations where it has been claimed that the state of the premises

Wooldridge (W) was a photographer injured at the 1959 National Horse Show at the White City Stadium, London. During the competition, W was knocked down and severely injured by a horse, 'Work of Art', owned by the first defendant (S) and ridden by a skilled and experienced horseman (H) employed by S. An appeal followed Barry J's finding in the High Court that the accident was caused by the negligence of H. In the Court of Appeal, the case was heard by Sellers, Danckwerts and Diplock LJJ. Importantly, in recognising that this was a novel case with 'no direct guidance or hindrance from authority', Diplock LJ emphasised that determining reasonable care in a particular circumstance would require 'inquiring whether the ordinary reasonable man would say that in all the circumstances the defendant's conduct was blameworthy'.[6] With this in mind, all Lords Justices of Appeal ruled to allow the appeal, providing instructive guidance not only on the precise standard of care required of a participant in competitive sport in relation to spectators but also with regard to defining sports negligence more generally.

Court of Appeal, Sellers LJ at 56–57:

. . . provided the competition or game is being performed within the rules and the requirement of the sport and by a person of adequate skill and competence the spectator does not expect his safety to be regarded by the participant. If the conduct is deliberately intended to injure someone whose presence is known, or is reckless and in disregard of all safety of others so that it is a departure from the standards which might reasonably be expected in anyone pursuing the competition or game, then the performer might well be held liable for any injury his act caused. . . . The relationship of spectator and competitor or player is a special one, as I see it, as the standard of conduct of the participant, as accepted and expected by the spectator, is that which the sport permits or involves. The different relationship involves its own standard of care.

Danckwerts LJ at 58–59

In the circumstances, the judge came to the conclusion that the accident was caused by the negligence of Mr. Holladay in the management of "Work of Art" and awarded damages to the plaintiff against the first defendant. The judge, however, said that no one attributed any sort of moral blame for this accident either upon the plaintiff or upon the rider of "Work of Art" or upon

---

has meant that they were not suitable for the reasonably safe hosting of the event in question. See, for instance, *Hall v Brooklands Auto-Racing Club* [1933] 1 KB 205 (CA); *Murray v Harringay Arena LD* [1951] 2 KB 529 (CA); *Browning v Odyssey Trust Co Ltd* [2014] NIQB 39. As in *Browning*, a Northern Irish case, such claims can now be brought under the 1957 Occupiers' Liability Acts.

6 *Wooldridge v Sumner* [1963] 2 QB 43, 66–67.

the organisers of the show. The judge also said that no one suggested that this was anything other than an isolated lapse on Mr. Holladay's part, for which there was a good deal of excuse because this was a contest in which three very well-known horses were involved and Mr. Holladay was very anxious indeed that his horse should win it.

. . .

If Mr. Holladay brought the horse at too fast a pace round the end of the arena, I cannot think that it can have been more than a slight error of judgment, which did not in fact cause the accident . . . in my view, Mr. Holladay was not guilty of negligence either in the speed at which he rode the horse or in his attempts to bring the horse into a course which would pass inside the line of the tubs and the benches and be in the view of the judges.

Diplock LJ at 66–71

To treat Lord Atkin's statement, "You must take reasonable care to avoid acts or omissions which you can reasonably foresee would be likely to injure your neighbour", as a complete exposition of the law of negligence is to mistake aphorism for exegesis. It does not purport to define what is reasonable care and was directed to identifying the persons to whom the duty to take reasonable care is owed. What is reasonable care in a particular circumstance is a jury question and where, as in a case like this, there is no direct guidance or hindrance from authority it may be answered by inquiring whether the ordinary reasonable man would say that in all the circumstances the defendant's conduct was blameworthy.

The matter has to be looked at from the point of view of the reasonable spectator as well as the reasonable participant; not because of the maxim volenti non fit injuria, but because what a reasonable spectator would expect a participant to do without regarding it as blameworthy is as relevant to what is reasonable care as what a reasonable participant would think was blameworthy conduct in himself. . . .

A reasonable spectator attending voluntarily to witness any game or competition knows and presumably desires that a reasonable participant will concentrate his attention upon winning, and if the game or competition is a fast-moving one, will have to exercise his judgment and attempt to exert his skill in what . . . is sometimes called "the agony of the moment". If the participant does so concentrate his attention and consequently does exercise his judgment and attempt to exert his skill in circumstances of this kind which are inherent in the game or competition in which he is taking part, the question whether any mistake he makes amounts to a breach of duty to take reasonable care must take account of those circumstances.

The law of negligence has always recognised that the standard of care which a reasonable man will exercise depends upon the conditions under which the decision to avoid the act or omission relied upon as negligence has to be taken. . . . It cannot be suggested that the participant, at any rate if he has some modicum of skill, is, by the mere act of participating, in breach of his duty of care to a spectator who is present for the very purpose of watching him do so. If, therefore, in the course of the game or competition, at a moment when he really has not time to think, a participant by mistake takes a wrong measure, he is not, in my view, to be held guilty of any negligence.

Furthermore, the duty which he owes is a duty of care, not a duty of skill. Save where a consensual relationship exists between a plaintiff and a defendant by which the defendant impliedly warrants his skill, a man owes no duty to his neighbour to exercise any special skill beyond that which an ordinary reasonable man would acquire before indulging in the activity in which he is engaged at the relevant time. It may well be that a participant in a game or competition would be guilty of negligence to a spectator if he took part in it when he knew or ought to have known that his lack of skill was such that even if he exerted it to the utmost he was likely to cause injury to a spectator watching him. No question of this arises in the present case. It was common ground that Mr. Holladay was an exceptionally skilful and experienced horseman.

The practical result of this analysis of the application of the common law of negligence to participant and spectator would, I think, be expressed by the common man in some such terms as these: "A person attending a game or competition takes the risk of any damage caused to him by any act of a participant done in the course of and for the purposes of the game or competition notwithstanding that such act may involve an error of judgment or a lapse of skill, unless the participant's conduct is such as to evince a reckless disregard of the spectator's safety".

. . .

The horse was deflected from its course before it reached the benches and no spectator would have been injured had not the plaintiff, in a moment of panic, stepped or stumbled back out of his proper and safe place among the other spectators in the line of benches into the path of the horse . . . a reasonable competitor would be entitled to assume that spectators actually in the arena would be paying attention to what was happening, would be knowledgeable about horses, and would take such steps for their own safety as any reasonably attentive and knowledgeable spectator might be expected to take.

. . .

The most that can be said against Mr. Holladay is that in the course of and for the purposes of the competition he was guilty of an error or errors of judgment or a lapse of skill. That is not enough to constitute a breach of the duty of reasonable care which a participant owes to a spectator. In such circumstances something in the nature of a reckless disregard of the spectator's safety must be proved, and of this there is no suggestion in the evidence. I, too, would allow this appeal.

92 Duty of care in context

In borrowing from Diplock LJ's judgment in *Wooldridge*, and recalling the necessity to distinguish between moral, ethical and legal duties of care as discussed in Chapter 1, there is a danger that the concept of the duty of care may potentially lead to mistaking 'aphorism for exegesis'. This appears likely to be the case when the concept of duty of care is adopted without any attempt to define what reasonable care actually is at common law. Moreover, in citing from the High Court judgment, Danckwerts LJ reiterated the need to distinguish between any sort of moral blame and breach of duty, and Diplock LJ emphasised the court's task of determining blameworthiness in a strictly legal sense.

On the crucial matter of defining negligence in the specific context of sport, the extracts just presented from *Wooldridge* reveal that full account must be taken of the particular circumstances inherent in the sporting activity in question. These particular circumstances, in the case of the duty owed to a spectator by a competitor and, when determining whether or not there has been a breach of duty to take reasonable care, include: (i) the rules and requirements of the sport; (ii) the special relationship between spectator and competitor, involving its own standard of care; (iii) recognition that slight errors of judgement or lapses in skill, in the context of a fast moving game/'agony of the moment', might reasonably be expected when participants exercise their judgement in a competitive sporting event; and (iv) that the expectations of both the defendant (i.e., participant) and the claimant (i.e., spectator) must be considered, which in *Wooldridge*, reinforced the fact that a reasonable participant will often focus their attention upon winning.

Although the duty owed was construed as a duty of care and not skill, there is a recognition in *Wooldridge* that a reasonable participant would possess an adequate level of skill and competence sufficient for their safe involvement in the relevant sporting event. Failing this, where a lack of skill by a participant would likely result in injury to a spectator, a finding of negligence liability may well be established. Further, Diplock LJ alluded to the fact that where a defendant holds themselves out as having a special skill, then there may be a duty to exercise this special skill.

Simply applied, as an expression of legal principle, *Wooldridge* is authority for the proposition that evidence of conduct that is deliberately intended to cause injury, or amounts to a reckless disregard of all safety of others, is likely to result in a finding of breach of duty by a sports participant. Nonetheless, it is clear that by taking into account the prevailing circumstances, the threshold of negligence liability is expected to be high and that there would not ordinarily be a breach of duty for a slight lapse of skill or error of judgement in a competitive and fast moving game. Commenting at the time of this judgment, Goodhart suggested that the emphasis placed on the reckless disregard standard seemed 'to introduce a novel element into the law, for it is unusual to find liability limited to recklessness'.[7] In elaborating on this issue, Goodhart highlighted the significant point that a finding of liability in negligence is in most cases supported by an error of judgement or a

---

7 AL Goodhart, 'The Sportsman's Charter' (1962) 78 *LQR* 490, 494. Interestingly, Goodhart made the further point that in practice it may be difficult to draw a distinction between recklessness and a lesser degree of negligence (at 496).

lapse of skill.[8] Indeed, and as will be discussed in detail in Chapter 6's case study, a claim of coach negligence has been supported when the coach momentarily took his 'eye off the ball'.[9] It should, however, be noted from the outset that as a matter of practical application, reckless disregard provides a sufficient, but not necessary, evidential guide in instances of sports negligence.[10] But, and of fundamental importance, the duty incumbent upon defendants remains that of reasonable care in the particular circumstances.

Some eight years later, these same legal principles were exposed to further scrutiny by the Court of Appeal following injuries suffered by spectators at a motor-cycle scramble.

Wilks v Cheltenham Homeguard Motor Cycle and Light Car Club [1971] 1 WLR 668 (CA)

At first instance in *Wilks v Cheltenham Homeguard Motor Cycle and Light Car Club*, Payne J had exempted the club from liability but found a motorcycle rider negligent, when for no explicable reason, he suddenly left the course and went into the spectators. Mr Wilks and his daughter, who were in the spectators' enclosure watching the motor-scramble organised by the club on 25 September 1966, suffered injury as a result. The rider, Mr Ward, appealed the High Court's decision.

Court of Appeal, Lord Denning MR, 670

Let me first try to state the duty which lies upon a competitor in a race. He must, of course, use reasonable care. But that means reasonable care having regard to the fact that he is a competitor in a race in which he is expected to go "all out" to win. Take a batsman at the wicket. He is expected to hit six, if he can, even if it lands among the spectators. So also in a race, a competitor is expected to go as fast as he can, so long as he is not foolhardy. In seeing if a man is negligent, you ask what a reasonable man in his place would or would not do. In a race a reasonable man would do everything he could do to win, but he would not be foolhardy. That, I think, is the standard of care to be expected of him.

We were referred to Wooldridge v. Sumner [1963] 2 Q.B. 43. It is, I think, different. It concerned a horse show where horses were to display their paces, but not to race. . . . In a race the rider is, I think, liable if his conduct is such as to evince a reckless disregard of the spectators' safety: in other words, if his conduct is foolhardy.

---

8 Ibid.
9 *Anderson v Lyotier* [2008] EWHC 2790 [120]. This poses the question of whether or not the standard of care required of coaches is modified to reflect the specific context of sport to the same degree that it is adapted when defining the duty of care owed by participants. See further, Chapters 5–7.
10 D McArdle and M James, 'Are you experienced? "Playing cultures", sporting rules and personal injury litigation after Caldwell v Maguire' (2005) 13(3) *Tort Law Review* 193, 207.

Edmund Davies LJ, 673–75:

But, in all the perplexing circumstances of this case, was it right to hold Mr. Ward guilty of negligence? Lord Denning M.R. has already referred to the decision of this court in Wooldridge v. Sumner [1963] 2 Q.B. 43 and I respectfully share his difficulty in accepting the view there expressed that a competitor in such events as this is to be held liable only if he acts in reckless disregard of the spectators' safety. For my part, I would with deference adopt the view of Dr. Goodhart in 78 L.Q.R. at p. 496 that the proper test is whether injury to a spectator has been caused "by an error of judgment that a reasonable competitor, being the reasonable man of the sporting world, would not have made". But the decision is, if I may say so, most valuable in pointing out those special features which are inherent in competitive events and which everyone takes for granted. I have here particularly in mind the observation of Sellers L.J., at p. 56, that, 'provided the competition or game is being performed within the rules and the requirement of the sport and by a person of adequate skill and competence the spectator does not expect his safety to be regarded by the participant'.

Nevertheless, although in the very nature of things the competitor is all out to win and that is exactly what the spectators expect of him, it is in my judgment still incumbent upon him to exercise such degree of care as may reasonably be expected in all the circumstances. For my part, therefore, I would hold him liable only for damage caused by errors of judgment or lapse of skill going beyond such as, in the stress of circumstances, may reasonably be regarded as excusable.

Applying that test here, what follows?

For my part, I cannot think that, in the difficult circumstances of the present case, it would be right to impute the defendant's loss of control to fault on his part. All happened in a split second, and (assuming the worst against him) even a slip or misjudgment too slight to be regarded as amounting to negligence could well account for this accident. Accordingly, while one must feel particularly sorry for the male plaintiff, I do not think it would be just to hold the second defendant [rider] liable.

Phillimore LJ, 675–76:

The duty owed by a competitor to a spectator was last considered by the Court of Appeal in Wooldridge v. Sumner [1963] 2 Q.B. 43. In considering whether conduct by a competitor which leads to injury to a spectator is to be termed negligent it is obvious that the conduct must be looked at in all

> the circumstances. Anyone who attends a cricket match as a spectator must accept the risk of a batsman hitting a six into the crowd. There must always be a risk at a race meeting, whether the race is between horses or cars or motorcycles, that a competitor who is riding or driving entirely properly may as a result of some unforeseen event be forced to leave the course, or at all events to collide with any barriers at the side of it.
>
> I confess that I find myself attracted to the sort of test propounded by Sellers L.J.[11].
>
> ... the words of Diplock L.J. might also provide a useful approach.[12]
>
> ...
>
> It is, however, important to remember that the test remains simply that of 'negligence' and that whether or not the competitor was negligent must be viewed against all the circumstances – the tests mentioned in Wooldridge v. Sumner are only to be applied if the circumstances warrant them.

In distinguishing this case from the somewhat similar facts found in *Wooldridge*, Lord Denning's comments emphasise that determining whether or not there has been a breach of duty will be highly fact- and context-specific. More fundamentally, the Court of Appeal in *Wilks* appears cautious to avoid introducing a new legal test,[13] or what might be regarded as a tort of reckless disregard,[14] that might apply in sports negligence cases. *Wilks* makes plain that the legal test to be applied in the context of sport, when determining whether or not there has been a breach of the duty of care owed, remains negligence in all the circumstances. That is, competitors in a race are still required to exercise such degree of care as may reasonably be expected in the particular circumstances. Nonetheless, foolhardy conduct, or conduct that shows a reckless disregard of the spectators' safety, appears sufficient as an evidential standard to amount to negligence in the circumstances of a fast moving contest. Correspondingly, by taking full account of all of the relevant circumstances, judicial allowance can, and should, be made for errors of judgement or lapses of skill that might be made by the reasonable person of the sporting world going 'all out' to win. Although the special features inherent in competitive events, as enunciated in *Wooldridge*, may be valuable in defining the standard of care incumbent upon competitors in sport, it would be wrong to assume that this is always the case. As insightfully observed by Phillimore LJ, and a material consideration in the next case considered concerning the liability of co-participants, the

---

11 See *Wooldridge* (n 6) 57: 'If the conduct...'.
12 See *Wooldridge* (n 6) 68: 'The practical result...'.
13 Clearly mindful of Goodhart's comments regarding the apparent introduction in *Wooldridge* of a novel element into the law. See (n 7).
14 M James, *Sports Law* (3rd edn, Croydon, Palgrave 2017) 86.

tests mentioned in *Wooldridge* will not always be warranted or engaged by particular sporting circumstances.

Duty of care owed by competitors to other participants

Harrison v Vincent [1982] RTR 8 (CA)

Harrison v Vincent is a case that appears to have been overlooked by the Court of Appeal in the later leading decision of *Condon v Basi*,[15] with Sir John Donaldson MR stating in 1995 that there was no previous authority regarding the standard of care which governs the conduct of players/participants in competitive sports. This was inaccurate. During a sidecar race on 12 September 1971, at a motorcycle racing circuit at Oliver's Mount near Scarborough, the passenger of a sidecar sustained serious injuries following an accident. The race in question was a final and involved speeds in excess of 100 miles an hour. The defendant sidecar rider experienced rear brake failure on the fastest part of the track, reducing his braking power by 40 per cent or so. Moreover, and although not regarded as blameful by the judge, the rider was also found to have missed his gear during this misadventure resulting in the sidecar careering along at a less reduced speed. Accordingly, the rider decided to escape from the track using a right-hand fork in the direction of the entrance to the paddock. In taking this evasive action, the sidecar subsequently collided with a vehicle which was parked almost entirely off the roadway but with two feet or so of its breadth on the road. As a result, the sidecar passenger sued the rider for negligence arising out of those circumstances.[16] In particular, the claim was based on the allegations that: (i) there was a negligent failure in fitting the brake mechanism by the rider; (ii) there was a failure to carry out a sufficient inspection of the equipment; and (iii) that there was a failure to drive at a sufficiently reduced speed. At first instance, Hodgson J found that the rider had been negligent. This decision was appealed.

> **Court of Appeal, Sir John Arnold P at 12–14 (Brandon and Watkins LJJ in agreement)**
>
> The evidence was, as regards the rider's equipment, that some days previously there had been a failure of a pin in the rear brake mechanism, that that had been investigated, and that the investigation had revealed a then existing misalignment of the caliper. That had led to a refit of the relevant equipment. There

---

15 *Condon v Basi* (1985) 1 WLR 866 (CA). Discussed below.
16 A claim was also brought against the race organisers based on the allegation that the state of the racetrack, due to partial blockage on the chosen escape route, meant that it was not suitable for the reasonably safe hosting of the race.

was evidence given by the rider, but not accepted by the judge, to the effect that that had taken place and had taken place wholly efficiently and had been the subject by him of inspection most recently at a time on the day of the race in question. There was, on the other hand, expert evidence to the effect that the only practical explanation of what was found to have happened at the time of the relevant accident, namely, the breaking of the pin and the consequent ejection of the pads, was such a misalignment, compounded by the circumstance that it was not discovered on an inspection. The judge had that explanation but no other theoretical explanation which involved anything other than negligence on the part of the rider – negligence, that is, measured by the standard of measurement the judge chose to adopt and which is challenged in this court.

...

The rider and his employers advanced however in this court contentions of law directed to the proposition that the judge applied the wrong standard of care, or at least the wrong measure of breach of duty of care. The point was first put quite broadly that, in circumstances of this sort, that is to say, in circumstances in which the passenger and the rider were associated together in a sport or other activity having an inherent element of danger, no duty of care whatsoever would be owed by the one to the other. That assertion was not founded on any discernible principle or on any cited authority. It seems to me that it must be a quite wrong proposition put as broadly as that in principle.

However the main thrust of the submission was to the effect that in such circumstances there was only a modified duty of care, so that only reckless disregard of the safety of the plaintiff or an intention to injure the plaintiff would constitute a relevant breach. That proposition was mainly based on Wooldridge v Sumner [1963] 2 QB 43.

...

That was a highly relevant and precisely applicable standard to be applied to this case in so far as the passenger might have based his claim on the rider missing his gear when he found that his brakes had failed. That would have been an act of a participant done 'in the course, and for the purposes of the game or competition'. . . . The act or acts which were complained of were not done in the flurry and excitement of the sport but were done in the relative calm of the workshop where the equipment is fitted and, I suppose, at the last opportunity, in the pits where the inspection should have been carried out. So it seems to me that the whole underlying differentiation between the normal standard of care and the modified standard of care applicable to violent sport, to use a slightly inaccurate but shorthand term, was totally absent. I can see, for my part, no reason whatever to suppose that the standard of care in relation to the maintenance and inspection of the mechanism was any standard of care other than that normally owed where a duty is owed to a neighbour. For my part I can see no justification for an attack on that ground on the judge's conclusion.

In dismissing the appeal, the Court of Appeal's judgment reveals four points of particular interest. First, expert witness evidence often plays a critical role in defining the standard of care, or measure of breach of duty of care, applied by the court. Second, any general suggestion that participants in a competitive sporting activity did not owe a duty of care towards other participants, in this instance the participants being a sidecar rider and his passenger, received short shrift. Third, the Court of Appeal rejected the argument that an evidential standard of reckless disregard of the safety of the plaintiff was necessary to constitute a breach of duty in a sports negligence case such as this. Finally, and more specifically, in scrutinising all of the prevailing circumstances, a crucial distinction was made between the standard of care that might be required in the course of a game or competition and the standard of care expected in the relative calm of the workshop. As will be revealed when examining cases brought in negligence against sports officials and referees, an opportunity for more considered thought and decision-making, for instance, during a stoppage in play, appears likely to be a material factor when defining the standard of care in sports negligence cases. By analogy, there will be circumstances in which sports coaching will be conducted in a controlled, supervised and tightly monitored environment whereby the coach may manipulate and determine the level of intensity, degree of competition and physical demands placed upon participants.

As will be highlighted in subsequent chapters, the principles established in *Harrison* may be of considerable relevance when defining the extent of a sports coach's duty of care. However, for present purposes, and also of considerable relevance to coach negligence enquiries, the following two Court of Appeal judgments are regarded as the leading authorities for co-participant liability.

Condon v Basi (1985) 1 WLR 866 (CA)

During a match between Whittle Wanderers and Khalso Football Club of the Leamington local league, the defendant performed a 'late' sliding tackle from about four yards distance away. In lunging at the plaintiff, with his studs showing at a height of approximately 9–18 inches from the ground, the defendant's tackle broke the plaintiff's right leg. In the opinion of the referee, the tackle constituted serious foul play and the defendant was sent off from the field of play. In finding that the tackle was made in a 'reckless and dangerous manner', His Honour Judge Wootton in the Warwick County Court ruled that the defendant had been negligent and awarded a sum of around £5,000 in damages. The defendant appealed this decision on the grounds that: (i) in all the circumstances, and with particular regard to a participant's consent to risk of injury in competitive sport, the defendant owed no duty of care to the plaintiff; and (ii) that the standard of care was subjective to the defendant and not objective.

Court of Appeal, Sir John Donaldson MR, 867–869 (Stephen Brown LJ and Glidewell J in agreement)

For my part I would completely accept the decision of the High Court of Australia in Rootes v. Shelton [1968] A.L.R. 33. I think it suffices, in order to see the law which has to be applied, to quote briefly from the judgment of Barwick C.J. and from the judgment of Kitto J. Barwick C.J. said, at p. 34:

> 'By engaging in a sport or pastime the participants may be held to have accepted risks which are inherent in that sport or pastime: the tribunal of fact can make its own assessment of what the accepted risks are: but this does not eliminate all duty of care of the one participant to the other. Whether or not such a duty arises, and, if it does, its extent, must necessarily depend in each case upon its own circumstances. In this connection, the rules of the sport or game may constitute one of those circumstances: but, in my opinion, they are neither definitive of the existence nor of the extent of the duty; nor does their breach or non-observance necessarily constitute a breach of any duty found to exist'.

Kitto J. said, at p. 37:

> 'in a case such as the present, it must always be a question of fact, what exoneration from a duty of care otherwise incumbent upon the defendant was implied by the act of the plaintiff in joining in the activity. Unless the activity partakes of the nature of a war or of something else in which all is notoriously fair, the conclusion to be reached must necessarily depend, according to the concepts of the common law, upon the reasonableness, in relation to the special circumstances, of the conduct which caused the plaintiff's injury. That does not necessarily mean the compliance of that conduct with the rules, conventions or customs (if there are any) by which the correctness of conduct for the purpose of the carrying on of the activity as an organized affair is judged; for the tribunal of fact may think that in the situation in which the plaintiff's injury was caused a participant might do what the defendant did and still not be acting unreasonably, even though he infringed the 'rules of the game'. Non-compliance with such rules, conventions or customs (where they exist) is necessarily one consideration to be attended to upon the question of reasonableness; but it is only one, and it may be of much or little or even no weight in the circumstances'.

I have cited from those two judgments because they show two different approaches which, as I see it, produce precisely the same result. One is to take a more generalised duty of care and to modify it on the basis that the participants in the sport or pastime impliedly consent to taking risks which otherwise would be a breach of the duty of care. That seems to be the approach of Barwick C.J. The other is exemplified by the judgment of Kitto J., where he is saying, in effect, that there is a general standard of care, namely the Lord Atkin approach in Donoghue v. Stevenson [1932] A.C. 562 that You are under a duty to take all reasonable care taking account of the circumstances in which You are placed, which, in a game of football, are quite different from those which affect You when You are going for a walk in the countryside.

For my part I would prefer the approach of Kitto J., but I do not think it makes the slightest difference in the end if it is found by the tribunal of fact that the defendant failed to exercise that degree of care which was appropriate in all the circumstances, or that he acted in a way to which the plaintiff cannot be expected to have consented. In either event, there is liability.

Having set out the test – which is the test which I think was applied by the judge in the county court – I ought to turn briefly to the facts, adding before I do so that it was submitted by Mr. Lee on behalf of the defendant that the standard of care was subjective to the defendant and not objective, and if he was a wholly incompetent football player, he could do things without risk of liability which a competent football player could not do. For my part I reject that submission. The standard is objective, but objective in a different set of circumstances. Thus there will of course be a higher degree of care required of a player in a First Division football match than of a player in a local league football match. But none of these sophistications arise in this case, as is at once apparent when one looks at the facts.

. . .

The judge said that he entirely accepted the 'value judgments' of the referee. He said:

> '[The tackle] was made in a reckless and dangerous manner not with malicious intent towards the plaintiff but in an "excitable manner without thought of the consequences."'

The judge's final conclusion is to be found in paragraph 13 of his judgment:

> 'It is not for me in this court to attempt to define exhaustively the duty of care between players in a soccer football game. Nor, in my judgment, is there any need because there was here such an obvious breach of the defendant's duty of care towards the plaintiff. He was clearly guilty, as I find the facts, of serious and dangerous foul play which showed a

> reckless disregard of the plaintiff's safety and which fell far below the standards which might reasonably be expected in anyone pursuing the game.'
>
> For my part I cannot see how that conclusion can be faulted on its facts, and on the law I do not see how it can possibly be said that the defendant was not negligent. Accordingly I would dismiss the appeal.

Condon makes plain that participants taking part in competitive sport owe a duty of care to all other participants. Importantly, whilst entertaining possible consideration of how implied sporting consent might modify a more generalised duty of care – on the assumption that sports participants impliedly consent to taking risks which otherwise would be a breach of the duty of care – the Court of Appeal ultimately shows preference for the recognition of a general standard of care (reasonableness) incumbent upon all participants in sport.[17] Crucially, this standard of care takes full account of the specific (sporting) circumstances. In setting out this legal test for negligence in competitive sport for co-participant liability, the court stipulates that this is an objective standard of reasonable care. Nonetheless, whilst broadly dismissing the possibility of variable standards of care reflective of the idiosyncrasies of individual defendants, the level of competition is acknowledged as a material aspect of the circumstances of sport, with Sir John Donaldson MR recognising that 'there will of course be a higher degree of care required of a player in a First Division football match than of a player in a local league football match'.[18] Interestingly, in emphasising the obvious breach of duty by the defendant in *Condon*, reference is made to dangerous foul play amounting to a reckless disregard of the claimant's safety. In the particular circumstances of this Leamington local league football match, such foul play fell far below the standards reasonably expected of players. Moreover, whilst breaking the rules, conventions or customs of a game would be a necessary consideration when establishing the negligence liability of participants in competitive sporting activities, it is by no means determinative and may actually be of little or no weight in the prevailing circumstances.

Condon has been criticised by Anderson for providing very limited and somewhat contradictory guidance in respect of defining the duty of care owed by participants to co-participants during competitive sporting activities.[19] In particular, acceptance of alternative formulations of the required standard of care as submitted by Barwick CJ and Kitto J in *Rootes v Shelton*, with the associated acknowledgement

---

17 This is, of course, in line with Lord Atkin's approach in *Donoghue v Stevenson* [1932] AC 562. See further, Chapters 1 and 2.
18 *Condon* (n 15) 454.
19 Anderson (n 5) 230.

that implied sporting consent could modify a more generalised duty of care, proved problematic in later cases until further clarification was provided by the Court of Appeal in the next case to be examined, *Caldwell v Maguire*.[20] By adding issues of consent into the definition of the duty owed by sports participants, and conflating standard of care and duty of care considerations, as argued by James, many of the sports negligence cases reported between 1985 and 2001 appear to be of limited legal value.[21] Nonetheless, the Court of Appeal's reliance in *Condon* on the Australian decision of *Rootes*, a case not directly involving the duty of care of a participant in sport but rather that of the driver of a towing boat for a waterskier, signifies the potentially wide application of legal principles derived from analogous and persuasive authority in this area.[22]

Caldwell v Maguire [2001] EWCA Civ 1054

The most recent decision of an appellate court in England and Wales concerning sports negligence generally, and the liability of sports participants in particular, is *Caldwell v Maguire*. In providing much-needed clarification to this area of sports law, *Caldwell* is undoubtedly one of the leading authorities in sports negligence jurisprudence. The facts of *Caldwell* concerned a serious injury suffered by a professional jockey whilst riding Fion Corn in a two-mile novice hurdle race at Hexham in September 1994. The accident occurred following an incident which obstructed and brought down Fion Corn, with the claimant jockey sustaining serious injury as a result. A stewards inquiry following the race found the two fellow jockeys guilty of careless riding. At first instance, Holland J dismissed the injured jockey's claim for personal injuries against these two fellow professional jockeys riding in the same race. The appeal was heard by the Court of Appeal in June 2001.

Court of Appeal, Lord Justice Tuckey (Giving the first judgment. Lord Woolf CJ agreed with the judgments of both Tuckey and Judge LJJ)

3. It was common ground that participants in competitive sport owe one another a duty of care. The appellant's complaint is that the judge set the standard of care too low; that he effectively required proof of deliberate or reckless disregard for safety. If he had applied the correct standard, in any event, he would or should have found that the respondents were negligent.

...

---

20 *Caldwell* (n 4).
21 James (n 14) 79. Although such cases remain of considerable factual interest.
22 See for instance, *Blake* (n 2).

Duty of care in the context of sport 103

11. As to the law, the judge said that the "primary guidance" for him must come from the Court of Appeal. He noted that this court had never had to consider an entirely similar situation, but had considered analogous situations in five cases, which he reviewed. From these cases he extracted five propositions:

'[1] Each Contestant in a lawful sporting contest (and in particular a race) owes a duty of care to each and all other contestants.
[2] That duty is to exercise in the course of the contest all care that is objectively reasonable in the prevailing circumstances for the avoidance of infliction of injury to such fellow contestants.
[3] The prevailing circumstances are all such properly attendant upon the contest and include its object, the demands inevitably made upon its contestants, its inherent dangers (if any), its rules, conventions and customs, and the standards, skills and judgment reasonably to be expected of a contestant. Thus in the particular case of a horse race the prevailing circumstances will include the contestant's obligation to ride a horse over a given course competing with the remaining contestants for the best possible placing, if not for a win. Such must further include the Rules of Racing and the standards, skills and judgment of a professional jockey, all as expected by fellow contestants.
[4] Given the nature of such prevailing circumstances the threshold for liability is in practice inevitably high; the proof of a breach of duty will not flow from proof of no more than an error of judgment or from mere proof of a momentary lapse in skill (and thus care) respectively when subject to the stresses of a race. Such are no more than incidents inherent in the nature of the sport.
[5] In practice it may therefore be difficult to prove any such breach of duty absent proof of conduct that in point of fact amounts to reckless disregard for the fellow contestant's safety. I emphasise the distinction between the expression of legal principle and the practicalities of the evidential burden.'

12. The judge then expressed his conclusions as follows:

'Each Defendant was guilty of lapses of care in their riding of their respective mounts away from the second last hurdle so as to contribute to the premature curtailment of the inside line otherwise to be followed by Royal Citizen – and thus so as to contribute to the Claimant's accident . . .

However, in neither instance was the lack of care, when evaluated in the circumstances prevailing in this horse race, of sufficient magnitude to constitute a breach of the duty of care respectively owed to the Claimant, that is to surmount the threshold for liability. . . . As I would evaluate the situation, all three jockeys were guilty of lapses of errors that must be an inevitable concomitant of adrenalin fuelled high speed racing with victory still a prospect. Turn back to the experts: in my judgment they did nothing to disabuse me of such evaluation of the significance of the identified lack of care.... We are a long way from the sort of conduct that triggers a response from the Courts as well as from the Stewards.'

...

17. Surprisingly, the court in Condon were not referred to three earlier Court of Appeal cases. The first two, Wooldridge v Sumner [1963] 2 QB 43, and Wilks v Cheltenham Homeguard Motor Cycle and Light Car Club [1971] 1 WLR 668, were spectator cases where the claimants were at a horse show (in Wooldridge) and a motorcycle scramble (in Wilks).

...

19. In the third case, Harrison v Vincent [1982] RTR 8, a sidecar passenger sued the motorcycle rider for injuries sustained during a race when he was unable to stop because he missed his gear and his brakes failed at the same time....

20. The last, and the most important of the cases considered by Holland J, is Smoldon v Whitworth (1997) ELR 249.[23]. ... Lord Bingham CJ, giving the judgment of the court, recorded that the defendant had invited the judge to say that nothing short of reckless disregard for the claimant's safety would suffice to establish a breach of the duty which the referee admittedly owed to the player. The judge, however, had adopted the test proposed by the claimant derived from Condon that the duty was to exercise such degree of care as was appropriate in all the circumstances. The court said that the judge was right to accept the plaintiff's approach....

21. The relevant principles to be applied to a case of this kind emerge clearly from the decision of this court in Condon and Smoldon, which are binding on us.

...

23. In his fourth and fifth propositions, the judge made it clear that he was referring to "the practicalities" of the evidential burden and not to legal principle. All he was saying was that, in practice, given the circumstances which he had identified, the threshold for liability was high.... The judge did not say that a claimant has to establish recklessness. That approach was specifically rejected by this court in Smoldon.

...

28. In such circumstances it is not possible to characterise momentary carelessness as negligence.... The Jockey Club's rules and its findings are of course relevant matters to be taken into account, but, as the authorities make clear, the finding that the respondents were guilty of careless riding is not

---

23 Discussed later.

determinative of negligence. As the judge said, there is a difference between response by the regulatory authority and response by the courts in the shape of a finding of legal liability.

29. I would dismiss this appeal. . . .

Lord Justice Judge

30. I agree. In an action for damages by one participant in a sporting contest against another participant in the same game or event, the issue of negligence cannot be resolved in a vacuum. It is fact specific.

. . .

34. I agree with Tuckey LJ's analysis of the legal principles. I would, however, emphasise two particular points. First, it is clear from the authorities that a finding that a jockey has ridden his horse in breach of the rules of racing does not decide the issue of liability in negligence.

. . .

37. Second, in the context of sporting contests it is also right to emphasise the distinction to be drawn between conduct which is properly to be characterised as negligent, and thus sounding in damages, and errors of judgment, oversights or lapses of attention of which any reasonable jockey may be guilty in the hurly burly of a race.

. . .

40. [Smoldon v Whitworth] involved an action against a referee. Referees have specific responsibility for the safety of the participants in the sport. . . . [A] referee would be entitled to escape liability in negligence for what was no more than oversight or error of judgment. It seems to me to follow that a participant who has caused injury to another participant in the same game or contest should be similarly entitled.

At first instance, Holland J's primary guidance had been provided by five analogous cases considered in this chapter: *Wooldridge*; *Wilks*; *Harrison*; *Condon* and (considered next) *Smoldon v Whitworth*.[24] In reviewing these decisions, the five propositions identified by Holland J, and cited with approval by the Court of Appeal, are of significant practical utility when defining the standard of care of defendants in all spheres of sports negligence. In addition to reiterating that sports participants owe a duty of care to each and all other competitors, the second proposition from *Caldwell* makes plain that the duty is to exercise objectively reasonable

---

24 *Smoldon v Whitworth* [1997] PIQR P133. This was regarded by the Court of Appeal as the most important of the cases reviewed.

care in the prevailing circumstances. This clarifies the possible confusion created by *Condon* discussed earlier.

However, without more, and as argued in Chapter 2, 'reasonableness' is a vague and elusive notion of limited meaningful application when defining the standard of care required in the prevailing circumstances of sport. This is where Holland J should be afforded much credit when at first instance he identified that the prevailing circumstances in cases of sports negligence include '[the sporting activity's] object, the demands inevitably made upon its contestants, its inherent dangers (if any), its rules, conventions and customs, and the standards, skills and judgment reasonably to be expected of a contestant'.[25] Crucially, this third proposition, by identifying the indicative criteria constituting the prevalent circumstances and enabling reasonableness to be defined, essentially formulates the legal test to be applied for injury caused by fellow competitors. More generally, by endorsing this approach, the Court of Appeal in *Caldwell* would appear to implicitly encourage the identification of specific guidelines that may be of assistance in the disposal of subsequent sports negligence cases.[26]

Furthermore, the fourth and fifth propositions succinctly expressed in *Caldwell* develop and refine the principles initially derived from *Wooldridge* when determining conduct that would amount to a breach of duty in the particular circumstances. Firstly, the fourth proposition recognises that in a fast-moving contest it is most unlikely that an error of judgement or momentary lapse in skill, by a competitor focused on winning, will be (sufficient) proof of a breach of duty – the threshold for liability is inevitably high – and these are to be regarded as mere incidents in the nature of sport. Simply applied, in this instance, momentary carelessness did not equate to negligence. Secondly, the final proposition submitted in *Caldwell* forcefully emphasises that a reckless disregard standard may be instructive when determining whether the evidential threshold of breach may have been crossed. Crucially, however, reference to reckless disregard in no way introduces a novel element into the law of negligence that is uniquely applicable in sports negligence cases. Put bluntly, there is no requirement in sports negligence cases for the claimant to establish recklessness. The legal test remains ordinary negligence in all the circumstances. Before concluding this section's analysis of the negligence liability of participants, a final important point from *Caldwell* which is explicitly mentioned by Lords Justices Tuckey and Judge, and an issue that the authorities make clear, is that a breach of the rules of the sport in question (i.e., a breach of The Jockey Club's rules due to careless riding) is by no means determinative of negligence liability.

Duty of care owed by referees to participants

When approving the five propositions integral to the legal test for a co-participant's liability identified by Holland J in *Caldwell*, Tuckey LJ regarded *Smoldon v Whitworth*

---

25 *Caldwell* (n 4) [11].
26 M James and D McArdle, 'Player violence, or violent players? Vicarious liability for sports participants' (2004) 12(3) *Tort Law Review* 131, 145.

as the most important of the analogous Court of Appeal authorities referred to for 'primary guidance' by the judge. In *Wooldridge*, another one of the cases referred to for primary guidance, Sellers LJ recognised the 'special relationship' between a spectator and a competitor and that this 'different relationship involves its own standard of care'. Both of these points, reasoning by analogy and the special relationship between claimant and defendant, represent central tenets when defining the duty of care owed by coaches to athletes. With this in mind, and having examined the general foundations of sports negligence jurisprudence in the UK, the legal principles highlighted above are brought into sharper focus and relevance by critical consideration of the analogous duty of care incumbent upon referees. As with sports coaches, given the functions of referees likewise often involve issues relating to player safety, the analogy between referee and coach is in many respects contended to be a particularly strong and instructive one. To date, the Court of Appeal has considered three cases concerning the negligence liability of referees, two of which are of the utmost relevance to the development of the legal principles fashioned in the context of sports negligence, *Smoldon v Whitworth* and *Vowles v Evans*.[27]

Smoldon v Whitworth & Nolan [1997] PIQR P133 (CA)

In *Smoldon v Whitworth*, the 17-year-old plaintiff was catastrophically injured during a rugby union match between Burton Colts and Sutton Coldfield Colts in October 1991. As the plaintiff was playing hooker, the scrum collapsed and his neck was broken. The initial claim brought by the plaintiff was against the first defendant, a member of the opposing team, and against the second defendant, the referee. At first instance, Curtis J dismissed the claim against the opposing player (for which there was no appeal) but found the referee liable in negligence. The judge held that: (i) the referee had not enforced safety requirements set out in the Laws of the Game requiring front rows to engage in a crouch – touch – pause – engage sequence and containing special provisions relating to players aged under 19; (ii) the number of collapsed scrums was approximately three or four times that ordinarily experienced in such a game; and (iii) as a consequence of the referee's failure to instruct the front rows adequately, and insist upon the crouch – touch – pause – engage sequence, the relevant scrum collapse and the consequential injuries suffered by the plaintiff were a result of a breach of the duty of care required of the referee. On appeal, counsel for the referee argued that the judge had incorrectly

---

27 *Smoldon* (n 24); *Vowles v Evans* [2003] EWCA Civ 318. The third case heard by the Court of Appeal is *Allport v Wilbraham* [2004] EWCA Civ 1668. It was accepted in *Allport* that if the referee had failed to call 'engage', as required by Law 20 of the then laws of the game, or had done so when the prop forwards were not properly engaged, this would have amounted to a breach of duty of care (at [11]). Such a failure would have resulted in an inadequate enforcement of the laws of the game designed to ensure safe and controlled scrummaging (at [4]). On the facts, that was not found to be the case. Moreover, this case offers little by way of defining the duty of care and turned on the credibility of the claimant's witnesses.

formulated the referee's duty of care. It was submitted that although a duty of care was owed to the plaintiff, that this duty would only be breached in circumstances where the referee had shown deliberate or reckless disregard for the plaintiff's safety. The Court of Appeal acknowledged that this appeared to be the first reported case in which a rugby player had sued a referee in negligence.

Court of Appeal, The Lord Chief Justice, delivering the judgment of the Court, 138–147:

The second defendant's [referee's] pleading was founded on observations of Sellers and Diplock L.JJ. in Wooldridge v. Sumner.[28]

. . .

The second defendant accepted that he owed a duty to the plaintiff, so that there was no issue whether any duty of care arose at all or whether any such duty was owed to the plaintiff. . . . The second defendant feared that if the test proposed by the plaintiff and upheld by the judge were held to be correct, the threshold of liability would be too low and those in the position of the second defendant would be too vulnerable to suits by injured players. We do not accept this fear as well-founded. The level of care required is that which is appropriate in all the circumstances, and the circumstances are of crucial importance. Full account must be taken of the factual context in which a referee exercises his functions, and he could not be properly held liable for errors of judgment, oversights or lapses of which any referee might be guilty in the context of a fast-moving and vigorous contest. The threshold of liability is a high one. It will not easily be crossed.

The position of a referee vis-à-vis the players is not the same as that of a participant in a contest vis-à-vis a spectator. One of his responsibilities is to safeguard the safety of the players. So although the legal duty is the same in the two cases, the practical content of the duty differs according to the quite different circumstances.

There was a narrow argument concerning the level of skill required of a referee such as the second defendant. In the second defendant's submission the court should consider whether he had fallen below the level of skill reasonably to be expected of a referee of his grade refereeing an Under 19 Colts match in October 1991. The plaintiff submitted that the level of skill required was determined by the function a referee was performing and not by his grade: accordingly, it was suggested that the level of skill required was that reasonably to

---

28 Discussed above.

be expected of a referee refereeing an Under 19 Colts match in October 1991, irrespective of the grade of the referee. In the present case, this difference of approach is academic, since the grade which the second defendant held (C1) was entirely appropriate to the match which he was refereeing. This is not a case of a referee taking charge of a match above his professed level of competence. We prefer the plaintiff's formulation, but we do not think it matters.

There can be no doubt that the scrummaging rules set out earlier were designed to minimise the risk of spinal injuries caused in collapsing scrums, this being a risk of which those managing or coaching rugby teams or refereeing or playing in matches were by October 1991 well aware. It is accepted that the second defendant owed the plaintiff a duty of care and skill. It is further accepted that serious spinal injury was a foreseeable consequence of a collapse of the scrum and of failure to prevent collapse of the scrum. If the second defendant was properly found to be in breach of his duty of care owed to the plaintiff by failing to take appropriate steps to prevent a collapse of the scrum, and if as a result of his failure a scrum did collapse and a player such as the plaintiff thereby suffered spinal injuries of the kind which the rules were designed to prevent, then in our judgment the second defendant would be liable in law for that foreseeable result of his breach of duty, despite the fact that (quantified statistically) it was a result which was very unlikely to eventuate. . . .

145–47:

5. Reports of Other Matches

The judge placed no reliance on reports of the second defendant's refereeing of other matches, most of which were favourable but one of which was critical of his failure to control the scrummaging. The second defendant accepted that such reports would be unhelpful if the complaint in this case were of a momentary lapse or failure, but submitted that since the complaint was of an overall failure to control the match and impose his authority it was relevant to take account of other matches in which he was reported to have shown proper control and authority. In our judgment the trial judge was entitled to take the view he did. The evidence was that this was the first Under 19 match which the second defendant had refereed since new rule changes had come into force. The judge was in our opinion right to concentrate his attention on the evidence of what heppened (sic) during this match, and to regard evidence of what had happened in other matches as unhelpful.

. . .

The judge was at pains to emphasise that his judgment in favour of the plaintiff was reached on the very special facts of this case, having regard in

> particular to the rule designed to afford protection to players aged under 19 and to the evidence that the number of collapsed scrums which were permitted to occur in the course of this match was well in excess of what any informed observer considered to be acceptable. He did not intend to open the door to a plethora of claims by players against referees, and it would be deplorable if that were the result. In our view that result should not follow provided all concerned appreciate how difficult it is for any plaintiff to establish that a referee failed to exercise such care and skill as was reasonably to be expected in the circumstances of a hotly-contested game of rugby football. . . .
> We would dismiss this appeal.

The weight afforded to *Smoldon* in the later decision of *Caldwell* (discussed earlier) makes plain that this is another leading authority in sports negligence jurisprudence. On closer analysis, it is suggested that *Smoldon* addresses six points worthy of particular mention and that prove highly instructive, especially when conducting a detailed assessment of the special features of sports negligence cases in order to define the duty of care owed. First, and by no means an entirely settled issue of law in 1997, it was accepted that the referee owed a duty of care to the 17-year-old Burton Colts plaintiff. Interestingly, and in contrast to the suggestion made in *Wooldridge*, where in the particular circumstances the duty owed was regarded as a duty of care and not skill, Lord Bingham CJ framed the duty incumbent upon the referee as a 'duty of care and skill'. Since one of the responsibilities of referees is to safeguard the safety of the players, this speaks to the special skill required of referees (and coaches) when doing so,[29] and is integral to the specific relationship between referee and player (and coach and athlete). It is contended that this distinction is significant and provides a more accurate representation of the duty required. Consequently, approaching the duty owed as a duty of care *and* skill better articulates the correct legal test when identifying the standard of care to be applied since requisite specialist skill is most likely to be a key circumstantial consideration. In other words, for reasonable care in all the circumstances to be defined, the specialist functions of the referee must be recognised.

The second point of interest, whereby the court calls for scrutiny of the full factual matrix in sports negligence cases, provides an endorsement of earlier judicial decisions where the view was expressed that errors of judgement or lapses of skill, in the context of fast-moving competitive sport, would not support a finding of breach of duty. By taking full account of the prevailing circumstances of the competitive sporting activity, and concomitantly regarding the threshold of liability as being a high one, the Court of Appeal in *Smoldon* dismissed the

---

29 See further, Chapter 3.

referee's submission that a standard of care premised on the ordinary law of negligence's liability threshold of reasonable care in all the circumstances was too low. Consequently, the suggestion that a finding of deliberate or reckless disregard of the plaintiff's safety should be a requirement in order for breach to be established is conclusively rejected by the court. This is underpinned by Lord Bingham CJ's crucial recognition that the threshold of liability would not easily be crossed.

In further extending the necessary detailed judicial examination of the specific context, the third point to be noted, and fundamental when attempting to define the content of the duty of care owed, was appreciation of the different/unique relationships found in various sporting situations. Put simply, and consistent with previous Court of Appeal reasoning in *Wooldridge* and *Wilks*, the practical content of the duty of care required must be reflective of the particular relationship involved (i.e., competitor and spectator; participant and co-participant; referee and player; coach and athlete). This key distinction was enunciated in *Smoldon* as follows:

> The position of a referee vis-à-vis the players is not the same as that of a participant in a contest vis-à-vis a spectator. One of his responsibilities is to safeguard the safety of the players. So although the legal duty is the same in the two cases, the practical content of the duty differs according to the quite different circumstances.

So clearly, and in looking ahead to the next chapter, the special relationship between a coach and athlete will demand the nature of the duty of care required of coaches to be more precisely defined, according to the quite different circumstances and more nuanced interdependent relationship between coach and athlete.

A fourth point of interest, and an issue revisited in the later decision of *Vowles v Evans*, was the narrow argument concerning the level of skill required of a referee. As will be argued, following subsequent analysis of the reasoning in *Vowles*, the Court of Appeal's preference in *Smoldon*, that the level of skill required should be determined by the function a referee was performing and not by her/his level of qualification, appears the correct approach.[30]

A further contested issue in *Smoldon* concerns the submission by counsel for the defendant referee that it was relevant to take account of other matches in which the referee was reported to have shown proper control and authority. At first instance, Curtis J placed no reliance on such reports. The Court of Appeal found that the judge was right to concentrate his attention on the evidence of what happened during the match in question and that it would have been unhelpful to have regard to evidence of what had happened in other matches. However, in light of the recent enactment of the Social Action, Responsibility and Heroism (SARAH) Act 2015 discussed in Chapter 2, and though still uncertain, providing evidence

---

30 Also see, N Partington, '"It's just not cricket". Or is it? *Bartlett v English Cricket Board Association of Cricket Officials*' (2016) 32(1) *Professional Negligence* 75.

of the defendant adopting a predominantly responsible approach when refereeing (or coaching) may be of some future relevance in sports negligence cases by affording defendants another statutory tool to call in assistance in support of their case.[31] Section 3 of the SARAH Act 2015 states that the court 'must have regard to whether the person, in carrying out the activity in the course of which the alleged negligence or breach of statutory duty occurred, demonstrated a predominantly responsible approach towards protecting the safety or other interests of others'. Despite being expressly invited to do so in *Smoldon*, and with this not being a mandatory requirement in 1997, this appears to be precisely what the Court of Appeal declined to do. Since it is contended that now requiring the court to have regard to whether the person sued demonstrated a predominantly responsible approach towards protecting the safety of others represents an actual (albeit 'modest') change in the law,[32] it will be interesting to follow related developments regarding the potential impact of the SARAH Act 2015 in this field. Nonetheless, whilst arguably better safeguarding persons functioning in connection with desirable activities, the SARAH Act appears to essentially duplicate a predominant benefit of section 1 of the Compensation Act 2006,[33] namely, concentrating the court's reasoning on wider aspects of the defendant's conduct. Indeed, since section 3 will not change the court's overall approach,[34] it seems difficult to establish how 'it may be the case that the requirement to consider this wider context will change the court's analysis'.[35] Although curiously, since the Government when introducing the SARAH Bill stated that it would welcome if the court's consideration of the Act's provisions tipped the balance in favour of a defendant in a finely balanced case,[36] defendant referees and sports coaches may perhaps potentially avail of this statutory provision.

A final and related issue of relevance, and which was directly and robustly addressed in both the High Court and Court of Appeal, was an acute awareness of the potential chilling effect of legal liability on volunteering in amateur sport, regarding it as 'deplorable if that were the result'. On this point, the Court of Appeal contended that the ordinary law of negligence's control mechanism of breach, when fully reflective of all of the relevant circumstances of competitive sport, afforded sufficient protection and reassurance to volunteers performing a socially desirable activity. In supporting this view, Caddell has suggested that:

> the test for breach of this duty has been sufficiently well formulated to discourage frivolous litigation, and claims for injuries sustained in circumstances

---

31 Reference to 'generally complimentary or very complimentary' match observation reports, and other evidence indicative of a predominantly responsible approach adopted by a rugby football referee, was also mentioned at first instance in *Vowles v Evans* [2002] EWHC 2612 [55]-[58].
32 Hansard HL vol 756 col 1573, (4 November 2014) (Lord Faulks).
33 Discussed in Chapter 2.
34 Explanatory Notes to the Social Action, Responsibility and Heroism Act 2015, [5].
35 Ministry of Justice, Social Action, Responsibility and Heroism Bill: European Convention on Human Rights memorandum (13 June 2014), [7].
36 Hansard (n 32).

over which it is near impossible for even the most diligent referee to have exercised any degree of preventative control will rightly be rejected. ... Such an 'arm's length' approach to liability should not pose any major disincentive for volunteers to come forward to act as match officials, while ensuring that dangerously substandard refereeing will attract the appropriate civil sanctions, given the serious injuries that may occur as a result.[37]

Clearly, in the circumstances of a fast-moving and vigorous contest, establishing liability in negligence of a referee is not easily satisfied by claimants and might necessarily constitute a high liability threshold that will not easily be crossed, a contended 'near impossible' finding of negligence liability in typical circumstances and 'dangerously substandard' refereeing. These pronounced legal and evidential parameters are potentially intensified by statutory provisions that might be regarded as tacitly inviting courts to raise the breach barrier. However, reassuring as these pronouncements may appear, *Bartlett v English Cricket Board Association of Cricket Officials*[38] provides a stark reminder that volunteer officials remain exposed to alleged negligence liability. Indeed, shortly after the Court of Appeal judgment in *Smoldon*, Opie insightfully and convincingly articulated that:

> [w]hile there is probably little prospect of the courts being flooded with claims against referees in the immediate future, one wonders whether the Court of Appeal is deluding itself to some degree in saying that protection will be provided by the difficulty in establishing breach. Reference need only be made to the standards today required of drivers, manufacturers, doctors and employers to realise that what was initially seen as limited scope for liability became much greater over time once placed on negligence's slippery slope.[39]

A number of these important themes evident in *Smoldon* were revisited some six years later by the Court of Appeal in *Vowles v Evans*.

Vowles v Evans [2003] EWCA Civ 318

Vowles v Evans concerned another claim by a seriously injured player against a rugby union referee. As in *Smoldon*, the injured claimant was playing hooker. It was during an amateur Rugby Football Club 2nd XV local Derby match between Llanharan and Tondu in January 1998, and following injury to a teammate of the claimant,

---

37 R Caddell, 'The Referee's Liability for Catastrophic Sports Injuries – A UK Perspective' (2005) 15 *Marq. Sports L. Rev.* 415, 424.
38 *Bartlett v English Cricket Board Association of Cricket Officials*, County Court (Birmingham), 27 August 2015.
39 H Opie, 'Referee Liability in Sport: Negligent Rule Enforcement and Smoldon v Whitworth' (1997) 5 *Torts Law Journal* 1, 7.

that a loose head prop from Llanharan had to leave the field. The referee was made aware that there was no trained or experienced front row forward available as a replacement. The referee informed the Llanharan captain that they could chose to either provide a replacement from within the scrum or, if they wished, choose non-contestable scrummages from that stage of the match. The leader of the Llanharan pack, having previously played as a front row forward occasionally a few years earlier and, at a lower level, said that he would 'give it a go'. The referee agreed to this course of action without enquiring about the previous experience of the replacement. The game proceeded until injury time when Tondu were aiming for a 'push-over' try to clinch victory. Following a problem as the two sets of forwards sought to engage, the claimant collapsed having suffered a serious injury. Since the amateur referee had been appointed by the Welsh Rugby Union Limited (WRU), they accepted that they would be liable under the principle of vicarious liability for a possible breach of duty by the first defendant referee. In the High Court, Morland J gave judgment in favour of the injured player and against the referee and the WRU. The referee and WRU, as appellants, challenged the findings of the High Court.

Court of Appeal, Lord Phillips MR, delivering the judgment of the Court:

The Laws of the Game

9. The match was being played under the 1997 version of the 'Laws of the Game', as issued by the Council of the International Rugby Football Board.

. . . .

[LAW 3] (12) In the event of a front row forward being ordered off, the referee, in the interests of safety, will confer with the captain of his team to determine whether another player is suitably trained/experienced to take his position; if not the captain shall nominate one other forward to leave the playing area and the referee will permit a substitute front row forward to replace him. This may take place immediately or after another player has been tried in the position

When there is no other front row forward available due to a sequence of players ordered off or injured or both, then the game will continue with non contestable scrummages which are the same as normal scrummages except that:

- there is no contest for the ball
- the team putting in the ball must win it
- neither team is permitted to push

. . .

13. Mr Leighton Williams submitted that, if referees are to be potentially liable in negligence for injuries to players, the supply of those prepared to referee without reward will be in danger of drying up. It is, he submitted, in the public interest that amateur referees should be prepared to referee amateur sports. It is not fair, just or reasonable to expose those prepared to offer their services for nothing to the risk of ruinous legal liability.

...

Was there a duty of care?

25. Rugby football is an inherently dangerous sport. Some of the rules are specifically designed to minimise the inherent dangers. Players are dependant for their safety on the due enforcement of the rules. The role of the referee is to enforce the rules. Where a referee undertakes to perform that role, it seems to us manifestly fair, just and reasonable that the players should be entitled to rely upon the referee to exercise reasonable care in so doing. Rarely if ever does the law absolve from any obligation of care a person whose acts or omissions are manifestly capable of causing physical harm to others in a structured relationship into which they have entered. Mr Leighton Williams has failed to persuade us that there are good reasons for treating rugby football as an exceptional case. A referee of a game of rugby football owes a duty of care to the players.

The standard of care

26. The standard of care to be expected of a referee must depend upon all the circumstances of the case. One of those circumstances is the nature of the game. As Lord Bingham CJ observed in Smoldon, a referee of a fast moving game cannot reasonably be expected to avoid errors of judgment, oversights or lapses. The threshold of liability must properly be a high one.

27. In Smoldon there was inconclusive discussion as to whether the level of skill to be expected of a referee depended upon the grade of the referee, or upon the grade of match he was refereeing. The answer to that question did not matter in that case, nor do we think that it matters in this. In Bolam v Friern Hospital Management Committee [1957] 1 WLR 582 at p. 586 McNair J., in addressing a jury in a clinical negligence action, made a statement of the law which has since been applied repeatedly to any situation in which a person undertakes a task which requires some special skill:

> '[W]here you get the situation which involves the use of some special skill or competence, then the test as to whether there has been negligence or not is not the test of the man on the top of the Clapham

omnibus, because he has not got this special skill. The test is the standard of the ordinary skilled man exercising and professing to have that special skill. A man need not possess the highest expert skill; it is well established law that it is sufficient if he exercises the ordinary skill of an ordinary competent man exercising that particular art.'

28. There is scope for argument as to the extent to which the degree of skill to be expected of a referee depends upon the grade of the referee or of the match that he has agreed to referee. In the course of argument it was pointed out that sometimes in the case of amateur sport, the referee fails to turn up, or is injured in the course of the game, and a volunteer referee is called for from the spectators. In such circumstances the volunteer cannot reasonably be expected to show the skill of one who holds himself out as referee, or perhaps even to be fully conversant with the Laws of the Game. That, however, is not this case. . . . [The referee's] qualifications were appropriate for the 2nd Division game that he was refereeing. He could reasonably be expected to be conversant with the Laws of the Game and competent to enforce them. The allegations of breach of duty made against him do not involve any higher standard of skill than this basic competence.

Breach of duty

29. The issue in relation to breach of duty was and is whether Mr Evans negligently failed to comply with the requirements of Law 3(12).

. . .

37. The contemporary evidence in Mr Evans' reports does not suggest that he satisfied himself that [CJ] was suitably trained/experienced to be tried in the front row, whatever the precise nature of that training/experience might be. On the contrary, that evidence indicates that Mr Evans left it to the Llanharan captain to elect whether to proceed with non-contestable scrummages or to try out his flanker as a front row prop. On no reading of the Law was it proper to offer him that option. We consider that the Judge rightly found that Mr Evans abdicated the responsibility which was his of deciding whether the situation had been reached where it was mandatory to insist upon non-contestable scrummages. This constituted a breach of his duty to exercise reasonable care for the safety of the players.

38. We stress that in reaching that conclusion we have well in mind that . . . this is a case in which the decision of the referee, which has been under scrutiny and which we have concluded amounted to a breach of duty, was taken while play was stopped and there was time to give considered thought to it. Very different considerations would be likely to apply in a case in which it was alleged that the referee was negligent because of a decision made during play.

. . .

48. To a greater or lesser degree, all the evidence showed that problems were experienced with the set scrum after [CJ] entered the front row which had not been experienced before, at least to the same degree. In the last set scrum of the game, the evidence suggests that the Llanharan front row failed to crouch and engage as a synchronised unit. Mr Vowles' accident resulted. There was, in our judgment, evidence upon which the Judge could properly conclude that the cause of this accident was that Mr Evans had, in breach of the Laws of the Game and negligently, permitted a player who lacked the suitable training and experience to play in the Llanharan front row. Accordingly we have concluded that this appeal must be dismissed.

Postscript

49. Mr Leighton Williams suggested that, if we upheld the Judge's finding that an amateur referee owed a duty of care to the players under his charge, volunteers would no longer be prepared to serve as referees. We do not believe that this result will, or should, follow. Liability has been established in this case because the injury resulted from a failure to implement a Law designed to minimise the risk of just the kind of accident which subsequently occurred. We believe that such a failure is itself likely to be very rare. Much rarer will be the case where there are grounds for alleging that it has caused a serious injury. Serious injuries are happily rare, but they are an inherent risk of the game. That risk is one which those who play rugby believe is worth taking, having regard to the satisfaction that they get from the game. We would not expect the much more remote risk of facing a claim in negligence to discourage those who take their pleasure in the game by acting as referees.

The Court of Appeal in *Vowles* had little difficulty in ruling that a referee of a game of rugby owes a duty of care to the players, not least since the role of the referee is to enforce the rules of the game, including those designed to protect the safety of players. Following *Wooldridge*, *Condon*, and the direct authority of *Smoldon* (albeit involving a Colts rugby match), this seems indisputable. Accordingly, perhaps the more interesting and instructive guidance provided by *Vowles* is in relation to defining this duty of care or, the standard of care required in the particular circumstances. With regard to the standard of care expected, *Vowles* approves and applies the approach adopted in *Smoldon*: reasonable care and skill in all the circumstances, with a corresponding high threshold of negligence liability for a finding of breach during play. Put simply, during a competitive and vigorous sporting contest, referees might reasonably be expected to make errors of judgement, have oversights or lapses in skill.

Significantly, whilst recognising that the duty owed is one of care and skill as per *Smoldon*, *Vowles* offers more explicit guidance when attempts are made to establish the level of skill to be expected of referees. In referring to the *Bolam* test, discussed in detail in the previous chapter, the court acknowledged that the functions of a rugby referee require some special skill. Accordingly, the level of skill required, and as informed by the legal principles derived from the field of professional negligence, was the ordinary skill of an ordinarily competent rugby referee exercising the required functions of a rugby referee in the prevailing circumstances. This extension of the reasoning of the same court in *Smoldon*, making plain that this represents an instance of professional liability, provides valuable clarity to instances of sports negligence. Indeed, and as revealed by this chapter's analysis of the relevant case law, developments in sports negligence jurisprudence have seen incremental refinement by the judiciary when tasked with defining the duty of care owed by different defendants in the context of sport. So whilst recognising that the precise content of the duty will be reflective of the special relationship between the claimant and the defendant, for example, referee–player, there now appears the development of established legal principles that are of more general application. For instance, recognition of a duty of care and not skill in *Wooldridge* was framed in *Smoldon* as a more nuanced duty of both care and skill. This was then further clarified and more fully articulated in *Vowles*, where it was explicitly regarded as a duty of care and special skill which is informed by the *Bolam* test. This presents important implications when defining the nature of the duty owed not only by referees but also by sports coaches, instructors and leaders.

Interestingly, the decision in *Vowles* toyed with going even further by revisiting what was regarded as an unresolved issue in *Smoldon*. That is, whether the level of skill to be expected of a referee depended upon the grade of the referee or upon the level of match s/he was refereeing.[40] It is suggested that the preferred approach identified in *Smoldon*, that the level of skill required should be determined by the function a referee has agreed to perform and not by her/his level of qualification, affords sufficient guidance to lower courts and practitioners. Accordingly, the correct approach when determining the degree of skill to be expected of a referee is to focus on the level of match being refereed and not upon the referee's grade. More problematically, though perhaps intended to provide reassurance to volunteers involved in the provision and delivery of sporting activities and address 'chilling effect' concerns raised by counsel for the appellants, the suggestion that a volunteer stepping in at short notice to referee cannot reasonably be expected to show the skill of one who holds themselves out as referee cannot be sustained. Simply applied, this submission by Lord Phillips appears to conceal the fact that an individual assuming a duty requiring the exercise of a special skill would be subject to the ordinary principles of the law of negligence if sued.[41] In short, an individual volunteering to step in at short notice to referee, in an effort to prevent cancellation of a fixture, is under a duty to do so properly. As such, should there be an alleged breach of duty by this same volunteer, this becomes an (albeit unusual) issue of professional liability.

40 *Vowles* (n 27) [28].
41 See Chapters 1 & 3.

In *Vowles*, the Court of Appeal stressed that scrutiny of the referee's decision, ultimately found to amount to a breach of duty, was taken during a stoppage in play. This enabled time for considered thought. Significantly, the judgment continued, '[v]ery different considerations would be likely to apply in a case in which it was alleged that the referee was negligent because of a decision made during play'.[42] This reasoning is consistent with *Harrison v Vincent*,[43] whereby a crucial distinction is made between the standard of care that might be required in the course of a race, game or competition, and the standard of care expected in the relative calm of the workshop. This distinction appears likely to be a material factor when determining the scope of a coach's duty of care given the differing contexts of practice sessions and competitive matches.

Having established the existence of a duty of care and the required standard of care, the Court of Appeal in *Vowles* deals straightforwardly with the issue of breach, since the referee failed to exercise reasonable care and skill for the safety of the players. Furthermore, in dismissing the referee's appeal, the court found that there was clear evidence for the conclusion that the referee's breach of duty caused the accident. Curiously, and somewhat unusually, the judgment concluded with a postscript which emphasised that a finding of negligence liability of referees will be rare and that this fact-specific decision should in no way discourage volunteers from being prepared to serve as referees. As previously mentioned, this echoes similar observations made by the same court in *Smoldon*. However, given the predominate reliance on amateur referees (and coaches) in sport,[44] and the emerging prospect of coaches/referees being sued for a breach of duty, as outlined in Chapter 2, the general tenor of the point raised by Mr Leighton Williams QC (counsel for the appellant referee in *Vowles*) still appears convincing when he stated: 'It is not fair, just or reasonable to expose those prepared to offer their services for nothing to the risk of ruinous legal liability'. More recently, in reiterating a further connected issue raised by Mr Williams, suggesting that the supply of volunteer referees will be in danger of drying up due to fears of legal liability, in *Bartlett v English Cricket Board Association of Cricket Officials*, the Senior Executive Officer called on behalf of the defendant highlighted that '[t]he amateur game is short of officials with many games not served by qualified officials and so those who officiate are to be treasured and not pilloried'.[45] Such issues, and in particular with regard to the education, training and development of coaches, in order to enable them to effectively discharge their duty of care, are considered more fully in the following chapters.

Conclusion

The courts in sports negligence cases in the UK, by taking full account of the prevailing circumstances, have fashioned a legal test for breach of duty with an

---

42 *Vowles* (n 27) [38]. See further, McArdle and James (n 10).
43 Discussed earlier.
44 See, for instance, P Tracey, 'Sports injury – should the referee be blamed?' (2000) 1 *JPI Law* 10.
45 *Bartlett* (n 38) [179].

intended generally high threshold. In the context of participants and referees exercising their duty of care in a fast moving and vigorous contest, this means that there should be no breach of duty for errors of judgement, oversights or lapses of skill. Indeed, in view of the propositions identified and approved in *Caldwell*, and following considerable development and refinement of the principles initially advanced in *Wooldridge*, this area of sports law now appears more settled. These legal principles derived from the cases discussed in this chapter provide the foundations and scaffolding used by the courts when defining the nature of the duty of care of defendants involved in sporting activities. Importantly, and as revealed in the following pages of this book, such principles remain of considerable relevance when determining the extent of a sports coach's duty of care. However, Lord Bingham in *Smoldon* insightfully emphasised that although the legal duty of reasonable care remains constant, the practical content of the duty owed (e.g., referee-player) differs according to quite different circumstances (e.g., versus participant-spectator as per *Wooldridge*). In the specific context of sports coaching, this involves a mutually dependent, or symbiotic relationship,[46] with coaches tasked with operating across an increasingly challenging range of performance levels and stages.[47] Moreover, and following *Harrison*, the circumstances in which coaches are practising, for instance, training sessions as compared with competitive matches, might also influence the nature of the duty of care owed. This reiterates a fundamental aspect of the intersection between sports coaching and the law of negligence – it is fact-specific. This raises difficult questions 'as to whether on the facts of any particular case there has been a breach of [that] duty'.[48] Accordingly, having examined the legal principles of general relevance to duty of care in sport inquiries, the following two chapters expose these to more precise, sustained and rigorous treatment by analysing the most pertinent emerging case law and the specific duties incumbent upon sports coaches.

---

46 See further, E Ryall and S Olivier, 'Ethical Issues in Coaching Dangerous Sports' in A Hardman and C Jones (eds), *The Ethics of Sports Coaching* (Abingdon, Routledge 2011) 187–88.
47 H Telfer, 'Coaching Practice and Practice Ethics' in J Lyle and C Cushion (eds), *Sports Coaching: Professionalisation and Practice* (Edinburgh, Elsevier 2010) 210.
48 *Blake* (n 2) [8].

5
DUTY OF CARE OF SPORTS COACHES

Introduction

General principles derived from the ordinary law of negligence are applied to the particular facts of individual sports negligence cases. Indeed, an understanding and appreciation of these established principles discussed in the previous chapters proves highly instructive when analysing the extent of the duty of care owed by coaches. Therefore, when defining more precisely the specific duties of sports coaches, consideration of established authority from the wider context of sport is often necessary, but given that the practical content of duties of care may differ according to the distinct duties involved (e.g., a referee's duty of care versus a coach's duty of care), a general awareness is by no means always sufficient or conclusive. The extremely fact-sensitive nature of coach negligence cases calls for robust and searching examination of the particular circumstances in which claims have been brought against coaches for a breach of duty. Accordingly, the aim of this chapter is to provide a detailed scrutiny of the duty of care required of modern sports coaches by engaging with the relevant jurisprudence in a sustained, informative and rigorous manner.

The cases discussed cover a range of sporting activities and performance levels, including the coaching of gymnastics, amateur rugby, professional football, hang gliding and paragliding, and elite level athletics and bobsleigh. There is also a case concerning a rugby football union coach-educator. As argued by Taylor and Garratt, there is often confusion and conceptual misunderstanding within the sports sector concerning terms such as coach, instructor, leader, teacher and so forth.[1]

---

1 B Taylor and D Garratt, 'The Professionalization of Sports Coaching: Definitions, Challenges and Critique' in J Lyle and C Cushion (eds), *Sports Coaching: Professionalisation and Practice* (Edinburgh, Elsevier 2010) 101.

Such definitions are likely to oversimplify the complex contextualised dynamics of coaching[2] which remains underpinned by a mutually dependent relationship.[3] Since this mutually dependent or symbiotic relationship is integral to a sports coach's, sports leader's and sports instructor's duty of care,[4] and not least given the core common functions of providing adequate instruction and supervision entailed with these roles, claims brought against sports leaders and instructors for negligence provide important analogous authority. Consequently, in addition to examining court decisions specifically listing coaches as defendants, the cases involving an alleged breach of duty by climbing guides, sports leaders and instructors, a fitness instructor and a mountain bike instructor deepen this chapter's critical analysis. Furthermore, in order to provide an original and engaging commentary, detailed extracts from these judgments are extensively cited and analysed in order to provide the reader with authentic and sustained insights that are both relevant and interesting.[5]

Context

When discharging their duty of care, sports coaches are under a legal duty to adopt objectively reasonable coaching practice, in the prevailing circumstances, so that athletes are reasonably safe and not exposed to unreasonable risk of personal injury. This duty involves taking all reasonable steps to minimise the dangers that athletes are exposed to, thereby ensuring that sporting activities are delivered as safely as is reasonably possible. Put simply, exposing athletes to unnecessary risk amounts to a breach of duty. In view of the specialist skill required of coaches, and consistent with the legal principles established in instances of professional negligence, the duty of care of coaches demands a standard of skill and care consistent with the ordinarily competent coach occupying the same role and/or coaching at the same level. As such, the duty of a coach is to adopt reasonable coaching practice so that reasonable care *and* skill is taken to ensure the reasonable safety of athletes and participants. However, and as previously argued, reliance on a touchstone of reasonableness offers only vague definitional parameters and provides limited guidance when defining the nature and extent of a coach's duty of care. It therefore proves necessary to define reasonableness more precisely in the specific context of sports coaching. Accordingly, although terminology making reference to specific duties may be regarded as technically misleading, since as highlighted in Chapter 2 the precise degree and scope of responsibilities owed by coaches more accurately

---

2 R Jones et al., *Sports Coaching Cultures: From Theory to Practice* (London, Routledge 2004) 1.
3 E Ryall and S Olivier, 'Ethical Issues in Coaching Dangerous Sports' in A Hardman and C Jones (eds), *The Ethics of Sports Coaching* (Abingdon, Routledge 2011) 187–88.
4 The cases discussed later reinforce this submission.
5 Throughout this chapter, the focus remains on defining the nature and practical content of the duty of care of modern sports coaches. To achieve this aim, it is imperative to concentrate on the conduct of defendants/coaches. Nonetheless, this is in no way intended to undermine or detract from the sometimes fatal and catastrophic injuries suffered by claimants/participants.

defines the standard of care, reference to the specific duties incumbent upon sports coaches provides an illuminating and helpful conceptual framework by which the legal duty of care of coaches can be clarified, unpacked and analysed. Indeed, *Clerk and Lindsell on Torts* recognises that formulating the standard of care in terms of a particular duty can be useful in a descriptive way.[6] Therefore, and in contrast to the case law analysis provided in the previous chapter which concentrated on different classes of plaintiff(s)/claimant(s) and defendant(s), the following critical discussion provides a searching and sustained examination of the specific duties required of coaches by providing a more thematic approach.

The specific duties of care of coaches have evolved,[7] previous academic commentary suggesting that coaches are required to discharge responsibilities that may be classified under three main headings: facilities and organisation; instruction and supervision; and medical care.[8] Moreover, and as outlined in Chapter 2, McCaskey and Biedzynski have argued convincingly that the specific duties of coaches when managing the risk of injury to athletes relate to: (i) supervision; (ii) training and instruction (including organisation); (iii) ensuring the proper use of safe equipment; (iv) providing competent and responsible personnel; (v) warning of latent dangers; (vi) providing prompt and proper medical care; (vii) preventing injured athletes from competing; and (viii) matching athletes of similar competitive levels.[9] Crucially, the following detailed analysis of emerging case law enables these classifications to be tested, clarified, further developed and rigorously scrutinised in a UK context. By more precisely defining the duty of care of modern sports coaches, this analysis provides important implications for coaching practice. For instance, the developing jurisprudence recognises a coach's duty to complete a suitable and sufficient risk assessment for the particular sporting activity in question, addresses the extent of the duty of coaches to provide warnings and, when planning and delivering group sessions, emphasises a coach's duty to pitch activities within the competence of the least able member of the group, following the necessary assessment of skill levels. The Court of Appeal has also considered the extent of a coach's duty to conduct pitch inspections prior to both training sessions and matches. Further tensions uncovered from these court judgments include a coach's duty not to make excessive demands of athletes, for instance, when pushing athletes outside of their 'comfort zones' and when determining training intensity levels. These issues speak to the threshold between reasonable and unreasonable coaching practice or, with regard to the legal duty of care owed, and for instance when seeking to optimise the performance levels of athletes, the boundary between forging champions and committing a tort. More fundamentally, a detailed scrutiny of the relevant

---

6 MA Jones and AM Dugdale (eds), *Clerk and Lindsell on Torts* (20th edn, London, Sweet and Maxwell 2010) [8–137].
7 AS McCaskey and KW Biedzynski, 'A Guide to the Legal Liability of Coaches for a Sports Participant's Injuries' (1996) 6 *Seton Hall J. Sport L.* 7, 15. Also see Chapter 2.
8 J Barnes, *Sports and the Law in Canada* (3rd edn, Toronto, Butterworths 1996) 302.
9 McCaskey and Biedzynski (n 7) 15–16.

case law consistently reiterates the importance of coaches following common and proper coaching practice when discharging their duty of care towards athletes and participants.

Common practice

Before turning to define the practical content of the duty assumed by coaches in more detail, and as somewhat of a preliminary issue following the analysis provided by Chapters 1–3, recognised and approved coaching practice remains a strong and useful touchstone when defining a coach's duty of care. This is because a coach's duty of care is ordinarily discharged by following coaching practice that is recognised and approved by a recognised body. In short, providing coaches meet the *Bolam* test, that is, satisfy the threshold of regular, approved, responsible and logically justifiable coaching practice, they will have discharged their duties with the requisite standard of skill and care.[10] A particularly telling illustration of the application of this test in practice is provided by *Woodroffe-Hedley v Cuthbertson*, albeit with the mountain guide failing to avail himself of the *Bolam* 'defence' given the particular facts of the case.[11]

Woodroffe-Hedley v Cuthbertson, 20 June 1997 (QBD)

Following the tragic death of an experienced climber on one of the peaks of the Mont Blanc Massif in 1990, a claim was brought against his alpine guide in *Woodroffe-Hedley*. The High Court accepted 'that Mr Cuthbertson owed a duty of care to Mr Hedley, and that the standard of care was that of a reasonably careful and competent alpine mountain guide'. Given the risk of rock fall at the time of the accident, the guide decided to use only a single screw for the last belay. In recognising this to be contrary to common practice, Dyson J stated that:

> [T]he starting point for the resolution of the issue in this case is that it is axiomatic that two ice screws should be used when belaying on ice. The papers include extracts from many climbing handbooks. This is the universal view.

Interestingly, Dyson J acknowledged that circumstances might justify deviating from practice universally accepted, for instance, in an emergency situation, but that such a decision must have a powerful and overriding justification:

---

10 As discussed in Chapter 3, this enables coaches to avail of the *Bolam* 'defence'.
11 *Woodroffe-Hedley v Cuthbertson*, 20 June 1997 (QBD). In the context of a school ski trip and, illustrating successful engagement of the *Bolam* 'defence', see *Woodbridge School v Chittock* [2002] EWCA Civ 915.

> I do not wish to suggest that there are absolutely no circumstances in which an alpine guide would be justified in allowing his client to be belayed to a single screw belay, but the importance of the two screw belay, which is universally recognised, means that there must be a powerful and overriding reason for making do with a single screw belay.

In holding that the facts of the case did not amount to such overriding reasons to dispense with the second screw, and given that the possibility of a fall was foreseeable, Mr Cuthbertson was found to have breached his duty of care by failing to act as a reasonably careful and competent alpine guide in judging that his actions were justifiable. Critically, in reiterating the distinction between 'heat of the moment' decisions[12] made in the context of a fast moving game,[13] as opposed to circumstances where there is time for considered thought and reflection,[14] it was significant that Mr Cuthbertson 'had ample time to make a calm assessment of the situation and make his decision'. Accordingly, Dyson J ruled:

> I have come to the clear conclusion that, in deciding to dispense with the second screw, Mr Cuthbertson fell below the standard to be expected of a reasonably competent and careful alpine guide. He was also negligent when he compounded that error by his decision not to use a running belay. . . . It is for the very reason that the consequences of a fall in such circumstances are so catastrophic that it is universally recognised good practice that two screws should be used in making a belay, and that running belays should be used.
> In my view, the risk of rock fall that was perceived by Mr Cuthbertson, whilst it was not groundless, came nowhere near to amounting to the kind of powerful and overriding reason which might, in an appropriate case, justify a guide in making do with a single screw belay.

The court acknowledged that there is no general rule as to the precise circumstances when a guide (or coach) would be justified in departing from established

---

12 See, for instance, *Wooldridge v Sumner* [1963] 2 QB 43 (CA). Discussed in Chapter 4.
13 Recognised in *Smoldon v Whitworth* [1997] PIQR P133 and applied in *Caldwell v Maguire* [2001] EWCA Civ 1054.
14 E.g., *Harrison v Vincent* [1982] RTR 8 (CA); *Vowles v Evans* [2003] EWCA Civ 318. See further, Chapter 4.

practice and that this would require a careful balancing of the relevant factors in the particular circumstances. In short, it is a matter of judgement and highly fact-specific. Moreover, in cautioning against opening the floodgates to claims against mountain guides following accidents, given the inherent dangers involved, Dyson J accepted that '[a]nyone who climbs with a guide is, as a matter of law, treated as consenting to the ordinary dangers of mountain climbing'.[15] Nonetheless, and with specific reference to the duty of care of the guide, a fundamental qualification was added to this statement by Dyson J:

> But it is the duty of a guide to take all reasonable steps to minimise the danger to his client of injury or death. If, but only if, he fails in that duty will a guide be liable for the consequences of any accident caused by his breach of duty.
>
> Sadly, for the reasons that I have given, in this case there was such a breach of duty.

Woodroffe-Hedley reiterates the important fact that the issue of coach negligence represents an instance of professional liability and that adopting common practice affords strong evidence of successfully satisfying the duty of care owed. With this in mind, this chapter next turns to unpack/clarify the specific duties of coaches in more detail. This is most effectively achieved by means of a thematic approach, namely, by focusing on the specific duties mentioned earlier and providing a critical analysis of the leading and most relevant judicial authorities under each of these headings. Nonetheless, such duties are by no means mutually exclusive, and so whilst the cases are presented in a logical and sequential manner, there are inevitable overlaps, with the most predominant duties of instruction and supervision representing material considerations in the vast majority of the cases analysed.

A. COACH'S DUTIES: INSTRUCTION; SUPERVISION; COMPETENCE; WARNINGS; COMMON/PROPER PRACTICE

This first section considers the extent of the duty of care of coaches with regard to instruction, supervision, ordinary competence and the provision of warnings. The importance of common or proper practice also remains a key theme. The court decisions discussed in detail include *Fowles v Bedfordshire County Council*, a case concerning the coaching of gymnastics. It is argued that this Court of Appeal decision remains the leading authority for instances of coach negligence and so merits

---

15 This reasoning appears consistent with *Condon v Basi* (1985) 1 WLR 866 (CA), with acknowledgement that implied sporting consent could modify a more generalised duty of care. However, following *Caldwell* (n 13), the better approach is recognition that the duty is to exercise objectively reasonable care in the prevailing circumstances. See further, Chapter 4.

an especially detailed discussion. Subsequent judgments used to further unpack and elaborate on the specific duties covered in this section, with *Fowles* cited with approval in two of them, include claims for a breach of duty by employed climbing instructors (*Pinchbeck v Craggy Island Ltd*), volunteer hang-gliding and paragliding coaches (*Petrou v Bertoncello*) and a professional fitness instructor (*Morrow v Dungannon*).

(i) Fowles v Bedfordshire County Council [1995] PIQR P380 (CA)

The plaintiff in *Fowles v Bedfordshire CC* was 21 years of age at the time of the accident and a university student. He suffered a catastrophic accident whilst performing a forward somersault on mats in the activities room at the Bedford Youth House (BYH) when he over-rotated and was catapulted into the wall. The plaintiff regularly attended BYH which catered for young people in the 16–25 age group. At first instance, Ognall J held that the defendant owed the plaintiff a duty of care and that this duty had been breached by the failure to provide a proper system of control, resulting in the use of mats for gymnastics in the absence of supervision. In contributing to his injury, the plaintiff was found two-thirds to blame for his accident. The decision was appealed.

Fowles concerned coaching by a trainee youth worker (RF), who was well qualified to teach trampolining but not gymnastics, and who had demonstrated to the plaintiff the technique of performing a forward somersault on the sports hall floor using gym mats and a crash mat. To avoid collision with any obstruction beyond the crash mat used for landing, RF arranged for it to be placed 10–15 feet away from the wall. Following several such demonstrations, RF supervised and supported the plaintiff when he attempted to follow suit. At trial, the plaintiff's expert described the forward somersault as:

> the most dangerous of the common gymnastic manoeuvres. . . . The forward somersault is not considered by teachers as a general gymnastics activity (recreation level) and is not included in the BAGA General Award Programme until level 3. It is contained in the syllabus for the highly specialised competitive men's syllabus at level 4. The requirements to take this award are very specific. . . . Under the recommendations of the Sports Council, the CCPR and the BAGA a coach of level [4] ability should have been present at all times of performance and teaching.

In citing this passage in the Court of Appeal, Otton LJ emphasised the significance of RF not holding a recognised qualification at the required level. Moreover, the judgment reiterated Ognall J's finding that the assistance of 'spotters', individuals directly present to provide immediate assistance if necessary, is an essential requirement for even skilled gymnasts performing this skill. At the time of the accident, the plaintiff and a friend were taking it in turns to attempt forward somersaults, having arranged the mats themselves, and in the words of the judge, with the far end of the crash mat 'as near as makes no difference hard up against the wall'. There was no supervision by RF or any other youth worker.

Fowles v Bedfordshire CC [1995] (CA) (Millett and Otton LJJ, with Nourse LJ in agreement)

Otton LJ p385–86

It was common ground that the forward somersault is a hazardous exercise with a clearly foreseeable risk of injury. There was no member of staff who was qualified to teach gymnastics, still less to the level required and recognised by independent bodies for the teaching of the forward somersault. A proper system of instruction would have included an express prohibition against practising the manoeuvre in the absence of a supervisor. It is also likely that such instruction would have included the correct and safe placing of crash mats, and impressing upon the learner the necessity of not placing it near to obstructions at the far end of the crash mat. To my mind it can readily be inferred that had [RF] been present on the day in question he would have seen immediately that the crash mat had been placed by the plaintiff in a dangerous position and would have required it to be moved. . . . If over-rotation, through enthusiasm and a desire to impress his audience, had occurred with the mat in free space, there would have been little or no risk of serious injury.

Furthermore, it is clear from the judge's findings that those senior members of staff who were constantly present at the premises were aware that young persons were regularly performing gymnastics on mats when there was no supervision. . . .

. . .

Consequently I am satisfied that the learned judge was entitled to come to the conclusion that the defendants were negligent in that "[t]hey issued no form of written warning or prohibitory notice, nor any verbal ones . . . they took no steps to prohibit such user".

. . .

The duty of care, as I have spelt it out to be, was a continuing duty and the breach which I have analysed was also continuing until the accident occurred. As I have indicated, if a supervisor had been present it is unthinkable that he would have permitted the mat to be placed in that position. Similarly, proper instruction would have included the necessity of placing the mat in a safe position. Proper supervision would have ensured that practising gymnastics unsupervised would have been discontinued and discouraged. I am satisfied that the learned judge correctly found that the defendants' negligence was a factor which was causative of the occurrence of the accident.

Millett LJ p388–391

Mr Fowles is almost 6ft tall. The judge found that the danger of his hitting the wall if he placed the mat where he did must have been obvious to him. Two expert witnesses called on behalf of Mr Fowles told the judge that, as professional gymnasts, they were "stunned by the utter foolishness" of what Mr Fowles had done. The judge found that he was two-thirds to blame. It is plain that he bears by far the greater part of the responsibility for the accident.

. . .

Mr Fowles had been taught gymnastics at school up to the age of 14, but he had not been taught the forward somersault. At the Bedford Youth House, however, one of the youth workers, [RF], showed him how to perform the exercise both on the trampoline and from the floor using the crash mat, and stood beside him and rendered assistance when he attempted it.

The forward somersault from the floor is too dangerous to be taught at school. If the recommendations of the Sports Council, the Central Council for Physical Education and the Amateur Gymnastics Association were followed, a coach of level 4 ability would be present at all times when the forward somersault was being taught or performed. The expert witnesses agreed that anyone aspiring to learn the forward somersault should have the theory and the inherent dangers carefully explained to him.

[RF] was employed by the defendants. He was not qualified to teach the forward somersault, and he did not warn Mr Fowles of the risks or impress upon him that he must never attempt the manoeuvre except in the presence of a qualified supervisor. Having assumed the task of teaching Mr Fowles how to perform the forward somersault, the defendants voluntarily assumed a duty to teach him properly and to make him aware of the dangers. They failed to do either; and then compounded their failure by providing unrestricted access to the crash mat, thereby encouraging him to use it to practise what he had been taught, without warning him that he must on no account do so without supervision.

Anyone who assumes the task of teaching the forward somersault is under a duty not only to teach the technique involved in the exercise and to explain the dangers associated with its performance but to teach the steps which must be taken to prepare for it, including the laying of the crash mat, and to explain the dangers of performing the exercise in an inappropriate environment. It matters not how obvious a danger may be; it should be pointed out.

> This is particularly the case where the danger of a minor accident (such as hitting an obstruction) may be obvious, but the risk of really serious injury is unlikely to be appreciated by the inexpert.
>
> Mr Fowles has brought a cross-appeal by which he seeks to reduce the share of the damage which he must bear himself. I would not be prepared to differ from the finding of the very experienced judge that Mr Fowles was two-thirds to blame; if anything, it was too favourable to Mr Fowles.
>
> I agree that both the appeal and Mr Fowles' cross-appeal should be dismissed.

Fowles is of fundamental importance and significance when defining the duty of care of modern sports coaches. As revealed by the critical analysis conducted in Chapter 1, and consistent with the principle derived from *Hedley Byrne & Co Ltd v Heller & Partner Ltd*,[16] *Fowles* makes plain that the existence of an assumption of responsibility by a coach or volunteer and reliance on this supervision and/or instruction by an athlete would typically give rise to a common law duty of care requiring the exercise of reasonable skill and care. In other words, and in paraphrasing Millett LJ, anyone who (voluntarily) assumes the task of teaching and coaching a sports skill assumes a duty to do so properly by exercising due skill and care.[17] Coaches possessing recognised qualifications, at the necessary level for the skill or activity being coached, are best placed to successfully satisfy this duty of care. As noted by the plaintiff's expert witness in *Fowles*, the requirements to take the coaching award which covers the forward somersault as part of its syllabus are highly specialised and very specific. The court recognised that the forward somersault is the most dangerous of the common gymnastic manoeuvres with a clearly foreseeable risk of serious injury. Accordingly, teaching the somersault properly and following the necessary preparatory steps requires careful sequential and progressive learning, qualified supervision, the presence of 'spotters' who can intervene to provide additional immediate support and recommended and approved use of equipment, including mats.[18] This demands the exercise of special skill and a degree of competence not ordinarily possessed by the ordinary reasonable person. Crucially, the standard of care expected of the defendant youth worker in discharging his duty of care in *Fowles*, irrespective of whether he was employed or acting as a volunteer, was that of the ordinarily competent gymnastics coach professing to have the necessary special skill. The court's emphasis on the standard of skill required, as approved by independent bodies, confirms this as an interesting instance of professional liability

---

16 *Hedley Byrne & Co Ltd v Heller & Partner Ltd* [1964] AC 465. See further, Chapter 1.
17 In a school context, see *Hammersley-Gonsalves v Redcar & Cleveland BC* [2012] EWCA Civ 1135; *Van Oppen v Clerk to the Bedford Charity Trustees* [1989] 3 All ER 389 (CA); and *Wright v Cheshire CC* [1952] 2 ALL ER 789 (CA). Also see *Gannon v Rotherham MBC* Unreported, Crown Court (Nottingham), 6 February 1991.
18 *Fowles v Bedfordshire CC* [1995] PIQR P380 (CA) P383, P385, P390.

and is entirely consistent with Chapter 3's analysis of the *Bolam* test in the context of sports coaching. Simply applied, and as most recently approved in *Shone v British Bobsleigh Limited*,[19] *Fowles* reiterates that the duty of coaches is to adopt reasonable coaching practice so that reasonable care is taken to ensure the reasonable safety of athletes. This emphasises the necessity of coaches assuming only duties of care that they are ordinarily competent and experienced to effectively discharge.

The particular duties of the coach scrutinised in *Fowles* concerned adequate instruction, supervision and the provision of warnings. Consistent with the findings of the Court of Appeal, athletes should not be allowed to practise unsupervised in circumstances where this exposes them to unacceptable levels of risk.[20] Given the obvious dangers associated with the performance of a forward somersault in gymnastics, once a duty of care had been established, the absence of adequate instruction and supervision in *Fowles* amounted to a breach of duty and was found to be the immediate cause of the accident. As succinctly noted by Otton LJ, '[P]roper instruction would have included the necessity of placing the mat in a safe position. Proper supervision would have ensured that practising gymnastics unsupervised would have been discontinued and discouraged.' Importantly, proper instruction during coaching sessions includes making athletes aware of dangers, regardless of how obvious such dangers may be.[21] This is in stark contrast to cases involving accidents during sporting activities where it has been held that there is no duty to warn of an obvious risk. For instance, in *Poppleton v Trustees of the Portsmouth Youth Activities Committee*[22] and *Maylin v Dacorum*,[23] where inherently risky activities (i.e., rock climbing activities) were voluntarily and freely undertaken by individuals,

---

19 *Shone v British Bobsleigh Limited* [2018] 5 WLUK 226.
20 Cf. *Porter v Barking and Dagenham LBC* (1990) Times, 9 April. No liability being found from a failure to supervise two 14-year-old pupils practising shot-put.
21 See, for instance, *Ahmed v MacLean* [2016] EWHC 2798 [94]-[95], discussed later. Also see *Murray v McCullough* [2016] NIQB 52. Cf. *Wai Yip Hin v Wong Po Kit* (No 1) [2009] 3 HKC 362. In *Wai Yip Hin*, following an injury suffered by the plaintiff during a Kendo (a Japanese martial art) class, the Court of First Instance in Hong Kong held that there was only a duty to warn of the risk of injury if such a risk was not obvious. The plaintiff had attended Kendo classes for about six months. Nonetheless, since this was the first time the plaintiff had worn a *men* (helmet) the court concluded that:

> 'The defendant has been in breach of duty by failing to take reasonable precautions. . . . He knew that being struck on the men for the first time would result in dizziness, discomfort and vibration to the head and it could be very painful. He failed to warn the plaintiff who put on the men for the first time that there was a risk of injury when being struck by the shinai [bamboo sword] on the men. There would have been no difficulty in giving such a warning' (at [64]).

22 *Poppleton v Trustees of the Portsmouth Youth Activities Committee* [2008] EWCA Civ 646.
23 *Maylin v Dacorum Sports Trust trading as XC Sportspace* [2017] EWHC 378. HHJ McKenna stating:

> 'There being, in my judgment, inherent and obvious risks in the activity which Miss Maylin was embarked upon, the law, as May LJ makes clear in Poppleton, does not require the Defendant to train, supervise or warn and again, as is made clear in Poppleton, it makes no difference that the Defendant charged Miss Maylin to use the bouldering wall and, as it seems to me, that the claim fails on that ground' (at [29]).

Also see, *Whittet v Virgin Active Ltd* [2019] 2 WLUK 779.

without the provision or reliance on any instruction or supervision, whilst using indoor climbing facilities provided by the defendant(s).[24]

The duty of a coach to warn athletes of dangers associated with the organised activity being delivered, no matter how obvious that danger might be, presents a fundamental issue in terms of the level of qualification, training and experience of coaches. Drawing from an analogous authority from the field of medical negligence, the Vice-Chancellor Sir Nicolas Browne-Wilkinson insightfully recognised that 'one of the chief hazards of inexperience is that nne [sic] does not always know the risks which exist'.[25] Previous sports coaching research has revealed some widespread concern regarding a possible 'skills gap', whereby coaches discharge a function beyond that for which they are qualified.[26] Indeed, Lyle and Cushion are mindful of situations whereby coaches may operate in circumstances for which they do not possess the appropriate qualifications or experience.[27] This is perhaps unsurprising, since as highlighted by Telfer, coaches are required to operate across an increasingly challenging range of performance levels and stages.[28] For instance, as performers progress to elite levels the required emphasis on more specialised training programmes creates new risks requiring coaches to ensure that they possess the necessary competence and expertise to operate safely in these amended circumstances.[29] A serious consequence of coaches lacking ordinary levels of competence and experience for the sporting activity in question would be a potential inability to recognise and account for the risks posed in the (amended) prevailing circumstances. This might very well prevent coaches from fulfilling their duty to adequately warn athletes of the dangers presented by specific skills, drills and training techniques, thereby resulting in inadequate levels of instruction and supervision. This situation might be compounded when coaching children and inexperienced performers in sporting activities where the dangers of minor accidents appear obvious but the full extent of serious injury is unlikely to be appreciated by participants.[30]

A further factor informing the standard of care required of coaches, and underpinning the foreseeability of injury, is the previous awareness and knowledge of the associated risk (i.e., in *Fowles* an awareness that young persons were regularly performing gymnastics on mats when there was no supervision).[31] Simply applied,

---

24 Cf. *Pinchbeck v Craggy Island Ltd* [2012] EWHC 2745, discussed later and where trained instructors provided advice and supervision to the claimant as part of an organised 'team-building' exercise.
25 *Wilsher v Essex AHA* [1987] QB 730 (CA) 777.
26 A Lynn and J Lyle, 'Coaching Workforce Development' in Lyle and Cushion (n 1) 199. See further, Chapter 7.
27 J Lyle and C Cushion, 'Narrowing the Field: Some Key Questions About Sports Coaching' in Lyle and Cushion (n 1) 247.
28 H Telfer, 'Coaching practice and practice ethics' in Lyle and Cushion (n 1) 210.
29 J Labuschagne and J Skea, 'The Liability of a Coach for a Sport Participant's Injury' (1999) 10 *Stellenbosch Law Review* 158, 166.
30 See, for instance, *Murray* (n 21).
31 See, for instance, *Woodroffe-Hedley* (n 11). Dyson J recognised that the staggering annual statistics of accidents on the Mont Blanc Massif provided frightening proof of the risk of falling on a mountain slope. Also see *Caldwell* (n 13) [12]; *Pinchbeck* (n 23); and *McErlean v MacAuley* [2014] NIQB 1 [11].

in circumstances where injury is more foreseeable, a heightened standard of care would be demanded of coaches.[32] Moreover, there is much force to the argument that a coach holding an advanced coaching qualification, and operating at a commensurate level, may reasonably be expected to have enhanced foresight of unacceptable risk to personal injury when coaching. Correspondingly, athletes more experienced in performing challenging skills and techniques safely may be able to take greater risks.[33] Nonetheless, during structured coaching activities it remains the duty of the coach to ensure that athletes are not exposed to unreasonable risk. In instances of coach negligence, and as was the case in *Fowles*, athletes may bear some responsibility for the injury suffered. Such contributory negligence may result in the apportionment of damages. However, the partial defence of contributory negligence does not negate the existence of a coach's duty of care and so coaches might still be found to be in breach of duty even when common sense clearly illustrates that the actions of claimants were negligent or foolish.

During organised coaching sessions, the duty to provide proper instruction and supervision is a continuing duty requiring the display of reasonable skill and care throughout the entire activity. As in *Fowles*, satisfying this duty may be highly problematic should the coach not be immediately present during the session. Nonetheless, when coaches are appropriately on hand to provide supervision, and national governing body (NGB) approved coach-participant ratios are followed, the standard of supervision required of coaches remains one of reasonableness in the particular circumstances. Indeed, and drawing from the analogous context of school sport, Pill LJ in the Court of Appeal recently emphasised that it should be 'obvious' that even the most observant physical education (PE) teacher cannot be expected to see every action of every pupil in a group activity, regardless of wherever the teacher positions themselves.[34] This represents a sensible and realistic approach. A less obvious and interesting complexity connected with this continuing duty of adequate instruction and supervision is when coaches might adopt a more 'relaxed' approach, for instance, perhaps towards the end of sessions. An instructive illustration of this is provided by *Pinchbeck v Craggy Island Ltd*.[35]

(ii) Pinchbeck v Craggy Island Ltd [2012] EWHC 2745

The claimant in *Pinchbeck v Craggy Island Ltd* was successful in a claim in negligence following an accident at an indoor climbing centre. The defendant company had been paid for instruction and supervision of a group comprising members of bank staff for a two-hour team-building exercise session. Most of the session involved the participants

---

32 WT Champion, 'The Evolution of a Standard of Care for Injured College Athletes: A Review of Kleinknecht and Progeny' (1999) 1 *Va. J. Sports & L.* 290, 295.
33 G Nygaard and T Boone, *Coaches' Guide to Sport Law* (Champaign, Human Kinetics 1985) 27; M James, *Sports Law* (Basingstoke, Palgrave Macmillan 2010) 75.
34 *Hammersley-Gonsalves* (n 17) [11].
35 *Pinchbeck* (n 24).

wearing a safety harness and ropes and climbing on a very high (competition) wall. For the final ten minutes or so, the claimant and a number of her colleagues experienced using the bouldering wall without any safety harness. The claimant's accident was sustained when she descended from the bouldering wall by jumping.

Prior to the session the claimant had signed a 'Course Acceptance Form' declaring that she was aware of and accepted the risks inherent in climbing and mountaineering activities. Moreover, this participant agreement stated in respect of the bouldering wall that descent from it should be made by climbing down since 'jumping or an uncontrolled fall can result in serious injury'.[36] For the vast majority of the session it was accepted that the instruction and supervision by staff employed by the defendants was careful, conscientious and thorough. This, combined with the effective use of appropriate safety equipment (i.e., harnesses and ropes), ensured that the participating individuals from the bank undertook the rope climbing part of the exercise safely. All of the climbing on the high competition wall was in a generally upward direction. When participants reached the top of the wall, they were lowered to the floor using ropes attached to their harnesses by instructors and so did not descend by climbing down. As noted by Judge Curran QC, no instruction was provided to participants about the method to be adopted when descending from the high climbing wall. With no more than ten minutes remaining in the session, the group was given the option of transferring to the bouldering wall by one of the climbing instructors. The judge found that the instructors, the claimant and her colleagues 'regarded the short spell on the bouldering wall as a warming-down session and they treated it with a significantly more relaxed attitude'.[37] Furthermore, only one instructor dealt with the bouldering wall group.

Given the above facts, the High Court in *Pinchbeck* reiterated that the provisions of the Unfair Contract Terms Act 1977 prevented the defendants from avoiding liability by means of the signed 'Course Acceptance Form'. Such terms were of no relevance in the circumstances and, in particular, with regard to 'risks which can be avoided or minimised by careful instruction and supervision'.[38] In summarising the relevant law, Judge Curran stated:

> It is accepted by the Defendant company that it owed a duty to the Claimant to provide her with appropriate instruction and supervision in her use of the premises, including the bouldering wall, and that included making it clear to her that she should not descend from the bouldering wall by jumping or dropping of [sic] it. The evidence called on behalf of the Defendants is that that is precisely what their staff did. I have found to the contrary.[39]

36 Ibid. [5].
37 Ibid. [34].
38 Ibid. [41]. Also see *Ahmed* (n 21).
39 *Pinchbeck* (n 24) [42].

The *Pinchbeck* judgment cites with approval the approach adopted by Millett LJ in *Fowles*. That is, when a defendant assumes a task involving instruction and supervision, the defendant assumes the duty to do so properly and to make the claimant aware of dangers inevitably involved in the sporting activity being undertaken. This is particularly the case when there is an absence of supervision.[40] In addressing the submission made by counsel for the claimant, arguing that the extent of the duty owed demanded maintaining the same levels of supervision and detailed instruction on the bouldering wall as had been provided on the climbing wall, and that this included a prohibition on jumping down from the bouldering wall, Judge Curran concluded:

> I agree that, in all the circumstances, the Defendants were under a duty in this respect as they had indeed assumed responsibility for the safety of the Claimant and, what is more, they knew of the previous accident, or possibly accidents, of which she was unaware. Moreover, they knew that she had practised only going upward (and had been lowered down by others) in the greater part of the time she had spent at the premises and had been carefully monitored throughout the previous one and three-quarter hours. If she were then left to her own devices at the bouldering wall they knew or ought to have known that that might put her at a disadvantage. In the circumstances, on the facts as I have found them to be, they failed to discharge their duty.[41]

To borrow a phrase from a coach/instructor negligence case where the claimant was very seriously injured during supervised skiing on the last day of a skiing holiday, and in view of the continuing duty of care incumbent upon the ski instructor (and coaches) to provide reasonable instruction and supervision throughout sessions, a coach momentarily taking their 'eye off the ball' may be in breach of duty.[42] Indeed, both the *Pinchbeck* and *Anderson v Lyotier* decisions, cases in which the defendant instructors were adopting a predominantly responsible approach towards the safety of individuals during socially desirable activities, appear to question the potency of section 1 of the Compensation Act 2006, and likewise perhaps in future the Social Action, Responsibility and Heroism Act 2015, in better protecting coaches from negligence liability.[43]

---

40 Ibid. [53].
41 Ibid. [55]. The claimant being found contributorily negligent and her damages reduced by one-third.
42 *Anderson v Lyotier* [2008] EWHC 2790 [120]. The next chapter conducts a detailed case study of this particularly relevant decision.
43 See further, Chapters 2 & 6. Also see, N Partington, 'Beyond the "*Tomlinson* trap": Analysing the Effectiveness of Section 1 of the Compensation Act 2006' (2016) 37(1) *Liverpool L Rev* 33.

Another relevant case citing *Fowles*, and informative when examining the duties of coaches in context, is *Petrou v Bertoncello*.

(iii) Petrou v Bertoncello [2012] EWHC 2286

Petrou v Bertoncello emphasises that negligence actions brought against volunteer coaches would most probably be approached, and framed, in terms of professional liability. Both the claimant and defendants in *Petrou* were members of the Dunstable Hang-gliding and Paragliding Club, an unincorporated members' club. On 10 October 2009, the claimant suffered catastrophic personal injury when he collided with the wing of the first defendant's paraglider. The first defendant was completing an 'Airspace' test, as required by the Club's rules, this familiarisation flight being conducted by the second defendant, the Club Chairman and qualified club coach. The third defendant was at all material times the Club's Safety Officer and also a qualified coach. The coaching awards held by the second and third defendants were granted by the British Hang-Gliding and Paragliding Association (BHPA).

As in *Fowles*, it seems plain that in assuming the duty to conduct the 'Airspace' test, it was incumbent upon the second defendant coach to complete this duty properly. Accordingly, it appears eminently sensible that counsel for the claimant submitted three strands to the claimant's case on liability:

> (i) the personal claim against the first defendant;
> (ii) the personal claims against the 2nd and 3rd defendants who were alleged to have failed to properly brief, assist, observe and/or supervise the 1st defendant and so being in breach of their duty of care arising from their roles as both Club coaches and Club office holders;
> (iii) what is called the 'organisational' claim against the 2nd and 3rd defendants – it being alleged that the club acting through its officers, negligently failed to operate and/or enforce separately landing and take-off area and so created a danger of collision such as that which occurred in this case; it is alleged that as officers of the club the 2nd and 3rd defendants were responsible for ensuring that the paragliding was organised in a safe way.[44]

Of particular interest for present purposes is the second strand to the claimant's submissions, regarding the duty and standard of care of the club coaches, this being a straightforward issue of alleged professional negligence. This professional liability is premised on the fact that

---

44 *Petrou v Bertoncello* [2012] EWHC 2286 [22].

by volunteering to act as BHPA Club coaches and as officers of the club, the 2nd and 3rd defendants voluntarily assumed a responsibility to carry out duties which included briefing, assessing, coaching, supervising, observing and guiding new members with reasonable care and skill.[45]

This reasoning appears convincing, and unsurprisingly Griffith Williams J concluded that there were indeed reasonable grounds for believing the case required a full investigation into the facts to avoid the risk of summary injustice.[46] Accordingly, *Petrou* provides a modern and important reminder that for both amateur and professional coaches, the benchmark of reasonableness against which their conduct would be measured would likely be premised on the standard of skill and care of the ordinarily competent coach exercising a specialist skill, regardless of whether or not they might be amateur. As such, and as approved in *Fowles*, it appears there would be a legal expectation for such duties to be discharged properly, irrespective of coaches being categorised as professional, amateur, 'professional amateur', qualified, (in)experienced or accredited by an NGB.[47]

A final case of considerable relevance to this section's analysis stemming from the Court of Appeal's decision in *Fowles*, and of direct relevance to a coach's duties regarding instruction, supervision, competence, the provision of warnings and common practice, is *Morrow v Dungannon*. Significantly, in fashioning the legal test in a claim of instructor/coach negligence, Gillen J in *Morrow* draws directly from established sports negligence principles discussed in Chapter 4.

(iv) Morrow v Dungannon and South Tyrone Borough Council [2012] NIQB 50

The claim in damages for personal injuries in *Morrow v Dungannon* centred on the negligence of the defendant fitness instructor when discharging duties relating to 'the instruction, supervision, management, control and assistance of the plaintiff whilst performing weightlifting exercises'.[48] The fitness instructor was fulfilling the role of 'spotter' when the injury was sustained to the plaintiff's shoulder/neck. Gillen J summarised the plaintiff's case thus: '[T]he plaintiff was not given any proper instruction, was encouraged to lift an excessive weight outside the range of safe practice and there was a failure to identify the risk of injury to him'.[49] Mr Taffee, the fitness instructor, had eight years of experience and made the case that he had

---

45 Ibid. [27]. *Fowles* was submitted by counsel for the claimant as an example of well-established case law showing that a volunteer can owe a duty of care arising out of their voluntary assumption of a responsibility within the Dunstable Hang-gliding and Paragliding Club.
46 Ibid. [35]-[36].
47 See further, Chapter 3.
48 *Morrow v Dungannon and South Tyrone BC* [2012] NIQB 50 [1].
49 Ibid. [12].

138 Duty of care in context

given the plaintiff an induction lasting about three hours over a four-day period. This included advice on each separate set of equipment. Moreover, Mr Taffee claimed that he had given advice and instruction on technique, posture, breathing and appropriate weights and, had spotted for the plaintiff on a number of occasions. Mr Taffee also claimed to have seen the plaintiff lifting 100 kilograms prior to the date of the accident and that he had told the plaintiff 'that the golden rule was that weights should never be increased by more than 5 kilograms on any lift (2½ kilograms on each side of the bar)'.[50] At the time of the accident, Mr Taffee claimed that the plaintiff was squatting using 98 kilograms and that it was on the third repetition of the second set when the accident occurred. Mr Taffee was observing the plaintiff's technique from immediately behind and saw nothing wrong.[51]

In identifying the legal principles applicable to the case, Gillen J succinctly stated:

> [18] Any physical exercise or sport carries with it a certain level of risk for those involved. A proper balance has to be struck between the benefits such activity confers on the participant and the risks involved. Injuries can sometimes occur that are not preventable and are simply part of the risk of the exercise itself. . . .
>
> [19] Gymnasiums and workout rooms present a risk area for weightlifters. This is particularly the case where persons are still learning proper techniques for weightlifting and exercise. The standard of care for those such as the defendant who provide such facilities and contract with persons such as the plaintiff to use them is that they owe the same duty of care to lawful visitors as any occupier and are governed by the same principles of negligence set out in Donoghue v Stevenson with a need to provide proper instruction, supervision and warning etc.
>
> [20] In arriving at the standard appropriate in any given case the court will take into account the prevailing circumstances including the sporting object, the demands made upon the participant, the inherent dangers of the exercise, its rules, conventions and customs, the standard skills and judgment reasonably to be expected of a participant and the standards, skills and judgment reasonably to be expected of someone such as the defendant and Mr Taffee in instructing monitoring and supervising the plaintiff.

Gillen J found Mr Taffee to be 'a conscientious fitness instructor who took a genuine interest in his work and in those lifting weights' and 'entirely believable'.[52] Consequently, the High Court ultimately determined that:

50 Ibid. [14]-[15].
51 Ibid. [16].
52 Ibid. [27].

> [T]his man [the plaintiff] has been injured in the course of an exercise which by its very nature carries a measure of risk. In this instance he has suffered a very rare injury in a sporting activity which he must have known carried some risk irrespective of the steps taken by the defendant to care for him. I find there was no blame attaching to Mr Taffee or the defendants. I consider that the plaintiff was lifting a weight he was used to in a safe environment which was properly organised with adequate facilities in circumstances where he had been properly instructed and monitored by an experienced and appropriately trained spotter. His injury was simply an unfortunate accident in the context of an exercise where the risk of injury is inherent.[53]

This straightforward, common sense and accessible judgment by Gillen J offers a clear illustration of the application of the relevant legal principles when courts are tasked with defining the extent of an instructor's (and coach's) duty of care. Furthermore, and consistent with *Fowles*, *Morrow* reiterates the requirement for coaches to discharge the specific duties of instruction, supervision and provision of warnings with reasonable skill and care. Importantly, and albeit without citing the particular authorities relied upon, it is clearly apparent that this decision draws from established sports negligence jurisprudence. This is perhaps most obvious when quoting directly from *Caldwell v Maguire*[54] to fashion the applicable legal test for instructor/coach negligence.[55] However, it is of significance that Gillen J elaborated on this cited passage from *Caldwell*, a case concerning a potential breach of duty by co-participants by adding 'and the standards, skills and judgment reasonably to be expected of someone such as the defendant and Mr Taffee in instructing monitoring and supervising the plaintiff'. Following *Fowles*, and as discussed in detail in Chapter 3, properly discharging the duties of a fitness instructor requires the standards, (special) skills and judgement to be expected of the ordinarily average and competent fitness instructor. Yet again, this underscores the fact that claims for a breach of duty by instructors/coaches represent an instance of professional negligence.

In ensuring that attempts to define the standard of care owed in the particular circumstances are realistic, Gillen J stressed that sporting activities carry a certain level of inherent risk and that a proper balance must be struck between the respective benefits and risks involved. Consistent with the operation of the ordinary law of negligence in the specific context of sport, and as discussed in relation to the

---

53 Ibid. [30].
54 *Caldwell* (n 13) [11]. The issue of sports negligence generally, and this case in particular involving a claim against two fellow professional jockeys riding in the same race, is discussed in detail in Chapter 4.
55 *Morrow* (n 48) [20].

legal duty of care incumbent upon coaches in Chapter 2, this should help to ensure that the standard of care is set at a sensible level. A final note worthy of mention from *Morrow*, and an issue in point in the next Court of Appeal decision to be considered, is that cases brought under the Occupiers' Liability Act 1957 can also be of relevance when considering the standard of care expected of coaches. As noted by Morris, this is because:

> An occupier does not need to make premises completely safe for a visitor but only to 'take such care as in all the circumstances of the case is reasonable to see that the visitor will be reasonably safe' for the purposes s/he is permitted to be there. This means that the usual negligence factors on breach come into play when setting the standard of care: the likelihood of harm; the gravity of harm; the cost of taking precautions and social utility.[56]

B. COACH'S DUTIES: PITCH INSPECTIONS; RISK ASSESSMENT; COMPETENCE; COMMON/PROPER PRACTICE

This second section considers the extent of the duty of care of coaches with regard to the appropriate use of safe facilities and the requirements of sufficient risk assessment. More generally, and in providing some overlap with section A, the significance of proper practice and the necessity of ordinary levels of competence are reiterated as key indicators when courts are tasked with determining whether or not a coach's duty of care has been successfully discharged. The discussion begins with another decision of the Court of Appeal, this time from the context of amateur rugby union, which proves instructive when defining the practical content of a coach's duty of care with regard to conducting pitch inspections (*Sutton v Syston RFC*). Both this duty and the requirement of coaches to conduct adequate risk assessments are subsequently further unpacked by scrutinising a case brought against a rugby union development officer and qualified coach (*Cox v Dundee City Council*). The final case considered in this section concerns the duty of care owed by the leaders of a formal army adventurous training exercise (*MacIntyre v Ministry of Defence*).

(i) Sutton v Syston RFC Ltd [2011] EWCA Civ 1182

Whilst taking part in a preseason training session, the 16.5-year-old claimant in *Sutton v Syston RFC Ltd* was injured during a game of tag rugby, which blended both under 16 and under 17 Colts, and which was supervised by three coaches. The claimant's right knee was gashed by a broken off part of a cricket boundary marker when he dived to score a try. The marker had been left behind by members

---

56 A Morris, 'Hayley Jane Liddle (personal representative of Sean Lesley Phillips Deceased) v Bristol CC (High Court of Justice Queen's Bench Division; HH Judge Gargan, 19 October 2018; [2018] EWHC 3673 (QB)) (2019) 2 *JPI Law* C63, C69. See for instance, *Tomlinson v Congleton BC* [2004] 1 AC 46 (HL) [34].

of a cricket club who had previously used the same area. The claimant argued that one of the three coaches should have inspected the pitch before the training session, and that if this had been done, the stub of the marker would have been discovered. The Club admitted that a duty of care was owed to those participating in the training session under the Occupiers' Liability Act 1957. This was a duty to take such care as was reasonable in all the circumstances to see that visitors, including the claimant, would be reasonably safe in using the Club's premises. Furthermore, the Club accepted that there should have been a general inspection of the pitch prior to the training session and that no such inspection took place. However, the Club asserted that such a general inspection would only be for obvious obstructions, and since the stub of the cricket marker did not obtrude above the surface of the grass, it would not have been discovered by a general inspection of the pitch.

When considering the scope of the required pitch inspection in the Court of Appeal, and after emphasising the necessity of conducting one, Longmore LJ drew from recognised and approved practice when he stated:

> The Rugby Football Union ("the RFU") itself provides risk assessment guidelines and states that such guidelines are for the purposes of identifying any unsafe condition. The RFU also provides a safety check list which includes at paragraph 2 a recommendation to check the ground for foreign objects "such as glass, concrete, large stones, dog waste". Although these guidelines refer to matches, it seems to me that this duty should also apply to training sessions and the Club did not seriously dispute that.[57]

In agreeing with the trial judge, Longmore LJ also rejected the suggestion that a quick walk over the pitch would be sufficient, but rather, that all of the ground should be covered 'at a reasonable walking pace'.[58] Moreover, and in providing instructive guidance concerning the nature of a coach's duty of care to inspect facilities, Longmore LJ concluded:

> The Club suggested in argument that it would be enough if the pitch were inspected by someone such as (in this case) one of the coaches walking round the perimeter; I would not accept that a limited inspection of that kind would discharge the Club's duty of care. There is, moreover, no suggestion in the RFU's own guidelines that such a limited inspection would be appropriate.

---

57 *Sutton v Syston RFC Ltd* [2011] EWCA Civ 1182 [9].
58 Ibid. [10].

> It is important that neither the game's professional organisation nor the law should lay down standards that are too difficult for ordinary coaches and match organisers to meet. Games of rugby are, after all, no more than games and, as such are obviously desirable activities within the meaning of section 1 of the Compensation Act 2006 (neither party suggested that this section in any way altered the common law position). I would therefore conclude that, before a game or training session, a pitch should be walked over at a reasonable walking pace by a coach or match organiser (or someone on their behalf) and that, if that is done, that will satisfy a Club's common law duty of care in relation to such inspection. If, of course, more than one coach or organiser is available, each such person could inspect a pre-agreed part of the pitch.[59]

On applying the identified requirement for coaches to conduct a pitch inspection by walking over the pitch at a reasonable walking pace, the Court of Appeal found that, on the balance of probabilities, such an inspection would not have revealed the stub's existence and so the Club's appeal was allowed. In recognising the disappointment caused to the claimant, the judgment emphasised that 'this court has to look at the case from a wider perspective than just his [the claimant's] own injury and must not be too astute to impose duties of care which would make rugby playing as a whole more subject to interference from the courts than it should be'.[60]

When defining the extent of a coach's duty of care, *Sutton* provides strong and convincing recognition for such duties to be reasonable and realistic, and more specifically, not too difficult for ordinary coaches to meet. *Sutton* also offers clarification regarding the precise scope of a coach's duty to inspect pitches for both practice sessions and matches. Importantly, many sports coaches operate in isolation and so *Sutton* provides a timely reminder of the requirement for such individual coaches to take all reasonable steps to ensure that the state of pitches and facilities does not expose athletes to unnecessary or unacceptable risk of injury. Failing to do so would amount to a breach of duty.

As highlighted by the guidance provided by the RFU, and cited by the Court of Appeal, risk assessment guidelines (and safety check lists) frequently appear instrumental when defining the nature of a coach's duty of care. Indeed, and as revealed in the following discussion of *Cox v Dundee City Council*, '[s]ometimes the failure to undertake a proper risk assessment can affect or even determine the outcome of a claim and judges must be alive to that and not sweep it aside'.[61]

---

59 Ibid. [12]-[13]. For further judicial recognition of the need to account for the social utility of physical activities when setting the standard of care of instructors, albeit in the specific context of a formal army adventurous (climbing) training exercise, see *MacIntyre v Ministry of Defence* [2011] EWHC 1690 [69].
60 *Sutton* (n 57) [18].
61 *Uren v Corporate Leisure (UK) Ltd* [2011] EWCA Civ 66 [41] (Smith LJ).

(ii) Cox v Dundee City Council [2014] CSOH 3

In *Cox v Dundee City Council*, the pursuer (claimant) was attending a rugby coach training course at Panmure Rugby Club, Dundee. The course was organised by Dundee City Council and being delivered by MC, a rugby development officer (and qualified coach) with the defenders (defendants). During a series of dynamic skills exercises at the start of the practical training conducted outside, including touch rugby, the pursuer was seriously injured when he side-stepped to avoid contact from opposition players. As ruled by Lady Scott, the case turned on a narrow dispute of fact:

> The underfoot conditions was the essential dispute in fact between the parties.
>
> There was no real dispute that if the condition of the ground was as spoken to by the pursuer's witnesses, then that would present an obvious risk of injury which ought to have been noted by a properly conducted risk assessment by the defenders' employee [MC] and which ought to have been remedied or guarded against. There was no dispute that the injury sustained by the pursuer was consistent with his evidence as to what happened. There was no suggestion of contributory negligence.[62]

Consistent with the Court of Appeal's decision in *Sutton*, Lady Scott in the Outer House, Court of Session recognised that the pursuer's witnesses agreed that:

> prior to any training session a risk assessment required to be carried out in respect of any hazards or risks of injury presented by the training facility involved. For an outdoor rugby training exercise this included an assessment of the underfoot conditions. This was achieved in an inspection by walking the area intended for use. . . .
>
> Importantly, all agreed that if there were any parts of the training area which were frozen or uneven and rutted or both then the ground was unsuitable. Further if the ground could not "take a stud" it was unsuitable or unusable. In such a situation the trainer required to consider what steps needed to be taken to remove the risk of injury presented. This may well involve either moving or cancelling the exercise. In addition, all agreed that if such areas of frozen or uneven ground existed, they should be obvious and identified in the course of a properly conducted risk assessment. Mr White suggested that if such areas existed and were missed, then the risk assessment could not have been properly conducted.[63]

---

62 *Cox v Dundee CC* [2014] CSOH 3 [5].
63 Ibid. [11]-[12].

The evidence given by the witnesses for the pursuer, suggesting the underfoot conditions were not suitable, and conversely for the defender, suggesting that the underfoot conditions were suitable, was in direct and marked contrast. In taking into account the qualifications and previous experience of the coach educator leading the session, and the weight afforded to the sufficient completion of an appropriate risk assessment, it is interesting to note from the judgment that:

> [MC] gave evidence that this was the first time he had led such a training course. He had in 2010, qualifications in coaching at SRU level 1 and UKCC level 1. He was unclear in his evidence what training he had received in respect of risk assessment prior to conducting this course. The record of his training programme with the defenders . . . [was] that at this time, he was on the waiting list for [the] same. However, in his evidence he stated he had received training for the conduct of risk assessment, but could not be clear when this was. Certainly subsequent to this course he had obtained qualifications which involved risk assessment. In general terms he agreed that if any part of an area used for training was frozen or uneven or rutted, then it would present a risk of injury and was unsuitable for the kind of exercises involved in the course. Further he agreed that if such unsuitable conditions existed and were not found by a risk assessment, then that assessment would be inaccurate.
>
> On the day in question he gave evidence that he had inspected the outside grounds and he had conducted a risk assessment prior to the arrival of the course participants. He had looked at the pitches and concluded the first fifteen pitch was unsuitable. He looked at the cricket area between the two pitches. He identified an area to the left hand side of the cricket square as suitable. He later suggested this area was within the fenced off cricket square. He accepted that in using this area the club "would not be too chuffed". He assessed the risk by walking the area. Initially he said he walked it wearing trainers, then he said he wore trailer shoes with a rugged sole and with moulded studs. He suggested if he were taking part in the exercise he would have worn boots with studs. He was clear in his evidence that the training area he identified was a good playing surface and no part was frozen, uneven or rutted. He completed the risk assessment form . . . after the course was completed.[64]

Despite the evidence provided by the defender coach, the court held that at least part of the ground used was too hard/frozen, uneven/rutted and would not 'take a stud'. Lady Scott also emphasised that all of the witnesses qualified to assess risk

64 Ibid. [19]-[20].

accepted 'that any part of an area which was too hard or uneven or rutted rendered the whole area unsuitable for use and presented a risk of injury'.[65]

Lady Scott expressed concerns over the credibility of the evidence relied upon by the defenders. In addressing this point, and offering weight to the submission that the failure to undertake a proper risk assessment can sometimes affect or even determine the outcome of a claim, the following passage from the judgment is particularly instructive when attempting to define a coach's duty to conduct a suitable and sufficient risk assessment:

> I was not convinced by [MC's] evidence that he had carried out a thorough risk assessment. He gave very little detail about testing the ground, he did not check the ground would take a stud by using rugby boots and he was inconsistent about what shoes he wore. His evidence that he told the participants to wear boots, did not sit well with his wearing some kind of trainer or trailer shoe, when carrying out the risk assessment. He did not complete the risk assessment form in the way recommended by Mr White – that is, using it as a checklist when conducting the assessment and completing it before commencement of the training session. Finally whilst he asserted he had undergone risk assessment training he could not say when and could not explain the training programme . . . which recorded that he was on the waiting list for training in risk assessment at this time.
>
> . . .
>
> All the witnesses qualified to give an opinion on the issue of risk assessment generally agreed on what was required and that either frozen ground that would not take a stud or ground that was uneven or rutted, would not be suitable for training exercises and present an obvious risk of injury. They also all agreed that any risk assessment which failed to identify such conditions could not have been accurately or properly conducted.
>
> Decision
> Accordingly having concluded on the evidence that these conditions existed at the relevant time, I was satisfied that such conditions present an obvious risk of injury and the risk assessment undertaken here by the defenders' employee, in the course of his employment, was inaccurate or inadequately conducted.[66]

As alluded to in *Cox*, completion of an accurate and adequate risk assessment enables coaches to identify (and address) conditions presenting an obvious risk of

---

65 Ibid. [23].
66 Ibid. [27], [31], [32].

injury, and thereby by fulfilling this duty, avoid exposing athletes and participants to unreasonable risk of injury. On the given facts, the coach in *Cox* was criticised for failing to complete an adequate risk assessment before commencing the session. However, and as revealed in the following case examined, the duty to complete an effective risk assessment by coaches also involves a dynamic process which is subject to continuous review.

(iii) *MacIntyre v Ministry of Defence* [2011] EWHC 1690

During a formal army adventurous training exercise, the claimant in *MacIntyre v Ministry of Defence* suffered a very serious injury in a climbing accident. The case turned on three main issues: (i) whether the leaders were adequately qualified and experienced; (ii) whether the assessment of risk was suitable and sufficient; and (iii) whether the climbing methods adopted by the leaders were proper. These issues clearly reiterate the fact that coaches have a duty to conduct adequate risk assessments and, more generally, that coaches with the relevant qualifications and experience, and those following recognised and proper practice, are best placed to effectively discharge their duty of care towards participants. On the facts, and accepting that the leaders 'owed the claimant a duty to take all reasonable steps to minimise the danger to him of injury or death' and, 'to see that the climbing undertaken was properly considered and that reasonable decisions were taken as to whether and where to climb',[67] Spencer J was not persuaded that there was any breach of duty.

In arriving at this judgment, Spencer J advocated a purposive construction with regard to the qualifications held.[68] This required the court to conduct a thorough consideration of the actual qualifications held in order to reveal a meaningful interpretation of whether the qualifications of the leaders were adequate in the particular circumstances. Given coaches may be accredited by different awarding bodies within the same sport, this approach appears entirely sensible.[69] There are two further points of interest raised by *MacIntyre* regarding the review of qualifications held by coaches when courts are tasked with establishing if there has been a breach of duty. First, in concluding that the leaders 'held the appropriate qualifications to be leading the climb on this mountain', Spencer J continued, '[e]qually important, they had very extensive practical experience to augment their formal qualifications'.[70] This observation explicitly reinforces the fact that when determining whether or not coaches are competent for the duties assumed, and notwithstanding the fact that formal accredited qualification(s) will generally provide the most conclusive evidence of this, practical coaching experience is also of considerable relevance. Second, and an

---

67 *MacIntyre* (n 59) [65]-[66]. According to the defendant, the Army General Administrative Instruction spelt out the duty of care owed (at [67]).
68 Ibid. [57].
69 For instance, in *Ahmed* (n 21) the court had to consider somewhat contrasting guidance provided by two different professional associations, the National Interscholastic Cycling Association and the Mountain Bike Instructors Award Scheme (at [91]). Discussed further later.
70 *MacIntyre* (n 59) [120].

extremely interesting observation when determining the boundary between reasonable and unreasonable coaching practice, was acceptance by the judge that:

> although Lieutenant Colonel Robson and Captain Williams were operating at the upper end of the limitations of their qualifications, this should in no way be regarded as undesirable. On the contrary, it is a positive and desirable feature of a training exercise that the leaders as well as the novices are stretched.[71]

Although this statement must be interpreted in the context of a formal army adventurous training exercise, by analogy, it appears reasonable to similarly accept that it may well be desirable for coaches working in performance sport with elite athletes to operate at the upper end of the limitations of their qualifications, and appropriately stretch athletes, in order to optimise performance.

The second main issue determinative of liability in *MacIntyre* concerned the leader's duty to adequately assess risk. Counsel for the claimant criticised the risk assessment carried out on the morning of the climb, submitting that a proper risk assessment would have 'involved a more precise estimation of the time for each section of the ascent' and 'shown that the proposed day's climbing was over ambitious and unrealistic'.[72] In addressing these submissions, three paragraphs from Spencer J's judgment reiterate risk assessment as an ongoing duty ordinarily achieved by effective completion of both a formal, or written risk assessment, and a dynamic risk assessment:

> the essence of effective risk assessment is that it is a dynamic process which must be subject to continuous review. Risk assessment is a process not a document. The question is whether, despite any shortcomings in the initial written risk assessment on the morning of the climb, there was a proper re-assessment of risk at every stage as the climb progressed.
>
> ...
>
> In my judgment it was reasonable for Lieutenant Colonel Robson and Captain Williams to take the decision to carry on despite the loose rock, provided they had that danger in mind and took all reasonable steps to minimise any risk arising from rock fall.
>
> ...
>
> (4) I am satisfied that at all material stages there was proper appraisal and assessment of risk, and that this was kept under continuous review.[73]

---

71 Ibid. [61].
72 Ibid. [81].
73 Ibid. [82], [95], [120]. See further, Chapter 6.

148 Duty of care in context

The final main issue on which this case turned concerned whether or not the climbing methods adopted by the leaders were proper. This included the climbing of the final pitch, the choice of route, and the demands placed upon the claimant. On detailed consideration and determination of the facts, the evidence provided by the experts, and relevant documentation, Spencer J found this to be an extremely well-led and well-managed expedition:

> Whatever the cause of the rock fall, however, I am quite satisfied that there was no fault (or lack of reasonable care) on the part of Lieutenant Robson or Captain Williams in the manner of their climbing the final pitch and establishing themselves on the final stance which caused or contributed to the rock fall and thus to the tragic accident to the claimant.
>
> . . .
>
> (3) It was not unreasonable to make an attempt on the summit by the Adam-Platte route. It was not unreasonable to take the route they did across the Herzl Terrace to the start of the Adam-Platte route, particularly as it was an established route, albeit not a route shown in the guide book.
>
> . . .
>
> (5) I am satisfied that although the day's climbing was ambitious and challenging, it was not beyond the competence of the claimant and Lieutenant Champion who were thoroughly enjoying the experience. But for the claimant's accident they would both have benefited from it greatly.
>
> (6) I am satisfied that the manner of the final climb on the Herzl Terrace was appropriate, despite the presence of loose rock. Neither parallel climbing nor climbing to the full extent of the rope was inappropriate. Nor did either cause or contribute to the accident.
>
> (7) I am satisfied that there was no negligence on the part of Lieutenant Colonel Robson or Captain Williams in the way in which they climbed the final pitch.[74]

In addressing questions concerning the adequacy of the leaders' qualifications and experience, the suitability of the risk assessment process and the appropriateness of the climbing methods adopted on the day of the accident, the reasoning of the High Court in *MacIntyre* displays a realistic and astute awareness of the specific context in which the leaders were performing their functions. Such an informed judicial appreciation and understanding of the particular circumstances in which

---

74 Ibid. [113], [120].

leaders, instructors and coaches discharge their duties is an essential requirement when courts determine whether or not there has been a breach of duty of care.

C. COACH'S DUTIES: PROMPT AND PROPER MEDICAL CARE; PREVENTING INJURED ATHLETES FROM COMPETING; TRAINING INTENSITY LEVELS

The third section of this chapter which explores the specific duties incumbent upon coaches begins by considering requirements relating to the referral of injured players and athletes for prompt and proper medical care. Closely linked to this is the extent of the duty of care of coaches to prevent injured athletes from training and competing. The two cases critically examined are from elite sport. The first, *Brady v Sunderland Association Football Club Limited*, involved the circumstances of professional football and a plaintiff footballer with excellent potential. The second, *Davenport v Farrow*, concerned a claim brought against a coach by an athlete of world-class potential. A material consideration before the court in both cases included determination of reasonable training intensity levels by the respective coaches involved.

(i) Brady v Sunderland Association Football Club Limited (Unreported, 2 April 1998 Queen's Bench Division)

Although *Brady v Sunderland Association Football Club Limited* is a case ultimately decided in the Court of Appeal,[75] it is the first instance judgment that is most instructive when defining the duty of care of coaches. The plaintiff in this case was a highly promising young footballer, having played for the Sunderland First Team and the Republic of Ireland Under-21 and Youth Teams. Due to a likely vascular problem in his right leg, and despite several operations, he was unable to pursue his career as a professional footballer. For present purposes, the action brought by the plaintiff essentially amounted to an allegation that the club had breached its duty of care owed to him by failing to properly heed or investigate obvious physical problems and/or complaints, with a subsequent failure to refer him to a doctor. It was alleged on behalf of the plaintiff that complaints by the player, and apparent difficulties in training, were attributed to an attitude problem and that any referral to a doctor would have led to a diagnosis of possible vascular problems which would have been investigated at a time when treatment would have been successful. The claim proved unsuccessful. However, detailed examination of the judgment from the perspective of a coach provides an important insight regarding the likely scrutiny by courts of the conduct of coaches should a claim be brought against a coach for a breach of duty of care.

---

75 *Brady v Sunderland Association Football Club Ltd*, 17 November 1998 (CA).

150 Duty of care in context

According to Martens, the medical responsibilities of a coach include making sure that the athlete's health is satisfactory prior to participation, determining when an athlete's illness or injury should prevent further participation and permitting athletes to return to active participation only when it is safe to do so.[76] Significantly, in *Brady*, when assessing the reasonableness of the Club's actions and, more specifically, the behaviour of the manager/coach, these were key issues for the court. Subsequently, given the particular facts of this case, the reasonableness of the instruction, supervision and referral to the club's physiotherapist for medical attention by the coach/manager were crucial matters in determining the outcome of the trial. As succinctly put by the trial judge, Mr Justice Buckley:

> [T]he real issues are whether the plaintiff complained of, as opposed to experienced, symptoms which should have led to an earlier referral to [the Club's honorary Doctor] or whether the Club, through [the Club's physiotherapist] or the manager . . . should otherwise have spotted them and made such a referral.

In prioritising the actions of the manager/coach, and consistent with this chapter's objectives of providing a detailed insight, and greater awareness of the scope of a coach's duty of care, interesting aspects of the plaintiff's submissions when seeking to make out the allegation of negligence included:

- During a training run, after complaining of severe pain in his calf to the manager, the plaintiff was told to keep running with the other players, the manager/coach saying he didn't care what the plaintiff had and that he could see the physiotherapist after training;
- The coach was repeatedly telling the plaintiff that he had an attitude problem, particularly in relation to training; and
- When referring to a six-mile run completed at a later date, in his witness statement, the plaintiff stated that the manager 'told me that he wasn't going to put up with any more nonsense. He told me that I couldn't stop and to keep going. He then sent the other players off in a different direction and he ran with me along the coast lecturing me about my attitude and telling me I just didn't like hard work. At the end of the run he told me I could go to see the physiotherapist'.

Whilst finding the plaintiff to be an honest witness, the court acknowledged the difficulty faced by him in recalling details from almost six years prior to the hearing of the case. Furthermore, the transient nature of the plaintiff's injury, combined

---

76 R Martens, *Successful Coaching* (3rd edn, Champaign, Human Kinetics 2004) 482.

with the admission that he did not like training without the ball, persuaded Buckley J that it had been understandable and reasonable for the manager to conclude that the plaintiff had an attitude problem. On this issue, the High Court's judgment concludes:

> [The manager/coach] agreed he did not like the plaintiff's attitude at times. He said he was a talented player, but one who needed to work harder. He was fine with the ball but not without it was how he described him. He felt the plaintiff did not work hard at stamina running or with weights and had a poor attitude to hard training generally. There is a measure of common ground here because the plaintiff was conscious that [the manager/coach] felt he had an attitude problem and he accepted he didn't like stamina training and preferred training with the ball. He was disenchanted with the coaching staff.

Crucially, the judgment of Buckley J at first instance, quite correctly, makes plain that, '[e]ven if [the manager's] attitude at the time was robust – and it probably was – in all the circumstances, that does not begin to amount to negligence'. The autocratic and authoritarian coaching style, perhaps prevalent within the culture in professional soccer,[77] and allegedly adopted by this manager/coach, was regarded by the court to have been reasonable in the circumstances of professional football at that time. Ultimately, the claims of a breach of duty of care by the Club, and its agents (including the manager/coach and physiotherapist), failed. Nonetheless, reflecting more widely on *Brady*, and although not established on the particular facts of this individual case, this judgment highlights the point that coaches may be in breach of duty as a result of: ineffective provision of medical care/referrals; negligent supervision and/or instruction; pressuring injured players to perform; and in failing to ensure that the intensity of training sessions and practices is within reasonable parameters of acceptable coaching.

The more recent case of *Davenport v Farrow* provides a further, and fuller, detailed illustration and unpacking of these specific duties owed by coaches to athletes under their charge and, in particular, the duty to provide prompt and proper medical care/referrals.

(ii) Davenport v Farrow [2010] EWHC 550

The defendant coach in *Davenport v Farrow* was extremely successful, holding the highest level of formal qualification accredited by UK Athletics. The claimant was

---

77 C Cushion and R Jones, 'Power, Discourse, and Symbolic Violence in Professional Youth Soccer: The Case of Albion Football Club' (2006) 23 *Sociology of Sport Journal* 142, 148.

an athlete of world-class potential, having broken the UK Junior record for the 400 metre hurdles at the World Junior Championships in 2004. The claimant's case, somewhat consistent with that argued by counsel in *Brady*, alleged that he sustained stress fractures in October/November 2004, causing significant pain which affected his ability to train, and which he drew to the attention of his coach. However, it was contended by the athlete that his coach ignored these complaints, dismissing them as symptomatic of a lack of motivation on the part of the claimant. Subsequently, it was submitted that in breach of his duties to the claimant the coach failed to take the complaints seriously, assuring the claimant that there was nothing wrong with him. It was further asserted that the coach ought to have advised the claimant to have the condition investigated, and that had an investigation then taken place, the stress fractures would have been treated conservatively with rest, and that, on the balance of probabilities, they would have united satisfactorily without surgical intervention. In short, the court was of the view that the claimant's case depended upon when the stress fractures occurred, since if the fractures predated October/November 2004, then there could be no causal relationship between the alleged failure on the part of the defendant coach to respond to the claimant's complaints of back pain during the relevant period and the injury, loss and damage for which the claimant contended.

Both sides in *Davenport* called other athletes trained by the defendant coach to provide evidence. One such athlete, EP, recalled how the defendant 'was continually on about the fact that [the claimant] was lazy and that there was nothing wrong with him'.[78] Crucially, in highlighting the potential significance of the specific circumstances of the case, including the coaching style adopted by coach, Owen J recognised:

> There is a further aspect of the evidence that bears on the issue. The claimant contends that the defendant was a forceful and controlling personality who demanded a high level of control over young athletes whom he coached. He gave evidence that the defendant wanted a say in all aspects of his life. The defendant would telephone on an almost daily basis, and would question his mother about what she was feeding him, wanting to control his diet.[79]

In terms of evidence regarding the authoritarian practice employed by the defendant coach, EP elaborated:

> Looking back at my time with [the defendant coach], I had not realised how controlling [he] was over his athletes. With hindsight, he was

---

78 *Davenport v Farrow* [2010] EWHC 550 [23].
79 Ibid. [27].

> incredibly controlling. He controlled everything. [He] told me what I could eat, he insisted that I weigh my food so I just got enough. He said that if I went to bed hungry then I would burn more fat whilst I slept and keep my weight down.[80]

Arguably, a more objective assessment of the defendant's approach to coaching, or coaching practice, was provided during the court hearing by the then Director of Coaching for Track and Field Events at Loughborough University:

> Knowing [the coach], he is pretty steadfast in his views on how someone should be coached and is not someone who readily listens to someone else's views. He is also controlling in the way in which he handles his athletes and he dictates how things are done. Younger athletes will tend to accept what their coach tells them in terms of how they train and what treatment they need and I can understand when [the claimant] says he accepted [his coach's] advice on things.[81]

As previously established, cases brought against coaches for a breach of duty are always extremely fact-sensitive and dependent upon the particular circumstances of each individual case. Accordingly, in *Davenport*, the defendant coach's relationship with the athletes that he trained and, more specifically, the coach's behaviour and practice, contextualised for the court assessment of the claimant's submissions in relation to his back pain. A further corresponding matter relating to both *Davenport v Farrow* and *Brady v Sunderland Association Football Club*, and likely to be of some relevance in future coach negligence cases, concerns what coaches frequently term an 'attitude problem' of the athlete(s) being coached. On this, the judgment of the court in *Davenport* found:

> Secondly the evidence as to the nature of their relationship is relevant in that the claimant contends that it provides an explanation as to why his complaints were ignored by the defendant. The evidence shows clearly that from December 2004 until they parted company, the defendant considered that the claimant lacked motivation and had an attitude problem.[82]

---

80 Ibid. [28].
81 Ibid. [30].
82 Ibid. [32].

Owen J continued:

> The claimant gave evidence that he thought that the defendant believed that the problem that he was reporting with his back was just an attempt to get out of training. [EP] recalled the defendant saying continually at this time that the claimant was lazy and that there was nothing wrong with him. [LP, another athlete] gave evidence that if you were someone who was lazy and lacked credibility, then any aches and pains would be met by the defendant with some cynicism.[83]

Whilst it may be reasonable for coaches, on occasions, to become frustrated with athletes due to a lack of commitment, hard work and intensity, the court's attention concentrates on how an ordinarily reasonable coach in the same circumstances would fulfil their duty of care. Crucially, this is an objective test of reasonableness which would not reflect the subjective idiosyncratic personal tendencies, for instance, possible excessive cynicism, of individual coaches. Simply applied, the negligence standard demands that defining the boundary between what might amount to appropriate coaching behaviour, as opposed to pushing athletes too hard, is a question of what is objectively reasonable and justifiable in the same circumstances. Consequently, a further contemporaneous source of information considered by the court in *Davenport*, and likely to be instructive and informative for coaches, was a screening report, compiled as part of a programme of regular screening due to the fact that the claimant had been enlisted in the UK Athletics programme for athletes with world-class potential. This 'SW Potential athlete report' contained the following statement on the claimant:

> From discussion with [the defendant coach] and feedback from Darcy appears training programme is all in place. However, concerns over controlling nature of relationship between coach and athletes . . . and strong possibility that athletes are being pushed too hard too early. Prevalence of injuries in whole group suggests this may be case.[84]

Following a detailed consideration of the issues, the High Court dismissed the claim against the defendant coach in *Davenport* since the claimant had not discharged the burden of proving that on the balance of probabilities the stress

---

83 Ibid. [35].
84 *Davenport* (n 78) [41].

fractures occurred in October/November 2004.[85] Importantly, Owen J found that the coaching regime undertaken in 2004–2005 'was within the range of acceptable coaching (level 4) for an athlete of his ability and aspirations', and the trial judge was 'not persuaded that there was a change in the level and intensity of training in September 2004 such as to provide an explanation for the development of spondyloyses'.[86]

Critical scrutiny of the judicial reasoning from both *Brady* and *Davenport*, and appreciation of the material facts presented to the court, reiterates the necessity for coaching practice to be reasonable and commensurate to the specific circumstances in which athletes are performing. This reinforces the good practice of coaches critically reflecting upon the suitability and appropriateness of their coaching behaviours, thereby ensuring that the coaching methods employed are rigorously justifiable. In this regard, should a claim be brought against a coach for a breach of duty, the court would likely be able to peruse expert witness testimony when seeking to determine what might amount to reasonable coaching practice in the same circumstances.

(D) COACH'S DUTIES: PROPER AND SAFE USE OF EQUIPMENT; PITCH OF COACHING SESSIONS

In further developing the previous section's discussion, the next case calling for critical analysis also concerns an injury sustained by an elite athlete of Olympic potential and whether or not the demands made of this athlete were reasonable and realistic. More specifically, this judgment from the particular circumstances of bobsleigh offers a detailed scrutiny of the extent of a coach's duty in relation to the proper use of safe equipment.[87]

Shone v British Bobsleigh Limited [2018] 5 WLUK 226

Shone v British Bobsleigh Limited is a recent case regarding a coach's duty to take reasonable steps to ensure the proper use of safe equipment. This case was initially mentioned in Chapter 1 when distinguishing between legal and moral duties of care. The claimant in *Shone* was an elite athlete who had previously competed for England and GB in athletics but, following a number of minor injuries, had started to consider competing in other sports. Following trials at the British Bobsleigh and Skeleton Association (BBSA) facilities in Bath in 2011, she was invited by the performance director to compete for GB in the forthcoming season. It was at

---

85 Ibid. [72].
86 Ibid. [59]. See further, the discussion of the law of negligence's control mechanism of causation in Chapter 2. Also see, the discussion of the *Woodbridge* principle in Chapters 2, 3 & 6–7.
87 In a school context, also see *Cassidy v Manchester CC*, 12 July 1995 (CA).

Winterberg, Germany, during a training session designed to allow the coaches to train, assess and observe the athletes on the track, that the claimant suffered serious spinal injuries in a bobsleigh accident on 26 October 2011. Essentially, the claimant's case was that the coaches:

> negligently allowed the claimant to ride as brakeman in a two-man bobsleigh which had not been customised for her, or at least which did not enable her to brace herself adequately within the bobsleigh by holding on to handles and by pressing her feet against foot pegs or against the back of the driver's seat, as a result of which she suffered injury in the crash.[88]

The BBSA accepted that a duty was owed to the claimant 'to take all reasonable actions to ensure she was reasonably safe in the course of her activities on the bobsleigh run, in accordance with the prevailing standard of reasonable practice in the sport of national bobsleigh'.[89] Whilst clearly correct, the submissions for the claimant more specifically addressed the practical content of this duty with regard to the proper use of safe equipment, maintaining that this duty included 'fitting out or customising the bobsleigh to the extent that it would reasonably have been required. The duty extended to preventing her from riding in a bobsleigh not fitted out or customised as would reasonably have been required'.[90]

The claimant was a complete novice and her practice run(s) on 24 October 2011 was the first time she had slid in a bobsleigh. On 26 October 2011 the claimant had three runs, with two different drivers, the third run of which involved the crash which was the cause of her injuries. When determining the circumstances of these runs, and in focusing on the scope of the duty owed by the coaches, the following detailed paragraphs from the judgment are most instructive and worth recalling in full.

Shone v British Bobsleigh Limited [2018] County Court (Swindon)

HH Judge Parkes QC

54 He [MW, GB Performance Coach] accepted that she [the claimant] said she felt worried, which is normal for any novice athlete competing at an elite

---

88 *Shone* (n 19) [2]. Accordingly, if successful, the BBSA would be found vicariously liable through the actions of its employees.
89 Ibid. [4].
90 Ibid. [5].

level for the first time. But, he said, there was no pressure on her. That may well have been the case from his perspective, and I accept that others . . . may have told her so, but it seems to me a wholly unrealistic and unimaginative attitude. The claimant was bound to regard herself as under assessment, even though these were only training runs. [MW] was her coach and the person best placed to assess her. As [MW] himself said, she was there to demonstrate that she had the skills to compete at the highest level and ultimately make the GB Olympic squad. That would have been the goal of the athletes present, he said, and 'so they did not need any motivation or pressure to compete'. That 'so' reveals an obvious non sequitur. Of course she felt herself under pressure to show herself made of the right stuff to go to the top. [MW], as an experienced coach, should have understood that.

. . .

63 [MW] did not recall a second discussion before the second run. As far as he was concerned, the claimant's first run with [FH] had been successful, and she had agreed to proceed with the third and final training run of the day. In my judgment he is wrong to say that she had agreed to anything of the kind. It is quite clear to me that the claimant had not expected to have to do a second run with [FH], and was very upset to be asked to do so. However, his evidence was that had she said she felt unsafe, he was certain that he would have told her not to slide: these were training sessions, and athletes were free to choose whether they took part or not. As I have said, while on one level the claimant was free to choose, the reality was that she felt that she had no choice, and [MW] should have understood that. It seems to me that his belief . . . that there was no pressure on the athletes simply cannot have been right. It is belied by the claimant's evidence of the tense attitude of [FH], and it is belied by the obvious reality that the athletes were being assessed by [MW] and others for potential Olympic skills.

. . .

Breach of Duty

66 I have referred above to the respective contentions of the parties about the extent of BBSA's duty of care towards the athletes. They are in essence agreed, and in my judgment rightly so, on the existence of a duty of care to the claimant to take all reasonable steps to ensure that she was reasonably safe when riding in a bobsleigh. I am doubtful that the duty is in any significant way qualified, at least not on the facts of this case, by the BBSA's coda 'in accordance with the prevailing standard of reasonable practice in the sport of national bobsleigh', although I accept that it must be seen in the context of a high risk sport that carries a high risk of injury and which involves a balance between performance and safety.

> 67 It is accepted on behalf of the BBSA that the level of control which it exercised over the bobsleigh teams was sufficient to impute liability to it for the actions of its coaches, especially [MW].
>
> 68 It seems to me quite clear, on my findings of fact, that the BBSA, through [MW] breached its duty to the claimant by allowing a frightened novice to go down the run from the top start when (to his knowledge) she could not brace with either hands or feet and felt unsafe to slide. . . .
>
> 69 It might have been different had she been frightened but well able to brace with hands and feet and therefore as safe as any brakeman, even a novice, could reasonably be: in those circumstances, I doubt whether it could have been said that there was any duty in [MW] to stop her sliding if, though frightened, she was prepared to go. What determines the matter on the facts that I have found is that she told him, and he knew, that she was not properly braced either with hands or feet, a situation in which (so he claimed in his witness statement) he would not have allowed the sled to leave the starting block.
>
> 70 It seems to me to be irrelevant that the FITB [Federation Internationale de Bobsleigh et Tobogganing] rules did not require handles or foot pegs in 2011. The claimant could not hold on to the chassis members, and she could not brace on the back of the driver's seat. Everyone was agreed on the need to hold on properly with the hands. If the claimant could not do so, either by grasping the chassis members or by firmly holding a loop of fabric, it is nothing to the point that the FITB did not require separate handles in 2011; and if the claimant could not brace on the driver's seat, as [MC, Operations Director for the BBSA and Race Organiser at Winterberg] eventually agreed she should have been able to do, it is nothing to the point that the FITB did not require foot pegs. Mr Meakin [counsel for the BBSA] argues that the BBSA was entitled to rely on the FITB rules as setting the standard for safety in the sport. That cannot be right, if simple reliance on the FITB requirements has the result that a brakeman is sent down a track unable to brace her body properly. The lie is given to that proposition by [MW's] claim that he would not have allowed the claimant to ride without being properly braced by hands and feet.

Of immediate relevance to a coach's duty regarding the proper use of safe equipment, and determinative in this case, is the fact that exposing athletes to an unreasonable level of risk amounts to a breach of duty of care. In short, the court found that the coach had been informed by the claimant athlete that she could not brace with either hands or feet and felt unsafe to slide. Proper and safe use of equipment was not possible. The coach had made plain in his witness statement that this was a situation in which he would have not allowed the sled to leave the starting block. This concession is undoubtedly appropriate, since exposing athletes to unnecessary risk of injury cannot be justified in any circumstances. The court recognised that this case involved 'a high-risk sport that carries a high risk of injury and which involves a balance between performance and safety'. Consequently, the court accepted that if the claimant could have used the equipment so that she was as safe as any brakeman (even a novice) could reasonably be, it appears most unlikely that the coach would have breached his duty of care in allowing her to slide. This would appear to remain the case even though the claimant may have been frightened but willing to give it a go. In these contrasting circumstances, the proper use of safe equipment would have enabled the elite athlete (claimant) to have been as reasonably safe as possible in the context of a high-risk performance sport where the claimant was being assessed for potential Olympic skills.

When discharging their duty of care, and particularly when determining the boundary between reasonable and unreasonable coaching practice in order to gain a competitive edge, coaches must be mindful of not placing athletes under too much pressure. Such possible excessive pressure – as discussed earlier in relation to a coach's duties to provide prompt and proper medical care, to prevent injured athletes from competing, to incorporate reasonable training intensity levels into training programmes, and as perhaps compounded by a perceived 'attitude problem' of athletes – also applies to the proper and safe use of equipment. In addressing this matter on the given facts in *Shone*, the view of HHJ Parkes was that as an experienced coach, MW was best placed to have a realistic appreciation of the considerable pressure that the claimant was under to complete a further run. In other words, when coaches are discharging their duty of care, and subject to the specific circumstances, the reality of the coach–athlete relationship means that coaches ought to be alive to the fact that athletes may perceive that they have no choice but to sometimes conform to the unreasonable demands of coaches.[91] Coaches lacking this empathy and awareness may find successfully discharging their duty of care problematic.

Moreover, this concern raises an important and connected issue yet to be tested before courts in the UK, namely, the extent of the duty of coaches to prevent athletes from exposing themselves to unreasonable risk of personal injury. For instance, with regard to sport-related concussion, and particularly in the absence of a qualified medical practitioner,[92] this would most certainly include coaches insisting upon players with a suspected concussion being removed from play and complying with all stipulated protocols. This would also cover circumstances where such players are determined to continue competing, which plainly exposes them to both unnecessary and unreasonable risks. Simply applied, coaches would be in breach of their duty of care by allowing a concussed player to continue to play and/or instructing a player to return to competition, or training, in the knowledge that the player is concussed or when the coach knows s/he is at risk of injury.[93]

---

91 An interesting corollary of this is the effect of peer pressure.
92 This being commonplace at amateur level.
93 T Meakin, 'The Evolving Legal Issues on Rugby Neuro-Trauma' (2013) 21(3) *British Association for Sport and Law Journal* 34, 37.

A final issue of note raised in *Shone* is the function of the rules promulgated by recognised bodies when defining a coach's duty of care. Although the FITB rules at the time of the accident did not require handles or foot pegs to be fitted to bobsleighs, HHJ Parkes regarded this as irrelevant since the fact remained that the claimant was sent down a track unable to brace her body properly. In other words, whilst the FITB rules may have been of some relevance when setting the standard for safety in the sport, this was essentially trumped by the coaches overriding duty to adopt reasonable coaching practice so that reasonable care is taken to ensure the reasonable safety of athletes. Complying with FITB rules was not sufficient to discharge this duty because such a reliance by the coaches had the effect of exposing the claimant to the unreasonable and unnecessary risk of foreseeable personal injury. Accordingly, in the particular circumstances, mere reliance on the FITB requirements could in no way be suggested to be logically justifiable.

(E) COACH'S DUTIES: MATCHING PARTICIPANTS; ASSESSMENT OF PARTICIPANTS; INSTRUCTION; SUPERVISION; ORGANISATION AND PITCH OF COACHING SESSIONS

In the final section of this chapter, the duties of coaches with regard to matching and assessing participants calls for particular emphasis. In so doing, by using a case involving a claim brought against a mountain bike instructor as the main focus, the High Court was somewhat inevitably also tasked with examining the extent of the instructor's duty when instructing, demonstrating, supervising and organising the session. This judicial scrutiny included consideration of the level of difficulty of the runs selected and the associated challenges, demands and expectations posed by the delivery of the course in question by the instructor.

Ahmed v MacLean [2016] EWHC 2798

At the time of the accident in *Ahmed v MacLean*, the claimant was taking part in a beginners' mountain bike tuition course in 2012. Although the claimant had owned a mountain bike for about 12 years, the court found that to all intents and purposes he was a novice mountain bike rider. The two other riders receiving group tuition at the same time, AN and KT, were considerably more experienced than the claimant. Another rider booked on the course failed to attend. The claimant suffered extremely serious personal injuries when he landed after going over the top of the handlebars when cycling down a slope, rendering him paraplegic. The claimant's action against the defendant mountain bike instructor alleged that the instructor had failed to take reasonable care of his safety on the course. The defendant instructor was originally a primary school teacher by profession, and after undertaking the MIAS (Mountain Bike Instructors Award Scheme) mountain bike instructor level 2 course in 2010, he became a full-time mountain bike instructor. Given the instructor's background, he was experienced in completing risk assessments. Deciding this case required the court to consider in detail the nature of the duty of care owed by the instructor/coach with regard to the duties of instruction and supervision. More specifically, in view of the different ability and experience levels of the individual group members, the duties of matching participants, and whether the participants possessed an adequate level of skills for the challenges presented on the course, called for rigorous scrutiny.

Ahmed v MacLean [2016]

Baker J

25. The defendant agreed that mountain biking is a potentially hazardous pursuit, so that the instructor's paramount focus was to ensure the minimisation of risk. He agreed that it was essential for instructors to know the level of individual expertise which each of the participants possessed prior to the commencement of the course, and for this to be monitored throughout the course. In so far as prior knowledge was concerned, he would have obtained this information from the booking form, and wouldn't ask any of them about their individual experience in the car park before setting off. The defendant said that in so far as monitoring their progress was concerned, he did this by observing those attending on his courses, and that if he observes that they can perform a particular skill, and they don't say that they are having any difficulty, then he assumes that they possess that skill. He agreed that it is not uncommon for individuals in a group to be embarrassed to admit that they are not keeping up with the others, and that it is therefore necessary to cater for the least able in the group. He said that so far as he was concerned, when he was at the top of the slope where the accident occurred, he believed that all three of the participants had shown equal riding ability prior to them attempting to ride down the slope for the first time. It was for this reason that he had treated the three participants equally that day, and had not provided any of them with any additional instruction or tuition.

...

27. The defendant agreed that on occasions he had introduced those who had attended for the beginners' course, to intermediate level skills ... albeit he would only do so, after he had assured himself that those participating had reached a sufficient skill level to be able to cope safely with the more advanced skills. He admitted that on occasions when he was instructing on these courses, including beginners' ones, he did push participants to the edge of their comfort zone. However, he said that he did not believe that he did so to the extent that any danger arose; albeit he agreed that on occasions this had resulted in the participants falling off their bikes.

...

71. [T]he matters to be determined are whether the claimant has established, on the balance of probabilities, that the accident was caused by the defendant having failed to exercise reasonable skill and care in providing him with tuition on the mountain bike beginners' course, or whether, as the defendant submits, the claimant was either wholly or in part responsible for the accident due to his own lack of care.

. . .

74. The defendant clearly has a passion for mountain biking, to the extent that he gave up his career as a primary school teacher, and, since 2010, has been a mountain bike instructor. Neither his demeanour in court, nor the evidence which I heard from those who attended on the course in March 2012, led me to believe that he was either a reckless or authoritarian individual. The impression which I gained was that in 2012 he had an enthusiastic easy-going manner of teaching, albeit, he had a tendency to be overly optimistic as to the ability of some of those attending his courses to keep pace with the instruction and training which he provided. . . [this] may explain why it was that, at the commencement of the course, instead of carefully ascertaining the individual abilities of each member, he appears to have set off from the car park without having made any such assessment.

75. In this regard I accept the evidence of Mr MacKay [expert witness], that such an assessment was a necessary prerequisite, which should have been undertaken by the defendant, so that he was able to appropriately pitch and progress his instruction and training during the course. It seems to me that this was particularly important in the present case, due to the fact that this was a group course, and, as the defendant accepts, it is likely that he knew from the booking forms that the pre-course mountain biking skills possessed by the various participants was significantly different, in that whereas the claimant possessed little or no mountain biking skills, [AN] was significantly more proficient. It was therefore essential that the defendant tailored his tuition to ensure the safety of the least able of those attending his course; a matter which I consider that he ultimately failed to achieve.

. . .

78. I accept the evidence of Mr MacKay, as reflected in the defendant's website, that repeated individual assessment of the claimant's ability to perform each of the necessary skills was required, in order to ensure that he had mastered them to a sufficient extent that it was safe for him to continue along the trail. . . .

. . .

81. I am disinclined to accept Mr Martin's [expert witness] opinion that the defendant's observations of the claimant, as he rode from the car park to the top of the slope in question, were sufficient to have allowed the defendant to adequately assess either the claimant's braking proficiency or any of the other

skills, which were necessary to enable the claimant to safely descend the slope where the accident took place.

82. It is unclear to me as to whether the defendant's failure to provide sufficient instruction, demonstration and assessment of the participants' mountain biking skills, other than the negotiation of small obstacles, before reaching the slope where the accident took place, was borne out of the time deficit caused by the nonattendance of one the participants. However, whatever its cause, it resulted in what I am quite sure was unjustified optimism by the defendant as to the claimant's ability to ride down the slope in question in safety. In that his belief that, by the time the group reached the top of the slope, all three of the participants had shown equal riding ability, one mirrored to an extent by [KT] and [AN], was founded on terrain which was significantly less challenging than the slope where the accident took place.

83. I am satisfied that the slope [where the accident took place] represented the most challenging part of the trail . . . the fact that [AN] didn't consider it particularly challenging, merely reflected his familiarity with mountain biking, and the skills which he possessed. Moreover, even he acknowledged that it would be a bit intimidating for those less experienced, and [KT] observed that the presence of the drop-off at the crest of the main route represented a "confidence moment". . . .

84. Although I accept that, on occasions, it may be appropriate for those under instruction to be taken slightly out of their "comfort zone" in order to make progress, I accept the evidence of Mr MacKay that, especially bearing in mind the risk of serious injury which it is acknowledged this slope presented, the defendant should have selected an alternative and less challenging slope upon which to teach the participants the skills which were necessary to negotiate it in safety; essentially those of balance, observation and braking. Moreover, I also accept that the defendant should only have permitted the group to ride down the slope where the accident took place, once each of them had not only gained sufficient mastery of these skills so as to be able to negotiate the slope in safety, but also with the necessary degree of confidence to meet the challenges presented by it. In my judgment had the defendant taken these steps, then it is likely that the accident would not have occurred, in that the claimant would have had sufficient confidence and ability to negotiate the slope in safety.

. . .

86. There is some conflict in the evidence as to whether the defendant provided the group with a choice of which of the two routes to take down the slope. . . . Not only did the main duty to assess whether the participants possessed an adequate level of skills to negotiate the slope in safety lie with the defendant, but he ought to have appreciated that any apparent choice, by any individual member of the group, may well be tainted by the effects

> of peer pressure. In this regard it is significant that the right hand route was considered, at least by [AN], to be the "chicken route".
>
> ...
>
> 96. I consider that the defendant is at least in part liable to the claimant for this accident, in that the accident was caused by his failure to carry out his tuition with reasonable skill and care, so as to enable the claimant to ride down the slope in safety. In summary, I consider that, having failed to carry out an adequate assessment of the claimant's individual skill level at the commencement of the course, he thereafter progressed the tuition which he provided to the group, without sufficient regard to the claimant's capabilities; in that he failed to make sufficient assessments of the claimant's ability to undertake the skills he was being taught, failed to teach the skills required to negotiate the slope where the accident took place in safety and thereafter permitted the claimant to attempt to negotiate the descent of the slope down the main route, and, on his second descent, encouraged him to do so at a speed which was likely to enhance the risk of serious harm being caused to him.

Before critically analysing some of the implications of this judgment regarding a coach's duty of care, it should be noted that the High Court was also tasked with considering the issue of contributory negligence. By informing the claimant that his technique was satisfactory, and advising him to ride down the slope at greater speed on his next attempt, it was accepted that the defendant instructor would likely have provided the claimant with a measure of false reassurance. Such false reassurance regarding the claimant's ability to ride down the slope for his second attempt in safety did not, however, totally eclipse the claimant's responsibility for his own safety. Consequently, given the claimant retained some insight into his own abilities, he was also to blame for not having informed the defendant that he considered that he did not have the capability to ride down the slope in safety. In finding this to be an instance of contributory negligence, Baker J determined that the appropriate amount of responsibility which the claimant was held to bear in relation to his contribution to the cause of the accident suffered was 20 percent.

As a preliminary issue, when defining his own duty of care, the mountain bike instructor in *Ahmed* agreed that ensuring the minimisation of risk was his paramount focus. Intuitively, one might suspect that without more considered and searching scrutiny that this might well be the view of most coaches. However, as the preceding pages of this book reveal, the duty of a coach is not to ensure the minimisation of risk. Since a wide range of sporting activity carries with it risks,[94] it may be both necessary and beneficial for coaches and instructors to on occasion expose participants to reasonable and worthwhile risks. Risk can be socially

---

94 *Scout Association v Barnes* [2010] EWCA Civ 1476 [22].

desirable; it is harm that should be avoided.[95] Accordingly, the duty of coaches is to take all reasonable measures to ensure that participants are reasonably safe by ensuring that participants are not exposed to unacceptable or unnecessary risk. This more precise, nuanced and fluid definition of the duty of care owed by coaches, in being able to more effectively account for the fact that taking part in many sports can be hazardous, socially beneficial and context specific, would help to prevent the law from laying down standards that are too difficult for ordinary coaches to meet.

Knowing the individual level of competence of each participant remains integral to satisfying the necessary standard of skill and care required of coaches, and more specifically, the duty of adequately matching participants. When matching participants, careful appraisal of contextual factors must be considered, including their age, height, maturity, weight, skill and experience.[96] The rules and guidelines provided by NGBs may emphasise this duty, for instance, with regard to age.[97] Physiological factors such as size and weight might arguably be more routinely considered by coaches when matching participants.[98] Nonetheless, as highlighted in *Ahmed*, a coach's duty of care also requires careful appraisal of the skill and experience of all participants being instructed and coached. As astutely recognised by Baker J when outlining the legal principles of relevance to this case, an effective assessment of the competencies of all of the participants was essential so that the defendant coach's tuition could be tailored to ensure the (reasonable) safety of the least able of those attending his course.

This duty appears coextensive with the duty of adequately assessing risk, not least since the assessment of the ability levels of participants ought to be conducted before the session (i.e., a formal, written or pre-session assessment) and continuously throughout the session (i.e., a dynamic or ongoing assessment). Importantly, this is a continuing duty that should be kept under constant review. Indeed, borrowing from terminology derived from research conducted in education proves instructive in this regard. For instance, this means that the duty of a coach to know the performance level of each participant, in order that coaching can be tailored to ensure the reasonable safety of all of those being coached, is best satisfied by adequate initial assessment (i.e., for group selection prior to commencement of activity), formative assessment (i.e., assessment for learning (AfL) conducted throughout sessions) and summative assessment (i.e., assessment of learning at the end of sessions to ensure appropriate continuity and progression between sessions). Such

---

95 T Kaye, 'Law and Risk: An Introduction' in G Woodman and D Klippel (eds), *Risk and the Law* (London, Routledge-Cavendish 2009) 8.
96 D Healey, 'Risk Management for Coaches' in F Pyke (ed), *Better Coaching: Advanced Coach's Manual* (2nd edn, Champaign, Human Kinetics 2001) 41.
97 See, for instance, *Mountford v Newlands School* [2007] EWCA Civ 21.
98 E.g., *Affuto-Nartoy v Clarke* (1984) Times, 9 February. Where a PE teacher participated in a rugby match with students during a games lesson and momentarily forgot that he was playing with young schoolboys, thereby committing an 'unlawful and dangerous tackle', resulting in a very serious accident for which the teacher was found to have been negligent.

regular checks and careful appraisal of performance and learning provides the evidence on which the pitch of sessions, and the pace of progression, can reasonably be decided. This is apposite to effective coaching practice. Indeed, it is submitted that the highly developed skills of observational analysis, as employed continuously by coaches to routinely assess the performance levels of participants, allows for the reasonably safe delivery of progressive and challenging coaching sessions. As such, critical scrutiny of a coach's duty of care from a legal perspective reinforces the importance of sufficiently assessing the skills of participants in the risk management process. Furthermore, it underscores the fundamental duty of coaches to provide adequate supervision during organised activities. In ultimately failing to satisfy these requirements and, therefore exposing the defendant to unreasonable risk of personal injury, the instructor in *Ahmed* failed to discharge his duty of care.

Effective coaching practice will appropriately stretch and challenge participants and, as recognised by Baker J, push participants 'slightly out of their "comfort zone" in order to make progress'. This is reasonable, ordinary and good coaching practice providing coaches are assured that participants have mastered a sufficient skill level to be able to cope appropriately with more advanced skills and demands. In this regard, an interesting factor revealed from *Ahmed*, and also in point in *Shone* and *MacIntyre*, is whether or not participants have sufficient confidence to effectively make a free and informed choice of whether or not they are prepared to accept the high expectations often demanded by coaches. In addition to reiterating a coach's duty to protect athletes from themselves, for instance, when participants might be willing to commit themselves to challenges creating unreasonable levels of risk, coaches must also be alive to the influence of coach and peer pressure in such scenarios. The emerging case law confirms that when scrutinising the full factual matrix of cases, courts are mindful of these factors when determining the extent of a coach's duty of care. Accordingly, given the standard of care for coaches when discharging their duties is premised on objective reasonableness, and as revealed in *Ahmed*, coaches should be cautious about being overly optimistic when ascertaining the ability and confidence of athletes to willingly meet the challenges posed.

A final issue of general (ir)relevance to the standard of care incumbent upon coaches concerns organisational difficulties frequently encountered by coaches. For example, in *Ahmed* this involved the nonattendance of a participant and prompted the judge to speculate whether the instructor's failure to provide sufficient instruction, demonstration and assessment of the participants' mountain biking skills was a result of the time deficit caused by this nonattendance. Other frequent difficulties encountered by coaches might include a leaking roof, a slippery court, or as in *Cox*, a frozen pitch. Simply applied, such difficulties in no way negate or detract from a coach's duty to perform their functions with reasonable skill and care to ensure that participants are not exposed to unreasonable risk.

Conclusion

The duty of care of a coach remains one of displaying reasonable care and skill to ensure the reasonable safety of athletes and participants when coaching.

Reasonableness is context-specific, and so defining the duty of care of coaches is highly fact-sensitive. Accordingly, by critically engaging with the emerging body of case law in the UK concerning claims of a breach of duty of care by coaches, leaders and instructors, this chapter has sought to define, clarify and analyse the duty of care incumbent upon modern sports coaches. As a starting point, framing the issue of coach negligence as an instance of professional liability reiterates the fundamental point that coaches who adopt regular, approved and logically justifiable coaching practice will be best positioned to successfully discharge their duty of care. Moreover, in contextualising and rigorously unpacking the somewhat nebulous notion of reasonableness in the particular context of sports coaching, identifying and examining the specific duties of coaches proves necessary and instructive. Building upon the approach adopted by some of the earlier research conducted in this area,[99] a thematic structural framework could be further developed, and refined, in order to better reflect advancements in coaching practice and a corresponding expansion in related jurisprudence.

Perhaps unsurprisingly, the case law analysis presented earlier confirms that the majority of cases brought against coaches for a breach of duty of care concentrate of what might be regarded as the main duties of providing adequate instruction and supervision. These duties are integral to the mutually dependent coach–athlete relationship. Whilst all of the duties of coaches discussed in sections (A)-(E) of this chapter must be discharged by coaches with reasonable care and skill, more recent case law reveals the greater importance placed by the courts on a coach's duty to complete suitable and sufficient risk assessments. Moreover, defining the boundary between reasonable and unreasonable coaching practice, for instance, when taking athletes and participants outside of their comfort zones, represents somewhat of an enduring tension that coaches must be mindful of. All of these issues were of relevance in *Anderson v Lyotier*.[100] Indeed, *Anderson* provides the most sustained consideration of the duty of care of instructors/coaches by a UK court and affords the most detailed and searching judgment regarding the practical content of a coach's duty of care. Therefore, in further extending this chapter's analysis and the principles established, whilst also offering an authentic and engaging insight of the application of the relevant law in action, the next chapter provides a case study of this highly informative High Court decision.

---

99 E.g., McCaskey and Biedzynski (n 7); Barnes (n 8).
100 *Anderson* (n 42). With regard to the framing of cases brought against coaches and instructors for alleged negligence, also see the recent case of *Craig v Tullymurry Equestrian Centre* [2019] NIQB 94.

6
CASE STUDY
Anderson v Lyotier

By adopting a sociolegal methodological framework, this book is intended to provide authentic insights of contemporary practical importance for coaching practice. In previous chapters, the emphasis has been on an examination of the law in the context of sport generally, and the domain of sports coaching in particular, in order to clarify and analyse the relevant legal principles and duties of care incumbent upon modern sports coaches. Following the establishment in Chapters 1–3 of the key legal concepts, Chapter 4 concentrated on different categories of claimants and defendants when scrutinising sports negligence jurisprudence. Subsequently, Chapter 5 engaged in a more thematic analysis of the various duties required of coaches. In further extending the preceding discussion, this chapter offers a complementary analytical lens by providing an extended focus on the 'law in action' in the individual case of *Anderson v Lyotier*.[1]

Introduction

Anderson v Lyotier represents the most sustained and rigorous scrutiny of the duty of care incumbent upon a sports instructor/coach by a UK court. Given the specific circumstances involved, it considers in detail the practical application of the duties of coaches discussed in Chapter 5 and, in particular, with regard to instruction, supervision and risk assessment. The judgment also engages with important duty of care issues of more general application, including the *Bolam* 'defence' (or test), the *Woodbridge* principle and the significant dangers of negligent entrenched practice when coaches are discharging their duty of care. Further, the court in *Anderson* was tasked with determining a matter likely to be of widespread interest

---

1 *Anderson v Lyotier* [2008] EWHC 2790.

to coaches, albeit in relation to the particular facts of this individual case, namely, the boundary between exposing athletes and participants to reasonable and/or unreasonable challenge(s). It is argued that although Foskett J gave detailed consideration to the full facts of the case in *Anderson*, ultimately, the threshold between negligent and non-negligent coaching practice was drawn too narrowly by the High Court. In adopting words used by Spencer J in the analogous case of *Pook v Rossall School*, it is submitted that the court in *Anderson* appeared too quick 'to condemn' the ski instructor 'as negligent and to substitute its own judgment for that of the [instructor]'.[2] Notwithstanding the force of such arguments, the *Anderson* judgment undoubtedly emphasises the importance of coaches (and sports law practitioners) appreciating the sometimes slender distinction between acceptable and unacceptable coaching practice when discharging their duty of care.

Facts

Mr Anderson, the claimant, sustained injuries that rendered him a complete tetraplegic at level C6 as a result of an accident when skiing off-piste[3] at a resort in the French Alps in 2004. The group with which Mr Anderson was skiing was of mixed skiing ability and experience.[4] The defendant ski instructor, M. Portejoie, provided instruction to the group from Monday–Saturday, with the accident occurring on the final day. The first two days of instruction focused on a general reintroduction to basic skills. On Wednesday, all members of the group successfully undertook a red run,[5] and some relatively unchallenging off-piste skiing, although the claimant did find aspects of the off-piste skiing difficult. Further off-piste skiing was completed on Thursday in the absence of one of the other group members, Mrs Anderson. This did not involve steep slopes or heavily wooded areas, but despite it being relatively easy off-piste terrain, both the claimant and another group member fell quite frequently. On Friday, with Mrs Anderson rejoining the group, the focus was on negotiating a steep red piste. No off-piste skiing took place on Friday. In summarising the progress and achievements of individual members of the group that week and, prior to the day of the accident, Foskett J established the following:

i) Mr Hall. He accomplished all that he attempted, including the off-piste work and a black run. He was enthusiastic about attempting more adventurous skiing

---

2 *Pook v Rossall School* [2018] EWHC 522 [33]. *Pook* involved a claim brought in negligence against a physical education (PE) teacher. See further, (n 9). Also see Chapter 2.
3 Off-piste being anything outside of the designated and marked plates or trails which are patrolled and generally prepared by machine (*Anderson* (n 1) [20]).
4 Interestingly, the court noted that the selection of the group was not claimed to be negligent or inappropriate (*Anderson* (n 1) [11]).
5 In ascending order of difficulty, the general hierarchy of piste runs is green, blue, red and black.

ii) Mr Tarquini. He had accomplished the skiing tasks set during the week, though he had found the off-piste skiing something of a challenge
iii) The Claimant. More or less the same comments as those made in respect of Mr Tarquini apply
iv) Mrs Anderson. She had managed one relatively untesting red run and one relatively undemanding off-piste experience, albeit the latter not being an experience she wished to repeat. She . . . managed one steep red run over a number of short sections with a lot of encouragement and support from M. Portejoie.[6]

Foskett J acknowledged that M. Portejoie had never seen the claimant coping competently on an off-piste slope. Moreover, with specific regard to the off-piste terrain where the accident occurred, the court found that it:

i) was steeper than any off-piste terrain any of the group had skied that week with M. Portejoie;
ii) that the snow conditions were such that they required more skill to negotiate than the on-piste conditions;
iii) whilst the terrain was not covered with large trees, there were trees (not just shrubs or saplings) on the slope, particularly to the right as the skier descended the terrain.[7]

Following a sustained examination of the particular facts and sporting context of this case, Foskett J delivered a robust and detailed judgment.

Decision

Anderson v Lyotier [2008] EWHC 2790, Foskett J

5. The central issue is whether the ski instructor . . . should have permitted or encouraged the Claimant to ski in an off-piste area where the accident occurred, the essential suggestion being that it was too difficult a terrain for the Claimant to negotiate successfully.

. . .

8 In essence, so far as the allegation of breach of duty is concerned, it is for the Claimant to establish that the ski instructor failed to provide his services to the Claimant with reasonable skill and care.

. . .

---

6 *Anderson* (n 1) [51].
7 Ibid. [82].

54. Whatever conclusion I may form about what it was the group was asked to do on the Saturday, the mere fact that members of the group had not coped particularly well with certain aspects of the tuition would not necessarily preclude the instructor from suggesting something more demanding thereafter. . . . In contemporary language it is necessary to move outside one's "comfort zone" in order to be able to progress. However, the question of where the dividing line is between the reasonable suggestion of something more challenging and the unreasonable suggestion is one to which I will have to return.

. . .

90. The position taken by the experts in the joint statement about the suitability of this off-piste section of terrain is demonstrated by the following paragraph in the joint statement:

'We are agreed that for at least some of the group members the slope was indeed a suitable choice. However . . . the instructor's judgement must always take into account the needs of the weakest member of the class. It is the opinion of Mr Exall that it was more likely than not that the slope was beyond the capabilities of the Claimant (and his wife) under the circumstances of the day. Mr Foxon and Mr Shedden on the other hand believe that it is more likely than not that at the time of the accident, the slope was suitable for the Claimant, albeit towards the upper end of what he would have been capable of descending.'

. . .

93. Before turning to other matters, it is also right to record the agreement of all the experts that 'when teaching, leading or guiding a ski group, the instructor's decisions should be based on the needs and capabilities of the weakest members of that group'.

. . .

112. It [the evidence] shows that in the seconds before his accident, the Claimant was 'struggling with the slope' and was anxious and concerned about making the turns. It evidences what, in my judgment, ought to have been the result of any prospective conscientious analysis of his capacity to undertake this slope before he did so, namely, that he would find it extremely difficult and would, more likely than not, fall and/or lose control of his skis if he attempted it. The evidence shows that he had not mastered to a sufficient level the skills necessary to undertake a piece of off-piste terrain of this nature in reasonable safety. . . . Had there been no trees of any sort, that might have made a difference – but any loss of control on a slope of this nature for someone of the Claimant's relatively limited acumen could . . . lead to an impact with a tree with potentially serious consequences. The snow conditions were such that skiing was more difficult than it would have been on-piste.

. . .

115. If I was to hold that M. Portejoie saw this first part of the descent, but that he did not feel that it was necessary to give any particular instructions about the final descent (e.g. for the Claimant to go far wider so as to avoid any prospect of colliding with the trees at all), I would be holding that he adopted a very cavalier attitude to what was happening. . . . I would have been very disinclined to draw such an adverse conclusion about someone who was a popular and approachable ski instructor. . . . However, if he did not see the Claimant's descent . . . one would wish to know why. . . . It is troubling that M. Portejoie was not watching the Claimant.

116. Whilst it is important not to be too critical, because his eyes could not be everywhere, the inference that I draw from this particular piece of evidence is that, as I think the other evidence demonstrates, M. Portejoie simply assumed that everyone in the group (a) was up to trying it and (b) wanted to do so. Not watching the Claimant suggests that he did not think that there was a problem.

117. The other compelling piece of evidence in this regard, in my judgment, is what I have taken as his presumption that Mrs Anderson was up for trying it and was capable of doing so safely. . . . [T]he fact that, in my judgment, M. Portejoie did not address the question of Mrs Anderson's capacity to undertake this slope is further evidence that he had not on this occasion considered conscientiously the capabilities of all members of the group. His duty was to choose activities for the group that were within the competence of the least able member of the group. . . .

118. For my part, on the evidence that I have heard and accepted, this slope was too much to ask of Mr Tarquini, the Claimant and Mrs Anderson. It was, on the basis of their experience and capacity, both generally and on the basis of what they did that week, a step too far and, if the question had been addressed by M. Portejoie, he ought to have seen it as such. Of course, I accept that Mr Tarquini in fact managed the slope safely (by concentrating carefully and following Mr Hall's tracks), but that is not the test. The test is whether, looked at prospectively and objectively, the terrain in the condition that it was in was a reasonably safe piece of terrain for all members of this group. Was it reasonably foreseeable that any one of these three individuals would have fallen or lost control of their skis when negotiating this terrain? The answer is "yes". That, of course, is not a determinative factor in relation to breach of duty: even the most skilled skier will fall from time to time. However, the next issue, in my judgment, is determinative in this case. If, as I have concluded, it was reasonably foreseeable that a member of the group might fall or lose control of their skis, was there a reasonably foreseeable risk of impacting with a tree in consequence? The answer too is plainly "yes" given the presence of the trees as the evidence demonstrates. Subject to the issue that has been raised of whether the seriousness of the injury to the Claimant was foreseeable . . . that establishes a breach of duty on M. Portejoie's part.

119. So why did M. Portejoie misjudge the situation? He was a very experienced ski instructor and, I am more than happy to accept, a generally conscientious one who is concerned for the safety and well-being of his students. There are two possible explanations, perhaps interrelated. First, he may have used this off-piste section regularly at the end of a week for an intermediate class, nothing untoward having occurred previously and it did not occur to him that there were any risks in taking the group there. . . . [H]e asserted that he had taken groups to the terrain on at least ten occasions that season. Second, he may have been over-influenced subconsciously by the obvious capacity of Mr Hall to undertake the slope safely. . . . If, as I think must have occurred, M. Portejoie treated them all as more or less of the same ability, then that was an unreasonable position to take.

120. I do not find it particularly palatable to have to find M. Portejoie in breach of duty. . . . However, if I may borrow an expression from another sporting field, I think that he took his eye off the ball on this particular occasion. I think that it can be characterised as involving a short period of inattention to the true capacity of all members of his group and, since it involves the Claimant particularly, the Claimant in particular. Had he stopped and thought about it, in my judgment it would have been clear, based on a proper analysis of what had gone before during the week, that this was asking too much of the Claimant. It may be of some comfort to M. Portejoie to know that there are very many distinguished and ordinarily highly competent and conscientious doctors, lawyers, accountants, engineers, surveyors and the like who, on an isolated occasion in their professional lives, are found to have been negligent within the meaning of the law.

121. I have been much pressed on behalf of M. Portejoie with the proposition that his decision as to the suitability of the slope was not negligent within the well-known Bolam principle. The argument was, to some extent, based on Chittock v Woodbridge School [2002] EWCA Civ 915, another claim arising from a skiing accident. There the claimant was on a school skiing trip. He had been disciplined for skiing off piste without permission and then later in the holiday he was injured when skiing on piste. The suggestion made on his behalf was that he should have been prevented from skiing altogether following the earlier incident. The Court of Appeal declined to hold that the failure to withdraw his skiing rights altogether was negligent. Auld L.J. said:

'Where there are a number of options for the teacher as to the manner in which he might discharge that duty, he is not negligent if he chooses one which, exercising the Bolam test. . . ., would be within a reasonable range of options for a reasonable teacher exercising that duty of care in the circumstances'.

. . .

123. Although on behalf of the Claimant the applicability of the use of the Bolam principle in the case . . . was conceded I have not found it particularly

helpful in analysing the issue of breach of duty because it is necessarily premised on the basis that all relevant risks and benefits have been taken into account in deciding on the course of action under review in the case. I have been unable to find that M. Portejoie did make a conscious exercise of judgment about the abilities of the Claimant to undertake the particular piece of off-piste terrain. The modern statement of the Bolam principle appears in Bolitho v City and Hackney Health Authority [1998] AC 232. It requires the body of opinion upon which reliance is placed to be capable of withstanding logical analysis such that it can be shown that all relevant risks and benefits of the course of action adopted have been weighed up to reach a defensible conclusion: per Lord Browne-Wilkinson pp. 242–244. I do not see that enunciation of the test as having much application in a situation such as this where, as I have said, the evidence does not permit me to find that M. Portejoie did weigh up the risks and benefits of what he asked the group to do.

124 Mr Davies [counsel for the defendant] submitted that M. Portejoie knew the resort very well, was there on the day and was able to take everything into account in making his decision about what the group were going to do. This comes perilously close to saying that whatever choice an experienced ski instructor makes must be right because his judgment will always be well-informed and within the band of reasonable decisions that could be made. I do not think that the law dictates such an approach.

The foreseeability of the Claimant's injuries

125. An argument foreshadowed in Mr Davies' initial Skeleton Argument was that, taking the case at its highest against M. Portejoie . . . the risks which he ought to have had in mind when assessing the suitability of the slope could not reasonably have included an accident of this sort resulting in an injury of this catastrophic nature.

126 [the argument] . . . appears to be that it would be imposing too high a standard of care on someone in M. Portejoie's position to seek to protect someone in the Claimant's position from the kind of harm suffered because it was not reasonably foreseeable that such harm could occur.

. . .

131. That serious injury can result from a skiing accident hardly needs evidence: even those who do not ski will probably know people who do who return from a skiing holiday with a broken arm or broken leg or, from time to time, with very much more serious injuries.

132. The potential for serious injury is clear. The potential for serious injury when impacting with a tree is obvious. Clearly, if the impact is with a young and flexible sapling, a serious injury would not necessarily be foreseeable. But any tree of any stature or substance must present a risk. Of course, such an

impact *may* not result in a serious injury, but there is a more than minimal risk that it will.

133. In my judgment, it is clear that there was a foreseeable risk of serious injury if anyone fell on this slope in the vicinity of the trees.

. . .

Contributory negligence

. . .

145. [I]t seems to me that the correct proportion is that M. Portejoie is 2/3 (two thirds) responsible and the Claimant 1/3 (one third) responsible. . . . [T]his seems to me fairly to reflect the proper balance between a ski instructor in whom his student invests significant trust but who, by failing properly to address the abilities of his student has asked him to do something beyond his abilities in an unsuitable location, and the adult student who recognises that what is being asked of him is either truly beyond his capabilities or is something about which he feels sufficiently concerned for his safety as to warrant making a protest or comment, but who fails to do so.

Discussion

Reasonable coaching practice and the Bolam 'defence'

Statements made by two of the expert witnesses in *Anderson* suggested that a reasonable instructor in the same circumstances may indeed have made the same decision as that taken by M. Portejoie when leading the group off-piste. The core dispute in this case of instructor/coach negligence centred on just what constituted reasonable practice in relation to the selection and suitability of this off-piste skiing for the claimant by the defendant instructor. In the prevailing circumstances of this individual sporting activity, a technical analysis of what might amount to accepted practice appears elusive, it being difficult to satisfy the implication that the procedure adopted by the ski instructor was (or ought to have been) widely followed.[8] For instance, consideration of the following non-exhaustive list of factors, indicative of many sporting activities, would suggest that it may not always be possible to identify approved practice which is widely followed in the context of sport: the particular off-piste slope; the snow conditions on the day of the accident; the previous experience of the claimant; the ability of the claimant; the previous sequential and progressive learning achieved in preparation for this attempt; and the previous experience (and knowledge) of the instructor gained from taking other groups on

---

8 See generally, M Jones, 'The Bolam Test and the Responsible Expert' (1999) 7 *Tort Law Review* 226, 240.

this particular run. Nonetheless, and as mentioned earlier and in Chapter 2, Spencer J in *Pook v Rossall School* emphasised that:

> the court should be slow to condemn a [PE] teacher as negligent and to substitute its own judgment for that of the teacher where the teacher can be expected to have knowledge of the school, the environment, the particular children in her charge and her experience.[9]

By analogy, when exercising his duty, M. Portejoie had knowledge of the particular off-piste terrain, the environmental conditions at the time (e.g., snow conditions and weather), the skiing ability of the group members and he was accepted as being a very experienced and generally conscientious ski instructor who was concerned for the safety and well-being of his students. Moreover, although the court remains the final arbiter when determining whether there has been a breach of duty, due regard must be taken of expert witness testimony. A form of risk-benefit analysis is employed by the court to weigh expert evidence.[10] Ultimately, in finding the ski instructor liable in negligence for the catastrophic personal injury suffered by the claimant when he collided with a tree, Foskett J held that the particular slope in question was a 'step too far', it being beyond the capability of the defendant (and other members of the group), thereby creating a foreseeable risk of serious injury. In short, Foskett J was not convinced that the decision of the instructor was reasonable, despite the joint statement of the experts indicating that the conduct of the instructor was not illogical, the judge having focused on a type of risk-benefit analysis of the expert evidence. *Anderson* was a finely balanced case,[11] yet the court did not appear to allow much leeway when accounting for the sometimes slender distinction between negligent and non-negligent coaching. As previously discussed in Chapter 2, and argued by Dobberstein, it can be problematic when courts fail to afford the discretionary decision-making practices of coaches appropriate latitude.[12]

Chapter 3 argues that the *Bolam* 'defence' may shield coaches from liability in negligence. Submissions to the court by counsel for the defendant instructor in *Anderson* strongly endorse this view. Importantly, even if a defendant (coach) had failed to balance the risks involved with a particular activity, s/he would still be able to invoke the *Bolam* principle in their defence.[13] Curiously, in *Anderson v Lyotier*, Foskett J highlighted how this may be problematic when stating, 'I do not see that

---

9 *Pook* (n 2).
10 Jones (n 8) 239. See, for instance, *Woodroffe-Hedley v Cuthbertson*, 20 June 1997 (QBD).
11 Ultimately, leave to appeal was granted, but the appeal was eventually compromised before being heard: see W Norris, 'The Duty of Care Owed by Instructors in a Sporting Context' (2010) 4 *JPI Law* 183, 184. Nonetheless, the case remains of considerable factual interest and proves highly instructive when examining the practical content of a coach's duty of care.
12 MJ Dobberstein, ' "Give Me the Ball, Coach": A Scouting Report on the Liability of High Schools and Coaches for Injuries to High School Pitchers' Arms' (2007) 14 *Sports Law Journal* 49, 69.
13 R Buckley, *The Law of Negligence* (4th edn, London, Butterworths 2005) 45.

enunciation of the [*Bolam*] test as having much application in a situation such as this where . . . the evidence does not permit me to find that M. Portejoie did weigh up the risks and benefits of what he asked the group to do'.[14] As discussed in detail in Chapter 3, it is respectfully submitted that this does not appear correct. Satisfying the *Bolam* test does not require adequate reasoning by coaches or instructors when deciding what amounts to proper practice in the prevailing circumstances. The focus of the court should remain on the practice adopted and not the decision-making process supporting this practice. As such, Foskett J should have considered the application of the *Bolam* 'defence' more fully in *Anderson*, especially in light of the joint statement of the experts.

However, the uniqueness and specificity of the particular off-piste skiing activity during which the accident occurred, combined with a lack of directly related uniform standards for instructors/coaches, may well have limited reliance on the *Bolam* 'defence' in *Anderson*. There will be other novel coaching contexts in which satisfying the *Bolam* test might prove challenging. Despite this, and as illustrated in cases including *Fowles v Bedfordshire CC*[15] and *Woodroffe-Hedley v Cuthbertson*,[16] for many sporting activities there will be examples of universal coaching practice that are recommended by a responsible body. Providing this universal practice is capable of withstanding logical scrutiny, it should always be adopted by coaches. Furthermore, and following *Woodbridge School v Chittock*,[17] the strong justification that the coach's decisions were 'within a reasonable range of options' when discharging their duty of care, or *Woodbridge* principle, represents a fluid and malleable variant of the *Bolam* test which is well suited to the specific circumstances of sports coaching.[18] Clearly, the *Bolam* test remains an instructive and valuable tool in protecting defendant coaches from liability in negligence.[19] Nonetheless, in circumstances where the *Bolam* 'defence' does not appear directly relevant, and in instances where coaches may be regarded as having made an error of judgement, further detailed analysis of whether the injury suffered by the claimant was reasonably foreseeable may often prove necessary.[20]

Matching participants

Coaches have a duty when matching participants to ensure that they are not exposed to unreasonable risk of personal injury due to the ability, experience,

---

14 *Anderson* (n 1) [123].
15 *Fowles v Bedfordshire CC* [1995] PIQR P380 (CA). Discussed in detail in Chapter 5.
16 *Woodroffe-Hedley* (n 10). See further, Chapter 5.
17 *Woodbridge School v Chittock* [2002] EWCA Civ 915.
18 See, for instance, *Davenport v Farrow* [2010] EWHC 550 [59].
19 E.g., *Davenport* (n 18). Also see Norris (n 11) 186.
20 This appears to have been the argument submitted on behalf of the defendant ski instructor in *Anderson* (n 1) at [125]-[133]. Also see Norris (n 11) 187–90. See further, Chapter 3.

age, maturity and height and weight of co-participants and opponents. Most obviously, this applies when coaching invasion games such as rugby and football but, and as demonstrated in *Anderson*, this duty of care has implications for decisions concerning the demands posed by all group activities. This includes the pitch, pace and progression of coaching sessions. Foskett J framed this as a duty 'to choose activities for the group that [are] within the competence of the least able member of the group'.[21] Such reasoning was also reiterated in *Ahmed v MacLean*,[22] it being clear that the level of difficulty posed by the drills and activities selected by coaches should be based on the needs and capabilities of the least able group members. This duty sounds deceptively simple. However, when seeking to appropriately challenge individual performers within group activities, such differentiation may not always be straightforward.

As reinforced in *Anderson*, this tension is compounded by the fact that it may often be necessary to move athletes outside of their 'comfort zone' in order to optimise learning and performance, with this case turning on the boundary between the reasonable suggestion of something more challenging and the unreasonable suggestion of something exposing the adult skier(s) to unacceptable risk. This emphasises the importance of ensuring that there are adequate systems in place so that athletes and participants are appropriately assessed and grouped accordingly prior to the commencement of coaching sessions. Whilst on the facts of *Anderson* there was no suggestion that the selection of the group was negligent, should the initial allocation of groups be inappropriate, fulfilling the ongoing duty of care of adequately matching participants in subsequent sessions may prove problematic. Moreover, this raises further important issues concerning a coach's duty to conduct suitable and sufficient risk assessments, the necessity of adequate supervision (and instruction), and the potential pitfalls associated with negligent entrenched practice. Interestingly, all of these issues were material considerations in *Anderson*.

Risk assessment, supervision and instruction

Clearly, in order to fulfil the duty of demonstrating reasonable skill and care when coaching, coaches must consciously consider the capability of all individual athletes. As alluded to in *Anderson*, this requires a prospective conscientious analysis of the capacity of participants and athletes to undertake the challenges posed during the supervised activity with reasonable safety. This is achieved by adequate completion of a risk assessment as discussed in Chapter 5. The starting point of any risk assessment may be regarded as identification of all reasonably foreseeable risks.[23] This involves appraisal of the potential risks associated with the particular activity

---

21 *Anderson* (n 1) [117].
22 *Ahmed v MacLean* [2016] EWHC 2798 [75], [96]. Discussed in Chapter 5.
23 *Uren v Corporate Leisure (UK) Limited* [2013] EWHC 353 [181] (Foskett J).

before its commencement,[24] by conducting what has been termed an *ex ante* assessment of risk.[25] Although strictly speaking there is no legal requirement for risk assessments to be confined to writing,

> there must be a systematic process which leads to their creation before the hazard is engendered and not afterwards. A proper system of assessing risk and generating the necessary documents well in advance is more likely to be a system in which the necessary control mechanisms are also properly implemented, rather than addressed haphazardly and adventitiously on the day.[26]

As highlighted in Chapter 5, and certainly of relevance in *Anderson*, as well as to the duty of coaches more generally, the High Court in *MacIntyre v Ministry of Defence* reiterated the importance of regarding risk assessment as 'a dynamic process which must be subject to continuous review'.[27] This requires a thoughtful appraisal of risk, as opposed to a document which might be completed in a tick-box fashion.[28] Such a dynamic risk assessment may be viewed as:

> a risk assessment that takes place during the operation or event in question rather than one carried out exclusively before. . . [involving] those responsible for providing the game [or activity] considering the game as it was played and intervening if it appeared to have become dangerous.[29]

Put simply, a dynamic risk assessment involves continuous monitoring and observation of activities, both before and during the event, whilst conducting the supervisory function of coach.[30] This requires coaching expertise developed and refined over time.[31] In *Anderson*, the court ruled that the ski instructor had failed to conduct a suitable and sufficient risk assessment. In elaborating on this point, Foskett J stated that it was 'troubling that M. Portejoie was not watching the Claimant' in the seconds before his accident when the claimant was '"struggling with the

---

24 *Kennedy v Cordia (Services) LLP* [2016] UKSC 6 [110].
25 *Uren* (n 23) [69].
26 *Risk v Rose Bruford College* [2013] EWHC 3869 [53] (Jay J).
27 *MacIntyre v Ministry of Defence* [2011] EWHC 1690 [82].
28 *Uren v Corporate Leisure (UK)* [2011] EWCA Civ 66 [44], Smith LJ drawing attention to the limitations of sometimes blunt risk assessment proformas that encourage a 'mechanistic or "tick-box" approach' to risk assessment.
29 *Uren* (n 23) [69].
30 P Whitlam, *Safe Practice in Physical Education and Sport* (Leeds, Coachwise 2012) 155. As noted by McArdle, a dynamic risk assessment recognises factors including the attitudes and maturity of participants, changing weather conditions and the confidence of instructors/coaches in their own competence in an open environment: see D McArdle, 'The Views from the Hills: Fatal Accidents, Child Safety and Licensing Adventure Activities' (2011) 31(3) *Legal Studies* 372, 383.
31 Whitlam (n 30).

slope" and was anxious and concerned about making the turns'.[32] Furthermore, the claimant was found to have failed to master 'to a sufficient level the skills necessary to undertake a piece of off-piste terrain of this nature in reasonable safety'.[33] Indeed, in the view of the court, adequately fulfilling his duties of supervision and risk assessment would have enabled M. Portejoie to realise that the particular slope in question was too much to ask of several members of the group and a 'step too far'.

Negligent entrenched practice

Foskett J identified two potentially interrelated and instructive explanations when concluding that M. Portejoie had breached his duty of care to the claimant. First, it was suggested that the instructor 'may have used this off-piste section regularly at the end of a week for an intermediate class, nothing untoward having occurred previously, and it did not occur to him that there were any risks in taking the group there'.[34] Second, the instructor 'may have been over-influenced subconsciously by the obvious capacity of Mr Hall to undertake the slope safely'.[35] Similar concerns in respect of coaches potentially having a tendency to be overly optimistic in terms of the competence levels of some participants in mixed ability groups were also expressed in *Ahmed v MacLean*. Whilst reinforcing the necessity of effectively discharging a duty of care to all participants, for instance, in order that the needs and capabilities of the least able member(s) of groups are accommodated, these posited explanations by Foskett J reinforce the dangers associated with coaches adopting negligent entrenched practice. Indeed, in acknowledging that much contemporary coaching practice appears to be underpinned by emulation, intuition and tradition, or 'uncritical inertia',[36] such scenarios described in *Anderson* appear feasible impediments to coaches satisfactorily discharging their duty of care. This poses important challenges and implications for coaching practice which are discussed more fully in the next chapter.

Legal vs moral duties of care

Another point raised in *Anderson* worthy of further consideration relates to the distinction made in Chapter 1 between legal and moral duties of care. Foskett J stated that he did 'not find it particularly palatable to have to find M. Portejoie

---

32 *Anderson* (n 1) [115], [112].
33 Ibid. [112].
34 Ibid. [119].
35 Ibid.
36 M Partington and C Cushion, 'An Investigation of the Practice Activities and Coaching Behaviors of Professional Top-Level Youth Soccer Coaches' (2013) 23 *Scand J Med Sci Sports* 374; AM Williams and NJ Hodges, 'Practice, Instruction and Skill Acquisition in Soccer: Challenging Tradition' (2005) 23(6) *Journal of Sports Sciences* 637; J Ehrmann, *InSideOut Coaching: How Sports Can Transform Lives* (New York, Simon & Schuster 2011) 80.

in breach of duty'.[37] In accepting that the breach of duty resulted from a 'short period of inattention', which according to Foskett J was not an uncommon situation experienced by very many distinguished and ordinarily highly competent and conscientious professionals, it could not be suggested that M. Portejoie was in any way morally at fault.[38] As stressed by Foskett J, M. Portejoie was more narrowly 'negligent within the meaning of the law'.[39] This reinforces how a coach's moral responsibility and legal duty of care can vary significantly in scope and content. Furthermore, it reiterates how momentarily taking your 'eye off the ball' might lead to a breach of duty by coaches, for example, as appears to have likewise been the case towards the end of the supervised indoor climbing activity in *Pinchbeck v Craggy Island Ltd*.[40]

Fact-specific nature of coach negligence

Finally, the court's decision in *Anderson* demonstrates the fundamental importance of the particular sporting context in all cases of coach negligence. This book's analysis reveals this to be a core consideration when courts are tasked with determining the nature of the duty of care owed by sports coaches. The previously cited extracts from *Anderson* demonstrate that the High Court was required to conduct a detailed examination of the full factual matrix of the case before it ruled that the off-piste slope was beyond the capability and competence of the claimant. Importantly, the court's reasoning in *MacIntyre v Ministry of Defence*[41] provides a sharp contrast to the ruling in *Anderson*. Indeed, given the very different circumstances in *MacIntyre*, involving a formal army adventurous training exercise, it can readily be distinguished from *Anderson*, with Spencer J accepting that the instructors in *MacIntyre* 'were operating at the upper end of the limitations of their qualifications, [but] this should in no way be regarded as undesirable. On the contrary, it is a positive and desirable feature of a training exercise that the leaders as well as the novices are stretched'.[42] Consequently, since coaches operate across a wide range of performance levels and stages,[43] defining the precise extent of a coach's duty of care will always be highly situation-dependent. The significance of the sometimes unique and particular circumstances in which coaches operate generates important implications for coaches discharging their duty of care. These implications are returned

---

37 *Anderson* (n 1) [120].
38 In *Woodroffe-Hedley* (n 10), Dyson J similarly found that the defendant alpine guide 'had Mr Hedley's best interests in mind when he made that fateful decision to move across to the rocks, without taking the elementary and fundamental precaution of making the belay safe for Mr Hedley by driving in a second screw'.
39 *Anderson* (n 1) [120].
40 *Pinchbeck v Craggy Island Ltd* [2012] EWHC 2745. See further, Chapter 5.
41 *MacIntyre* (n 27).
42 Ibid. [61].
43 H Telfer, 'Coaching practice and practice ethics' in J Lyle and C Cushion (eds), *Sports Coaching: Professionalisation and Practice* (Edinburgh, Elsevier 2010) 210.

to in the following chapter when analysing specific background considerations associated with coaching.

Conclusion

The most rigorous and informative judgment by a UK court concerning the issue of coach/instructor negligence remains that provided by Foskett J in *Anderson*. In citing relevant and detailed passages from the case, this chapter has provided an authentic insight into the law in action. Moreover, *Anderson* illustrates how Foskett J was tasked with considering many of the main issues discussed throughout this book with regard to a coach's duty of care. This included the common practice or *Bolam* 'defence' and the practical content of an instructor's/coach's duty of care in relation to: (i) instruction; (ii) supervision; (iii) risk assessment; (iii) the organisation and pitch of sessions; (iv) matching and assessing participants; (v) the boundary between reasonable and unreasonable coaching expectations; (vi) the dangers of negligent entrenched coaching practice; and (vii) the crucial distinction between a legal and moral duty of care. Despite Foskett J's reservations in relation to the application of the *Bolam* test in *Anderson*, it is argued that both the *Bolam* 'defence' and *Woodbridge* principle will remain of considerable practical utility in future claims of coach negligence.

Foskett J in *Anderson* was correct to acknowledge that it frequently proves necessary for coaches to challenge participants to move outside of their 'comfort zones' in order to improve and achieve desired outcomes. As a key aspect of much sporting activity, and given the mutually dependent coach–athlete relationship, this represents a common and prevailing circumstance of many structured coaching environments. However, having expressed his approval of such an approach, it appears somewhat curious why, and contrary to the consensus view provided by the experts, Foskett J then draws the boundary between negligent and non-negligent coaching so narrowly. Nonetheless, the reasoning adopted by Foskett J makes plain that irrespective of the difficult challenges faced by coaches when seeking to differentiate coaching activities, so as to ensure that individuals within mixed ability groups are personally stretched and challenged, under no circumstances is it reasonable to expose the least able performer to unacceptable risk. Consequently, conscientious and committed coaches and instructors, as in *Anderson* and *Ahmed*, must resist any tendency, or perhaps instinctive desire, to be overly optimistic or ambitious when making decisions about pushing participants beyond their 'comfort zones' and, not least, during mixed ability coaching sessions.

This chapter's detailed case study of *Anderson v Lyotier* generates a considerable number of important implications for coaches exercising their duty of care, including the requirement for the coaching practices adopted to be logically and rigorously justifiable. These implications are critically analysed in the next chapter.

PART III
Implications and future developments

7
IMPLICATIONS FOR COACHING PRACTICE

Introduction

The responsibility of sports coaches in discharging their duty of care, by adopting reasonable coaching practice when interacting with athletes, is becoming more pronounced. This poses significant implications for modern sports coaches. As the previous chapters reveal, the legal duty of care incumbent upon coaches would be breached when the conduct of a sports coach falls below the required objective standard ascertained by the court, when guarding against reasonably foreseeable risk, in the specific circumstances of the individual case. This benchmark of objective reasonableness is defined to safeguard the legitimate and genuine right of athletes not to be exposed to unreasonable risks. Crucially, however, providing coaches discharge and meet this standard of care and skill, there can be no breach of duty. Simply applied, the duty of a coach remains a requirement to adopt reasonable coaching practice so that reasonable care is taken to ensure the reasonable safety of athletes. It has previously been argued that the legal test of reasonableness may be regarded as vague, nebulous and uncertain, which promotes the view that there is no 'transparent, fixed and universally accepted boundary . . . between appropriate and inappropriate coaching conduct'.[1] Nonetheless, and as discussed in detail in Chapters 5 and 6, a coach's duty of care demands that definitions of appropriate or reasonable coaching practice must be capable of being logically justified and withstanding searching and robust judicial scrutiny. As will be contended in this chapter, whilst regular and approved coaching practice remains integral to defining reasonableness in this context, there appears strong support for further

---

1 A Hardman and C Jones, 'Sports coaching and virtue ethics' in A Hardman and C Jones, *The Ethics of Sports Coaching* (Abingdon, Routledge 2011) 78.

discussions concerning legal (and ethical) dilemmas drawn from practical coaching scenarios in order to support coaches in developing proper and effective coaching practices.[2] In this regard, the previous detailed analysis of sports negligence case law generally,[3] and instances of alleged coach negligence in particular,[4] prove instructive and insightful.

Accordingly, this book's critical analysis of the relationship between coaching, sport and the law is drawn together in this chapter to identify important implications for coaches exercising their duty of care. When defining a coach's duty of care an extremely useful starting point is the acknowledgment that '[i]n law context is everything',[5] and 'the issue of negligence cannot be resolved in a vacuum. It is fact specific'.[6] This chapter, therefore, begins by discussing some of the specific background considerations connected with coaching. These considerations include a number of challenges faced by modern sports coaches associated with possible excesses of coaching behaviour, the dangers of negligent entrenched practice, the differing environments in which coaches perform their functions and the tendency for the prevailing standards required of coaches to heighten over time. Following this contextualisation, key findings from the critical analysis of the emerging and fact-specific case law in the previous chapters are consolidated to uncover important implications for coaching practice. These implications are of particular relevance when reflecting on the (un)reasonableness of some coaching behaviours and on the benchmark of regular and approved coaching practice and the associated *Bolam* 'defence'. Moreover, this chapter's analysis also calls for distinctions between formal qualifications and experience, as indicators of coaching competence, to be more fully explored. The focus of this discussion relates to the full range of the duties of coaches. However, in view of the increased judicial attention afforded to the risk assessment process, as reiterated in Chapters 5 and 6, a coach's duty of care regarding this aspect of risk management warrants discrete examination. The chapter concludes by highlighting a number of broader considerations related to coach education, training and development, and the role of national governing bodies (NGBs) in adequately preparing coaches so that they can effectively discharge their duty of care.

Context

As the principal supervisors of organised sporting activities, coaches must appreciate that participation in sport frequently leads to injury.[7] Accidents can and do

---

2 T Cassidy et al., *Understanding Sports Coaching: The Social, Cultural and Pedagogical Foundations of Coaching Practice* (2nd edn, London, Routledge 2009) 169.
3 See Chapter 4.
4 See Chapters 5 and 6.
5 *Regina (Daly) v Secretary of State for the Home Department* [2001] 2 AC 532 (HL) [28] (Lord Steyn).
6 *Caldwell v Maguire* [2001] EWCA Civ 1054 [30] (Judge LJ).
7 A Miles and R Tong, 'Sports Medicine For Coaches' in RL Jones and K Kingston (eds), *An Introduction to Sports Coaching: Connecting Theory to Practice* (2nd edn, Abingdon, Routledge 2013) 178.

happen without fault. However, in circumstances where sporting injury was caused by a breach of duty of care, or negligent coaching, legal liability may increasingly eventuate. The interpersonal relationship between coach and athlete creates the capacity for a lack of 'empathy with or care and concern for the wellbeing of the other person'.[8] Some coaches may seek to gain any 'edge' possible when conforming to the 'win at all costs' mentality frequently prevalent in a range of competitive sports.[9] Such expectations and pressures may promote what might be termed as the 'sport ethic', with over-conformity to this ideology reinforcing the acceptance of unreasonable risks by both coaches and athletes, as evidenced by an over-emphasis on the pursuit of winning and a refusal to accept appropriate and necessary limitations.[10] Many admired and respected coaches are arguably held in such high regard because of this notable commitment and insistence on an excessive 'win-at-all-costs' ethos.[11] It is argued by Alexander, Stafford and Lewis that young athletes in the UK may 'accept a culture where training through discomfort, injury and exhaustion is seen as normal'[12] and that some coaches encourage athletes, or 'guilt' them, into continuing to participate in these same circumstances in order to avoid letting teammates down. As suggested by Coakley and Pike, coaches may:

> take great care to control deviant underconformity, but they often ignore or encourage overconformity, even though it may lead to injuries and have long-term negative implications for the health and well-being of athletes. Therefore, in the culture of high-performance sports, these norms are accepted uncritically, without question or qualification, and often followed without recognizing limits or thinking about the boundaries that separate normal from deviant.[13]

Excesses of coaching behaviour may not be confined to high-level competitive sport since a culture of control and authoritarianism appears deeply embedded, even at the lower levels of the sports performance pyramid.[14] For instance, reputation and kudos at the amateur level may facilitate adoption by coaches of high-risk

---

8   J Lyle, 'Coaching Philosophy and Coaching Behaviour' in N Cross and J Lyle (eds), *The Coaching Process: Principles and Practice for Sport* (Philadelphia, Butterworth-Heinemann 1999) 43.
9   L Jamieson and T Orr, *Sport and Violence: A Critical Examination of Sport* (London, Elsevier 2009) 95.
10 Ibid. 80–81.
11 K Young, 'From Violence in Sport to Sports-Related Violence' in B Houlihan (ed), *Sport and Society: A Student Introduction* (2nd edn, London, Sage Publications 2008) 189; K Young, *Sport, Violence and Society* (London, Routledge 2012) 81–82; J Ryan, *Little Girls In Pretty Boxes: The Making and Breaking of Elite Gymnasts and Figure Skaters* (London, Warner Books Edition 1995) 220–21.
12 K Alexander et al., *The Experiences of Children Participating in Organised Sport in the UK* (Edinburgh, University of Edinburgh/NSPCC Child Protection Research Centre 2011) 14.
13 J Coakley and E Pike, *Sports in Society: Issues and Controversies* (2nd edn, New York, McGraw-Hill Education 2014) 160.
14 Cassidy et al. (n 2) 32.

practices with the potential to cause physical harm,[15] it being assumed that some coaches at the non-professional level appear unsympathetic to athletes complaining of being injured.[16]

Arguably, authoritative and oppressive interaction between coaches and players, and possible implementation of punishment type drills and practices, may become regarded as routine and acceptable in certain circumstances.[17] Take, for example, some of the conditioning/punishment type drills modelled, reinforced and portrayed as necessary and effective coaching practice in contemporary films such as *Coach Carter, Remember the Titans* and *Best Shot*. Included is a high-intensity shuttle-sprint training drill, commonly referred to as 'suicides'. Whilst many coaches will, no doubt, utilise such methods reasonably, as this book's legal analysis reveals, coaches must be cautious when using exercise drills as a form of punishment.[18] In advocating the avoidance of such terminology as 'suicide' drill by coaches, Appenzeller notes that this and similar terms 'could come back to haunt you in court should an injury occur'.[19] Put bluntly, it may be particularly challenging for coaches engaging in such coaching methods as a matter of habit, routine or 'uncritical inertia'[20] to justify such practice as being objectively reasonable. As broadly alluded to in Chapters 5 and 6, such practice appears a possible scenario with the potential for negligent entrenched practice to be 'accepted uncritically, without question or qualification, and often followed without recognizing limits or thinking about the boundaries that separate normal from deviant'.[21] In short, contextualisation of modern sports coaching emphasises the considerable scope for the practices sometimes adopted by some coaches to cross the boundary between that which is reasonable in optimising performance and that which would amount to negligence.

15 K Young, 'The Role of the Courts in Sports Injury' in K Young (ed), *Sporting Bodies, Damaged Selves: Sociological Studies of Sports-Related Injury* (Oxford, Elsevier 2004) 343.
16 K Young and P White, 'Threats to Sport Careers: Elite athletes talk about injury and pain' in J Coakley and P Donnelly (eds), *Inside Sports* (London, Routledge 1999) 208; H Charlesworth and K Young, 'Why English Female University Athletes Play with Pain' in Young (n 15) 167; E Pike and A Scott, 'Safeguarding, injuries and athlete choice' in M Long and M Hartill (eds), *Safeguarding, Child Protection and Abuse in Sport: International Perspectives in Research, Policy and Practice* (London, Routledge 2015) 174. Similarly, at the professional level, some coaches would also appear unsympathetic to athletes complaining of being injured. See, for instance, D McRae, 'Alex Corbisiero: "Even Now People Will Frown if You Need a Rest"' *The Guardian* (London, 5 May 2016) <www.theguardian.com/sport/2016/may/05/alex-corbisiero-rugby-union-england-lions?CMP=share_btn_tw> accessed 28 October 2019.
17 P Kellett, 'Football-as-War, Coach-as-General: Analogy, Metaphor and Management Implications' (2002) 5 *Football Studies* 60, 70; J Ehrmann, *InSideOut Coaching: How Sports Can Transform Lives* (New York, Simon & Schuster 2011) 80.
18 G Wong, *Essentials of Sports Law* (4th edn, Oxford, Praeger 2010) 111.
19 H Appenzeller, *Ethical Behavior in Sport* (Durham, Carolina Academic Press 2011) 153.
20 M Partington and C Cushion, 'An Investigation of the Practice Activities and Coaching Behaviors of Professional Top-Level Youth Soccer Coaches' (2013) 23 *Scand J Med Sci Sports* 374. Discussed further later.
21 Coakley and Pike (n 13) 160.

This somewhat nebulous dividing line is of critical importance when defining the duty of care owed by coaches to athletes under their charge.

Sports coaching involves both rapid and intuitive decision-making in the environments of training and competition,[22] with associated and necessary structured improvisation.[23] However, an important distinguishing factor in the circumstances of sports coaching, as contrasted with the case law derived from instances of co-participant liability discussed in Chapter 4, may relate to a void of special allowance for 'errors of judgment' or 'lapses of skill' made in the preparation for competition as opposed to during competition.[24] Preparation for matches and competitions by coaches would sometimes appear more analogous with *Harrison v Vincent*,[25] where failure to maintain a motorcycle before a race led to a finding of negligence. Given the significance of context when defining a coach's duty of care, there may be scope for the argument that in the circumstances of a competitive match the standard of care and skill required of coaches may differ from that needed during a practice session. Coaches can more readily control environmental factors, including the level of intensity and pace of activities, during training sessions. However, application of such a principle may become somewhat limited with some experienced and advanced coaches seeking to replicate, if not surpass, the physical and psychological pressures of match competition in training sessions, the widely held view being that 'perfect practice makes perfect'. Nonetheless, the supervisory function of the coach during practice sessions clearly allows for 'a stoppage in play, thereby enabling time for considered thought'.[26] As such, and in paraphrasing the observations of Lord Phillips in *Vowles v Evans*, very different considerations might apply when defining the extent of a coach's duty of care during a practice session as compared with a fast-moving competitive match.[27] Accordingly, whilst consideration of the specific context of sport may enable the court to distinguish between the expression of objective reasonableness and the practicalities of the evidential burden of 'reckless disregard',[28] as with other professionals, it does not necessarily follow that a coach would be exonerated from negligence liability for a mere 'error of judgment'.[29] Indeed, and as revealed in Chapter 6, in *Anderson v Lyotier*, the defendant ski instructor was found to be in breach of duty since 'he took his eye off the ball on this particular occasion'.[30]

---

22 H Telfer, 'Coaching Practice and Practice Ethics' in J Lyle & C Cushion (eds), *Sports Coaching: Professionalisation and Practice* (Edinburgh, Elsevier 2010) 214.
23 See generally, C Cushion and J Lyle, 'Conceptual Development in Sports Coaching' Lyle and Cushion (n 22) 4.
24 See generally, MA Jones and AM Dugdale (eds), *Clerk and Lindsell on Torts* (20th edn, London, Sweet and Maxwell 2010) [8–145].
25 [1982] RTR 8. Discussed in detail in Chapter 4.
26 *Vowles v Evans* [2003] EWCA Civ 318 [38].
27 Ibid.
28 E.g., *Caldwell* (n 6) [11]. See further, Chapter 4.
29 See Jones and Dugdale (n 24) [10–03].
30 *Anderson v Lyotier* [2008] EWHC 2790 [120].

More generally, the standard of skill and care incumbent upon coaches continues to evolve, since it is the responsibility of coaches to be up-to-date with sport-specific knowledge, given techniques in sport are subject to rapid change.[31] For instance, the management of sport-related concussion represents a contemporary example of advances in knowledge leading to the publication of best practice protocols by NGBs.[32] However, there may also be general improvements in the standards of skill and care provided by particular professions, regardless of associated advances in knowledge, similarly heightening the standard of the reasonably competent practitioner.[33] In this situation, practice previously viewed as tolerable may come to be regarded as negligent,[34] reinforcing the need for coaches to be familiar with the publication of written recommendations by NGBs, including approved codes and guidelines reflecting the best practices of the 'profession'. Nonetheless, the standards observed by the ordinarily skilled and competent coach would be judged by the standards prevailing at the time of their acts or omissions, and so should not to be affected by the wisdom of hindsight.[35] This was succinctly articulated in *Villella v North Bedfordshire BC*, when Otton J recognised the need to be careful when determining reasonable coaching practice so as not to 'import into 1980 standards which may have evolved at a later stage with the wisdom of hindsight and the increased sophistication of this particular sport'.[36]

Coaching practice

The pivotal issue should a coach be sued in negligence (for a breach of duty) concerns whether or not the coach's actions, conduct or behaviour satisfied the required standard of reasonable care and skill, as defined by the court, after taking full account of the prevailing circumstances of the case. This obligation encompasses both acts and omissions (i.e., negligent instruction and inadequate supervision). In the context of sports coaching, this would relate to coaching practices that have an explicit impact on the athlete, most typically, direct coaching interventions and interactions in the particular circumstances of training, practices, competitions and fixtures.

Much contemporary coaching practice appears to be derived from tradition and 'uncritical inertia'.[37] This may 'authenticate certain types of collective knowledge

---

31 G Nygaard and T Boone, *Coaches Guide to Sport Law* (Champaign, Human Kinetics 1985) 24. Also see, J Gardiner, 'Should Coaches Take Care?' (1993) 143 *NLJ* 1598.
32 As noted by Meakin, this may be the case despite inconclusive medical evidence regarding the issue of causation: T Meakin, 'The Evolving Legal Issues on Rugby Neuro-Trauma?' (2013) 21(3) *Sport and the Law Journal* 34.
33 J Powell and R Stewart, *Jackson and Powell on Professional Liability* (7th edn, London, Sweet and Maxwell 2012) [2–135].
34 Ibid.
35 *Eckersley v Binnie* [1988] 18 ConLR 1 (CA).
36 *Villella v North Bedfordshire BC*, 25 October 1983 (QBD).
37 Partington and Cushion (n 20); AM Williams and NJ Hodges, 'Practice, Instruction and Skill Acquisition in Soccer: Challenging Tradition' (2005) 23(6) *Journal of Sports Sciences* 637; Ehrmann (n 17) 80.

with the resulting discourse giving certain practices an entrenched legitimacy'.[38] Problematically, in circumstances where this entrenched legitimacy exposes athletes to unreasonable risk of injury, coaches are in breach of their duty of care. This fact illustrates the need for coaches to have the prerequisite self-awareness to understand both the positive and negative implications of their behaviour.[39] These observations appear to be of considerable relevance when coaches are discharging their duties, with research indicating that coaches may demonstrate low self-awareness about their coaching practice and conduct.[40] Consequently, the reasonableness of demands made of athletes by coaches may not always be sufficiently appraised, evaluated and reflected upon.

A significant ethical and legal dilemma facing modern sports coaches and, not least, when working with young athletes, concerns determination of training intensity levels.[41] As a judgement call, this is an area where individual coaches have considerable leeway to decide what is reasonable in the specific circumstances.[42] According to Martínková and Parry:

> The dangers of over-training and inappropriate methods have long been recognized, as have the duties of the coach to be knowledgeable and well informed, to take care over the appropriate design of training session schedules, and to monitor athletes for signs of weariness and distress.[43]

In terms of appropriate coaching practice, Cross and Lyle continue:

> [C]oaches have a responsibility to implement a coaching process, especially with elite and high-level performance athletes, which is comprehensively planned, adequately and frequently monitored and in which, through careful regulation of the training loading factors, the athlete's progress and wellbeing are constantly emphasised in order to avoid 'overtraining'.[44]

Yet despite this suggested long recognition of the risks posed to athletes by over-training and inappropriate training methods and practices, research would indicate that excessive training, both in terms of the intensity and duration of sessions,

---

38　C Cushion and M Partington, 'A Critical Analysis of the Conceptualisation of "Coaching Philosophy"' (2014) 21(6) *Sport, Education and Society* 851, 857.
39　C Cushion, 'Coach behaviour' in Lyle and Cushion (n 22) 53.
40　Partington and Cushion (n 20) 381; S Harvey et al., 'A Season Long Investigation into Coaching Behaviours as a Function of Practice State: The Case of Three Collegiate Coaches' (2013) 2(1) *Sports Coaching Review* 13, 14.
41　See, for instance, Miles and Tong (n 7) 188–89; J Lyle, *Sports Coaching Concepts: A Framework for Coaches' Behaviour* (London, Routledge 2002) 240; J Oliver and R Lloyd, 'Physical Training as a Potential Form of Abuse' in Long and Hartill (n 16) 163. See further, Chapter 5.
42　Cassidy et al. (n 2) 154–55.
43　I Martínková and J Parry, 'Coaching and the Ethics of Performance Enhancement' in Hardman and Jones (n 1) 177–78.
44　N Cross and J Lyle, 'Overtraining and the Coaching Process' in Cross and Lyle (n 8) 192.

remains a concern.[45] Consistent with this book's legal analysis, overtraining, or training requiring an unreasonable level of intensity, may provide the foundation for a cause of action in negligence.[46] Further, coaches must be mindful to avoid exerting undue pressure or influence on players returning from injury, in addition to discharging responsibilities regarding appropriate medical care of athletes, including pertinent referral to relevant specialist medical practitioners and adherence to stipulated protocols.[47]

Effective coaching practice will appropriately stretch and challenge participants, and as recognised by the High Court in both *Anderson v Lyotier* and *Ahmed v MacLean*, move or push participants to outside of their 'comfort zone' in order to make progress.[48] Pushing athletes outside of their comfort zones is reasonable, routine and effective coaching practice in situations where athletes have demonstrated the necessary competence to cope safely with more advanced demands.[49] Nonetheless, and as revealed in Chapter 5, coaches must guard against the possibility of being overly optimistic or too blasé when ascertaining the ability and confidence of athletes to willingly meet the challenges posed. Such a failure by coaches may result in athletes and participants being exposed to an unacceptable risk of injury and, concomitantly, a breach of duty of care by coaches.

There is evidence to suggest that coaches develop some of their preliminary notions and conceptions of how to coach from experience as athletes.[50] Socialisation of coaches within respective sports is likely to shape perceptions of ethically correct approaches to coaching.[51] However, relying on idiosyncratic, subjective and perhaps ill-considered judgements of acceptable practice, given the apparent lacuna in coach education and training focused on legal and ethical issues, appears problematic.[52] Further, as pressures grow to optimise levels of performance, associated

---

45 Alexander et al. (n 12); Oliver and Lloyd (n 41) 163.
46 See, for instance, *Davenport v Farrow* [2010] EWHC 550. Discussed in Chapter 5.
47 See, for instance, *Brady v Sunderland Association Football Club* Ltd, 2 April 1998 (QBD). Discussed in Chapter 5.
48 *Anderson* (n 30) [54]; *Ahmed v MacLean* [2016] EWHC 2798 [84]. See further, Chapters 5 & 6.
49 Coaches will be better informed when determining if participants can cope safely with more demanding challenges by keeping written records of such things as training sessions delivered, schedules of training programmes, attendance registers, injuries sustained by participants, performance and fitness assessments, and depending on the level at which the coach is operating, medical screening test results and records of progression reviews/meetings. Other relevant records, as discussed later, include risk assessments. See further, J Barnes, *Sports and the Law in Canada* (3rd edn, Toronto, Butterworths 1996) and P Whitlam, *Case Law in Physical Education and School Sport* (Worcester, BAALPE 2005).
50 C Mallett, 'Becoming a High Performing Coach: Pathways and Communities' in Lyle and Cushion (n 22) 122. See further, C Cushion et al., 'Coach Education and Continuing Professional Development: Experience and Learning to Coach' (2003) 55 *Quest* 215; G Bloom et al., 'The Importance of Mentoring in the Development of Coaches and Athletes' (1998) 33 *International Journal of Sports Psychology* 410.
51 Telfer (n 22) 216.
52 Ibid. See, for instance, the analysis of *Davenport* (n 46) in Chapter 5.

tensions relating to legal and ethical considerations are amplified.[53] Broadly speaking, as the principles of coaching are constantly assessed and revised,[54] so too is the legal standard of care required of coaches.[55] This may prove precarious for talented and experienced coaches, perhaps even former professional athletes themselves, working in isolation or unreceptive to the latest developments in coaching and the constantly evolving legal context in which coaches discharge the duty of care incumbent upon them. The importance of this is heightened by the fact that practice ethics appears to be an undervalued aspect of the 'craft' of coaching and perhaps indicative of a somewhat 'underdeveloped awareness, or understanding, of duties associated with professional practice' by some coaches.[56] Significantly, and as argued by Duffy et al., addressing such complexities of coaching should become a priority, reinforcing the necessity for coach education, training and systematic continuing professional development (CPD) to more fully engage with legal/duty of care considerations.[57]

Bolam 'defence'

The methods adopted by ordinarily competent professionals exercising specialist skill are underpinned by regular, approved and responsible practice. Since this common practice would be logically justifiable, should an athlete suffer personal injury whilst under the coach's charge, customary practice, so defined, would provide a strong indication of reasonable coaching and instructing.[58] In such circumstances, coaches would be ideally positioned to engage the *Bolam* 'defence' discussed in Chapter 3. Put simply, providing the standards, skills and judgement of coaches are reasonable, there would be no breach of duty. In *MacIntyre*, the actions of the climbing leaders were to be:

> judged by the standards of the reasonable climbing leader in such circumstances. It is not sufficient to show that a different decision might have been better. Rather the test is whether no reasonable climbing leader would have done what they did.[59]

Consequently, the threshold of reasonable coaching should only be breached in circumstances where no other reasonable coach would have done what the defendant

---

53 Telfer (n 22) 217.
54 Cassidy et al. (n 2) 130–31; B Taylor and D Garratt, 'The Professionalisation of Sports Coaching: Relations of Power, Resistance and Compliance' (2010) 15(1) *Sport, Education and Society* 121, 124.
55 See generally, Powell and Stewart (n 33) [2–135].
56 Telfer (n 22) 211.
57 P Duffy et al., 'Sport Coaching as a "Profession": Challenges and Future Directions' (2011) 5(2) *International Journal of Coaching Science* 93, 104.
58 E.g., *Davenport* (n 46) [59]; *Morrow v Dungannon and South Tyrone BC* [2012] NIQB 50 [27]-[30].
59 *MacIntyre v Ministry of Defence* [2011] EWHC 1690 [70].

did. Also, given the courts' recognition of the discretionary professional judgement of expert practitioners, or *Woodbridge* principle endorsing decision-making 'within a reasonable range of options',[60] at first glance, satisfying this benchmark of the reasonably average coach does not appear particularly onerous. Indeed, as with cases of medical negligence pre-*Bolitho*,[61] this creates the impression that providing a coach might be able to find an expert from the field to endorse her/his actions or omissions, a finding of breach of duty would be prevented. However, and perhaps unsurprisingly, this represents a dangerous oversimplification of the approach taken by the judiciary. Since the shift towards the professionalisation of sports coaching continues to be a work in progress, unlike evaluations of due care and skill exercised by medical practitioners, judges may not be so hesitant to declare a widespread practice employed by some coaches to be negligent.[62] Furthermore, Chapter 6's case study of *Anderson v Lyotier* reveals the scope for a somewhat narrow application of the *Bolam* 'defence' in particular circumstances. Nonetheless, coaches employing approved practice (i.e., advocated by a responsible coaching organisation/NGB), which is logically justifiable for the requirements of the coaching post held (i.e., appropriate to the performance level in question), remain extremely well positioned to successfully exercise their duty of care since these propositions are the hallmarks of reasonable coaching practice.[63]

Distinctions between formal qualifications and experience

Coaching is dependent upon volunteers. As such, it is largely unregulated and devoid of a commonality of occupational practice.[64] This is illustrated in the UK, for instance, by the fact that around 76 percent of coaches are volunteers, including some parents, with approximately half of the coaches in this jurisdiction not holding a coaching qualification.[65] Importantly, attainment of a formal coaching qualification, delivered by an approved body such as an NGB, is a strong indicator of necessary competence and specialist skill. This was reiterated when the Court of Appeal considered the level of qualification required and recognised by independent bodies for the teaching of the forward somersault in the leading authority for coach negligence, *Fowles v Bedfordshire County Council*.[66] Nonetheless, not all enquiries of the competency of coaches will be so clear-cut, there being a wide range of reasons

---

60 *Woodbridge School v Chittock* [2002] EWCA Civ 915 [27]. Discussed in Chapters 2, 3 & 5–6.
61 *Bolitho v City of Hackney Health Authority* [1998] AC 232 (HL). See further, Chapter 3.
62 See generally, Jones and Dugdale (n 24) [10–03].
63 For instance, the *Bolam* test was essentially successfully satisfied in: *Davenport* (n 46); *Morrow* (n 58) and *Woodbridge School* (n 60). In the context of school sport, also see *Wright v Cheshire CC* [1952] 2 ALL ER 789.
64 A Lynn and J Lyle, 'Coaching Workforce Development' in Lyle and Cushion (n 22) 205.
65 Sports Coach UK, *Coach Tracking Study: A Four-Year Study of Coaching in the UK* (Leeds, Coachwise 2012) 17.
66 *Fowles v Bedfordshire CC* [1995] PIQR P380 (CA). Discussed in detail in Chapter 5.

why experienced and highly proficient coaches may not always become formally accredited at all or, alternatively, at a level reflective of their expertise. Conversely, the typically unregulated nature of the coaching 'profession' appears somewhat deficient in preventing coaches, perhaps with only entry level type qualifications, from operating at levels beyond their level of recognised competence and therefore lacking the specialist skill needed to effectively discharge their duty of care. In the unfortunate circumstances whereby an athlete may suffer serious personal injury, and legitimately seek redress through the courts, determining the relevance of the coach's qualifications and previous experience, and the possible existence of a skills gap, requires careful scrutiny of the full factual circumstances of the individual case. Although judges will often be equipped with the opinions of experts in the relevant field regarding what constitutes reasonably safe practice,[67] the lack of formal accreditation of coaches poses a difficult challenge for courts, often compounded by the specificity of sport. However, despite coaching being regarded as a 'new' profession, in applying the principles of professional liability to claims of coach negligence, as with architects, solicitors and doctors, a coach should not be viewed as incompetent just because the judge fancied 'playing' coach.[68] As with the more traditional learned professions, judges lack the required expertise to appropriately define proper coaching practice, a particularly pertinent issue in the absence of formal accreditation.

On this point, and as highlighted in Chapter 4, the Court of Appeal in *Smoldon v Whitworth* was faced with conflicting arguments about whether the required competence of a rugby union referee should be determined by the qualification held or the level of sporting performance at which the special skill was being employed. In delivering the court's judgment, the Lord Chief Justice disregarded the case as being an instance of a possible skills gap.[69] The qualification held by the referee was entirely commensurate with the level of match he was officiating. The Court of Appeal expressed the view that the level of skill required in the circumstances should be determined by the function a referee was performing and not by her/his grade.[70] Following *Wilsher v Essex Area Health Authority*,[71] this reasoning seems correct.[72] Applying this formulation in a coaching context enables account to be taken of both formal qualifications and, importantly, the level of performance at which the specialist skill is employed, when ascertaining whether coaches are

---

67 M Brazier and J Miola, 'Bye-Bye Bolam: A Medical Litigation Revolution?' (2000) 8(1) *Med Law Rev* 85, 87. See further, Chapter 5.
68 Ibid.
69 *Smoldon v Whitworth* [1997] PIQR P133 (CA), P139. See further, Chapter 4. The implications of a possible skills gap of coaches are discussed further later.
70 This same reasoning was recently adopted by Judge Lopez in *Bartlett v English Cricket Board Association of Cricket Officials*, County Court (Birmingham), 27 August 2015.
71 *Wilsher v Essex AHA* [1987] QB 730 (CA). See further, Chapters 2 & 3.
72 See further, N Partington, '"It's Just Not Cricket". Or Is It? *Bartlett v English Cricket Board Association of Cricket Officials*' (2016) 32(1) *Professional Negligence* 75, 79.

sufficiently competent.[73] The diverse composition of the coaching 'workforce', and lack of commonality of occupational practice, also endorses this approach. Furthermore, volunteers may not always be in a position to fully engage with education and training opportunities,[74] with the balance between formal qualifications and practical experience in this area unlikely to resemble more established professions.[75] Baroness Tanni Grey-Thompson's Duty of Care in Sport Report recognised that more needs to be done to ensure coaches have the appropriate qualifications and called for the consideration of a national coach licensing scheme, with the creation of a register of licensed coaches.[76] This book's analysis of the duty of care required of coaches strongly endorses this view.

Since parents often volunteer to become involved in sport to support the active involvement of their children, it is forcefully (though not without being mindful of the potential wider repercussions) submitted that they, and indeed all volunteer coaches, should only be prepared to coach should they possess the skill of the ordinarily competent coach for that particular level. In protecting the legitimate safety and welfare interests of both athletes and volunteer coaches, this stance is absolutely consistent with the legal expectations and obligations revealed by this book's analysis of a coach's duty of care. Subjectively speaking, there will no doubt be highly committed and enthusiastic volunteers prepared to step in at a moment's notice in order to unselfishly prevent cancellation of matches and practice sessions. Despite such altruistic actions, in objectively determining if the standard of care and skill has fallen below that expected in the particular circumstances, it appears that courts may place limited weight on the positive intentions of highly committed volunteers.[77] In short, it is imperative that all coaches are fully aware of their limitations and only operate at levels entirely commensurate with their expertise and competence.

Although formal qualification and accreditation remains the ideal indicator of requisite skill, *Wilkin-Shaw v Fuller*[78] provides an instructive illustration of the approach taken by courts when competence is not readily demonstrable by means of formal qualifications. The first defendant teacher in the tragic case of *Wilkin-Shaw* was responsible for the training of pupils for the Ten Tors Expedition on Dartmoor. Since the Kingsley School Bideford Trustee Co. Ltd, as employer,

---

73 In *Davenport* (n 46) [59], for instance, the court took account of the athlete's ability and aspirations and the fact that 'DF' was a level 4 coach (the highest athletics award available at the time of the alleged breach of duty in 2004).
74 H Campbell, 'Work with Us', Presentation by Scottish Council for Voluntary Organisations (1999) cited in M Graham and M Foley (eds), *Volunteering in Leisure: Marginal or Inclusive?* (Eastbourne, LSA 2001) 50.
75 Duffy et al. (n 57) 110.
76 Baroness Tanni Grey-Thompson, 'Duty of Care in Sport: Independent Report to Government', Department for Digital, Culture, Media & Sport, 21 April 2017, 18, 20, & 32.
77 E.g., *Scout Association v Barnes* [2010] EWCA Civ 1476.
78 *Wilkin-Shaw v Fuller* [2012] EWHC 1777. Also see, *MacIntyre* (n 59).

would have been vicariously liable for the negligent acts or omissions on the part of the first defendant, Owen J determined that:

> [T]he school was under a duty to ensure that the first defendant was competent to organise and to supervise the training, and that the team of adults assisting him in the training exercise had the appropriate level of experience and appropriate level of competence to discharge any role required of them.[79]

Problematically, although the experts agreed that formal qualifications including, for instance, the Walking Group Leader Award, was reflective of the standard against which the defendants should be judged, the first defendant did not hold any formal qualifications relevant to such activities.[80] Significantly, whilst recognising that formal qualifications represent the easiest way to demonstrate competence, the High Court acknowledged that qualifications were not the only means to do so.[81] The competence of the first defendant to act as a team leader was ultimately based on his experience and the measures taken to prepare the group for the Ten Tors.[82] Consideration of all of the prevailing circumstances in negligence claims brought against coaches would likewise be expected to account for the experience levels of the defendant coach. This is consistent with Lord Bingham's observations in *Smoldon*, it clearly being feasible that highly competent and proficient coaches, though possessing experience commensurate to the coaching being conducted, may lack official qualifications relevant to this same level. Although this logical and common-sense approach by the judiciary should provide some reassurance to (suitably experienced) coaches, formal qualification remains the 'gold standard' in evidencing competence and every effort should be made to promote the formal accreditation of all coaches. Consequently, before a person can be referred to as a coach, every reasonable attempt should be made to ensure the achievement of appropriate minimum criteria, with the monitoring of such compliance, and removal of related barriers and obstacles, an important priority for NGBs and scUK (sports coach UK).[83]

Risk assessment

The aim of effective risk assessment is to eliminate harm, not necessarily risk, by means of sensible and informed risk management. As such, in the context of sports coaching, a risk assessment is intended to promote the effective determination,

---

79 *Wilkin-Shaw* (n 78) [40].
80 Ibid. [56].
81 Ibid. [57].
82 Ibid. [59].
83 See generally, C Nash, 'Volunteering in Sports Coaching – A Tayside Study' in Graham and Foley (n 74) 54.

evaluation and management of reasonable risk. Detailed examination of recent case law reveals realistic judicial reasoning and expectations when establishing what might be regarded as suitable and sufficient assessment of risks in particular circumstances. For instance, as in *Blair-Ford v CRS Adventures Limited*, this included recognition that it may not always be necessary to complete a formal risk assessment for all activities,[84] since formal risk assessments are 'a less effective tool where a lot of variables may come into play'.[85] This concurs with Spencer J's ruling in *MacIntyre*, which was discussed in Chapter 5.[86] Suitable and sufficient assessment of risk is a process and not a document. However, an informed and well-considered formal risk assessment provides a critical and robust foundation from which a proper and continuous reassessment of risk can be effected.[87] Indeed, a flawed initial formal risk assessment somewhat negates the identification of what might be regarded as acceptable risk in the prevailing circumstances, since the necessary balancing exercise (i.e., a risk-benefit assessment) is compromised.[88] Put bluntly, should an initial formal risk assessment be inadequate, there may not be 'a subsequent opportunity for a proper dynamic risk assessment to inform and improve upon the earlier risk assessment'.[89] This is a serious potential pitfall which coaches must guard against when discharging their duty of care.

Evidence of intelligent and well-informed reasoning, or lack thereof, would appear to be the pivotal issue when coaches seek to identify acceptable risk.[90] The clear expectation that coaches should employ a 'thoughtful appraisal of risk' when completing risk assessments,[91] speaks to the requirement of the approach adopted being justifiable and therefore capable of withstanding logical scrutiny.[92] In short, whenever possible, coaches should adopt regular and approved approaches to risk

---

84 E.g., in *Blair-Ford v CRS Adventures Limited* [2012] EWHC 2360 [62], Globe J held that 'although there was a formal risk assessment of the Mini-Olympics as a whole, there was no formal risk assessment and no advance plan as to the method of handicapping for the teachers before the welly-wanging event was about to begin. That, though, is not decisive'. Also see *Wilkin-Shaw* (n 78) [70]; *Risk v Rose Bruford College* [2013] EWHC 3869 [53]; *Uren v Corporate Leisure (UK) Limited* [2013] EWHC 353 [181].
85 *Uren v Corporate Leisure (UK) Ltd* [2011] EWCA Civ 66 [42] (Smith LJ). Also see *Blair-Ford* (n 84) [62].
86 *MacIntyre* (n 59) [120].
87 Ibid. [82], [92].
88 Jones and Dugdale (n 24) [8–145]. Recognition of such potentially erroneous reasoning in *Uren v Corporate Leisure (UK) Limited* [2010] EWHC 46 provided sufficient grounds for a successful appeal. As noted by Jones and Dugdale, '[i]f the risk assessment was flawed that threw into question whether the appropriate balance between the degree of risk and the social value of the game had been reached'. Curiously, attaching too much/little weight to the social desirability of activities would appear to have a similar impact. See, for instance, *Scout Association* (n 77).
89 *Uren* (n 84) [165].
90 *Uren* (n 85) [45].
91 Ibid. [44].
92 As explained by Lord Browne-Wilkinson in *Bolitho* (n 61) 242, 'in forming their views, the experts have directed their minds to the question of comparative risks and benefits and have reached a defensible conclusion on the matter'.

management that they have thought carefully about. This assertion is endorsed by the emerging jurisprudence in this area.[93] Clearly, adequate risk assessment extends far beyond a purely back-covering, evidence generating, tick-box type paper exercise. This reinforces the importance of a proactive approach to effective risk management by coaches since it should not be necessary to await a sufficiently substantial or significant incident before the likelihood of its occurrence is envisaged.[94] Curiously, in *Cox v Dundee City Council*,[95] although Lady Scott did not find the defendant coach educator at all reliable or credible, his vagueness about when he received risk assessment training, or where and exactly how he carried out his risk assessment on the day of the incident,[96] may be insightful in revealing the somewhat diminished importance that might on occasion be afforded to risk assessments by some coaches. In view of the duty of a coach to adequately assess risk, this possible absence of reflective and thoughtful practice appears to signify some cause for concern.

Best practice in assessing risk clearly warrants completion of a formal risk assessment before amending regular and approved practice, or adopting innovative training methods, with accompanying dynamic assessment of risks also necessary. Coaches make frequent and extensive use of corrective and instructive concurrent feedback to enhance learning and performance. By honing highly proficient skills of observational analysis, this process simultaneously facilitates the opportunity for a continuous assessment of risk. Generally speaking, this is routine practice and enables appropriate intervention by coaches in a timely and effective manner to ensure that athletes are not exposed to unacceptable or unreasonable risk. This approach is one of the hallmarks of dynamic risk assessment. In this context and, as noted in *Blair-Ford v CRS Adventures Limited*, 'spur of the moment' decisions may be necessary due to factors including the weather and the individual needs of participants.[97] Nonetheless, the careful forethought evidenced in a suitable and sufficient written risk assessment should minimise the need for spur of the moment decisions. Moreover, the suitability and sufficiency of dynamic risk assessments is more likely to be acceptable when coaches have been trained to use their knowledge, experience, initiative and common sense when continuously assessing risk.[98]

---

93 As revealed in Chapter 5. See, for instance, *Macintyre* (n 59) [79], [120], [122]. Also see, *Blair-Ford* (n 84) [61], [62], [65].
94 *Uren* (n 84) [179].
95 *Cox v Dundee CC* [2014] CSOH 3. See further, Chapter 5.
96 Ibid. [19], [26].
97 *Blair-Ford* (n 84) [27].
98 Ibid. Also see *Uren* (n 88) [52], Field J highlighting that Professor Ball, an expert witness, explained that when he assesses the risks of an activity he extrapolates from his technical knowledge, experience of life and comparable activities. Similar such intelligent and informed reasoning is no doubt frequently employed by coaches, teachers and instructors.

Coach education, training and development

Somewhat reassuringly, it has been suggested that greater emphasis is now being placed on the duty of care required by law during coach education courses.[99] Notwithstanding such progressive developments, questions remain over the value of introductory coaching qualifications, often of between four and six hours duration, with successful certification frequently dependent only on attendance.[100] This general tendency to deliver coach education training programmes over short periods of time results in coaching certificates representing the minimum level of expertise at a specific level.[101] Additionally, in order to stay up-to-date, there are demands placed on coaches to avail of learning opportunities since the science of coaching continues to expand.[102] These factors appear probable obstacles to the achievement and maintenance of a level of specialist skill reflective of the ordinarily competent coach and necessary for adequate fulfilment of the duty of care required of coaches. In further elaborating on some of these very considerable limitations of coach education, training and accreditation, Telfer has stated the following:

> Dealing with performers who are on the whole young and impressionable and led by coaches whose education and training may be limited to a mere handful of hours over a few weekends demonstrates a clear need for greater investment in the way in which sport seeks to develop expertise in their coaches. Expertise takes time to develop and there is certainly an argument that novice coaches should be made more aware of the limitations of coaching individuals or teams armed only with the most basic coaching level award. Although governing bodies of sport generally try to emphasise that an early coaching role should be that of supporting more qualified coaches, this is poorly regulated.[103]

These observations speak to legitimate safeguarding interests of both athletes, often young and impressionable, and coaches, whose expertise must be commensurate to the level of coaching being delivered. Coaches must have an awareness and appreciation of their own limitations and developmental needs and priorities. Importantly, there is evidence to indicate that volunteers are less prepared to commit themselves to CPD opportunities than those in employment.[104] Furthermore, whilst it has been recognised that required attendance at training courses may boost the confidence of some volunteers, 'this was countered by the belief that

---

99 Telfer (n 22) 210.
100 Nash (n 83).
101 P Trudel et al., 'Coach Education and Effectiveness' in Lyle and Cushion (n 22) 149.
102 Ibid.
103 Telfer (n 22) 211.
104 Campbell (n 74).

the additional burden in terms of time and cost would deter others'.[105] Research conducted with 19 Scottish governing bodies of sport revealed some widespread concern of a possible skills gap, whereby coaches discharge a function beyond that for which they are qualified.[106] This concern is reiterated by Lyle and Cushion, who are also mindful of situations where coaches may operate in circumstances for which they do not possess the appropriate qualifications *or* experience.[107] Certainly, and as argued by Nash, unqualified coaches working unsupervised with children represents a substantive ethical (and legal) issue.[108]

Intuitively, although the altruistic motives of volunteer coaches may encourage a reluctance to politely refuse requests to coach in contexts extending beyond the coach's level of expertise or competence, this must be resisted. Put bluntly, the duty of care derived from the law of negligence is premised on objective reasonableness. By analogy, and although relating to the contributory negligence of an adult skier,[109] it appears plain that '[t]he human reaction not to want to appear awkward, difficult or. . . "faint-hearted" is quite understandable from a subjective viewpoint, but objective analysis does suggest that serious concerns must be ventilated'.[110] Correspondingly, should coaches have concerns about a possible skills gap, this represents a serious issue that must be ventilated, since objective analysis of a coach's duty of care demands that when coaches assume a particular coaching task there is a duty of care to discharge it properly.

National governing bodies of sport

Curiously, it seems that NGBs may often assume that coaching codes of conduct enable coaches to sufficiently resolve many of the associated issues and tensions, with regard to the effective discharge of their duty of care, discussed earlier. In essence, when attempting to address many of the ethical (and potentially legal) dilemmas encountered by coaches, there would appear to be an unexamined and superficial reliance by NGBs and coaching organisations on codes of conduct.[111] Since the assumption seems to be that ethical considerations regarding coaching practice will be understood and grasped intuitively by coaches,[112] the extent to which codes

---

105 R Groom et al., 'Volunteering Insight: Report for Sport England' (Manchester Metropolitan University 2014) 58.
106 Lynn and Lyle (n 64) 199.
107 J Lyle and C Cushion, 'Narrowing the Field: Some Key Questions About Sports Coaching' in Lyle and Cushion (n 22) 247.
108 Nash (n 83) 44.
109 *Anderson* (n 30).
110 Ibid. [142].
111 A Hardman and C Jones, 'Ethics For Coaches' in Jones and Kingston (n 7) 126. See further, M McNamee, 'Celebrating Trust: Virtues and Rules in the Ethical Conduct of Sports Coaches' in M McNamee and S Parry (eds), *Ethics & Sport* (London, E & FN Spon 1998) 165.
112 Telfer (n 22) 210–11.

of conduct impact and shape coaching behaviour appears open to conjecture and debate.[113] Developing in coaches a greater knowledge and understanding of the emerging interface between sports coaching and the law of negligence represents a significant opportunity to address this potential void, given the qualified overlap between legal and ethical obligations.[114] Indeed, an unexamined and superficial reliance on coaching codes of conduct fails to sufficiently account for the evolving legal context in which coaches discharge the duties incumbent upon them. Since an aim of relevant and engaging coach education courses should be to assist coaches in constructing (context-specific) knowledge rather than merely receiving it,[115] instructive scenarios derived from the relevant case law examined in previous chapters should be designed to stimulate critical reflection on pertinent legal (and ethical) issues. In transcending some of the present limitations of codes of conduct, such action would more effectively guide and support coaches in defining their duty of care by providing an awareness and understanding of the dynamic relationship between sport, coaching and the law. Significantly, this would also provide real-world illustrations of what constitutes (un)reasonable coaching practice.

Conclusion

This chapter's analysis highlights important implications for practitioners exercising the specialised 'art' of coaching. Most notably, established jurisprudence confirms that coaches would be judged according to the benchmark of the ordinarily competent/reasonably average coach when exercising their duty of care. This is regardless of coaches being categorised as amateur, professional, qualified and/or (in)experienced. Further, as a 'new' and emerging profession, rigorous and searching judicial scrutiny of what might amount to proper or approved practice, or *Bolam* 'defence', emphasises the requirement for coaches to adopt universal good practice whenever possible. Moreover, practices employed by coaches must always be responsible and robustly justifiable. Simply applied, when discharging their duty of care, the hallmarks of reasonable coaching are (i) regular and approved coaching practices; that are (ii) logically justifiable; and (iii) suitable for the post or position of the coach. When critically evaluating and reflecting upon their own coaching practice, successfully satisfying these three legal propositions, or tests, should ensure that coaches adequately discharge their duty of care and skill. In short, coaches

---

113 B Taylor and D Garratt, 'The Professionalization of Sports Coaching: Definitions, Challenges and Critique' in Lyle and Cushion (n 22) 109; T Cassidy, 'Exploring Ethics: Reflections of a University Coach Educator' in S Harvey and RL Light (eds), *Ethics in Youth Sport: Policy and Pedagogical Applications* (London, Routledge 2013) 153. Also see McNamee (n 111) 155.
114 M Mitten, 'The Coach and the Safety of Athletes: Ethical and Legal Issues' in R Simon (ed), *The Ethics of Coaching Sports: Moral, Social, and Legal Issues* (Colorado, Westview Press 2013) 216.
115 RL Jones, 'Toward a Sociology of Coaching' in RL Jones & KM Armour, *Sociology of Sport: Theory and Practice* (London, Pearson 2000) 34; C Nash, 'How Coaches Learn and Develop' in C Nash (ed), *Practical Sports Coaching* (Routledge 2015) 182.

with the developed self-awareness to continuously evaluate the appropriateness of their coaching methods and behaviour, and thereby successfully satisfy these propositions which are indicative of reasonable coaching, would be shielded from negligence liability.

Whether application of the ordinary principles of professional liability in the context of voluntary sports coaching is fair, just and reasonable, or whether this establishes unrealistic expectations,[116] remains debatable.[117] Nonetheless, the legal obligations of coaches, derived from the law of tort, reinforce the urgency of coach education and CPD affording considerably more importance to legal (and ethical) issues likely to be encountered by ordinary coaching practitioners. There is a pressing need for greater investment in the way in which sport seeks to develop expertise in coaches and, not least in view of the evolving legal context in which coaches discharge their duty of care. This must become a priority. In the same manner in which 'the contemporary coach needs to be "professional" in terms of the acquisition of new forms of knowledge',[118] the contemporary coach must also be more fully aware and informed of the practical content of the duty of care they assume. Bespoke coach education resources, derived from the developing coach negligence case law, would provide the most authentic, engaging and accurate means of achieving this aim. Ultimately, it is hoped that this chapter's suggested implications for coaching practice will be of considerable practical relevance and engender further debate concerning the legal duty of care of modern sports coaches. In addition to emphasising the safety and welfare of athletes, the coach education and training provision argued for should enable a coach's acts or omissions to be more capable of withstanding robust and searching judicial scrutiny in any future claims brought against coaches for a breach of duty of care.

---

116 See generally, G Nichols and P Taylor, 'The Balance of Benefit and Burden? The Impact of Child Protection Legislation on Volunteers in Scottish Sports Clubs' (2010) 10(1) *European Sport Management Quarterly* 31, 46.
117 See, for instance, N Partington, 'Beyond the "*Tomlinson*" Trap": Analysing the Effectiveness of Section 1 of the Compensation Act 2006' (2016) 37(1) *Liverpool L Rev* 33.
118 Taylor and Garratt (n 54).

CONCLUSION

This book offers a detailed analysis of the duty of care incumbent upon modern sports coaches. The interdependent coach–athlete relationship represents the most fundamental instance of a duty of care in sport, requiring coaches to display the levels of care and specialist skill ordinarily expected of the reasonably average coach in the same circumstances. Defining this standard of objectively reasonable coaching practice, at first glance, may appear straightforward and a matter of common sense. However, as this book's critical analysis reveals, reasonableness is a vague and elusive concept which offers little by way of more precise and concrete guidance when attempts are made to define the practical content of a coach's duty of care in particular sporting circumstances. Similarly, the extant academic literature offers only limited detailed analysis of a coach's duty of care and, moreover, clarification of what may amount to a breach of this duty. This book addresses this gap by adopting an interdisciplinary approach within a broader sociolegal methodological framework. As such, authentic insights of contemporary importance for coaches have been identified through an analytical lens that seeks to make an interconnection between different academic disciplines and, in particular, tort law, sports law and sports coaching in order to critically examine the practical application of the law of negligence in the specific context of sports coaching. This is a highly fact-dependent and evolving area of the law. Therefore, sustained and rigorous analysis of the emerging case law is not only necessary but, by providing actual and engaging scenarios that illustrate common challenges faced by coaches when discharging their duty of care, enables the perspective of the coach to remain central throughout. It has been argued that the ubiquity of sport and a commonly adopted legal standard of reasonableness means that the requisite duty of care of sports coaches may be regarded to a large extent as being generally similar everywhere. This means that many of the suggested implications highlighted in this book will transcend geographical and jurisdictional boundaries. Put simply, the previous pages offer an original and bespoke analysis of a hitherto seldom examined core complexity of sports coaching which is of widespread importance and relevance.

For ease of reference, the findings and implications of this analysis are presented in this conclusion in the following three sections that focus primarily on: (i) coaches and coaching practice; (ii) sports law; and (iii) national governing bodies of sport (NGBs). Whilst this structure is intended to better consolidate and emphasise the arguments made throughout the book, inevitably there will remain substantial overlaps regarding the importance of this research for these different constituent groups. Also, the issues raised will, no doubt, be of considerable interest and relevance to readers from other related backgrounds (e.g., tort law, physical education, sports ethics and sports policy).

Coaches and coaching practice

Crucially, coaches must be attuned to the fact that duty of care is a dynamic concept, the extent of which (i.e., standard of care) has a tendency to heighten, and be more challenging to discharge over time. This is compounded by many of the various complexities of coaching, including mutually dependent relationships spanning a wide and demanding range of performance levels and the rapidly advancing environment in which coaches perform. Whilst it is inescapable that the relationship between a coach and those under the coach's charge is reflective of the emerging interface between sport and the law, accurately defining a coach's duty of care requires full account to be taken of all of the prevailing circumstances. This requirement emphasises the importance of developing in coaches an informed awareness of evolving legal standards when discharging the specific duties discussed in Chapters 5 and 6 in their own coaching contexts and, as highlighted in Chapter 7, presents notable implications for coaching practice, coach education and training, and sports policy and development.

In aiming to stimulate and encourage further discussion on the application of duty of care principles in the context of sport generally, and the circumstances of sports coaching in particular, this book's detailed and rigorous analysis of the relevant case law is contended to be especially instructive and insightful. As discussed in the following section, this analysis uncovers established legal principles of broad application in this field.[1] More specifically, by identifying and investigating situations that do/do not amount to a breach of duty of care by coaches, barometers of acceptable and unacceptable coaching practice have been revealed through detailed and sustained examination of individual cases. These cases cover a range of sporting activities, from the coaching of gymnastics, football, skiing, bobsleigh, mountain

---

1 As argued, and most particularly in Chapters 1 & 3, this book's critical analysis is of relevance to not only sports coaching but a general range of duty of care inquiries and the broader field of professional negligence. Indeed, the sustained analysis of tort law principles in the specific circumstances of sport/sports coaching should also prove instructive for practitioners specialising in personal injury law.

biking and athletics to coaching delivered by a rugby football union coach educator during a training course. They also include participation in both elite and grassroots sport and involve both amateur and professional coaches. To date, such a sustained, transparent and authentic illustration of the level of due care and skill necessary for coaches to effectively discharge the duty of care owed to athletes has been lacking. These illustrations, combined with a greater recognition and understanding of the 'calculus of risk' discussed in Chapter 2, and which is used by courts to reflect the balancing of the magnitude of risk against the cost of preventative measures and the social utility of the activity giving rise to the risk, should support coaches in devising a proactive risk assessment lens.

The foregoing examination of relevant case law presents real-life scenarios affording informative and engaging illustrations of a coach's duty of care in action. A coach's duty of care represents a somewhat hidden complexity of coaching given the tendency to focus on the bioscientific aspects of sports science, and practical skills and associated knowledge, in present sports coaching scholarship. Simply applied, this book's discussion should more effectively enable coaches to critically reflect on the appropriateness of their own coaching behaviours with regard to legal (and ethical) dilemmas and, importantly, encourage/restrict the assumption of duties of care in/to clearly identified circumstances in which these said duties can be discharged properly. Significantly, coaches with the developed self-awareness to systematically evaluate the appropriateness of their coaching practice(s), and successfully satisfy the propositions indicative of reasonable coaching analysed in previous chapters, would be best placed to effectively discharge their duty of care and thereby better protect the safety and welfare of athletes.

Critical reflections on coaching practice must account for factors likely to extend the duty of care expected of modern sports coaches. As revealed, whilst the standard expected of sports coaches is fixed conceptually as the duty to take reasonable care, the specific duties required of coaches have, and will continue, to evolve. This is due to advances in sports science, technical developments in certain sports, societal expectations and general improvements connected to the further professionalisation of sports coaching.

Chapter 3 makes plain that these factors are integral to this area of professional negligence, despite the majority of coaches being amateur volunteers. Such advances will increase the scope and degree of the duty of care owed by progressively placing more responsibilities on coaches. Indeed, as the principles of coaching are continuously assessed and revised, the legal standard of care required of coaches when exercising their duty of care will correspondingly be prone to constant review since it represents a fluid and malleable benchmark.[2] Raising the standards expected of ordinarily competent coaches in a considered and incremental manner, in order to protect the legitimate safety interests of athletes, is both

---

2 This underscores the necessity of judging coaches by the standards prevailing at the time of any alleged breach of duty and not with the wisdom of hindsight.

positive and desirable. However, there remains a danger that the pervading duty of care in sport narrative risks conflating legal, moral and social duties of care. As argued in Chapter 1, this reiterates the need for a more precise, nuanced and informed understanding of the duty of care in sport in order to avoid extending the nature of a coach's legal duty of care beyond its intended sphere of application.

Broadly speaking, established jurisprudence in the UK perhaps unsurprisingly reveals that the specific duties of care of coaches relate predominantly to the reasonableness of supervision, training and instruction when managing the risk of injury to athletes. Nonetheless, the emerging case law also reveals judicial scrutiny of the duties of coaches with regard to: suitable and sufficient risk assessment;[3] adequate provision of warnings; pitch inspections; the matching of participants; the organisation, pitch and pace of coaching sessions; decisions made to take athletes and participants outside of their comfort zones; determination of what might appropriately satisfy the requirements of common practice or *Bolam* 'defence'; and ultimately, the boundary between reasonable and unreasonable coaching practice. These duties are context- and circumstance-specific and will be prone to further refinement and modification in the future, and not least in response to the ever-developing protocols and best practice recommendations promulgated by NGBs (e.g., with regard to sport-related concussion). Coaches mindful of, and responsive to, applicable developments will be best positioned to effectively discharge their evolving duty of care, avoid the pitfalls associated with negligent entrenched practice and ensure that the coaching practices adopted are reasonable and capable of being logically justified.

To this end, this book provides sensible guidelines for coaches when discharging their duty of care, it being imperative that modern sports coaches are aware of legal developments affecting sports participation and continuously reflect upon their own coaching practices and methods through a proactive risk assessment lens. This is a hallmark of best practice since '[s]uccessful coaches are those who can learn new skills, who are flexible enough to change old ways when change is needed, who can accept constructive criticism, and who can critically evaluate themselves'.[4] Simply applied, this book's clarification and analysis of the requisite duty of care of coaches consistently stresses the requirement and importance of all coaches:

- Always adopting reasonable coaching practice so that reasonable care and skill is taken to ensure the reasonable safety of athletes;
- Following recognised and approved coaching methods that are capable of withstanding logical analysis and are appropriate for the level of sports performance;

---

3 Given the increased judicial scrutiny of this aspect of risk management, the issue of risk assessment is returned to in the following section.
4 R Martens, *Successful Coaching* (3rd edn, Champaign, Human Kinetics 2004) vii.

- Only deviating from recognised and approved practice in exceptional circumstances and when there is a compelling and convincing justification to do so;[5]
- Refraining from assuming duties beyond their competence, qualifications and/or experience by being more conscious of their potential limitations or a possible skills gap;[6]
- Understanding and appreciating the necessity of relevant coach education, qualifications, training and continuing professional development (CPD);
- More confidently establishing what might amount to objectively reasonable coaching practice in their own specific coaching contexts;
- Being sensitised to the dangers of negligent entrenched practice and coaching behaviours premised on 'uncritical inertia' and 'entrenched legitimacy';
- Incorporating best practices in risk management into their own coaching practices (e.g., with respect to risk assessments, the provision of warnings, ensuring the proper use of safe equipment etc.); and more generally,
- Being better aware and knowledgeable with regard to the implications posed by the dynamic legal landscape in which they operate.

In returning to a question first posed in the preface to this book, the previous chapters are designed to support coaches in rigorously identifying (and justifying) the boundary between forging champions and committing a tort when pushing athletes outside of their comfort zones and determining the pitch, pace and intensity of coaching sessions. Interestingly, in addition to the intended objective of supporting coaches in effectively and assuredly discharging their duty of care, a systematic and informed appraisal of litigation risk would be likely to correspondingly enhance the safety and welfare of athletes, thereby coincidentally minimising the loss of availability of athletes for sports participation.[7]

Sports law

For the sports law student, teacher and practitioner, this book provides a rigorous analysis of the legally significant features of sports negligence jurisprudence generally and, more specifically, the emerging body of coach negligence case law in the UK.

This sustained treatment of the relevant case law emphasises important statements of legal principle. Before reiterating and discussing these applicable principles, there are three elemental points that have previously been mentioned but, for present purposes, merit further prominence. These considerations are integral when analysing the interaction between the law of negligence and sport. Indeed,

---

5 See further, *Woodroffe-Hedley v Cuthbertson*, 20 June 1997 (QBD), discussed in Chapter 5.
6 Albeit this sometimes appearing to contradict the very essence and motivations for volunteering to coach.
7 M Mitten, 'The Coach and the Safety of Athletes: Ethical and Legal Issues' in RL Simon (ed), *The Ethics of Coaching Sports: Moral, Social, and Legal Issues* (Colorado, Westview Press 2013) 227.

they are of fundamental importance to the decisive factor on which the vast majority of cases brought in negligence against coaches are decided, namely, determination of the required standard of care in all the circumstances and the law of negligence's control mechanism of breach. First, as forcefully articulated by Jackson LJ in *Scout Association v Barnes*, '[i]t is not the function of the law of tort to eliminate every iota of risk or to stamp out socially desirable activities'.[8] Without question, sport represents an activity of immense social value. As such, section 1 of the Compensation Act 2006 and the Social Action, Responsibility and Heroism Act 2015 should afford defendant coaches statutory tools to call in assistance in support of their case if sued for a breach of duty.[9] Second, in *Sutton v Syston RFC*, Longmore LJ stressed that the law must not 'lay down standards that are too difficult for ordinary coaches . . . to meet'.[10] This must be correct and yet, as previously argued, it remains questionable whether this objective is always achieved in practice. Moreover, given the potential conflation of social and moral duties with legal duties of care in grassroots sport, thereby creating legal obligations, from a strict legal perspective, the standards required of volunteer coaches may well in future become increasingly difficult to meet.[11] And third, 'the issue of [sports] negligence cannot be resolved in a vacuum. It is fact specific'.[12] As revealed most expressly in Chapters 5 and 6, the full factual matrix of coach negligence cases can be varied and often more complex than other aspects of sports negligence, demanding searching judicial scrutiny alongside detailed consideration of expert witness testimony. Put simply, these three statements made in the Court of Appeal are of foundational importance when defining the practical content of the duty owed by defendants in the circumstances of sport. Significantly, these broad points contextualise the issue of coach negligence and bring into sharper focus the following highlighted statements of legal principle.

Given the extensive cross-pollination of tortious principles between different jurisdictions, and as argued in the introduction, this book's critical analysis is intended to be of widespread relevance. For instance, the cases discussed in the previous chapters should provide a potential source of strong and useful persuasive authority both within and outside the UK. This is particularly the case since coach negligence represents a hitherto seldom analysed but nonetheless frequently mentioned and emerging area of professional negligence. Accordingly, by examining the principles of professional liability in a context where the majority of defendants are predominantly amateur volunteers, Chapter 3 proves instructive in analysing the *Bolam* test. This analysis reveals that reliance on the so-called *Bolam* 'defence' can be made in circumstances where defendants may be unqualified and

---

8 *Scout Association v Barnes* [2010] EWCA Civ 1476 [34] (dissenting).
9 See further, N Partington, 'Beyond the "*Tomlinson* Trap": Analysing the Effectiveness of Section 1 of the Compensation Act 2006' (2016) 37(1) *Liverpool L Rev* 33.
10 *Sutton v Syston RFC Ltd* [2011] EWCA Civ 1182 [13].
11 This issue is discussed in detail in Chapter 1.
12 *Caldwell v Maguire* [2001] EWCA Civ 1054 [30] (Judge LJ).

may not have embarked upon a responsible decision-making process, providing the approved and justifiable standards of the reasonably skilful coach are met. Furthermore, the related *Woodbridge* principle,[13] providing decisions about coaching methods are 'within a reasonable range of options', should afford coaches considerable latitude in their discretionary judgement making. Undoubtably, both the *Bolam* 'defence' and *Woodbridge* principle will remain of considerable practical utility in future claims of coach negligence.

The legal test fashioned by the UK courts for breach of duty, as illustrated in Chapter 4 and in cases including *Wooldridge v Sumner*,[14] *Smoldon v Whitworh*[15] and *Caldwell v Maguire*,[16] by taking full account of all of the relevant sporting circumstances, is designed to set the standard of care at a reasonable and realistic level for defendants. Ordinarily, in the context of a competitive sporting activity, the threshold of liability is intended to be high and not easily crossed. As such, for participants and referees it appears most unlikely that there would be a breach of duty of care resulting from an error of judgement or lapse in skill during fast moving games. This is despite these same lapses in the majority of negligence cases, including those outside of sporting activities and in most claims of professional negligence, leading to a finding of liability. Nonetheless, there remains no requirement in sports negligence cases for the claimant to establish that the defendant acted with a reckless disregard for their safety. A standard of reckless disregard or foolhardiness provides a sufficient but by no means necessary evidential guide in claims of sports negligence. Crucially, the test for breach remains one of ordinary negligence in all the circumstances, with the propositions approved by the Court of Appeal in *Caldwell* expressly identifying the indicative criteria constituting the prevalent sporting circumstances and enabling reasonableness to be defined.

As in *Morrow v Dungannon*,[17] these propositions derived from *Caldwell* may sometimes be directly applicable in cases of coach negligence without requiring the need for much adaptation. However, the issue of breach of duty by sports coaches represents a distinctively nuanced instance of sports negligence since the interdependent coach–athlete relationship gives rise to its own peculiar circumstances. So although the legal duty of all defendants in the context of sport remains premised on a reasonableness standard, the practical content of a coach's duty of care will be reflective of specific circumstantial considerations. Accordingly, although the special features inherent in competitive sporting activities espoused in *Caldwell* may be extremely valuable in defining the standard of care in claims of coach negligence, it would be a precarious representation of legal principle to assume that this application will be universal. For instance, both *Anderson v Lyotier*[18] and *Ahmed*

---

13 *Woodbridge School v Chittock* [2002] EWCA Civ 915.
14 *Wooldridge v Sumner* [1963] 2 QB 43 (CA).
15 *Smoldon v Whitworth* [1997] PIQR P133.
16 *Caldwell* (n 12).
17 *Morrow v Dungannon and South Tyrone BC* [2012] NIQB 50.
18 *Anderson v Lyotier* [2008] EWHC 2790.

v MacLean[19] are blunt illustrations of how a momentary error of judgement or lapse in skill by a coach or instructor can amount to a breach of duty and a finding of negligence liability.

The requirement for refinement of the legal principles established by the leading authorities for sports negligence, when fashioning the breach test for coach negligence, is further underscored by a careful reading of *Vowles v Evans*[20] and *Harrison v Vincent*.[21] As in *Vowles*, coaching practice will often enable time for considered thought, thus providing very different considerations than would be likely to apply in circumstances where there is an alleged breach of duty during a fast-moving game or activity. As recognised by Dyson J, this was a material factor in *Woodroffe-Hedley v Cuthbertson*,[22] since it was found that the mountain guide 'had ample time to make a calm assessment of the situation and make his decision'. Similarly, following *Harrison v Vincent*, the 'relative calm' of the workshop could be argued to appear analogous with the 'relative calm' of some practice sessions delivered by some coaches. In these circumstances, a more exacting degree of care than that required in the 'heat of a game' would most typically be demanded.

A fundamental principle established by sports negligence jurisprudence in the UK is that the requisite standard of care takes full account of the specific sporting circumstances, including any inherent dangers of the activity. Consequently, it is unnecessary to consider how implied sporting consent might modify a more generalised duty of care.[23] Such a modification would be based on the assumption that athletes consented to taking risks which otherwise would be a breach of the duty of care. Whilst this alternative approach was considered in *Condon*,[24] as revealed in Chapter 4, preference for a standard of care formulation premised on the requirement that reasonable care is taken in all the circumstances has become the adopted approach when determining fault in sports negligence cases in this jurisdiction.[25] As demonstrated in *Shone v British Bobsleigh Limited*,[26] this malleable test can be effective when courts are tasked with scrutinising the issue of consent as an important constituent component of the prevailing circumstances. This considerable flexibility and breadth for judicial interrogation of the issue of consent in coach negligence cases is significant, not least since the question of consent during sporting activities can be especially complex due to the increasing pressures faced by athletes to perform.[27] Also, as discussed in Chapter 7, this might be compounded

---

19 *Ahmed v MacLean* [2016] EWHC 2798.
20 *Vowles v Evans* [2003] EWCA Civ 318.
21 *Harrison v Vincent* [1982] RTR 8 (CA).
22 *Woodroffe-Hedley* (n 5).
23 This was the approach advocated by Barwick CJ in the decision of the High Court of Australia in *Rootes v Shelton* [1968] ALR 33.
24 *Condon v Basi* (1985) 1 WLR 866 (CA). Discussed in detail in Chapter 4.
25 *Caldwell* (n 12).
26 *Shone v British Bobsleigh Limited* [2018] 5 WLUK 226.
27 P Vines, 'Doping as Tort: Liability of Sport Supervisors and the Problem of Consent' in U Haas and D Healey (eds), *Doping in Sport and the Law* (Oxford, Hart 2016) 190.

by the normalisation of the so-called 'sport ethic' and possible excesses of coaching behaviour.

Related to this is the defence of volenti non fit injuria, or voluntary assumption of risk. Volenti is premised upon the notion of consent, but as previously mentioned, since the issue of consent is reflected in the scope of the practical content of the duty owed in all of the circumstances, volenti appears to be of extremely limited practical application in cases of coach negligence. Unsurprisingly, there has been no reported successful reliance on the defence of volenti in claims brought against sports coaches or instructors for negligence in England and Wales. As such, the only legally sustainable denial of liability for coach negligence appears to be establishing that the duty of care has not been breached.[28] This observation reinforces the importance of the partial defence of contributory negligence for defendants, with a finding of contributory negligence in successful claims brought against coaches not uncommon.[29]

Alongside the partial defence of contributory negligence, and not least in view of recent judgments giving rise to a modern theory of the doctrine,[30] it seems probable that there will be an increase in the number of claims of vicarious liability in cases of coach negligence. As with findings of contributory negligence, the issue of vicarious liability in instances of coach negligence will often be an arguable matter.[31] Following the *Christian Brothers'* case[32] and *Cox v Ministry of Justice*,[33] and as discussed in Chapter 2, crystallisation of the 'akin to employment' category appears likely to encompass some amateur volunteer coaches in certain circumstances. Moreover, and as will be elaborated upon later, the increasing scope of vicarious liability may pose serious implications for NGBs.

An integral aspect of risk management discussed in detail in Chapters 5, 6 and 7 is the risk assessment process. This book's case law analysis strongly endorses Smith LJ's insightful acknowledgement that the failure to undertake a suitable and sufficient risk assessment can sometimes affect or even determine the outcome of a claim.[34] Coaches, just like judges, must be alive to this fact. For instance, the adequacy/inadequacy of the risk assessment process in *MacIntyre v Ministry of Defence*,[35] *Cox v Dundee City Council*[36] and *Anderson v Lyotier*[37] proved to be a decisive factor in determining if there had been a breach of duty. Furthermore, the risk assessment

---

28 See generally, D McArdle and M James, 'Are You Experienced? "Playing Cultures", Sporting Rules and Personal Injury Litigation After Caldwell v Maguire' (2005) 13(3) *Tort Law Review* 193, 200–01.
29 E.g., *Fowles v Bedfordshire CC* [1995] PIQR P380 (CA) P383; *Anderson* (n 18); *Ahmed* (n 19). The partial defence of contributory negligence is discussed further in relation to NGBs below.
30 *Cox v Ministry of Justice* [2016] UKSC 10 [24].
31 *Shone* (n 26); *Petrou v Bertoncello* [2012] EWHC 2286; *Morrell v Owen* (1993) Times, 14 December.
32 *Catholic Child Welfare Society v Various Claimants* (the '*Christian Brothers'* case) [2012] UKSC 56.
33 *Cox* (n 30).
34 *Uren v Corporate Leisure (UK) Ltd* [2011] EWCA Civ 66 [41] (Smith LJ).
35 *MacIntyre v Ministry of Defence* [2011] EWHC 1690.
36 *Cox v Dundee City Council* [2014] CSOH 3.
37 *Anderson* (n 18).

guidelines produced by the Rugby Football Union were afforded considerable force by the Court of Appeal in *Sutton v Syston RFC Ltd*.[38] Simply applied, evidence of a thoughtful, intelligent and informed appraisal of risk by coaches may prove conclusive in determining whether the probability and seriousness of the injury suffered by the claimant was reasonably foreseeable, in other words, such that it might reasonably be expected that the ordinary reasonable coach would/would not have anticipated it.[39]

National governing bodies of sport

At first glance, NGBs may not appear directly connected to a sports coach's duty of care. However, as the previous pages of this book reveal, NGBs have an instrumental role to play in this context. This role pertains to the training, accreditation and education of coaches, enabling practising coaches to remain up-to-date with their own CPD. The identification and dissemination of best practice guidelines and protocols relating to coaching practice by NGBs is necessary to protect the safety of participants. From a legal perspective, and following *Watson v British Boxing Board of Control*,[40] it is argued that since NGBs are associations with specialist knowledge giving advice to coaches on the understanding that this information will be relied upon, reasonable care ought to be exercised by them in order to safeguard coaches from legal liability due to a breach of duty.[41] A prospective risk analysis would alert NGBs, and other awarding bodies and policy makers, to the increasing potential for instances of coach negligence given the evolving intersection between sports coaching and the law. Accordingly, NGBs and those organisations providing training and support for coaches have a responsibility to ensure that the guidance and CPD afforded to coaches is reflective of the dynamic and emerging relationship between modern sports coaching and the law of negligence.

In short, coach education and accreditation must explicitly recognise the legal duties and obligations of coaches as being a foundational complexity of coaching and effectively account for the demands this makes in relation to modern coaching practice in a proactive manner. NGBs, therefore, have a duty to make coaches fully aware of recognised and approved coaching methods that would withstand logical analysis, best practice risk management policies and procedures and, crucially, to equip coaches with the knowledge and expertise needed to realistically determine the practical content of their requite duties in their own coaching contexts. Whilst recognising that conscientious and progressive bodies may have procedures already in place to effectively protect and safeguard coaches from some of the legal

---

38 *Sutton* (n 10).
39 See, *MacIntyre* (n 35) [70]; *Whippey v Jones* [2009] EWCA Civ 452 [16]; *Perry v Harris* [2008] EWCA Civ 907 [38].
40 *Watson v British Boxing Board of Control* [2001] QB 1134 (CA).
41 N Partington, 'Legal Liability of Coaches: A UK Perspective' (2014) 14(3–4) *International Sports Law Journal* 232, 239.

vulnerabilities highlighted in this book,[42] as with other posts and positions requiring a specialist skill, the standards required of modern sports coaches will continue to become more exacting and challenging to meet in future. Consequently, it is entirely appropriate that all NGBs consider conducting a comprehensive prospective risk assessment covering all facets of coach negligence to ensure that their legal duties and obligations, and those of the coaches involved in their respective sports, continue to be successfully discharged.

The negligence liability of NGBs for sports injuries is the area of sports negligence least explored.[43] *Gannon v Rotherham Metropolitan BC*[44] appears to be the first decision in the UK where an NGB has been found directly liable in negligence as a result of personal injury suffered during an event under its control.[45] The court in *Gannon* had to address a number of issues that are of relevance when considering the potential scope for claims brought in negligence against NGBs following instances of coach negligence. For present purposes, there are four main issues demanding particular attention. The first three, a claim by the injured athlete, vicarious liability and contributory negligence, relate to established legal principles and so are essentially straightforward to frame. The fourth, a claim by the coach whose negligence caused the athlete's injury, builds upon the Court of Appeal's reasoning in *Watson* and would represent an incremental development of the law of negligence in order to create a new duty situation. Importantly, with regard to all of these matters, a failure by an NGB to provide effective coach education and training may prove decisive.

In *Gannon*, a breach of duty of care by a PE teacher/coach resulted in the claimant breaking his neck when diving off starting blocks into the shallow end of a swimming pool. The instruction provided by the coach was found by the court to be inadequate. The Council, as the coach's employer, was held vicariously liable.[46] Importantly, in addition to succeeding in his claim against the coach, the claimant was also successful in a claim against the NGB, the Amateur Swimming Association (ASA), for a failure to issue swim instructors/coaches with sufficient warnings with regard to the associated dangers when teaching this skill.[47] In view of the claimant's

---

42 In this regard, as an essential minimum requirement, appropriate insurance provision (e.g., provided through NGBs) should mean that in a successful coach negligence action, individual coaches should not be required to provide damages from their own personal resources (although see *Woodland v Maxwell* [2015] EWHC 820 [9]). However, the stress of being sued, and negative labelling potentially associated with a finding of a breach of duty of care, appears highly unlikely to be negated through public liability insurance coverage, indicating that insurance may be necessary but not always sufficient in safeguarding coaches. More fundamentally, adequate insurance provision offers little in terms of clarifying and defining the practical content of a coach's duty of care.
43 M James, *Sports Law* (3rd edn, Croydon, Palgrave 2017) 111.
44 *Gannon v Rotherham Metropolitan Borough Council* Unreported, Crown Court (Nottingham), 6 February 1991.
45 J Anderson, *Modern Sports Law: A Textbook* (Oxford, Hart 2010) 248–49.
46 James (n 43) 102.
47 D Griffith-Jones and N Randall N, 'Civil Liability Arising Out of Participation in Sport' in A Lewis and J Taylor, *Sport: Law and Practice* (3rd edn, Haywards Heath, Tottel 2014) 1639.

age and experience, he was held contributory negligent.[48] *Gannon* demonstrates how, in particular circumstances, a breach of duty by a coach can make NGBs susceptible to a number of claims in negligence.

As discussed previously, given recent developments, vicarious liability looks likely to be a broadening head of liability in this area. Even prior to judicial approval and construction of the 'akin to employment' categorisation, in the context of claims of sports negligence involving amateur volunteer defendants, an acceptance of vicarious liability on the part of NGBs has not been uncommon.[49] More specifically, courts have held NGBs vicariously liable in cases of coach negligence where defendant coaches have been both professional[50] and amateur volunteers.[51] So whilst situations in which coaches are employed, or appointed centrally by NGBs, most obviously satisfy the requirements for the doctrine of vicarious liability to be applicable, its scope could become materially wider in future. Consequently, NGBs are advised to be mindful of recent legal developments in this area, not least because suing a recognised body may be a financially more attractive proposition for claimants rather than solely pursuing the individual tortfeasor (coach), since the prospect of a successful recovery of any award of damages would most certainly be strengthened.

The fourth issue of pressing curiosity is whether the coach may have a cause of action against the NGB. Such a claim is not yet based on direct authority and so may be regarded as a considerably more speculative proposition. Nonetheless, it is contended to certainly be arguable. Taking this point at its highest, the following scenario is used for illustrative purposes. In this scenario, an athlete is seriously injured during a sporting activity as a result of poor and dangerous technique when executing a skill. The technique causative of the injury was performed by the athlete in the exact same manner in which s/he had been instructed to do so by her/his volunteer coach. Moreover, this same technique was precisely how the coach had been advised to teach and coach it when completing the appropriate level of coaching qualification award organised and delivered by the NGB. Although inadequate, this technique had been approved by the NGB for over 20 years. However, the technique exposes athletes to unreasonable and unnecessary risk, represents an instance of negligent entrenched practice and on closer analysis can in no way be regarded as logically justifiable. The injured athlete could, no doubt, bring a claim against the coach for a breach of duty of care due to poor and inadequate

---

48 Anderson (n 45) 249; K Lines, 'Thinking Outside the Box(-ing Ring): The Implications for Sports Governing Bodies Following Watson' (2007) 4 *International Sports Law Review* 67, 73.
49 E.g., *Vowles* (n 20); *Bartlett v English Cricket Board Association of Cricket Officials*, County Court (Birmingham), 27 August 2015. Also see *Scout Association* (n 8).
50 E.g., *Shone* (n 26). Also see *Cox* (n 36) where a Council was found vicariously liable for the negligence of a rugby development officer. Both of these cases are discussed in detail in Chapter 5.
51 E.g., *Morrell* (n 31). *Morrell* is discussed in Chapter 2. More generally, see: *Fowles* (n 29) and *Petrou* (n 31). *Fowles* and *Petrou* are examined in detail in Chapter 5.

instruction.[52] Following *Gannon*, the injured athlete may also perhaps consider a claim against the NGB.[53] Depending upon the particular circumstances and, as discussed earlier, this claim may pose issues of vicarious liability (and contributory negligence by the claimant) for the NGB.

On the given facts, it would seem reasonable to expect the NGB to intervene to settle any claim brought against the volunteer coach in circumstances where the coach had been following the coaching methods advocated by the NGB. However, let us assume that this is not the NGB's preferred course of action. The claim in negligence against the coach would succeed and so damages would be awarded against the defendant coach and to the claimant athlete. It follows that since the NGB provided 'specialist' knowledge to the coach on the understanding that this information would be relied upon, it would appear that the coach may have a cause of action against the NGB for the provision of negligent coach education and training which resulted in loss. For instance, this claim would relate to economic and reputational harm suffered by the coach due to the negligence of the NGB. This would be an arguable case and involve asking the court to incrementally extend the law of negligence to create a new duty situation. Nonetheless, following the precedent set by *Watson*, it would appear that such a potential claim against an NGB might prove persuasive before the UK courts.

The merits to the coach's claim in this fictional scenario would include the degree of control exercised by the NGB over the sport and, in particular, with regard to the provision and award of coaching qualifications; the fact that NGBs profess to possess specialist knowledge or competence; the proximity between the NGB and the coach; the fact that there is a known and determinate class of qualified and accredited coaches; the reasonable foreseeability of injury to those under the coach's charge due to the deficient technique being endorsed and followed; and the fact that NGBs are private law bodies[54] and, therefore, take on a more limited public interest role than statutory regulators.[55] In short, it would appear fair, just and reasonable[56] for the defendant coach in this posited scenario to respond to a claim against them in negligence by arguing that they relied on the NGB to provide coach education and training with reasonable care and skill. Whilst this submission would need to be tested before the courts, combined with the established authorities discussed earlier, it is certainly the case that NGBs should be on notice regarding the necessary and reasonable measures the emerging relationship between the law and sports coaching demands of them when adequately

---

52 E.g., *Fowles* (n 29); *Van Oppen v Clerk to the Bedford Charity Trustees* [1989] 3 All ER 389 (CA).
53 For instance, in this scenario, the NGB created the risk by means of the inadequate training of coaches and could be seen to support the activity through the licensing of its coaches. See generally, Lines (n 48) 71.
54 M Beloff et al., *Sports Law* (2nd edn, Oxford, Hart 2012) 30–31; Anderson (n 45) 28–29.
55 For further detailed consideration of these issues, see J George, '*Watson v British Boxing Board of Control*: Negligent Rule-Making in the Court of Appeal' (2002) 65 *MLR* 106; Lines (n 48).
56 *Caparo Industries Plc v Dickman* [1990] 2 AC 605.

Conclusion 217

safeguarding coaches from negligence liability. Given that techniques in sport can change remarkably over relatively short periods of time,[57] the duty of NGBs in this context seems to encompass a requirement to continuously re-evaluate the dissemination of recognised and approved coaching methods, in light of current knowledge and events, in a proactive manner.[58]

On a more general point, and in recognising that traditionally the technical and bioscientific aspects of coaching may have been held in higher regard by some coaches and coach educators, a particular challenge facing NGBs in this area would appear to be in implementing manageable educative provision and disseminating suitable resources that are engaging and relevant. Risk assessment proformas, mentoring schemes and meaningful/applied codes of ethics and conduct may afford valuable platforms and opportunities to consider a coach's duty of care. However, the most robust, objective and authentic illustrations of reasonable and/or unreasonable coaching practice are provided by the case law. As revealed in the introduction to this book, judges can to a large extent be regarded as the hypothetical reasonable person's/coach's spokesperson, with the judgments of courts referring to instructive factual scenarios from which judicial pronouncements of reasonableness have been drawn. Since this body of case law provides the most authoritative reference point with regard to defining a coach's duty of care, it provides a primary source of insightful information and guidance that ought to be more fully maximised and mobilised in an accessible fashion. As such, it is hoped that this book's analysis of sports negligence jurisprudence in general, and coach negligence in particular, might be utilised to provide and/or devise realistic and informative case studies (e.g., as in Chapter 6) for coaches to engage with. By enabling the scope and practical content of a coach's duty of care to be more fully and precisely defined, identifying, discussing and critically reflecting on scenarios informed by rich and detailed contemporary case law will empower coaches to more confidently discharge their duty of care in the particular sporting circumstances in which they coach.

Final remarks

Whilst the focus of this book has been on the duty of care owed by coaches towards athletes, in order to ensure that athletes are not exposed to unacceptable and unnecessary levels of risk in structured coaching environments, it would be remiss of the author not to warn against potential unintended consequences should coaches be faced with unrealistic expectations. For instance, should an extralegal duty of care in sport narrative be left unchecked and escape robust and searching scrutiny, this may inadvertently extend the duties of coaches beyond reasonable limits. This is

---

57 G Nygaard and T Boone, *Coaches' Guide to Sport Law* (Champaign, Human Kinetics 1985) 24.
58 Lines (n 48) 73. Although Lines is making reference to the rule-making function of NGBs, it is contended that this argument is equally applicable to the recognition and approval of coaching methods which are modelled and disseminated as part of formal NGB coach education training courses.

at a time when there is a burgeoning body of case law in which claims have been brought against coaches for a breach of duty of care, when it is now well established that sports coaching is exposed to negligence's slippery slope and, moreover, when coaches appear concerned about the possible exposure to negligence liability.[59] Indeed, it is recognised that anxieties regarding perceived professional malpractice may be displacing considerations of coaching pedagogy.[60] These factors highlight some of the possible tensions created by potentially placing too high a burden, in terms of discharging their functions with reasonable care and specialist skill, on sports coaches. As mentioned previously, the legal duties and obligations demanded of coaches are undoubtedly an evolving core complexity of modern sports coaching. As these responsibilities inevitably become more extended and pronounced, the standard of care required of coaches remains destined to rise. Provided such an extension in the nature of a coach's duty of care is done in a deliberate, informed and precise fashion, coaches should not be unduly compromised or unwittingly exposed to liability in negligence. However, at present, the assumption appears to be that coaches are responsible for the reasonable safeguarding of athletes from personal injury but, problematically, it remains questionable whether the same level of due care is applied to the adequate safeguarding of coaches from the prospect of breaching the duty of care incumbent upon them. This book's analysis of the duty of care of coaches should equip practising coaches, all bodies involved in the training and development of coaches and students and teachers in related fields with the necessary awareness, knowledge and understanding to accurately and rigorously define a coach's duty of care, thereby helping to ensure that it remains within reasonable limits and is always successfully discharged.

---

59 S Greenfield, 'Law's Impact on Youth Sport: Should Coaches Be "Concerned About Litigation"?' (2013) 2(2) *Sports Coaching Review* 114, 121.
60 D Garratt et al., '"Safeguarding" Sports Coaching: Foucault, Geneology and Critique' (2012) 18(5) *Sport, Education and Society* 615, 626.

REFERENCES

Adams v Rhymney Valley District Council [2001] PNLR 4 (CA)
Affuto-Nartoy v Clarke (1984) Times, 9 February
Agar v Hyde [2001] HCA 41
Ahmed v MacLean [2016] EWHC 2798
R Ahmed, 'The Influence of Reasonableness on the Element of Conduct in Delictual or Tort Liability – Comparative Conclusions' (2019) *Potchefstroom Elec. L.J.* DOI: 10.17159/1727–3781/2019/v22i0a6122
K Alexander, A Stafford and R Lewis, *The Experiences of Children Participating in Organised Sport in the UK* (Edinburgh, University of Edinburgh/NSPCC Child Protection Research Centre 2011)
Allport v Wilbraham [2004] EWCA Civ 1668
Anderson v Lyotier [2008] EWHC 2790
J Anderson, 'Personal Injury Liability in Sport: Emerging Trends' (2008) 16 *Tort Law Review* 95–119
J Anderson, *Modern Sports Law: A Textbook* (Oxford, Hart 2010)
J Anderson and N Partington, 'Duty of Care in Sport: Time for a Sports Ombudsman?' (2018) 1 *International Sports Law Review* 3–10
H Appenzeller, *Ethical Behavior in Sport* (Durham, Carolina Academic Press 2011)
G Applebey, '"The Butcher's Cart and the Postman's Bicycle": Risk and Employers' Liability' in G Woodman and D Klippel (eds), *Risk and the Law* (Abingdon, Routledge-Cavendish 2009) 172–183
HAP Archbold, AT Rankin, M Webb, R Nicholas, NWA Eames, RK Wilson, LA Henderson, GJ Heyes and CM Bleakley, 'RISUS study: Rugby Injury Surveillance in Ulster Schools' *Br J Sports Med* 600–606 Published Online 23 December 2015. DOI: 10.1136/bjsports-2015–095491
K Armour, 'The Learning Coach . . . the Learning Approach: Professional Development for Sports Coach Professionals' in J Lyle and C Cushion (eds), *Sports Coaching: Professionalisation and Practice* (Edinburgh, Elsevier 2010) 153–164
Atkin Lord, 'Law as an Educational Subject' (1932) *J Soc'y Pub Tchrs L* 27–31
Austin v Miami University, (2013) – Ohio – 5925

D Ball and L Ball-King, *Public Safety and Risk Assessment: Improving Decision Making* (London, Earthscan from Routledge 2011)
R Banakar and M Travers, *Theory and Method in Socio-Legal Research* (Oxford, Hart 2005)
Barclays Bank v Various Claimants [2020] UKSC 13
J Barnes, *Sports and the Law in Canada* (3rd edn, Toronto, Butterworths 1996)
Barnett v Chelsea and Kensington Hospital Management Committee [1969] 1 QB 428
J Barr Ames, 'Law and Morals' (1908) 22 *Harvard Law Review* 97–113
G Barrell, *Teachers and the Law* (5th edn, London, Methuen 1978)
Bartlett v English Cricket Board Association of Cricket Officials, County Court (Birmingham, 27 August 2015)
M Beloff, T Kerr, M Demetriou and R Beloff, *Sports Law* (2nd edn, Oxford, Hart 2012)
Blair-Ford v CRS Adventures Ltd [2012] EWHC 2360
Blake v Galloway [2004] EWCA Civ 814
G Bloom, N Durand-Bush, R Schinke, and JH Salmela, 'The Importance of Mentoring in the Development of Coaches and Athletes' (1998) 33 *International Journal of Sports Psychology* 410–430
Blyth v Birmingham Waterworks (1856) 11 Ex 781
Bolam v Friern Hospital Management Committee [1957] 1 WLR 582
Bolitho v City of Hackney Health Authority [1998] AC 232
Bolton v Stone [1951] AC 850
Brady v Sunderland Association Football Club Limited (QBD, 2 April 1998)
Brady v Sunderland Association Football Club Ltd (CA, 17 November 1998)
J Braithwaite, 'Negotiation Versus Litigation: Industry Regulation in Great Britain and the United States' (1987) *American Bar Foundation Research J* 559–574
M Brazier and J Miola, 'Bye-Bye Bolam: A Medical Litigation Revolution?' (2000) 8(1) *Med Law Rev* 85–114
SP Broglio, R Vagnozzi, M Sabin, S Signoretti, B Tavazzi and G Lazzarino, 'Concussion Occurrence and Knowledge in Italian Football (Soccer)' (2010) 9 *Journal of Sports Science and Medicine* 418–430
Browning v Odyssey Trust Co Ltd [2014] NIQB 39
Q Bu, 'The Good Samaritan in the Chinese Society: Morality vis-à-vis Law' (2017) 38 *Liverpool L Rev* 135–157
R Buckley, *The Law of Negligence* (4th edn, London, Butterworths 2005)
Caldwell v Maguire [2001] EWCA Civ 1054
R Caddell, 'The Referee's Liability for Catastrophic Sports Injuries – A UK Perspective' (2005) 15 *Marq. Sports L. Rev.* 415–424
P Cane, *Responsibility in Law and Morality* (Oxford, Hart Publishing 2002)
P Cane, 'Morality, Law and Conflicting Reasons for Action' (2012) 71(1) *Cambridge Law Journal* 59–85
Canterbury Banks Town Rugby League Football Club Ltd. v Rogers [1993] Aust. Torts Reports 81–246
Caparo Industries Plc v Dickman [1990] 2 AC 605
T Cassidy, 'Exploring Ethics: Reflections of a University Coach Educator' in S Harvey and RL Light (eds), *Ethics in Youth Sport: Policy and Pedagogical Applications* (London, Routledge 2013) 149–160
T Cassidy, R Jones and P Potrac, *Understanding Sports Coaching: The Social, Cultural and Pedagogical Foundations of Coaching Practice* (2nd edn, London, Routledge 2009)
Cassidy v Manchester City Council (CA, 12 July 1995)
Catholic Child Welfare Society v Institute of the Brothers of the Christian Schools [2012] UKSC 56
Cavalier (Pauper) v Pope [1906] AC 428

WT Champion, 'The Evolution of a Standard of Care for Injured College Athletes: A Review of Kleinknecht and Progeny' (1999) 1 *Va. J. Sports & L* 290–307

A Chappell, 'Teaching Safely and Safety in PE' in S Capel and M Whitehead (eds), *Learning to Teach Physical Education in the Secondary School: A Companion to School Experience* (4th edn, London, Routledge 2015) 184–203

H Charlesworth and K Young, 'Why English Female University Athletes Play with Pain' in K Young (ed), *Sporting Bodies, Damaged Selves: Sociological Studies of Sports-Related Injury* (Oxford, Elsevier 2004) 163–180

R Clancy, 'Judo Mats, Climbing Walls, Trampolines and Pole Vaulters' (1995) 3(1) *Sport and the Law Journal* 28

J Coakley and E Pike, *Sports in Society: Issues and Controversies* (2nd edn, London, McGraw-Hill Education 2014)

Condon v Basi (1985) 1 WLR 866 (CA)

Cooper v Hobart [2001] 3 SCR 537

R Corbett, H Findlay, and D Lech, *Legal Issues in Sport: Tools and Techniques for the Sport Manager* (Toronto, Emond Montgomery Publications 2010)

F Cownie and A Bradney, 'Socio-Legal Studies: A Challenge to the Doctrinal Approach' in D Watkins and M Burton (eds), *Research Methods in Law* (London, Routledge 2013)

Cox v Dundee CC [2014] CSOH 3

N Cox and A Schuster, *Sport and the Law* (Dublin, First law 2004)

P Craig and P Beedie (eds), *Sport Sociology* (2nd edn, Exeter, Learning Matters 2010)

Craig v Tullymurry Equestrian Centre [2019] NIQB 94

C Cronin and K Armour, '"Being" in the Coaching World: New Insights on Youth Performance Coaching from an Interpretative Phenomenological Approach' (2017) 22(8) *Sport, Education and Society* 919–931

N Cross and J Lyle, 'Overtraining and the Coaching Process' in N Cross and J Lyle (eds), *The Coaching Process: Principles and Practice for Sport* (Philadelphia, Butterworth-Heinemann 1999) 192–209

C Cushion, 'Coach behaviour' in J Lyle and C Cushion (eds), *Sports Coaching: Professionalisation and Practice* (Edinburgh, Elsevier 2010) 43–62

C Cushion, K Armour and R Jones, 'Coach Education and Continuing Professional Development: Experience and Learning to Coach' (2003) 55 *Quest* 215–230

C Cushion and R Jones, 'Power, Discourse, and Symbolic Violence in Professional Youth Soccer: The Case of Albion Football Club' (2006) 23 *Sociology of Sport Journal* 142–161

C Cushion and J Lyle, 'Conceptual Development in Sports Coaching' in J Lyle and C Cushion (eds), *Sports Coaching: Professionalisation and Practice* (Edinburgh, Elsevier 2010) 1–14

C Cushion and M Partington, 'A Critical Analysis of the Conceptualisation of "coaching philosophy"' (2014) 26(1) *Sport, Education and Society* 851–867

D v East Berkshire Community Health Authority [2005] 2 AC 373

Davenport v Farrow [2010] EWHC 550

P David, 'Sharp Practice: Intensive Training and Child Abuse' in M McNamee (ed), *The Ethics of Sport: A Reader* (Abingdon, Routledge 2010) 426–434

Davis Contractors Ltd v Fareham UDC [1956] AC 696

T Davis, 'Tort Liability of Coaches for Injuries to Professional Athletes: Overcoming Policy and Doctrinal Barriers' (2008) 76 *UMKC L. Rev* 571–596

P De Prez, 'Something "Old" Something "New", Something Borrowed . . . The Continued Evolution of Bolam' (2001) 17 *Professional Negligence* 75–92

S Deakin and Z Adams, *Markesinis and Deakin's Tort Law* (8th edn, Oxford, Oxford University Press 2019)

S Deakin, A Johnston, and B Markesinis, *Markesinis and Deakin's Tort Law* (7th edn, Oxford, Oxford University Press 2013)

M Dickinson, 'Coaches Unite Over Bullying', *The Times* (London, Wednesday 21 November 2018)

Dickson v Northern Lakes Rugby League Sport & Recreation Club Inc & Anor (No 2) [2019] NSWDC 433

MJ Dobberstein, ' "Give Me the Ball Coach": A Scouting Report on the Liability of High Schools and Coaches for Injuries to High School Pitchers' Arms' (2007) 14 *Sports Law Journal* 49–70

Dolby v McWhirter [1979] OJ No. 4154

Donoghue v Stevenson [1932] AC 562

Dorset Yacht Company v Home Office [1970] AC 1004

S Drewe, 'An Examination of the Relationship Between Coaching and Teaching' (2000) 52 *Quest* 79–88

P Duffy, H Hartley, J Bales, M Crespo, F Dick, D Vardhan, L Nordmann and J Curado, 'Sportcoaching as a "Profession": Challenges and Future Directions' (2011) 5(2) *International Journal of Coaching Science* 93–123

Dyck v Manitoba Snowmobile Assn [1982] MJ No. 13

Eckersley v Binnie [1988] 18 Con LR 1 (CA)

J Ehrmann, *InSideOut Coaching: How Sports Can Transform Lives* (New York, Simon & Schuster 2011)

A Epstein, *Sports Law* (Mason, Cengage Learning 2013)

European Commission, *White Paper on Sport* [2007] COM (2007) 391 final

H Evans, 'Negligence and process' (2013) 29(4) *Professional Negligence* 212–222

Evans and Others v Waitemata District Pony Club, East Coast Bays Branch And Others [1972] NZLR 773

Fairchild v Glenhaven Funeral Services [2003] 1 AC 32

Falconer Lord, *Compensation Culture* (Health and Safety Executive Event, 22 March 2005)

E Finch and S Fafinski, *Legal Skills* (7th edn, Oxford, Oxford University Press 2019)

Fink et al. v Greeniaus [1973] OJ No. 2283

G Fletcher, 'The Right and the Reasonable' (1985) 98 *Harv L Rev* 949–982

Fowles v Bedfordshire County Council [1995] PIQR P380 (CA)

Frazer v Johnston [1989] Aust Torts Reports 80–248

Froom v Butcher [1976] QB 286 (CA)

J Fulbrook, *Outdoor Activities, Negligence and the Law* (Abingdon, Ashgate 2005)

C Fuller, 'Implications of Health and Safety Legislation for the Professional Sportsperson' (1995) 29 *Br J Sp Med* 5–9

L Fuller, *The Morality of Law* (Revised edition, London: Yale University Press 1969)

Gannon v Rotherham Metropolitan Borough Council Unreported, Crown Court (Nottingham, 6 February 1991)

J Gardiner, 'Should Coaches Take Care?' (1993) 143 *New Law Journal* 1598

S Gardiner, M James, J O'Leary and R Welch, *Sports Law* (3rd edn, London, Cavendish 2006)

D Garratt, H Piper and B Taylor, ' "Safeguarding" Sports Coaching: Foucault, Geneology and Critique' (2012) 18(5) *Sport, Education and Society* 615–629

GHK, *Study on Volunteering in the European Union* (2010) Report for DG EAC (Directorate-General for Education and Culture)

Glasgow Corporation v Muir [1943] AC 448

G Glendenning, *Education and the Law* (Dublin, Butterworths 1999)

Gold v Haringey Health Authority [1988] QB 481
Goldstein v Levy Gee (A Firm) [2003] EWHC 1574
Goode v Angland [2016] NSWSC 1014
AL Goodhart, "The Sportsman's Charter" (1962) 78 *Law Quarterly Review* 490–494
Goshen v Larin, [1974] NSJ No. 248
J Goudkamp, 'Restating the Common Law? The Social Action, Responsibility and Heroism Act 2015' (2017) 37 *Legal Studies* 577–598
Gravil v Carroll, Redruth Rugby Football Club [2008] EWCA CIV 689
A Gray and A-M Blakeley, 'Child Protection' in A Lewis and J Taylor (eds), *Sport: Law and Practice* (2nd edn, Haywards Heath, Tottel 2008) 779–813
A Gray, A-M Blakeley and J Mulcahy, 'Child Safeguarding' in A Lewis and J Taylor (eds), *Sport: Law and Practice* (3rd edn, Haywards Heath, Bloomsbury Professional 2014)
E Grayson, *Sport and the Law* (3rd edn, Haywards Heath, Tottel 1999)
S Greenfield, 'Law's Impact on Youth Sport: Should Coaches Be "Concerned About Litigation"?' (2013) 2(2) *Sports Coaching Review* 114–123
S Greenfield, K Karstens, G Osborn and JP Rossouw, 'Reconceptualising The Standard Of Care In Sport: The Case Of Youth Rugby In England And South Africa' (2015) 18(6) *Potchefstroom Elec. L.J* 2183–2219
T Grey-Thompson Baroness, *Duty of Care in Sport: Independent Report to Government* (Department for Digital, Culture, Media & Sport, 21 April 2017)
D Griffith-Jones, *Law and the Business of Sport* (Haywards Heath, Tottel 2007)
D Griffith-Jones, 'Civil Liability Arising Out of Participation in Sport' in A Lewis and J Taylor (eds), *Sport: Law and Practice* (2nd edn, Haywards Heath, Tottel 2008) 711–752
D Griffith-Jones and N Randall, 'Civil Liability Arising Out of Participation in Sport' in A Lewis and J Taylor (eds), *Sport: Law and Practice* (3rd edn, Haywards Heath, Tottel 2014) 1610–1653
R Groom, W Taylor and L Nelson, *Volunteering Insight: Report for Sport England* (Manchester Metropolitan University 2014)
Hall v Brooklands Auto-Racing Club [1933] 1 KB 205 (CA)
A Hall and M Mannis, 'In Loco Parentis and the Professional Responsibilities of Teachers' (2001) 7 *Waikato Journal of Education* 117–128
M Hamilton, 'Coaching, Gamesmanship, and Intimidation' in R Simon (ed), *The Ethics of Coaching Sports: Moral, Social, and Legal Issues* (Colorado, Westview Press 2013) 137–149
Hammersley-Gonsalves v Redcar & Cleveland Borough Council [2012] EWCA Civ 1135 (CA)
Hamstra et al v British Columbia Rugby Union [1989] 1 CCLT (2d) 78
A Hardman and C Jones (eds), *The Ethics of Sports Coaching* (Abingdon, Routledge 2011)
A Hardman and C Jones, 'Sports Coaching and Virtue Ethics' in A Hardman and C Jones (eds), *The Ethics of Sports Coaching* (Abingdon, Routledge 2011) 72–84
A Hardman and C Jones, 'Ethics For Coaches' in RL Jones and K Kingston (eds), *An Introduction to Sports Coaching: Connecting Theory to Practice* (2nd edn, Abingdon, Routledge 2013) 113–130
V Harpwood, *Modern Tort Law* (6th edn, London, Cavendish 2005)
N Harris, *The Law Relating to Schools* (2nd edn, Croydon, Tolley 1995)
Harrison v Vincent [1982] RTR 8 (CA)
HLA Hart, 'Positivism and the Separation of Law and Morals' (1959) 71 *Harvard Law Review* 593–629
HLA Hart, *The Concept of Law* (3rd edn, Oxford, Oxford University Press 2013)
H Hartley, *Sport, Physical Recreation and the Law* (Abingdon, Routledge 2009)

J Hartshorne, 'Confusion, Contradiction and Chaos within the House of Lords Post Caparov. Dickman' (2008) 16 Tort Law Review 8–22

S Harvey, C Cushion, E Cope and B Muir, 'A Season Long Investigation into Coaching Behaviours as a Function of Practice State: The Case of Three Collegiate Coaches' (2013) 2(1) Sports Coaching Review 13–32

D Healey, 'Risk Management for Coaches' in S Pyke (ed), Better Coaching: Advanced Coach's Manual (2nd edn, Leeds, Human Kinetics 2001) 39–48

D Healey, Sport and the Law (4th edn, Sydney, UNSW Press 2009)

A Hecht, 'Legal and Ethical Aspects of Sports-Related Concussions: The Merril Hoge story' (2002) 12 Seton Hall J. Sports L 17–64

Hedley Byrne & Co Ltd v Heller & Partner Ltd [1964] AC 465

J Herring, Medical Law and Ethics (5th edn, Oxford, Oxford University Press 2014)

R Heuston, 'Donoghue v Stevenson in Retrospect' (1957) 20(1) Modern Law Review 1–24

R Heywood, 'The Logic of Bolitho' (2006) 22 Professional Negligence 225–235

R Heywood and P Charlish, 'Schoolmaster Tackled Hard Over Rugby Incident' (2007) 15 Tort Law Review 162–171

Hide v The Steeplechase Company (Cheltenham) Ltd [2013] EWCA Civ 545

Honnor v Lewis [2005] EWHC 747

T Honoré, 'The Dependence of Morality on Law' (1993) 13 Oxford J Legal Studies 1–17

T Honoré, 'The Necessary Connection between Law and Morality' (2002) 22(3) Oxford J Legal Studies 489–495

D Howarth, 'Many Duties of Care – Or a Duty of Care? Notes from the Underground' (2006) 26(3) Oxford J Legal Studies 449–472

Humphrey v Aegis Defence Services Ltd [2016] EWCA Civ 11

TR Hurst and JN Knight, 'Coaches' Liability for Athletes' Injuries and Deaths' (2003) 13 Seton Hall J. Sports L 27–51

Hyde v Agar [1998] 45 NSWLR 487

R Jackson, 'The Professions: Power, Privilege and Legal Liability' (2015) 31(3) Professional Negligence 122–139

M James, Sports Law (Basingstoke, Palgrave Macmillan 2010)

M James, Sports Law (2nd edn, Basingstoke, Palgrave Macmillan 2013)

M James, Sports Law (3rd edn, Croydon, Palgrave 2017)

M James and D McArdle, 'Player Violence, or Violent Players? Vicarious Liability for Sportsparticipants' (2004) 12(3) Tort Law Review 131–146

James-Bowen v Commissioner of the Police of the Metropolis [2018] UKSC 40

L Jamieson and T Orr, Sport and Violence: A Critical Examination of Sport (Oxford, Elsevier 2009)

M Jones, 'The Bolam Test and the Responsible Expert' (1999) 7 Tort Law Review 226–250

M Jones and A Dugdale (eds), Clerk and Lindsell on Torts (20th edn, London, Sweet and Maxwell 2010)

R Jones, 'Toward a Sociology of Coaching' in RL Jones & KM Armour (eds), Sociology of Sport: Theory and Practice (London, Pearson 2000)

R Jones, K Armour and P Potrac, Sports Coaching Cultures: From Theory to Practice (London, Routledge 2004)

R Jones, 'Coaching as Caring (The Smiling Gallery): Accessing Hidden Knowledge' (2009) 14(4) Physical Education and Sport Pedagogy 377–390

T Kaye, 'Law and risk: an introduction' in G Woodman and D Klippel (eds), Risk and the Law (Abingdon, Routledge-Cavendish 2009) 3–20

P Kellett, 'Football-as-War, Coach-as-General: Analogy, Metaphor and Management Implications' (2002) 5 Football Studies 60–76

Kennedy v Cordia (Services) LLP [2016] UKSC 6

Kent v Griffiths [2001] QB 36 (CA)

J Kessler, 'Dollar Signs on the Muscle . . . And the Ligament, Tendon, and Ulnar Nerve: Institutional Liability Arising from Injuries to Student-Athletes' (2001) 3 *Va. J Sports & L* 80–114

R Kidner, 'The Variable Standard of Care, Contributory Negligence and Volenti' (1991) 11(1) *Legal Studies* 1–23

J Kircher, 'Golf and Torts: An Interesting Twosome' (2001) 12 *Marq. Sports L. Rev* 347–363

D Kirk, 'Towards a Socio-Pedagogy of Sports Coaching' in J Lyle and C Cushion (eds), *Sports Coaching: Professionalisation and Practice* (Edinburgh, Elsevier 2010) 165–176

RS Kretchmar, 'Soft Metaphysics: A Precursor to Good Sports Ethics' in M McNamee and S Parry (eds), *Ethics & Sport* (London, E & FN Spon 1998) 19–34

J Labuschagne and J Skea, 'The Liability of a Coach for a Sport Participant's Injury' (1999) 10 *Stellenbosch Law Review* 158–183

Law Reform Commission of Ireland, *Civil Liability of Good Samaritans and Volunteers* (LRC 93 2009)

Letang v Cooper [1965] 1 QB 232 (CA)

Lewis v Buckpool Golf Club [1993] SCT 43

K Lines, 'Thinking Outside the Box(-ing ring): The Implications for Sports Governing Bodies Following Watson' (2007) 4 *International Sports Law Review* 67–75

W Lucy, *Philosophy of Private Law* (Oxford, Oxford University Press 2007)

M Lunney, D Nolan and K Oliphant, *Tort Law: Text and Materials* (6th ed, Oxford, Oxford University Press 2017)

M Lunney and K Oliphant, *Tort Law: Test and Materials* (5th edn, Oxford, Oxford University Press 2013)

J Lyle, 'Coaching Philosophy and Coaching Behaviour' in N Cross and J Lyle (eds), *The Coaching Process: Principles and Practice for Sport* (Philadelphia, Butterworth-Heinemann 1999) 24–46

J Lyle, *Sports Coaching Concepts: A Framework for Coaches' Behaviour* (London, Routledge 2002)

J Lyle, and C Cushion, 'Narrowing the Field: Some Key Questions About Sports Coaching' in J Lyle and C Cushion (eds), *Sports Coaching: Professionalisation and Practice* (Edinburgh, Elsevier 2010), 361–382

A Lynn and J Lyle, 'Coaching Workforce Development' in J Lyle and C Cushion (eds), *Sports Coaching: Professionalisation and Practice* (Edinburgh, Elsevier 2010) 193–207

MacFarlane v Tayside Health Board [2000] 2 AC 59

MacIntyre v Ministry of Defence [2011] EWHC 1690

U Magnus, 'Tort law in general' in JM Smits (ed), *Elgar Encyclopedia of Comparative Law* (Cheltenham, Edward Elgar 2006) 719–729

C Mallett, 'Becoming a High Performing Coach: Pathways and Communities' in J Lyle and C Cushion (eds), *Sports Coaching: Professionalisation and Practice* (Edinburgh, Elsevier 2010) 119–134

D Mangan, 'The Curiosity of Professional Status' (2014) 30(2) *Professional Negligence* 74–89

B Markesinis, 'The not so Dissimilar Tort and Delict' (1977) 93 *Law Quarterly Review* 78–123

R Martens, *Successful Coaching* (3rd edn, Champaign, Human Kinetics 2004)

I Martínková and J Parry, 'Coaching and the Ethics of Performance Enhancement' in A Hardman and C Jones (eds), *The Ethics of Sports Coaching* (Abingdon, Routledge 2011) 165–184

Mattheson v The Governors of Dalhusey University and College (1983) 57 NSR (2nd) 56; 25CCLT 9l (SC)

Maylin v Dacorum Sports Trust Trading as XC Sportspace [2017] EWHC 378

D McArdle, 'The Views from the Hills: Fatal Accidents, Child Safety and Licensing Adventure Activities' (2011) 31(3) *Legal Studies* 372–391

D McArdle and M James, 'Are You Experienced? "Playing Cultures", Sporting Rules and Personal Injury Litigation After Caldwell v Maguire' (2005) 13(3) *Tort Law Review* 193–211

McCarty v Pheasant Run Inc 826 F2d 1554 (1987)

AS McCaskey and KW Biedzynski, 'A Guide to the Legal Liability of Coaches for a Sports Participant's Injuries' (1996) 6 *Seton Hall J. Sport L* 7–125

P McCrory, WH Meeuwisse, M Aubry, B Cantu, J Dvořák, RJ Echemendia, L Engebretsen, K Johnston, JS Kutcher, M Raftery, A Sills, BW Benson, GA Davis, RG Ellenbogen, K Guskiewicz, SA Herring, GL Iverson, BD Jordan, J Kissick, M McCrea, AS McIntosh, D Maddocks, M Makdissi, L Purcell, M Putukian, K Schneider, CH Tator and M Turner, 'Consensus Statement on Concussion in Sport: The 4th International Conference on Concussion in Sport Held in Zurich, November 2012' (2013) 47 *Br J Sports Med* 250–258

McErlean v MacAuley [2014] NIQB 1

McMahon v Dear [2014] CSOH 100

M McNamee (ed), *The Ethics of Sport: A Reader* (Abingdon, Routledge 2010)

M McNamee, 'Celebrating Trust: Virtues and Rules in the Ethical Conduct of Sports Coaches' in M McNamee and S Parry (eds), *Ethics & Sport* (London, E & FN Spon 1998) 148–168

M McNamee and S Parry (eds), *Ethics & Sport* (London, E & FN Spon 1998)

MJ McNamee, B Partridge and L Anderson, 'Concussion in Sport: Conceptual and Ethical issues' (2015) 4 *Kinesiology Review* 190–202

D McRae, 'Alex Corbisiero: "Even Now People Will Frown if You Need a Rest"' (London, *The Guardian*, 5 May 2016)

T Meakin, 'The Evolving Legal Issues on Rugby Neuro-Trauma?' (2013) 21(3) *Sport and the Law Journal* 34–42

Michael v Chief Constable of South Wales Police [2015] UKSC 2

R Michaels, 'American law (United States)' in J Smits (ed), *Elgar Encyclopaedia of Comparative Law* (Cheltenham, Edward Elgar 2006)

A Miles and R Tong, 'Sports Medicine For Coaches' in RL Jones and K Kingston (eds), *An Introduction to Sports Coaching: Connecting Theory to Practice* (2nd edn, Abingdon, Routledge 2013) 177–196

M Mitten, 'The Coach and the Safety of Athletes: Ethical and Legal Issues' in R Simon (ed), *The Ethics of Coaching Sports: Moral, Social, and Legal Issues* (Colorado, Westview Press 2013) 215–233

Mocharski v Young Men's Christian Assn. of Greater Vancouver [2004] BCJ No. 1898

J Montrose, 'Is Negligence an Ethical or a Sociological Concept?' (1958) 21 *Modern Law Review* 259–264

M Moran, *Rethinking the Reasonable Person: An Egalitarian Reconstruction of the Objective Standard* (Oxford, Oxford University Press 2003)

P Morgan, 'Vicarious Liability and the Beautiful Game – Liability for Professional and Amateur Footballers?' (2018) 38(2) *Legal Studies* 242–262

Morrell v Owen (1993) Times, 14 December 1993

A Morris, '"Common Sense Common Safety": The Compensation Culture Perspective' (2011) 27(2) *Professional Negligence* 82–96

A Morris, 'Spiralling or Stabilising? The Compensation Culture and Our Propensity to Claim Damages for Personal Injury' (2007) 70 *Modern Law Review* 349–378

A Morris, 'Hayley Jane Liddle (Personal Representative of Sean Lesley Phillips Deceased) v Bristol CC (High Court of Justice Queen's Bench Division; HH Judge Gargan, 19 October 2018; [2018] EWHC 3673 (QB)), (2019) 2 *JPI Law* C63-C70

Morrow v Dungannon and South Tyrone Borough Council [2012] NIQB 50

Mountford v Newlands School [2007] EWCA Civ 21

R Mulheron, 'Trumping Bolam: A Critical Legal Analysis of Bolitho's Gloss' (2010) 69 *Cambridge Law Journal* 609–638

R Mulheron, *Principles of Tort Law* (Cambridge, Cambridge University Press 2016)

R Mullender, 'The Reasonable Person, The Pursuit of Justice, and Negligence Law' (2005) 68(4) *Modern Law Review* 681–695

Mullin v Richards [1998] 1 WLR 1304 (CA)

Murray v Harringay Arena LD [1951] 2 KB 529 (CA)

Murray v McCullough [2016] NIQB 52

C Nash, 'Volunteering in Sports Coaching – A Tayside Study' in M Graham and M Foley (eds), *Volunteering in Leisure: Marginal or Inclusive?* (Eastbourne, LSA 2001)

C Nash, 'How Coaches Learn and Develop' in C Nash (ed), *Practical Sports Coaching* (Abingdon, Routledge 2015) 177–189

Nettleship v Weston [1971] 2 QB 691 (CA)

J Neyers, 'Distilling Duty: The Supreme Court of Canada Amends Anns' (2002) 118 *Law Quarterly Review* 221–225

G Nichols and P Taylor, 'The Balance of Benefit and Burden? The Impact of Child Protection Legislation on Volunteers in Scottish Sports Clubs' (2010) 10(1) *European Sport Management Quarterly* 31–47

W Norris, 'Perry v Harris – Case Comment Following the Ruling in the Court of Appeal' (2008) 4 *JPI Law* 258–259

W Norris, 'The Duty of Care to Prevent Personal Injury' (2009) 2 *JPI Law* 114–134

W Norris, 'The Duty of Care Owed by Instructors in a Sporting Context' (2010) 4 *JPI Law* 183–191

W Norris, 'A Duty of Care in Sport: What It Actually Means' (2017) 3 *JPI Law* 154–167

G Nygaard and T Boone, *Coaches' Guide to Sport Law* (Champaign, Human Kinetics 1985)

J Oliver and R Lloyd, 'Physical Training as a Potential Form of Abuse' in M Long and M Hartill (eds), *Safeguarding, Child Protection and Abuse in Sport: International Perspectives in Research, Policy and Practice* (Abingdon, Routledge 2015) 163–171

H Opie, 'Referee Liability in Sport: Negligent Rule Enforcement and Smoldon v Whitworth' (1997) 5 *Torts Law Journal* 1–10

Orchard v Lee [2009] EWCA Civ 295

Overseas Tankship (UK) Ltd v Morts Docks & Engineering Co Ltd (Wagon Mound No 1) [1961] AC 388

Overseas Tankship (UK) Ltd v The Miller Steamship CoLtd (Wagon Mound No 2) [1967] 1 AC617

Paris v Stepney Borough Council [1951] AC 367

M Partington and C Cushion, 'An Investigation of the Practice Activities and Coaching Behaviors of Professional Top-Level Youth Soccer Coaches' (2013) 23 *Scand J Med Sci Sports* 374–382

N Partington, 'Legal Liability of Coaches: A UK Perspective' (2014) 14(3–4) *International Sports Law Journal* 232–241

N Partington, 'Professional Liability of Amateurs: The Context of Sports Coaching' (2015) 4 *JPI Law* 232–242

N Partington, 'Beyond the "Tomlinson Trap": Analysing the Effectiveness of Section 1 of the Compensation Act 2006' (2016) 37(1) *Liverpool L Rev* 33–56

N Partington, ' "It's Just Not Cricket". Or is it?' (2016) 32(1) *Professional Negligence* 75–79
N Partington, 'Murray v McCullough (as Nominee on Behalf of the Trustees and on Behalf of the Board of Governors of Rainey Endowed School)' (2016) 67(2) *NILQ* 251–255
N Partington, 'Sports Coaching and the Law of Negligence: Implications for Coaching Practice' (2017) 6(1) *Sports Coaching Review* 36–56
N Partington, 'Volunteering and EU Sports Law and Policy' in J Anderson, R Parrish and B Garcia (eds), *Handbook on EU Sports Law* (Cheltenham, Edward Elgar 2018) 98–119
R Percy and C Walton (eds), *Charlesworth & Percy on Negligence* (9th edn, London, Sweet & Maxwell 1997)
Perry v Harris [2008] EWCA Civ 907
Petrou v Bertoncello [2012] EWHC 2286
T Petts, 'Visualising a Parent with a Very Large Family: The Liability' (2017) 1 *JPI Law* 13–18
S Peyer and R Heywood, 'Walking on Thin Ice: The Perception of Tortious Liability Rules and the Effect on Altruistic Behaviour' (2019) *Legal Studies* 266–283. DOI: 10.1017/lst.2018.39
Phee v Gordon [2013] CSIH 18
Phelps v Hillingdon London Borough Council [2000] LGR 651
Pinchbeck v Craggy Island Ltd [2012] EWHC 2745
E Pike and A Scott, 'Safeguarding, Injuries and Athlete Choice' in M Long and M Hartill (eds), *Safeguarding, Child Protection and Abuse in Sport: International Perspectives in Research, Policy and Practice* (London, Routledge 2015) 172–180
Pitcher v Huddersfield Town Football Club (QBD, 17 July 2001)
Plumb (Guardian ad litem of) v Cowichan School District No. 65, [1991] BCJ No. 3709
Pook v Rossall School [2018] EWHC 522
Poppleton v Trustees of the Portsmouth Youth Activities Committee [2008] EWCA Civ 646
Porter v Barking and Dagenham LBC (1990) Times, 9 April
Potozny v Burnaby (City), [2001] BCJ No. 1224
J Powell and R Stewart, *Jackson and Powell on Professional Liability* (7th edn, London, Sweet and Maxwell 2012)
R v Barnes [2004] EWCA Crim 3246
R v Cey [1989] 48 CCC (3d) 480
R M Turton & Co (in liq) v Kerslake & Partners [2000] 3 NZLR 406
J Raz, 'Legal Positivism and the Sources of Law' in J Raz (ed), *The Authority of Law. Essays on Law and Morality* (Oxford, Clarendon Press 1979) 37–52
Read v Lyons [1947] AC 156
Regina (Daly) v Secretary of State for the Home Department [2001] 2 AC 532
Risk v Rose Bruford College [2013] EWHC 3869
D Roan, 'Was 2017 the Year British Sport Lost Its Way?' *BBC News* (29 December 2017)
D Roan, 'Player Welfare: How Big a Problem Is Football Facing? And What Is Being Done?' *BBC News* (10 August 2018)
S Roberts, M Baker, M Reeves, G Jones and C Cronin, 'Lifting the Veil of Depression and Alcoholism in Sport Coaching: How Do We Care for Carers?' (2018) *Qualitative Research in Sport, Exercise and Health* 510–526 DOI: 10.1080/2159676X.2018.1556182
Robinson v Chief Constable of West Yorkshire Police [2018] UKSC 4
W Rogers, *Winfield and Jolowicz: Tort* (18th edn, London, Sweet & Maxwell 2010)
Rootes v Shelton [1968] ALR 33
E Ryall and S Olivier, 'Ethical Issues in Coaching Dangerous Sports' in A Hardman and C Jones (eds), *The Ethics of Coaching Sport* (Abingdon, Routledge 2011) 185–198

J Ryan, *Little Girls in Pretty Boxes: The Making and Breaking of Elite Gymnasts and Figure Skaters* (New York, Warner Books Edition 1995)

Scout Association v Barnes [2010] EWCA Civ 1476

S Shavell, 'Law Versus Morality as Regulators of Conduct' (2002) 4(2) *American Law and Economics Review* 227–257

Shone v British Bobsleigh Limited [2018] 5 WLUK 226

R Simon, 'Coaching, Compliance, and the Law' in R Simon (ed), *The Ethics of Coaching Sports: Moral, Social, and Legal Issues* (Colorado, Westview Press 2013) 187–192

Smith New Court Securities Ltd v Scrimgeour Vickers (Asset Management) Ltd [1997] AC 254

Smoldon v Whitworth [1997] ELR 115, 46

Smoldon v Whitworth [1997] PIQR P133 (CA)

H Spamann, 'Contemporary Legal Transplants: Legal Families and the Diffusion of (Corporate) Law' (2009) 2009 *BYU L Rev* 1813–1878

Spartan Steel & Alloys Ltd v Martin & Co (Contractors) Ltd [1973] QB 27 (CA)

J Spengler, P Anderson, D Connaughton and T Baker, *Introduction to Sport Law* (Champaign, Human Kinetics 2009)

J Spengler, D Connaughton and A Pittman, *Risk Management in Sport and Recreation* (Champaign, Human Kinetics 2006)

Sports Coach UK, *Coach Tracking Study: A Four-Year Study of Coaching in the UK* (Leeds, Coachwise 2012)

J Steele, *Tort Law: Text, Cases and Materials* (2nd edn, Oxford, Oxford University Press 2010)

R Stevens, *Torts and Rights* (Oxford, Oxford University Press 2007)

A Stirling, G Kerr and L Cruz, 'An Evaluation of Canada's National Coaching Certification Program's Make Ethical Decisions Coach Education Module (2012) 6(2) *International Journal of Coaching Science* 45–60

MH Stober, *Interdisciplinary Conversations: Challenging Habits of Thought* (Stanford, Stanford University Press 2011)

Stovin v Wise [1996] AC 923

Sutherland Shire Council v Heyman [1985] 60 ALR 1

Sutton v Syston RFC Limited [2011] EWCA Civ 1182

B Taylor and D Garratt, 'The Professionalisation of Sports Coaching: Relations of Power, Resistance and Compliance' (2010) 15(1) *Sport, Education and Society* 121–139

B Taylor and D Garratt, 'The Professionalization of Sports Coaching: Definitions, Challenges and Critique' in J Lyle & C Cushion (eds), *Sports Coaching: Professionalisation and Practice* (Edinburgh, Elsevier 2010) 99–118

H Telfer, 'Coaching Practice and Practice Ethics' in J Lyle & C Cushion (eds), *Sports Coaching: Professionalisation and Practice* (Edinburgh, Elsevier 2010) 208–220

N Thompson, *Theory and Practice in Human Services* (Oxford, Oxford University Press 2003)

Thornton v School Dist. No. 57 (Prince George) Bd. Of School Trustees [1976] 5 WWR 240, 73 DLR (3d) 35 (BCCA)

D Thorpe, A Buti, C Davies, S Fridman and P Johnson, *Sports Law* (Oxford, Oxford University Press 2009)

Tomlinson v Congleton Borough Council [2004] 1 AC 46

P Tracey, 'Sports Injury – Should the Referee Be Blamed?' (2000) 1 *JPI Law* 10–12

P Trudel, W Gilbert and P Werthner, 'Coach Education and Effectiveness' in J Lyle and C Cushion (eds), *Sports Coaching: Professionalisation and Practice* (Edinburgh, Elsevier 2010) 135–152

Uren v Corporate Leisure (UK) Limited [2010] EWHC 46

Uren v Corporate Leisure (UK) Limited [2011] EWCA Civ 66

Uren v Corporate Leisure (UK) Limited [2013] EWHC 353

Unruh (Guardian ad litem of) v Webber (BCCA), [1994] BCJ No. 467

US v Carroll Towing Co 159 F2d 169 (1947)
Van Oppen v Clerk to the Bedford Charity Trustees [1989] 1 All ER 273
Van Oppen v Clerk to the Bedford Charity Trustees [1989] 3 All ER 389 (CA)
Vaughan v Menlove (1837) 3 Bing NC 468
R Ver Steeg, 'Negligence in the Air: Safety, Legal Liability, and the Pole Vault' (2003) 4 *Tex. Rev. Ent. & Sports L* 109–180
D Vick, 'Interdisciplinarity and the Discipline of Law' in D Cowan, L Mulcahy and S Wheeler (eds), *Law And Society*, Vol 1 (London, Routledge 2014)
Villella v North Bedfordshire BC (QBD, 25 October 1983)
P Vines, 'Doping as Tort: Liability of Sport Supervisors and the Problem of Consent' in U Haas and D Healey (eds), *Doping in Sport and the Law* (Oxford, Hart 2016) 189–203
Vowles v Evans [2002] EWHC 2612
Vowles v Evans [2003] EWCA Civ 318
Wai Yip Hin v Wong Po Kit (No 1) [2009] 3 HKC 362
Watson v British Boxing Board of Control [2001] QB 1134 (CA)
CT Watson and R Hyde (eds), *Charles Worth & Percy on Negligence, First Supplement to the Thirteenth Edition* (London, Sweet and Maxwell 2015)
Watt v Hertfordshire County Council [1954] 1 WLR 835 (CA)
Wattleworth v Goodwood Road Racing Co Ltd [2004] EWHC 140
J Weir, *An Introduction to Tort Law* (2nd edn, Oxford, Oxford University Press 2006)
Wells v Full Moon Events Ltd [2020] EWHC 1265
S Wheeler and P Thomas, 'Socio-Legal Studies' in D Hayton (ed), *Law's Future(s)* (Oxford, Hart 2002)
Whippey v Jones [2009] EWCA Civ 452
P Whitlam, *Case Law in Physical Education and School Sport* (Worcester, BAALPE 2005)
P Whitlam, *Safe Practice in Physical Education and Sport* (8th edn, Leeds, Coachwise 2012)
Whittet v Virgin Active Ltd [2019] 2 WLUK 779
Wilkin-Shaw v Fuller [2012] EWHC 1777
Wilks v Cheltenham Homeguard Motor Cycle and Light Car Club [1971] 1 WLR 668 (CA)
Williams v Eady (1893) 10 TLR 41
K Williams, 'Doctors as Good Samaritans: Some Empirical Evidence Concerning Emergency Medical Treatment in Britain' (2003) 30 *Journal of Law & Society* 258–282
AM Williams and NJ Hodges, 'Practice, Instruction and Skill Acquisition in Soccer: Challenging Tradition' (2005) 23(6) *Journal of Sports Sciences* 637–650
Wilsher v Essex Area Health Authority [1987] QB 730 (CA)
C Witting, 'The Three-Stage Test Abandoned in Australia – Or Not?' (2002) 118 *Law Quarterly Review* 214–221
C Witting, 'Tort Law, Policy and the High Court of Australia' (2007) 31 *Melb U L Rev* 569–590
G Wong, *Essentials of Sports Law* (4th edn, Oxford, Praeger 2010)
Woodbridge School v Chittock [2002] EWCA Civ 915
Woodland v Maxwell [2015] EWHC 820
Woodland v Swimming Teachers Association [2013] UKSC 66
Woodroffe-Hedley v Cuthbertson (QBD, 20 June 1997)
Woods v Multi-Sport Holdings PTY Ltd [2002] HCA 9
Wooldridge v Sumner [1963] 2 QB 43 (CA)
Wright v Cheshire County Council [1952] 2 ALL ER 789 (CA)
G Yaffe, 'Reasonableness in the Law and Second-Personal Address' (2007) 40 *Loy L A L Rev* 939–976

K Young, 'The Role of the Courts in Sports Injury' in K Young (ed), *Sporting Bodies, Damaged Selves: Sociological Studies of Sports-Related Injury* (Oxford, Elsevier 2004) 333–353

K Young, 'From Violence in Sport to Sports-Related Violence' in B Houlihan (ed), *Sport and Society: A Student Introduction* (2nd edn, London, Sage Publications 2008) 174–204

K Young, *Sport, Violence and Society* (London, Routledge 2012)

K Young and P White, 'Threats to Sport Careers: Elite Athletes Talk About Injury and Pain' in J Coakley and P Donnelly (eds), *Inside Sports* (London, Routledge 1999) 203–213

Young Lord, *Common Sense Common Safety* (October 2010)

Young v Kent County Council [2005] EWHC 1342

Yuen Kun Yeu v Attorney-General of Hong Kong [1988] AC 175

B Zipursky, 'Reasonableness In and Out of Negligence Law' (2015) 163 *U. of Pa. L. Rev* 2131–2170

INDEX

ability levels 58, 83, 101, 161
Adams, Z. 8, 47, 52
agony of the moment 90, 92
Ahmed, R. 6–7
Alexander, K. 187, 192
amateur coaches 23, 30, 71
Amateur Gymnastics Association 129; *see also* British Gymnastics
amateur sport 36–37, 58, 112, 119; *see also* volunteers
Amateur Swimming Association 214
Anderson v Lyotier case study 168–182
Anderson, J. 17–18, 42–43, 46, 53, 62, 71, 73, 88, 101, 214–216
archery 56–57
Army, The *see* Ministry of Defence (MoD)
army adventurous training exercise 142–147, 181
aspirational standards 20, 30, 32, 36–37
assessment of athletes/participants 157, 160–166, 179–180, 192
assumption of responsibility 19, 21, 23, 32, 130
assumption of responsibility/reliance test 32
athlete aspirations 58–60, 155
athletics 151, 154–155
attitude problems (athletes) 149–151, 153, 159
Australia 3–4, 6–8, 10, 99, 102
autocratic/authoritarian coaching style *see* coaching style

balance of probabilities 60, 142, 152, 162
balancing exercise 12, 59, 66, 198

Barnes, J. 47, 51, 65, 123, 167, 192
Beloff, M. 18, 24, 42, 46, 48, 58, 216
Biedzynski, K.W. 31, 42–43, 47–48, 123, 167
bioscientific aspects of sports science/sports coaching 44–45, 206, 217
Bolam 'defence' 65, 175–177, 193–194
Bolam test 64, 68, 74–84, 177
Bolitho test 65, 78; *see also Bolam* test
Boone, T. 71, 133, 190, 217
boundaries: forging champions vs committing a tort 34, 44, 72, 123, 208; negligent and non-negligent coaching 54, 169, 176; *see also* breach of duty
breach of duty 42, 72, 135, 157–158, 193; *Anderson v Lyotier* 170–174, 181; barometers of acceptable/unacceptable coaching practice 74, 131, 142, 205; case law 90, 97, 103, 109, 116, 126, 157; context specific/prevailing circumstances 9, 92, 95, 119, 153, 210; customary practice 64–65; expert witnesses 98, 155, 176, 194; foreseeability 53; legal test 5, 8, 110–111, 139, 210–212; moral blame vs breach of duty 22–23, 92; national governing bodies of sport 213–215; pivotal issue 70, 190; professional liability 38, 79, 118, 139, 167; unacceptable risk 192; volenti non fit injuria 61
British Amputee and Les Autres Sports Association *see* British Les Autres Sports Association (BLASA)
British Bobsleigh and Skeleton Association (BBSA) *see* British Bobsleigh Ltd.

British Bobsleigh Ltd. 155–156
British Boxing Board of Control 3, 213
British Gymnastics 1
British Hang-Gliding and Paragliding Association (BHPA) 64, 136
British Les Autres Sports Association (BLASA) 56
burden of proof *see* balance of probabilities

Caddell, R. 3, 113
calculus of negligence 53, 66, 206
Caldwell propositions 103–106, 210
Canada 3, 6, 10, 51
Cane, P. 18, 26, 28
Caparo test 3–4
careful parent test 51
case study 168–182
Cassidy, T. 31, 33, 44, 49–50, 57, 186–187, 191, 193, 202
causation 6, 41, 45, 59–61, 190
Champion, W.T. 43, 55, 133
Charlish, P. 43, 60
child protection 2, 42, 45
children 35, 48, 52–54, 62, 75, 132, 176, 196, 201
chilling effect *see* fears of being sued
civil law 6
Clancy, R. 30, 55
climbing 124, 126–127, 131–135, 146–148
coach-athlete relationship 2, 47, 59, 159
coach competence 31, 37, 51–52, 57, 77, 126–149, 186, 194–197, 201, 208
coach education 43–45, 67, 77, 82, 192–193, 200–203, 213–216
coach educators 217
coaches being stretched 181
coaching behaviour *see* coaching practice
coaching disabled athletes 56–57
coaching experience 67, 71, 77, 88, 131–132, 137–139, 144, 146
coaching methods *see* coaching practice
coaching practice 33–35, 59, 159–160, 166–169, 175–177, 186–188, 190–193, 205–208; commonalities 3, 35, 124, 194, 196; complexities 10, 44–45, 193, 205–206; reasonable 13, 28–32, 41, 66, 122–124, 131, 147
coaching qualifications *see* qualifications
coaching style 44, 151–152
coach's duties: assessment of participants 123, 160–167, 178–180; common/proper practice 67, 78–79, 124–126; competence 31, 37, 51–52, 57, 77, 126–149, 186, 194–197, 201, 208; fact specific 48, 66, 181–182; instruction 126–140, 160–167, 178–180, 207, 214; matching participants 160–166, 177–178; organisation and pitch of coaching sessions 160–166; pitch inspections 123, 140–146, 207; preventing injured athletes from competing 48, 123, 149–155; prompt and proper medical care 48, 123, 149–155, 159; proper and safe use of equipment 155–160; risk assessment 140–149, 167, 178–180; supervision 31, 47–48, 65, 123, 126–140, 160–167, 178–180; training intensity levels 13, 33, 123, 149–155, 159, 191
coach training and development *see* coach education
Coakley, J. 187–188
codes of conduct 70, 201–202
comfort zones 72, 123, 161–163, 166–167, 171, 178, 182, 192, 207–208
common law 2, 5–8, 27–28, 99, 142
common law family 3–6, 41, 88
common practice 67, 78–79, 124–126, 193–194
compensation culture 43, 75
complexities in coaching practice 10, 44–45, 193, 205–206
concussion 36–37, 49, 159, 190
confidence: athletes/participants 163, 166, 192; coaches 73, 179, 200, 208
consent 61, 98, 100–102, 126, 211–212
context of sports coaching 19–22, 42–45, 71–73, 122–124, 181–182, 186–190; *see also* coach's duties
continuing professional development (CPD) 65, 74–77, 84, 200, 213; *see also* coach education
contributory negligence 62, 133, 135, 143, 164, 175, 201, 212
control devices 23, 45, 60–61, 74, 82
control mechanisms 41, 75; *see also* control devices
co-participants 5, 12, 45, 101, 139, 178
cost of preventative measures 53–54, 66, 206; *see also* calculus of negligence
Cox, N. 18, 42, 51, 53, 55, 57
cricket 63, 95, 113, 119, 140–141
cross-pollination of legal principles 3, 7, 41, 209; *see also* persuasive authority
Cushion, C. 44, 78, 132, 151, 180, 188–192, 201
customary practice *see* common practice

Deakin, S. 8, 22, 25, 47, 52–53, 59
defences 61–62, 79

defensive practice *see* fears of being sued
definition of coach's duty of care 29–30, 122, 131; *see also* coach's duties
Department for Digital, Culture, Media and Sport (DCMS) 1, 19, 38
De Prez, P. 74–75, 79, 81, 124
descriptive sports ethics *see* empirical sports ethics
desirable activities 21, 53–55, 112, 135, 142, 209
developments in coaching practice 31, 49, 67, 77, 193, 206–207
differentiation 178
different jurisdictions 4–10, 209
disability sport *see* coaching disabled athletes
discretionary decision making *see* *Woodbridge* principle
discus 56–57
distinctions between formal qualifications and experience 194–197
Dobberstein, M.J. 54, 176
doctrinal approach 10, 22, 88
Donaghue v Stevenson 5, 19, 24–25, 46, 100, 138
Duffy, P. 31, 68, 70–71, 73–74, 193, 196
Dugdale, A. 30, 47, 70, 76, 78, 123, 189, 194, 198
duties of care of coaches *see* coach's duties
Duty of Care in Sport: Independent Report to Government (DoC in Sport Report) 1, 26, 34–38
dynamic risk assessment 147, 179, 198–199

elite sport 44, 48, 57, 71, 149
empirical sports ethics 20
employers' liability *see* vicarious liability
English Cricket Board Association of Cricket Officials 63, 113, 119
English Rugby Football Union 141–142
error of judgment 90–91, 94, 103, 105, 189
ethical dilemmas 186, 206; *see also* tensions
ethics 19–20, 34, 73, 193, 217
Evans H. 80, 82
excesses of coaching practice 186–187, 212
expertise 35, 51–52, 57, 179, 195–196, 200–203
expert witnesses 98, 129–130, 175–176
extended principle in *Hedley Byrne* 32, 130
extralegal vs legal duties 2, 21, 25, 217

fact specific 10, 55, 59; *see also* coach's duties
fast moving contests 46, 92, 106, 110, 125

fault *see* breach of duty
fears of being sued 42–43, 73, 119, 218
football: amateur 98, 100–101, 178; professional 4, 44, 56, 74, 149, 151, 153
foreseeability 58, 83, 132, 174, 216
formal risk assessment 198–199
Fulbrook, J. 43, 55
Fuller, L. 21, 26

Gardiner, J. 32, 76, 190
Gardiner, S. 42–43, 61, 64
Garratt, D. 68–70, 72–73, 121, 193, 202–203, 218
golf 58, 60
Goodhart, A.L. 9, 92, 94–95
good practice 37, 65, 67, 84, 125, 155, 202
grassroots sport 206, 209; *see also* amateur sport
Grayson, E. 18, 42, 50
Greenfield, S. 6–7, 18, 42, 44, 56, 72, 218
Grey Thompson, Baroness, T. 1, 17, 19, 26, 38, 196
Griffith-Jones, D. 10, 18, 24, 42–46, 49, 56, 61, 214
guidelines 43, 70, 106, 165, 207–208
guides (climbing) 126
gymnastics 51, 126–132

Hall, A. 50, 52
Hand formula/test 52–53
Hardman, A. 30, 45, 185, 201
Hart, HLA 18, 22
Hartley, H. 18, 33, 42–43
hazards 51, 66, 128, 143, 161
Healey, D. 33, 35, 48, 67, 165
health and safety 33, 36, 74
heightening standard of care 31, 49, 190
Heuston, R. 24, 28, 35
Heywood, R. 32, 43, 60, 79
higher standard of care 52, 76; children 56; disabled athletes 56–57; foreseeable risk 55
Hong Kong 9, 27, 131
Honoré, T. 18, 20, 26, 34
horse race 103
Hurst, T.R. 34, 44, 72

implied sporting consent *see* consent
incremental approach 4, 37, 88, 118, 206–207, 214, 216
individual responsibility 131–132, 164, 175; *see also* contributory negligence
inherent risks 55, 61, 66, 115–117
injuries 65, 67, 109, 117, 138, 154, 174, 187

in loco parentis 41, 46, 49, 50–52
instruction 31–32, 41, 47–48, 51; *see also* coach's duties
insurance 64, 70, 73, 75, 214
interdisciplinary 2, 12, 41, 204
International Council for Coaching Excellence (ICCE) 73
International Rugby Football Board 114

Jackson, R. 19
James, M. 18, 42, 44, 46, 59, 61–62, 64–65, 73, 93, 95, 102, 106, 119, 133, 212, 214
Jockey Club, The 104, 106
jockeys 102–105
Jones, C. 30, 45, 185, 201
Jones, M. 30, 47, 68, 70, 76, 78, 123, 175–176, 189, 194
Jones, R. 20, 44, 122, 151, 202

Kendo 9, 131
Kessler, J. 48, 55
Kidner, R. 61–62, 69, 74
Knight, J.N. 34, 44, 72

Labuschagne, J. 31, 47–49, 57, 77, 132
lapse in skill 103, 106, 210–211
legal vs moral duties of care 18–28, 31, 35–38, 180–181, 209
licensing scheme 196
limitations *see* skills gap
Lines, K. 44, 215–217
Lucy, W. 20, 34
Lunney, M. 24, 70, 76
Lyle, J. 33, 35, 45, 72–73, 78, 132, 187, 189, 191, 194, 201
Lynn, A. 35, 72, 132, 194, 201

Magnus, U. 6, 41
Mangan, D. 69–70, 75–76, 81, 84
Mannis, M. 50, 52
Martens, R. 48, 150, 207
Martínková, I. 191
matching participants 160–167, 177–178
McArdle, D. 44, 61, 64, 93, 106, 119, 179, 212
McCaskey, A.S. 31, 42–43, 47–48, 123, 167
McNamee, M. 19–20, 36, 201–202
Meakin, T. 93, 190
methodology 2, 10, 168, 204
Miles, A. 33, 36, 186, 191
minimum requirements 20, 70, 75, 197, 200, 214
Ministry of Defence (MoD) 146–149, 179, 181

Mitten, M. 33–34, 65, 73, 202, 208
momentary lapse 103, 106, 109
Montrose, J. 26, 79
morality 18–22, 25–26, 34, 38; *see also* legal vs moral duties of care
Morgan, P. 63–64
Morris, A. 42, 75, 140
motor sport 93–98
Mountain Bike Instructors Award Scheme 146, 160
mountain biking 160–166
mountain climbing 79, 124–126, 134, 146, 211; *see also* climbing
Mulheron, R. 28, 47
Mullender, R. 4–5, 7

Nash, C. 31, 35, 71, 197, 200–202
national governing bodies of sport (NGBs) 28, 36, 63–65, 165, 197, 201–202, 213–217
National Horse Show 89
National Interscholastic Cycling Association 146
negligence (overview and framework) 45–61
negligent entrenched practice 57, 59, 65, 67, 180, 188, 207–208
neighbour principle 19, 24, 38, 40, 46
New Zealand 4, 8–9
no-duty-to assist 19, 27–28
Norris, W. 2, 23, 25, 27–28, 30, 32–33, 35, 37, 47, 55, 83, 176–177
Northern Ireland 12, 89, 137–140
novices 9, 29, 147, 156–160, 181, 200
Nygaard, G. 71, 133, 190, 217

objective reasonableness 74–75
obvious risks 131
occupiers' liability 89, 140–141
Oliphant, K. 70, 76
omissions 5, 24, 115, 190
Opie, H. 113
optimising performance 44, 57, 123, 132, 147, 157, 159, 178, 188, 191–193
organisation and pitch of coaching sessions 160–167
over-commitment 187; *see also* sport ethic

parents 35, 50, 52, 194, 196
Parry, J. 19, 191
Partington, M. 180, 188, 190–191
Partington, N. 17–18, 22–23, 28, 30, 34, 38, 47, 50, 54–55, 65, 69, 71–72, 84, 111, 135, 195, 203, 209, 213
peer pressure 159, 164, 166

Percy, R. 25, 38, 49
performance levels 71, 120–121, 166, 181
persuasive authority 4–5, 8–10, 102, 209
Petts, T. 50, 52
physical education (PE) 43, 51, 129, 133, 169, 205
Pike, E. 187–188
pitch inspections 123, 140–146, 207
Powell, J. 11, 31, 38, 70, 76, 78, 190, 193
practical content of coach's duty of care *see* standard of care
practice ethics 193
pressuring athletes 157, 159, 166, 187, 192, 211
probability of injury 53; *see also* calculus of negligence
professionalisation of coaching 73–74
professional liability *see* professional negligence
professional negligence 23, 32, 65, 69–71, 74–84, 209–210
professional sport 4, 48, 77, 102–106, 149–151
proper and safe use of equipment 155–160
proximity 27, 216
punishment drills 188

qualifications 34–35, 60, 111, 118, 127–133, 146–148, 181, 194–197

reasonable average 76–78
reasonable coaching practice 3, 13, 28–32, 66, 74, 122–123, 194, 207–208
reasonableness 5–8; context specific 30, 45, 49, 106, 167, 210; fluidity 211; objective reasonableness 74–75; reasonable range of options (*see Woodbridge* principle); standard of conduct 68, 101, 122, 133, 137, 189, 201; vagueness 55, 57, 66, 122, 185
reasonable person of the sporting world 94–95
reckless disregard 44, 75, 91–98, 101–108, 111, 189, 210
recreational sport 31, 71; *see also* grassroots sport
referees 46, 98, 106–120, 210
regular and approved practice 65, 79, 185–186, 199, 202; *see also* common practice
reliance *see* assumption of responsibility/ reliance test
risk assessment 67, 123, 140–149, 178–180, 197–199, 207–208, 212–213; *see also* coach's duties
risk assessment lens 43, 206–207

risk-benefit assessment 53, 65–66, 138–139, 148, 164, 174, 177, 198
risk management 45, 74, 166, 186, 197, 199, 208, 212–213
Rugby Football Union (RFU) 141–142
rules of the game/sport 45, 61, 89, 92, 101–106, 115, 158, 160, 165

safeguarding 2
school sport 18, 48, 53, 133, 194; *see also* physical education
Schuster, A. 18, 42, 51, 53, 55, 57
scope of coach's duty of care *see* standard of care
Scotland 143–146, 201
Scott, A. 188
Scout Association 54, 63, 209
seriousness of injury 54, 172, 213; *see also* calculus of negligence
Simon, R. 33
Skea, J. 31, 47–49, 57, 77, 132
skiing 135, 168–182
skills gap 77, 132, 195, 201, 208
social utility 53–54, 67, 140, 142, 206; *see also* desirable activities
sociolegal 2–3
South Africa 6–7
spectators 88–96
Spengler, J. 37, 57
sport ethic 187, 212
sport-related concussion *see* concussion
sports coach UK 31, 35, 197
Sports Council 127, 129
sports ethics 11, 20
sports governing bodies; *see* national governing bodies of sport (NGBs)
sports instructors 127, 135, 137–139, 160, 168
sports law 42, 66, 102, 120, 208–213
sports negligence 87–120, 209–211
sports officials *see* referees
standard of care 23, 52–59; children 53, 56, 75; coaching 30–33; different jurisdictions 6, 9; different relationships 89–90, 92, 107; disabled athletes 56; dual function 74–75; expectations of participants 59, 66; foreseeability 132–133; game vs stoppage in play 98, 119, 189; hazardous activities 51, 75, 165; heightening standard of care 31, 49, 190; higher standard of care 52, 76; level of sport 77, 100–101; objective 100, 105–106, 166, 196; pivotal issue 12, 40, 209; prevailing circumstances 49, 51, 101, 210–211; specialist skill 28, 76, 124, 130, 136

statutory provision 112
Steele, J. 42–43, 52–53, 61–62, 75
Stewart, R. 11, 31, 38, 70, 76, 78, 190, 193
Sunderland Association Football Club Limited 149
supervision 31, 47–48, 65, 123, 126–140, 160–167, 178–180
Swim England *see* Amateur Swimming Association

Taylor, B. 68–69, 70, 72–73, 121, 193, 202–203
teaching 51–52, 66, 130
Telfer, H. 30, 34, 70–72, 74, 78, 120, 132, 181, 189, 192–193, 200–201
tensions 34, 123, 192–193
Tong, R. 33, 36, 186, 191
training intensity levels 13, 33, 123, 149–155, 159, 191

UK Athletics 151, 154
United States 5, 10

Ver Steeg, R. 31
vicarious liability 62–64, 114, 215

volenti non fit injuria 61–62, 212; *see also* defences
voluntary assumption of risk *see* volenti non fit injuria
volunteers 12, 31, 69, 71–72, 83, 112, 117–118, 200–201

Walking Group Leader Award 197
Walton, C. 25, 38, 49
warnings 126, 131, 207–208
weightlifting *see* weight training
weight training 48, 137–138
Weir, J. 26
Welsh Rugby Football Union 114
Whitlam, P. 50–51, 65–66, 179, 192
win at all costs 187
Witting, C. 3–4
Wong, G. 10, 64, 188
Woodbridge principle 80, 177, 194, 210
written risk assessment 147, 199; *see also* formal risk assessment

Young, K. 187–188

Zipursky, B. 5–7

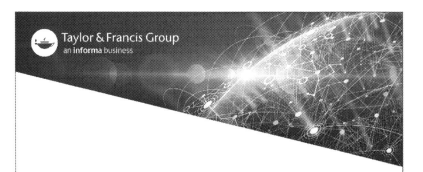

Printed in the United States
by Baker & Taylor Publisher Services